The Adventures of a Modern Renaissance Academic in Investing and Gambling

World Scientific Series in Finance
(ISSN: 2010-1082)

Series Editor: William T. Ziemba *(University of British Columbia (Emeritus) and London School of Economics, UK)*

Advisory Editors:
Greg Connor *(National University of Ireland, Maynooth, Ireland)*
George Constantinides *(University of Chicago, USA)*
Espen Eckbo *(Dartmouth College, USA)*
Hans Foellmer *(Humboldt University, Germany)*
Christian Gollier *(Toulouse School of Economics, France)*
Thorsten Hens *(University of Zurich, Switzerland)*
Robert Jarrow *(Cornell University, USA)*
Hayne Leland *(University of California, Berkeley, USA)*
Haim Levy *(The Hebrew University of Jerusalem, Israel)*
John Mulvey *(Princeton University, USA)*
Marti Subrahmanyam *(New York University, USA)*

Published*:

Vol. 8   Risk, Value and Default
        by Oliviero Roggi (University of Florence, Italy & New York University, USA)

Vol. 9   Great Investment Ideas
        by William T. Ziemba (University of British Columbia, Canada & London School of Economics, UK)

Vol. 10 Problems in Portfolio Theory and the Fundamentals of Financial Decision Making
        by Leonard C. MacLean (Dalhousie University, Canada) & William T. Ziemba (University of British Columbia, Canada & London School of Economics, UK)

Vol. 11 The Strategic Analysis of Financial Markets (In 2 Volumes)
        Volume 1: Framework; Volume 2: Trading System Analytics
        by Steven D. Moffitt (Stuart School of Business, USA & Market Pattern Research, Inc., USA)

Vol. 12 The Adventures of a Modern Renaissance Academic in Investing and Gambling
        by William T. Ziemba (University of British Columbia, Canada & London School of Economics, UK)

*To view the complete list of the published volumes in the series, please visit:
www.worldscientific.com/series/wssf

World Scientific Series in FINANCE vol. 12

The Adventures of a Modern Renaissance Academic in Investing and Gambling

William T Ziemba
University of British Columbia, Canada
London School of Economics, UK

World Scientific

NEW JERSEY · LONDON · SINGAPORE · BEIJING · SHANGHAI · HONG KONG · TAIPEI · CHENNAI · TOKYO

Published by

World Scientific Publishing Co. Pte. Ltd.
5 Toh Tuck Link, Singapore 596224
USA office: 27 Warren Street, Suite 401-402, Hackensack, NJ 07601
UK office: 57 Shelton Street, Covent Garden, London WC2H 9HE

Library of Congress Cataloging-in-Publication Data
Names: Ziemba, W. T., author.
Title: The adventures of a modern renaissance academic in investing and gambling /
    authored by William T. Ziemba.
Description: Hackensack, NJ : World Scientific Publishing Co. Pte. Ltd., [2017] |
    Series: World scientific series in finance, 2010-1082 ; Vol 12 | Includes bibliographical references.
Identifiers: LCCN 2016049905| ISBN 9789813148284 | ISBN 9789813148291
Subjects: LCSH: Ziemba, W. T. | Capitalists and financiers--Biography. | Investments. | Gambling.
Classification: LCC HG172.Z54 Z54 2017 | DDC 332.6092 [B] --dc23
LC record available at https://lccn.loc.gov/2016049905

British Library Cataloguing-in-Publication Data
A catalogue record for this book is available from the British Library.

Copyright © 2018 by World Scientific Publishing Co. Pte. Ltd.

All rights reserved. This book, or parts thereof, may not be reproduced in any form or by any means, electronic or mechanical, including photocopying, recording or any information storage and retrieval system now known or to be invented, without written permission from the publisher.

For photocopying of material in this volume, please pay a copying fee through the Copyright Clearance Center, Inc., 222 Rosewood Drive, Danvers, MA 01923, USA. In this case permission to photocopy is not required from the publisher.

Desk Editor: Lum Pui Yee

Typeset by Stallion Press
Email: enquiries@stallionpress.com

Printed in Singapore

Review Quotes

1) Bill's many interests have taken him through the worlds of academia, investing and gambling. This memoir adds human background to his prolific writings, which range from finance, horse-racing and lotteries, to oriental rugs.

— Edward O. Thorp, author of *Beat the Dealer and Beat the Market*

2) For more than 3 decades, a major passion of mine has been to encourage professional school faculty to draw research inspiration from industry. Bill embodies this ideal more completely than anyone I've ever known.

— Arthur Geoffrion, James A. Collins, Chair in Management Emeritus, UCLA Anderson School

3) This book is remarkable in several ways. It recounts Bill's adventures throughout his life, and the amazing number of things he has done, places he has visited and people he has known and worked with. Many of those people were among the most brilliant in their respective fields, and Bill recounts his interactions, adventures and often collaborations with them. But the book is not just fun, it also provides keen insights into how to make money in the stock market and horse racing. It is a matter of looking for the special situations, the anomalies, where distinctive opportunities open up, and Bill backs this up with his careful and exhaustive research. The book is an adventure in life and money from beginning to end.

— Willard (Bill) Zangwill, Booth School of Business, University of Chicago

4) Most academics in finance, even if they consult, keep to a mainstream efficient markets approach. Indeed they often suggest investing in index funds. Since that beats three-quarters of all investors with low cost it's a useful strategy. Ziemba strives for more. In each market — be it the stock market, lotteries, football, horse racing betting or owning top horses — he looks at the behavior of the participants, the institutional practices, mean reversion of prices and biases to generate superior risk-adjusted returns. This requires more study, research and execution work, but it does pay off. All throughout this book you will find interesting stories and creative solutions in various markets with very colorful people, many of whom have been extremely successful focusing on the data and research. His story covers a lot of what happened in the financial markets over the last 50 or so years. He embeds his academic and practical sides with lots of travel both to conferences and for fun. It's an amazing journey that very few have been willing take. There is a lot here for all types of individuals.

— Frank J. Fabozzi, Professor of Finance, EDHEC Business School and Editor, *Journal of Portfolio Management*

This book is dedicated to the memory of some greats I was fortunate to know and work with or take classes from

Kenneth J. Arrow, Frederick Balderson, David Blackwell, C West Churchman, Thomas M Cover, George B Dantzig, Gerard Debreu, William S. Jewell, In Ho Kim, Ernest Koenigsberg, Gerald Lieberman, Edmund Malinvaud, Joseph Sol Marcus, Jacob Marshak, Charles Bartlett McGuire, Merton H Miller, John Nash, Andras Prekopa, Stephen A Ross, Sidney Schloffer, Arthur F Veinott Jr, Paul A Samuelson, Ronald Sheppard, Douglass Wilde, Philip Wolfe, Gene Woolsey and Arnold Zellner

A grateful William T Ziemba, Bergamo, May 30, 2017

Acknowledgments

Special thanks University of Massachusetts economics Professor Sidney Schoeffler who steered me to Berkeley in 1963. It was the experience there that shaped my research and teaching career. A lecture by University of Texas Professor Douglass Wilde at the University of Connecticut was very important and introduced me to Management Science/Operations Research.

My UMass background was good but Berkeley was at another level. There I met my wife, Sandra Schwartz, and that led to lots of good adventures together, the production of this book being one of her many contributions. Special thanks to our daughter Rachel Ziemba who has become successful in the political economics arena working with Nouriel Roubini. It has been great giving lectures together, discussing topics, doing the two books based on our Wilmott columns and thanks for very helpful advice on this memoir/financial history volume.

Many Berkeley professors were very helpful as well as some close by at Stanford. Bart McGuire was especially helpful as were Roger Wets, David Blackwell, and Dale Jorgensen. My closest friends at Stanford were Tom Cover who was probably the top information theorist around and a gambling expert and Arthur (Pete) F. Veinott, Jr who prided himself as my grandfather having supervised Bill Zangwill my PhD supervisor, Alan Manne who died at 80 from a polo accident, and the great economic theorist, Kenneth Arrow who died this year in his mid-90s. I was pleased to have good dealings with all of these giants. Now, we only have Wets and Jorgenson left. I dedicate this memoir cum history of investment book to these greats and the nice memories I have of my dealings with them.

In my investment and gambling research and practice and the search for excellence, I have been greatly influenced by Bill Benter, Warren Buffett, Blair Hull and especially Edward O Thorp who has been an inspiration to work with the past 40 years. Long-time relationships with Donald B Hausch and Leonard C MacLean have been very beneficial for all of us.

Special thanks to the wonderful collection of co-authors and colleagues I worked with over the years, including Abdul Akatir, Michael Alen-Buckley, Carol Alexander, Mukhtar Ali, Ed Altman, Amin Amershi, William Anthony, Kenneth J. Arrow, Phillipe Artzher, Orley Ashenfelter, Mordicai Avriel, Warren Bailey, Rod Bain, Egon Balas, G. Balla, Vijay Bawa, Adrian Bell, Aaron Ben-Tal, Bill Benter, Klaus Berge, Johnathan Berk, Marida Bertocchi, Sandra Betton, Andy Beyer, James Bicksler, Enrico Biflis, Ron Bird, John Birge, George Blazenko, John Board, David Booth, Lawrence Booth, Steve Bradley, Richard Brealey, Michael Brennan, Menachem Brenner, Rick Brooks-Hill, Sid Browne, Shelby Brumelle, Kelly Busche, John Butterworth, Charles Cadsby, Elio Canestrelli, Brian Canfield, David Cariño, Peter Carr, Hurricane Carter, Randy Chapmon, Robert Cheung, Ross Clark, Luis Comolli, Greg Connor, Giorgio Consigli, Andrea Consiglio, George Constantinides, Kathyrn Cootner, Tom Copeland, Richard Cottle, John Cox, Rita D'Eclessia, George Dantzig, Ron Dattero, Mark Davis, Werner DeBandt, Michael Dempster, Albert Dexter, Giorgio di Girgio, Fram Dimshaw, Elroy Dimson, Elroy Dimson, James Douglass, Andrew Dowden, Darrell Duffie, Philip Dybvig, Constantine Dzhabarov, Curtis Eaves, Espen Eckbo, David Edelman, Chanaka Edirishinghe, George Elford, Steve Ellis, Stuart Ethier, Igor Evstingneev, Frank Fabozzi, Bruce Fauman, Wayne Ferson, Jerry Fetham, Steve Figlewski, Stein Fleten, Hans Foellmer, Jim Forbes, Cary Fotias, Murray Frank, David Fuller, Saul Gass, Horand (Gus) Gassmann, Antoine Gautier, Art Geoffrion, Olivier Gergaud, Alois Geyer, S. Ghosh, Sam Ginsburg, Christian Gollier, Marshall Gramm, Robert Grauer, Peter Griffin, Mark Grinblatt, Richard Grinold, Martin Gruber, John Guerard, Mustafa Gultekin, Nils Hakansson, Yasashi Hamao, Yasuchi Hamao, Bob Hammond, Gabriel Hawawani, Thorsten Hens, Chris Hensel, Wolfgang Herold, John Hicks, Julie Higle, David Hirshleifer, Stewart Hodges, C. C. Huang, Donald Iglehart, Gerd Infanger, Shegeri Ishi, David Jackson, Robert Jarrow, Harry Joe, Johnny Johnsson, Dale Jorgenson, Sherry Judah, Mitch Julis, Peter Kall, Jerry Kallberg, M. Kallio, Basil Kalymon, Anti Kanto, Andrew Karolyi, Kiyoshi Kato, Harry Katz, Donald Keim, Woo Chang Kim, Alan King, Dennis Kira, Bruce Kittle, Alan Kleidon, Ernest Koenigsberg, Matti Koivu, Asaji Komatsu, Kourad Kontriner, S P Kothari, Roy Kouwenberg, Bjarni Kristiansson, Paul Krokhmal, Martin Kusy, Dan Lane, Liam Larkin, Hayne Leland, Siew Meng Leong, Haim Levy, Kian Guan Lim, Sebastien Lleo, Andy Lo, Victor

Lo, Jim Lodas, Francois Louveaux, David Luenberger, C. B. MaGuire, Max Maksimovic, Burton Malkiel, Tassos Mallarias, Olvi Mangasarian, Alan Manne, Jim Mao, Harry M. Markowitz, Paul Marsh, Terry Marsh, Jacob Marshak, Joseph Mayo, Piera Mazzolini, Bruce McConnachie, C. Bartlett McGuire, David McKenzie, Harry McPike, Robert Merton, Merton Miller, Dick Mitchell, Jack Mitten, Perigrine Moncrief, John Mulvey, Gulnar Muradoglu, Katta Murty, Stewart C Myers, David Myers, Vasant Naik, Edwin Neave, Maureen O'Hara, James Ohlson, Otto Optiz, Gian Marco Ottaviano, Celik Parkan, Jacopo Patrizi, Teemu Pennanen, Georg Pflug, Max Phua, James Poterba, William Poundstone, Gordon Pye, David Pyle, Richard Quandt, James Quinn, Zari Rachev, Pierluigi Riva, Mark Reinganum, Juan Rendon, Jay Ritter, Peter Robinson, Terry Rockafellar, Juan Rodriguez, Oliviero Roggi, Steve Roman, Jerry Rosenwald, Zvi Ruder, Markus Rudolf, Ren Ruren, David Rutenberg, Romesh Saigal, Paul A Samuelson, Raphael Sanegre, Kats Sawaki, Siegfried Schaible, Thomas Schneeweis, Suvrajeet Sen, Bill Sharpe, Julian Shaw, Klaus Shenk-Hoppe, H. Shin, Hiroshi Shintani, Gordon Sick, Larry Siegel, Max Smith, Bruno Solnik, Klaus Spreemann, Hal Stern, Joseph Stiglitz, Doug Stone, Karl Storchmann, Michael Stutzer, Marti Subrahmanyhan, Suresh Sundaresan, Charles Sutcliffe, John Swetye, Giorgio Szego, Tom Tenkhoff, Anjan Thakor, Dan Tudball, Andy Turner, Jun Uno, Richard Van Slyke, Maria Vassalou, Ilan Vertinsky, Raymond G Vickson, Alan Wagner, Patrick Waldron, Stein Wallace, Jarrod Wilcox, Paul Wilmott, Robert Wilson, John Woods, Gene Woolsey, Owen Wu, Jeff Yass, Johnny Yu, Stavros Zenios, Mikhail Zhitlukhin, Y. Zi, Alex Ziegler, J P Zigrand, and Constantin Zopoundis.

Wow! that's a lot of people and I am sure I have forgotten some — some of whom I would like to forget, others I am sorry to have slighted.

Contents

Review Quotes		v
Acknowledgments		ix
About the Author		xv
1	Beginning	1
2	The Early Days in Adams and at the University of Massachusetts in Amherst	7
3	Reminiscences of the Early Days in Berkeley	15
4	The Start of a New Department in Vancouver	21
5	Travels on a Flying Carpet	29
6	The Canadian Sports Pool and a New Name, Dr Z, 1982	61
7	*Fortune's Formula*: How the Pros Wager	69
8	The Invention of the Place and Show Betting System	83
9	The Turn-of-the-Year 1982/1983	95
10	Testing the Dr Z System with Ed Thorp	101
11	The 2 Minute Sprint	123
12	Susquehanna	129
13	What is Japan Doing Right to Get All that Money? Will they Lose It?	133

14	The Bond–Stock Earnings Yield Crash Prediction Model	147
15	Arbitrage and Risk Arbitrage	159
16	Bill Benter Letter	165
17	Scenario Optimization in Action — The Russell–Yasuda Kasai Financial Planning Model	171
18	Anomalies Research at Frank Russell, 1989–1998	179
19	Risk Management and Planning in the Vienna Siemens Pension Model, InnoALM	195
20	Evaluating the Greatest Investors	201
21	How to Lose Money in Derivatives and Some Who Did	211
22	Trend Following in the Bahamas	261
23	The Internet Bubble Crash, 2000–2002	267
24	The US Housing Bubble, Credit Crisis, Crash and Recovery 2006 to 2015	271
25	The Flash Crash and High Frequency Trading	275
26	The Greek Crisis and Why It is Important	283
27	Inefficiencies and Anomalies: Other Crashes and How They Fit the Models	297
28	Dealing with Madoff and Other Swindlers	315
29	An Adventure in the Bed and Breakfast Business, British Columbia Real Estate over the Years	321
30	Two Tries in the Horse Ownership Business	327
31	Travels to Universities and Academic and Professional Conferences over the Years	385
Epilog		435
Bibliography		443
Index		455

About the Author

William T Ziemba is the Alumni Professor (Emeritus) of Financial Modeling and Stochastic Optimization in the Sauder School of Business, University of British Columbia where he taught from 1968–2006. His PhD is from the University of California, Berkeley. He currently teaches part time and makes short research visits to various universities. At present he is the Distinguished Visiting Research Associate, Systemic Risk Centre, London School of Economics. He has been a Visiting Professor at Cambridge, Oxford, London School of Economics, University of Reading and Warwick in the UK, at Stanford, UCLA, Berkeley, MIT, University of Washington and Chicago in the US, Universities of Bergamo, Venice and Luiss in Italy, the Universities of Zurich, Cyprus, Tsukuba (Japan), KAIST (Korea), and the National University and the National Technological University of Singapore. He has been a consultant to a number of leading financial institutions including the Frank Russell Company, Morgan Stanley, Buchanan Partners, RAB Hedge Funds, Gordon Capital, Matcap, Ketchum Trading, and in the gambling area to the BC Lotto Corporation, SCA Insurance, Singapore Pools, Canadian Sports Pool, Keeneland Racetrack, and some racetrack syndicates in Hong Kong, Manila and Australia. His research is in asset-liability management, portfolio theory and practice, security market imperfections, Japanese and Asian financial markets, hedge fund strategies, risk management, sports and lottery investments, and applied stochastic programming. His co-written practitioner paper on the Russell–Yasuda model won second prize in the 1993 Edelman Practice of Management Science Competition. He has been a futures and equity trader and hedge fund and investment manager since 1983. He has published widely in journals such as *Operations Research, Management Science, Mathematics of OR, Mathematical Programming,*

American Economic Review, Journal of Economic Perspectives, Journal of Finance, Journal of Economic Dynamics and Control, JFQA, Quantitative Finance, Journal of Portfolio Management and *Journal of Banking and Finance* and in many books and special journal issues. Recent books include *Applications of Stochastic Programming* with S W Wallace, SIAM-MPS, (2005), *Stochastic Optimization Models in Finance*, 2nd edition with R G Vickson, World Scientific (2006) and *Handbook of Asset and Liability Modeling*, Volume 1: *Theory and Methodology* (2006) and Volume 2: *Applications and Case Studies* (2007) with S A Zenios, North Holland, *Scenarios for Risk Management and Global Investment Strategies* with Rachel Ziemba, Wiley, (2007), *Handbook of Investments: Sports and Lottery Betting Markets*, with Donald Hausch, North Holland, 2008, *Optimizing the Aging, Retirement and Pensions Dilemma* with Marida Bertocchi and Sandra Schwartz (2010, 2015 (2nd edn.) and *The Kelly Capital Growth Investment Criterion* (2010), with legendary hedge fund trader Edward Thorp and Leonard MacLean, *Calendar Anomalies and Arbitrage, The Handbook of Financial Decision Making* (with Leonard MacLean) and *Stochastic Programming* (with Horand Gassman), published by World Scientific in 2013 and 2012. In progress is Handbook on the *Economics of Wine* (with O Ashenfelter, O Gergaud and K Storchmann) and published in 2015 is the Handbook of Futures Markets (with T Mallaris). He is the series editor for North Holland's Handbooks in Finance, World Scientific Handbooks in Financial Economics and Books in Finance, and previously was the CORS editor of INFOR and the department of finance editor of *Management Science*, 1982–1992. He has continued his columns in *Wilmott* and his 2013 book with Rachel Ziemba have the 2007–2013 columns updated with new 2018 with real bets material published by World Scientific. Ziemba, along with Hausch, wrote the famous *Beat the Racetrack* book (1984), which was revised into *Dr Z's Beat the Racetrack* (1987), which presented their place and show betting system and the *Efficiency of Racetrack Betting Markets* (1994, 2008) — the so-called bible of racetrack syndicates. Their 1986 book *Betting at the Racetrack* extends this efficient inefficient market approach to simple exotic bets. Ziemba is revising *BATR* into *Exotic Betting at the Racetrack* (World Scientific) which adds Pick 3, 4, 5, 6, etc., and provides updates to be out in 2016 with real bets he made across the world. Finally he has just completed *Travels with Dr Z: The Adventures of a Modern Renaissance Academic in Investing and Gambling*, a memoir and financial history of his investment activities over the last fifty years, *Great Investment Ideas*, which has all twelve of his applied investment papers published in the *Journal of Portfolio Management*. These hard to find papers cover many important topics including the evaluation of the greatest investors. Finally *Stock Market Crashes: Big and Small and what to do about them* was published in 2017.

Chapter 1

Beginning

On his deathbed on May 2, 1519, in the castle of French King Francois I at Amboise, Leonardo di Vinci, my greatest hero, died saying "I have so much more to do." Well he did a lot as the world's greatest scientist, painter, sculptor, inventor, geologist, anatomist, mathematician, engineer, writer and all the myriad of other things he did living until 67 from his April 15, 1452 birth in Vinci, near Florence.

There is no way my travels and experiences can begin to match Leonardo's but at least I set a high goal. In this book, I trace a career from a small town in Massachusetts to the big time as a graduate student at Berkeley in the 1960s which then was the greatest university in the world and then on to a life mostly in British Columbia with many visits across the world to do research, visit universities, attend conferences, consult and write books and work on some very interesting financial market research with some major institutions and very wealthy investors. Along the way, I moved across fields starting with chemical engineering at the University of Massachusetts in Amherst where I spent four delightful but difficult years from 1959–1963. Then the question was where to go to graduate school — I actually applied in five fields: chemical engineering, metallurgy (inspired by a summer doing work at Penn State University), patent attorney, one I forgot and an MBA in business.

Doug Wilde, a red-headed colorful and exciting speaker from the Chemical Engineering Department at the University of Texas gave a stimulating talk on network optimization using dynamic programming — an important theory of how best to make multiperiod decisions. That was a very influential lecture for me and was at the University of Connecticut in Storrs where a group of us from UMass went to have a joint function with their students and hear Doug's lecture.

That was a serious introduction to operations research and optimization — the way to do things the best way. Doug beat out my Korean University of Massachusetts mass transport teacher In Ho Kim who used to say "got to go to MIT" for a choice position at Stanford where I would have many visits and gave many talks over the years up to the present. UMass was a good school but a visit to MIT's Chemical Engineering Department and walking down the hall and seeing door after door the names of the textbooks we were using made a big impact. MIT was the big time. Later in 2005, I was pleased to teach at MIT. Discussions with my economic theory teacher Professor Sidney Schloeffler sealed the deal. Why not go to the best school and that was Berkeley which was even more famous than MIT or Harvard the top Massachusetts schools. Economic theory was slick and elegant but made strict assumptions and we know to this day its successes and failings.

Schloffler suggested the MBA program at Berkeley. I was accepted and turned down the other schools and headed to Berkeley. Despite its fame it was cheap to go there and by the second year I was a California resident and tuition was only $100 each of the three quarters. This was a much simpler era than now and my truck driver father with three children to send to college with a stay at home wife had funds so I did not need to take on any debt.

Berkeley was tough with really good students and famous professors and I drifted into operations research where Berkeley and Stanford were #1 and #2 ahead of #3 and #4 MIT and Cornell. I did a masters thesis on the optimization of the inventory control system of The Berkeley Lawrence Radiation Laboratory which was in the hills above Berkeley. My advisor C Bartlett McGuire was a gem at the business school helping all sorts of students. Bart did not have a PhD but was plugged in having spent time at the Cowles Commission at Yale, the Rand Corporation in Santa Monica, California and other good places. He got me a summer job at the Institute for Defense Analysis, Arlington, Virginia at the aptly named 400 Army Navy Drive, where I was part of the team studying the possible United States supersonic aircraft. We built a linear programming model of the world and it bought airplanes to serve the world's demand for air travel and cargo. It was cargo that was my role to figure out what it was worth. I visited Pan Am in New York and got the data on the cargo's contribution to earnings. I learned that Pan Am executives did not know much about their business and I was able to determine what shipping the cargo was worth. Blind Rochester economics professor Walter Oi was part of the team which was headed by Bill Niskanen who later became the head of the Cato Institute. It turned out that the 747 dominated the supersonic so that and the pollution killed the SST. So 200K was enough as the project budget to save the US the billions that France and the UK lost.

One day I ventured into the library. My fellow Berkeley student colleague Stewart was looking at a globe. I asked what are you doing? He said finding cities in Russia to bomb on my simulation. He was working for the Weapons System Evaluation Group (WSEG) on a classified floor of the building.

I had a nice drive with a few Berkeley friends through the US to get to Washington, DC. The summer was hot and muggy (typical DC weather). I shared a room with Art Frass. After the summer I drove myself up to Adams then to Montreal and across Canada to Banff in Alberta and then to British Columbia and down the coast to Berkeley. It took 12 days but was a good trip.

Another summer I got a job at the Norwegian Computing Centre in Oslo and wrote a computer code for the transportation program which is how to ship from A to B through a complicated network of intermediate trans-shipment points. I played on the local rugby team with mostly a bunch of English beer drinkers but I survived uninjured. While there I bought a cross country ski outfit: skis, boots and poles for $25 which I still have. That was enjoyable.

The business PhD at Berkeley had a lot of flexibility and I was able to complete it with essentially no more business courses beyond the MBA but rather I could focus on operations research, statistics (also #1 and #2 with Stanford) and Economics which was also at the top. There was lots of contact with and visits to Stanford which was close by. So I had access to two great places. At the time I did not realize the greatness of some of the teachers — some later won the Nobel Prize in Economics like Gerard Debreu, Daniel Mc Fadden and John Harsanyi and some were arguably just as important like Roy Radner and Dale Jorgenson. And the most brilliant of all to me at the time was David Blackwell of the statistics department who was my best teacher ever. I took his class in dynamic programming (the study of multiperiod decision problems) in 1963 and no matter how vague the student questions were he always explained them clearly. One of his 12-page papers on dynamic programming had so much in it that it became a whole course at Berkeley. The breath, depth and diversity of the courses at Berkeley gave me a great advantage as I was ahead of others in important areas, especially portfolio theory.

The University of British Columbia in Vancouver was just getting going and my Berkeley roommate now one of Canada's most distinguished economists Erwin Diewert pushed Vancouver — the homeland he would say. With no offer from Stanford — they hired someone less talented than I but arguably a better teacher who they got rid of a few years later — I was off to UBC. My girlfriend Sandra Schwartz, a brilliant thinker in economics and public policy came up and we were later married in a giant ceremony in Carson City with a judge and a witness. She has been my mentor and companion since. UBC had its ups and downs but I was able to do good work there in lots of areas and it was a good base to work from and there was a good research atmosphere and some good colleagues and Vancouver was always a great city to live in.

But as the years went by and I got more famous instead of being treated better I was not liked. Creative people were not liked especially if they were inventors of new fields and traveled a lot. I was simply too creative for the place and fields like risk management and stock market anomalies not to mention oriental carpets and horse racing were not popular. Jealousy was rampant as it is in many universities but UBC Commerce was sure in the tail. What the Deans wanted was boring xerox copy people who show up 9–4:30 and pal around. Some were excellent but got ruined by the excess administration but most were mediocre. The good ones mostly left eventually and went to better Universities in the US and Europe. There was a time of excellence in the 1970s and 1980s that decayed later with the poor vision of the sequence of Deans who had no idea who was good. The late Bruce Fauman, who coined the name Dr Z for me, put it this way, writing from the 1984 Breeder's Cup, see Chapter 10, he said:

> ... back home there are two types — some don't realize the breadth and depth of his work so resent him. Others do but cannot keep up with him so resent him more ... and trying to talk to him was like drinking out of a fire hydrant

And has it changed in 2017, as I finish this book? Well, the last president, a computer science researcher, was trying to reform the whole university to focus more on higher quality faculty, stronger in research and less on administrators taking the vast bulk of resources. Well, he is now a visitor back where he started at the University of Toronto. Reform is tough and the administrators were able to kick him out.

I recall one dean telling me when I asked gently for a raise to fair value based on superior research and strong innovative research. His response: I don't care what the faculty handbook says, I decide what to give people.

But, UBC and Vancouver in particular had some advantages which were better in the early days-a long summer, frequent sabbaticals (once after 4 years of teaching at 60% pay), a great city, some good courses to teach, some good students, lovely mountains, beaches and skiing. As a base I could do a lot of things. Much was academic and I became a star in the operations research/management science approach to finance community. This led to lots of jealousy from the pure efficient market types so I had to be somewhat of a loner. It was good to start out as a theorist in mathematical and stochastic programming armed with my great Berkeley training and then be a pioneer in quantitative finance, risk management, asset-liability management and portfolio theory and its applications to horse racing and other areas.

Along the way I was always interested in horse racing having gone to the local track Saratoga near my Berkshires home in Adams, Massachusetts. That took me down the path of gambling research. It was this combination of solid academic training and research and knowledge of gambling that attracted the many billionaires and other investment people to search me out.

I hope you readers enjoy my story, which is a combination of my experiences embedded into the modern advances in the financial markets, and I have been pleased to write it all down. Along the way, I interacted with many academic and trading greats from Nobel Prize winners to a number who started with nothing and became fabulously rich. Most of them won't write their stories so I hope my account is sufficient.

Why am I not a billionaire? Well, I suppose I could have been extremely wealthy. Actually my family and I are comfortable and we all can do what we want. But the billionaires are very focused, disciplined individuals who generally focus on one thing and do that well. They do not usually write books or give lectures all around the world. Well, George Soros is an exception and so is my colleague Ed Thorp. I like to be thorough and explain my ideas and help others. After more than 30 books and 200 research papers, the fun of writing took a lot of time but records and discusses lots of interesting things.

Chapter 2

The Early Days in Adams and at the University of Massachusetts in Amherst

I was born on August 30, 1941 in Adams, Massachusetts. I had the same birth date as my boyhood hero Ted Williams, arguably the greatest pure hitter in baseball history. Later, I discovered that Warren Buffett an investment hero, also shared the day.

To Ted Williams, hitting was a science. Each ball in the display case has Ted Williams' estimate of his batting average should the ball be thrown there. His eyesight was so good that he would not swing at a ball if it was a half inch outside the strike zone. Hence, the umpires realizing this knew if he did not swing it should be a ball.

Me at six months

Wedding of my mother and father, on the far right. On the far left is my mother's sister Rose, in the middle are my father's sisters Annie and Helen

My father with a new car

My mother, Mary Moser

My father, a great fisherman, truck driver and gas station owner, was very generous to his oldest son, me

My mother with my younger brother Gary and me

Me with sister Carol, who later worked at the Clark Art Museum in Williamstown (part of the Getty Museum) and little brother Gary

Merry Christmas

The three of us children, me, Carol and Gary posing for our Christmas card

Adams, a small town in the Berkshires was a very good place to grow up. Travel was mostly to Boston to see a Red Sox baseball game or to the Saratoga race track. My father, a truck driver and later gas station owner, was very generous and provided well for his family. He bought our house for $7,000 in 1941. We lived at 6 Forest Park Avenue on a quiet street near the downtown. I was the oldest with one brother and one sister. Growing up we were all very involved in various sports, especially me. In my teens, in the summer we would play basketball for 6 or 8 hours daily. I liked golf and used to play at a course just up the street from our house. I liked to caddy and most remember participation in the NCAA finals at Williams College. To get there I hitch hiked to North Adams then to Williamstown, then caddied for the day and returned to Adams. The young sure have a lot of energy. I was an altar boy at the local church, St. Thomas Aquinas. When I was 12, I and another young boy lit all the candles in the church. But we got out of that mess ok.

I was a decent but not great student and just barely got into UMass, Amherst. I had wanted to go to Georgia Tech but my mother nixed that idea. On day one at UMass, the engineering dean said look to your left and look to your right, only one of you three will make it. We had tough

On the left: Me with Sandra and Rachel with my mother and sister at the 1985 Kentucky Derby. In the 80s the dosage theory gave us the winner of the Kentucky Derby virtually every year. That year the two dual qualifiers were Spend a Buck who went wire to wire to win the race and Stephan's Odyssey. The $2 exacta paid $118.
On the right: My mother, Rachel and me on the bottom row with my mother's sister Lena and husband Otto, sister Rose and husband Fred.

The Early Days in Adams 11

Our church were I was an altar boy

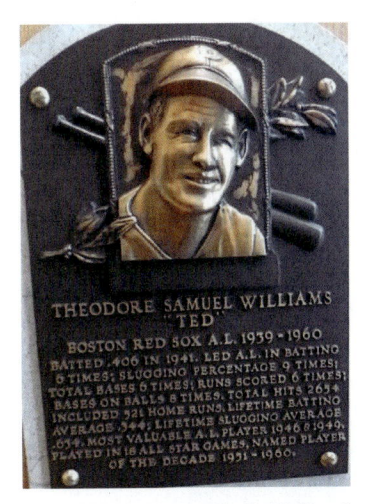

Ted Williams Baseball Hall of Fame Plaque

(Williams' assumed batting average at each spot in the strike zone)

loads with 7 courses. In the fall freshman term I got 4 Ds. A 69.2 D in calculus from Henry Skilling was tough to swallow but I always had a good attitude towards learning and was more interested in learning than the actual grades. I persevered and each semester trended higher in grades. A most excellent 99 in the physical chemistry exam from J Harold Smith in my junior year was a big accomplishment. By the fourth year I made

Tau Beta Pi, the engineering honors society and got a BS in Chemical Engineering. My colleagues in chemical engineering and chemistry were very good and I keep up with a few of them even now including Joseph Mayo, a chemistry major, who is now a pediatrician.

After my third UMass year I had an interesting job in Penn State with a group studying the strength and ductivity of various metals in the metallurgy department. We had a grand time that summer with a nice group working under our professor and traveling around the region near Penn State.

My strength and weakness has always been that I am interested in everything. So I applied to graduate schools in five fields and took Berkeley. That was a smart move. When Rachel was considering colleges and she was looking at Amherst, I returned to UMass and the engineering building. I was pleased to see a tribute to physics Professor "Flunking Joe" Marcus. I had statics and dynamics from this dynamic teacher. On day one he read the class roll, gave a pop quiz in the second class, in the third class he handed each of the some 40 students their paper individually, knowing all the names. He was a legend and got the flunking moniker because he was tough. But he was fair and we all learned a lot. I got decent grades from his class.

The university has expanded and is a top state school. The hedge fund alternative investment group is a strong one and I published two papers

Me in the Joseph Sol Marcus Atrium

Left: With my cousin from Trento in Venice. On the right: With my aunt Rose Kurpiel, my mother's sister was a champion runner and good tennis player.

in their journal the *Alternative Investment Analyst Review*[1] which publishes papers similar to the *Financial Analysts Journal* and the *Journal of Portfolio Management*.

Note

[1] See Lleo, S. and W. T. Ziemba (2014), How to lose money in financial markets: Examples from the recent financial crisis, *Alternative Investment Analyst Review*, *3*(3), 22–35 and W. T. Ziemba (2016), Understanding the Kelly Capital Growth Investment Strategy, *Alternative Investment Analyst Review*, *5*(2), 49–54.

Chapter 3

Reminiscences of the Early Days in Berkeley

This chapter is based on a talk given at the retirement of Professor Roger Wets at the University of California, Davis on October 10, 2008. Roger influenced my studies and research starting with a PhD course in stochastic programming in 1967. While Willard (Bill) Zangwill was my official PhD thesis advisor, with Jacob Marschak and Romesh Saigel as my committee, it was Wets who advised me the most in my dissertation on *Stochastic Programming and the Theory of Economic Policy*.

Roger's Retirement Party

While we had a very good day of talks in Roger's honor, I knew he was not really retiring just moving on from his full time position in the University of California, Davis mathematics department. The organizers invited a number of top researchers most of whom I knew well. These included Dick Cottle of Stanford, Alan King of IBM Research, John Birge of the University of Chicago, Suvrajeet Sen of Ohio State University now the University of Southern California and Terry Rockafellar of the University of Washington. These were all people who I know well and were interested in stochastic programming with ties to Roger's work. In my talk, I traced my arrival and days at Berkeley. I arrived in the fall of 1963 having picked Berkeley and their MBA program over studies in chemical engineering, metallurgy and patent law. From the start I was always interested in many subjects and that continued during my entire career into end May 2017 when I finished these memoirs.

Berkeley was the big time and it was exciting to be there. My initial courses were fine but I was keen to finish those basic courses and move onto more advanced research courses.

An early event I recall was walking in the main square on November 22, 1963 and learning of the assassination of US president John F Kennedy from my home state of Massachusetts. That was a great shock for all including me. It was a turning point for the world.

I did well in my courses and drifted towards the economics, operations research and statistics departments where I focused during my PhD in management science. After the first year I became a California resident and then had tuition of only $100 a quarter. So I could go to the top university in the world at that time for basically nothing. Along the way I picked up some scholarships and research assistantships and that plus financial help from my father. My father was always supportive and sadly I lost him on October 10, 1967 just prior to my finishing at Berkeley.

What was great at Berkeley was outstanding students and professors to push you to new levels of intellectual thinking. Each course was taught by a famous professor and each department was one of the top or the top one in the US and the world. Economics had several Nobel laureates in waiting such as Gerald Debreu and Daniel McFadden who I took courses with plus equally deserving Nobel potential winners such as Dale Jorgenson and Roy Radner. Both of these I studied with and they have moved on to Harvard and NYU, respectively, but other actual Nobel winners arrived later such as George Akerlof, the husband of Fed Chair Janel Yellen, herself a Berkeley business school professor as well.

The business school also had future Nobel laureates John Harsanyi and Oliver Williamson. A big star was philosopher C West Churchman. And the most useful was C Bartlett McGuire, a very versatile non-PhD who seemed to be helpful to all of us PhD students. Bart supervised my masters thesis, an inventory control system for the Lawrence Radiation Laboratory on the hill above the campus. Statistics had the best teachers or so I assumed when four of us, none from statistics, picked our best teacher and the result was four different members of the Berkeley statistics department. My choice was David Blackwell. I had Blackwell for dynamic programming which was a pure delight. No matter how vague the question he was always on top of it with a very clear response. It was greats like him I remember most from my Berkeley days plus courses so tough they pulled you up to a level higher and higher.

On left: With Roger and me in the salt mines in eastern Europe. On right: Roger Wets in Potsdam, 2004

Operations research was also #1 or #2 just like statistics. While star linear programming Professor George Dantzig left for Stanford in 1965, the remaining professors such as Bill Jewell, Robert Oliver, Ron Wolff were top notch. At the same time, Stanford was in competition with Berkeley in these areas and we had many visits there as students. They had an all star cast as well and it was Stanford where over the years I gave the most talks after leaving Berkeley.

The photos show Roger and I in a salt mine in eastern Europe, Roger in Potsdam in 2004, a 1981 conference with George Dantzig, Ellis Johnson, Philip Wolfe, Richard Cottle, Wets and others and finally a 2012 conference in Singapore.

Roger Wets visited Potsdam in 2004 during a stay at the Humboldt University in Berlin. I had pleasant visits to Humboldt twice, once was to lecture with Hans Foellmer on convex risk measures that I worked on with Terry Rockefellar; and at an international conference on stochastic programming in Berlin organized by Werner Roemish. My own international conference on stochastic programming in 1998 had a banquet at the wonderful UBC Anthropology Museum. I served as general chairman and Wets and I were program chairs. My strategy was very simple: who are the best 15 people in the field in the world, they are my plenary speakers. We edited a book with these lectures in Peter Hammer's series in the *Annals of Operations Research*. Other conferences since then have used

The picture shows a 2012 meeting in Singapore on variational inequalities. Roger Wets, third from the far left, stands out. Two positions to his left is Jong-Shi Pan and three positions to his left is his scientific grandson Defeng Sun

a different format but I had felt I wanted the main speakers to be the very best.

Roger Wets was from Belgium and first went to the Berkeley business school but he moved quickly to the mathematics department. He took courses that would have eventually led him to a degree in mathematics however, after one or two weeks, he realized that he would be stuck in partial differential equations and changed to engineering science. There was no operations research degree at that time. That allowed him to get his PhD exam in mathematical analysis, optimization and probability. Wets had an all star PhD committee including Economic Nobel Prize winner Gerard Debreu,[1] statistician David Blackwell,[2] and George B Dantzig.[3] Wets, extremely talented as well, made major contributions to stochastic and mathematical programming and various mathematical areas. He introduced me to stochastic programming in 1967 and I took operations research, statistics and economics courses doing my PhD in the business school. While I cannot keep up with him in mathematics, I learned a lot that has been useful since.

Shown are the participants in a 1981 Brazil-Germany-USA conference. The father of linear programming, George Dantzig is in the middle (white shirt) with nonlinear programming great Philip Wolfe from IBM Research on his right, Dick Cottle of Stanford is on the far right, left of Dantzig is Terry Rockefellar (who studied at Harvard and is from the University of Washington, perhaps the world's top convexity expert), and Ellis Johnson (from Georgia Tech a discrete optimization expert). Johnson and Cottle were from Berkeley just before me. A young slender Wets is the fourth from the left in the second row

Notes

[1] Debreu had a lucky opportunity to come to the US. A member of the staff of the Cowles Commission at Yale University told a professor in France that he had a position for one good young French mathematical economist. The professor had two good candidates: Debreu had the good fortune to win the coin toss and get the position. Later he moved to the Berkeley economics department and worked with Kenneth Arrow on the work related to Arrow-Debreu securities for which he won the Nobel prize in economics.

[2] I recall four of us grad students including Richard Grinold (who later went to Barra and Wells Fargo), Steve Stigler (son of economics Nobel prize winner George Stigler and now professor of statistics at the University of Chicago) and Steve Bradley (who went to the Harvard Business School). We discussed who was the best teacher we had at Berkeley. All of us had taken courses in several departments. We each had a different person but each was a member of the Berkeley statistics department. My choice by a wide margin was David Blackwell, who I had for dynamic programming. Blackwell, who was an African-American taught at Howard University and because of his brilliance was recruited to Berkeley. He had eight children and no phone in his house. In the class, no matter how vague the question asked by the student, he would

respond by saying I understand and give a perfect answer. He wrote one paper on discrete dynamic programming that was twelve pages long, published in the *Annals of Statistics* that was an entire Berkeley course.

[3] Dantzig was the father of linear programming and much of optimization. When he was a PhD student at Berkeley, he was once late for a class. On the blackboard were two problems that he assumed were homework problems. He was very disappointed that he could only solve one of them. Little did he know that these two problems were very famous unsolved problems in statistics put on the board by the famed statistician Jersey Neyman. The previously unsolved problem he solved became his PhD thesis.

Chapter 4

The Start of a New Department in Vancouver

I left Berkeley in late summer 1968 and headed to Vancouver. My heart was set on a position at Stanford or the second choice UCLA but I did not get offers in either place after interviews. At Stanford, the person who beat me out was thought to have the potential to be a better teacher. Despite them thinking I was better at research, they took him. As I predicted then, he did not get tenure as he did not publish enough. I do not know about the teaching but top research universities like Stanford rarely will tenure weak researchers. I did get offers at Rochester and Northwestern but chose the new school University of British Columbia (UBC). In 1968, the business school, then called the Faculty of Commerce, was just starting. Like me, most of the faculty were young newly minted PhDs from top US universities. One of my Berkeley graduate school days roommates, Erwin Diewert was from Vancouver and always pushed the UBC case. He actually went to the University of Chicago but moved to the UBC economics department 2 years later.

Given that the school was new all the courses were new ones. So we could devise our own courses. The loads were high, three courses one term and two the other but the terms were short and the teaching was over by May. There was a long summer and after 4 years of teaching there was a 60% paid sabbatical. The top schools have yearly loads of two or three courses. Later, when I had a chaired professorship I had a load of four and used the chair money to buy off the fourth course bringing it down to three. In 1968, I got into the grant application business right away and got the first National Science and Engineering Research Council (NSERC) grant awarded to the business school for $4,000. When I left UBC in 2006 to take early retirement, I had a 5 year $52,000 or $260,000 in total grant and the current grants are even higher. The grants did not provide salary but they paid for research trips to conferences, computer supplies and equipment, secretarial assistance to type papers and reports, etc. So this was very helpful and especially good was the way NSERC viewed research. If it was published in very top journals, they were happy. So it was a US style approach to promote publishing. The other granting agency, the Social Science and Humanities Research Council of Canada (SSHRC) was more project oriented and you had to focus on more specific deliverables. But over the years I got a number of SSHRC grants and I had NSERC grants my whole career there from 1968 to 2006.

Besides some good courses to teach, we were forced to teach some undergraduate courses where the students were weak and hated the courses. Basic statistics was such an example. My teaching is such that the best students always love it as I bring together so many things, but the weak ones are threatened. This happened not only at UBC. I found in 2005 that even at the esteemed MIT, students can mark you down as a bad teacher even if your lectures and course materials are terrific. Having a fair but tough teaching assistant at MIT turned some of my class against me as they feared — they would not get the highest grade — something they were

Attending a UBC graduation with colleague George Gorelik

used to their whole career. So there was one group which thought I was wonderful and another group which felt threatened by the heavy load and risk of not getting the top grade.

Eventually, I was able to move to a more pleasant teaching load and in my last years at UBC I had a yearlong PhD sequence on nonlinear programming and portfolio theory in the fall and applied stochastic programming and asset-liability management in the winter. Then I had two MBA modules that were half courses adding up to the third course on large scale financial planning models and world stock markets: anomalies and behavioral finance. This was a nice load.

In 1974, I had my first class in stochastic programming with a great group of PhD students and we studied asset-liability management. This led to the early papers in *Management Science* and *Operations Research* and eventually to the Russell Yasuda Kasai and other models at Frank Russell and the Siemens Austria InnoALM model and a number of important books.[1]

The management, who never liked me much, felt I had too good a deal, but I was always well respected by the best people around the world and I have had to be satisfied with that.

The focus of the department was changing. When the school was reorganized with fewer departments and operations research and transportation were merged. In the new department most members were into logistics, production and supply chain management and the name was changed to operations and logistics which was not good for my finance work. At the same time, the finance department lost most of their good people and were left with weaker theorists who did not appreciate anomalies, asset and asset-liability management and the other things I was interested in. The management was mean to the end, moving all the materials in my office into unmarked boxes in a small room in another building a week before I returned from MIT so it was hard to find things. Then later they forced me to vacate even that. So I needed to rent storage which I still have to pay for.

For a variety of reasons, including the chance to teach at MIT and the University of Washington in 2005, I took early retirement as of the end of June 2006. Needless to say, there was no retirement party for me! The rest of the book interweaves the stories of the things I did while UBC served as my home base.

Vancouver and UBC were popular for outside visitors and with my travel and work in the operations research-management science community, I had

24   *The Adventures of a Modern Renaissance Academic*

With Gordon Sick in 1990 in Ephesus, Turkey

With Len in Venice

many connections. Our group was strong in theory so we had a first class seminar series. The emphasis was on theory and, in fact, there was an endless search for the so-called senior applied guy. One colleague, Shelby Brumelle, remarked that maybe I had become that person. In the early days, the seminar organizer got a half course credit for arranging the speakers and the other half could be made up supervising a PhD thesis. In the end, after 36 years, I had chaired 10 PhDs in various areas including financial modeling, theoretical stochastic programming, energy policy, stochastic dominance and accounting theory, which I believe is more than any other professor there.

While others found seminar organizing hard work, it was fun for me, since I had a vast knowledge of people, I could draw top talent to UBC who were always keen to come. We were always great hosts and people liked the city and we enjoyed taking them on walks around Stanley Park. In my stochastic programming class in the winter term I would invite skiers such as Dan Rosen of Algorithmics in Toronto, Gerd Infanger working with George Dantzig at Stanford, Georg Pflug of the University of Vienna and Alan King of IBM to Whistler which became Whistler–Blackcomb, the site of the 2010 Olympics. Not everyone was a skier as there were visitors in the fall term as well such as Suvrujeet Sen of the University of Arizona. A superstar visitor was Egon Balas of Carnegie Mellon.[2] They all gave good seminar talks and spoke in my nonlinear programming and portfolio theory, and applied stochastic programming and asset-liability management courses. Leonard MacLean of Dalhousie University came on sabbatical to work with me and from the start we established a good working relationship and friendship that continues into 2017.

I gave the nonlinear programming and portfolio theory and practice course in the fall and applied stochastic programming and asset-liability management in the winter. Over about a 20 year period I had about 4–8 students in each class, not a lot but there were good students

- Some from the mathematics department like Harry Zhang, now at the Imperial College Mathematics Department in London.
- Finance like Gordon Sick who went to work with Steve Ross at Yale and is now at the University of Calgary.
- Dennis Kira who went to Lakehead College and later Concordia.
- Visitors from Europe like Erik Fleten from Norway.
- Markus Rudolf from the University of Zurich now a major professor and Dean at WHU in Germany.

- Plus our own PhD students I supervised or co-supervised such as Amin Amershi who was hired at Stanford in accounting and later went to the University of Minnesota.
- Jerry Kallberg who went to NYU and later the Thunderbird School in Arizona and then to Washington State University in eastern Washington near the great wine producing centre around Walla Walla.
- Martin Kusy who went to Concordia and is now the Dean of the Brock University Business School.
- Donald Hausch who became my racetrack betting co-author on five books and is now a Dean at the University of Wisconsin after a Northwestern PhD.
- Horand Gassmann who I convinced to move to our PhD program and later supervised him and he went to Dalhousie University in Halifax, Nova Scotia; we edited the book based on the Halifax International Conference on Stochastic Programming in 2010.[3]
- Kats Sawaki from Japan was in the 1974 stochastic programming course and later became a major administrator in Nanzan University in Nagoya.

It was frontier times in BC then. The operations research team at the lumber giant MacMillan Bloedel had to go to San Francisco to find a computer powerful enough to run their linear program which took 24 hours. Then there were the visits by Colorado School of Mines applied OR crusader Gene Woolsey who, when he gave a seminar, planted the flag and talked about tripping over things in Mexico and how much he improved efficiency in the plant by just organizing the tool boxes. Before Japanese management became popular, OR had already recognized the importance of paying attention. Woolsey was a priceless speaker on a mission to force the mighty Stanford, the symbol of operations research theory, to do more applications. In fact, despite their tremendous power in theory, they did do a lot of applications but they were a symbol of how the field had gone too far in the direction of theory. Woolsey was eventually successful as the field turned more toward applications and he was a good visitor for us. We were in the 1970s to 2000 area on the top research circuit and I became friends with major researchers all over the world. Stanford had three departments with Operations Research being the most prestigious. The Engineering Systems Department had high powered talent like Ron Howard and David Luenberger who worked on novel applications. Finally, the low prestige Industrial Engineering Department was into standard applications. As time evolved they all merged when Condolezza Rice was provost prior to joining the Bush administration. Then the status reversed with the IE people at the top in status.

My UBC department Chair Jack Mitten was into interesting social activities and among them was the building of an igloo in the local Cypress mountain. There was a good collegiality in the 1970s and 1980s which waned later as more people left and the school became more politicized.

My closest colleague in the Management Science Department was Shelby Brumelle who I recruited from Berkeley when I was set up to go to UBC. He was a Cal Tech undergraduate and a deep thinker. We did some papers and one book together, mostly related to lottery research. He was a top theorist in stochastic processes, queuing theory and related modeling. Sadly we lost him to cancer around the time of the September 11, 2001 attack on New York and Washington.

This chapter is a synopsis of teaching at UBC, even with its difficulties, I was able to pursue a variety of interests: it was near the mountains for skiing and camping, ferry rides to the islands felt like cruises. Through visitors at UBC, I forged life long friendships around the world but have few ties to the current business school. However, I do work with people in the statistics and computer science departments. Chapter 31 is a tour through the wonderful academic travel and related experiences that I was able to have.

Notes

[1] See Ziemba and Mulvey (1998), Wallace and Ziemba (2005) and Zenios and Ziemba (2006, 2007).

[2] Balas was in Romania and escaped the country and went to Hungary as a stamp collector then came to the US with a first class reputation as one of the world's top experts in integer programming and discrete optimization. He was first at the University of Toronto then became an Institute Professor at Carnegie Mellon University in Pittsburgh. His own memoir, *Will to Freedom: Journey through Fascism and Communism*, Syracuse University Press, 2000, is wonderful to read and relates the story of solitary confinement in communist prisons for him and his wife who is also a professor at Carnegie Mellon. At 94 he is still active. I met with him at the July 2015 International Conference on Mathematical Programming in Pittsburgh.

[3] Gassmann, H. and W. T. Ziemba (2012). *Stochastic Programming: Applications in Finance, Energy, Planning and Logistics*. Singapore: World Scientific.

Chapter 5

Travels on a Flying Carpet

My wife, Sandra, got the travel bug early. She was part of a very strong class in honors economics at the University of California, Berkeley — others included famous economists Robert Hall (Stanford) and Thomas Sargent (economics Nobel Prize winner, 2011 at NYU). She did research with star Professor Roy Radner, one of those possibly better than many economics Nobel Prize winners. Radner was friendly with Andreas Papandreau and became involved with the Center for Planning and Economic Research in Athens. Sandra went there on a fellowship after her undergrad for the academic year 1964–1965. There she met University of Wisconsin professor Arthur Goldberger which led to her going to Madison for an MA in Economics. She had two summers traveling around Europe and at Christmas went to Turkey and Israel with an overnight transit in Cyprus. It was her year of three divided cities: Berlin, Jerusalem and Nicosia. Indeed, she liked to travel!

The Samaria Gorge

In 1970, we married on a late Friday afternoon on April 24, 1970 in a big ceremony in Carson City, Nevada with two witnesses. We were camping in Nevada and California. We had a summer off from UBC teaching and bought a red VW camper bus for $3,000, picked it up at the German factory and traveled throughout Europe. We drove through Italy, the painted monasteries of Romania, ate yoghurt in Bulgaria, traveled down the coast of Yugoslavia, walked the Samaria George on Crete and visited many other great places. We saw the Danube in flood, found ourselves at a rally in Yugoslavia, misread a no parking sign and had our new van towed while we were shopping to outfit it, and panned for gold in Northern Greece on the road to Istanbul. The picture shows Sandra in a peasants outfit. We wanted to buy one but to get one we would have to send money and get it made later. Unfortunately, we did not follow up. The picture of me is on the Danube and in one of our camps.

The Samaria Gorge trip was especially good. It was undeveloped then so we took a bus from the delightful Chania and stayed at a local inn in Omalos which was 4 kilometers from the beginning of the longest and deepest gorge in Europe. In the morning we walked to the edge and descended switch backs for more than an hour, about a kilometer through a pine and cypress forest and then walked the 18 kilometers along the river trail to

Me in my flooded Danube hat

Sandra trying out a peasant outfit near the Pec Pass in Yugoslavia

the Mediterranean on the south side of Crete. We saw only two people on that trip. Then there was a boat ride to the town of Agia Roumela which had good food and retsina (we drank too much). We camped out in the woods so that we could get up in time for the 6 am bus back to Chania the next day. We took photos and almost got a National Geographic article. In later years we would make three more hikes through the gorge. In 1980, we carried our 1 year old daughter with one carrying her and one the diaper bag. The later trips were fine, but the event was discovered, so was more and more crowded with easier ways to get there and back.

Some delightful Rachel as a young child follow with Sandra and in Efes, Turkey.

When we arrived in Turkey, it was an exotic place with great treasures. But we were novices. I was the buyer enjoying the bargaining process with Sandra the one who saw the better quality pieces. We drove around Turkey and had a great first trip there.

In Kayseri we bought our first carpet — quite an emotional experience. The salesperson even had us go to another stall and ask if we had gotten a good deal... of course the other vendor just nodded assent! That first carpet — a prayer carpet — cost $65. A lot of money when we were

Northeast Anatolian prayer kilim and kilim as a door

living on $5/day! In Urgup in the Cappadocia area, we met a carpet dealer, Abdulkadir (Kadir) Akatay, and became friends. He looked like an Oxford don with his perfect English and nice dress. Later, we met him in Kuşadasi, near Ephesus, a gem of a Roman ruin, high on the list of places to see in Turkey. Later, we were to co-author a book on Turkish kilims with Kadir. In Kuşadasi we bought more weavings and leather coats. Kilims have many uses as the one here hanging as a mosque door. Later, in 1973 we took another long trip, again picking up a new VW camper in Germany but starting in the winter. At this time Sandra was into yoga practice and we set out to get to India. Though we didn't make it to India, we did have a fantastic trip lasting from January to the end of May going from Germany to Afghanistan and back through ancient Persia up to Herat. Herat was a gem with all sorts of antiques and carpets for sale.

I had a sabbatical after 4 years of teaching at UBC and visited Stanford for the spring quarter of 1972 (UBC classes ended in March so it was convenient). Bill Sharpe, future economics Nobel laureate, was kind and arranged that visit. I taught statistics in the business school. The thing I remember most was the Hewlett Packard hand held calculators. At the midterms, there were a few of them fighting for the electrical outlets and by the final exam, virtually all of the students had the calculators and did not need the electric outlets. We had a great time and started doing pottery, jewelry making and making a nice dining table with Turkish tiles. I recall that quarter as the one that I worked the hardest. The reason for that was an invitation to speak in Coimbra, Portugal at a NATO conference. I had NSERC grants which covered the travel. I was scheduled to give four talks right after the world's top nonlinear programmer, Philip Wolfe of IBM. It was tough to follow Wolfe as he was a giant and a great lucid speaker but I managed to do it and he was generous and friendly to a young professor. I wrote three good papers based on those lectures including: one on portfolio theory with stable distributions. Eugene Fama and Paul Samuelson had simple papers on this but I did it much better in the one asset and multi-asset cases. The paper is still the standard for allocating these fat tailed assets. Coimbra had great white and blue pottery and we bought a tea set; there were also colorful floral designs on white background. After the conference, we traveled across Portugal and Spain.

We returned to Stanford. In the summer I had the pleasure of seeing the great Kenneth Arrow in action. Each day at 4 pm there was a mathematical economics seminar. The room was filled with great visitors like Karl Shell of Cornell, the editor of the *Journal of Economic Theory*. I was working on the book *Stochastic Optimization Models in Finance* (later with co-editor Raymond Vickson) which became a great book and helped in my promotion to full professor. But I missed one thing — options — which were just starting. Shell said to include the famed Black and Scholes 1973 paper — the book was in his Academic Press series, but I did not pick that up until later. Now I am an options trader in the equity index futures markets. Anyway, in each day's seminar, some usually young professor from a top US school would present a talk that they had worked on for months.

Me in a cave in Deriyinku

Cappadocia

Buying embroideries from a local in Cappadocia

These were the cream of the US economists and they would discuss in a noisy fashion the paper. Then at the end there would be complete silence and Arrow would start to talk. And he would raise the discussion to a new level and provide better ways to do the paper and what was wrong with it. Arrow is a very nice pleasant person, he was just 100 times smarter than everyone else in the room. So day after day he would do this no matter what the topic — theoretical, applied, data, etc. It was just amazing to watch him. To this day I have never seen such an impressive performance. The best most impressive talk during my days in Berkeley was by Richard Bellman, the inventor of dynamic programming — I recall two great seminars he gave in Berkeley with no notes — he just took his jacket off and began filling the blackboard with equations. Another giant was Lev Pontryagin who formulated and proved the maximum principle in control theory which is related to the optimal way to do things. He was blind and spoke in his native Russian. My Berkeley control theory professor Lucien Polak translated to english but each time he made a mistake, Pontryagin corrected him in english. At Berkeley and Stanford there were many other great speakers, but Arrow was the best though I never saw the famous physicist Richard Feynmann of Cal Tech, reported to be at Arrow's level. I have always gotten along well with the greats and I learned from one of them at Berkeley, C West Churchman, that they are so big they have no trouble bending over to talk to everyone. It is the mediocre people that give me trouble.

A very interesting book to read is Englund (2008). Economics Nobel Laureate and Harvard Professor Michael Spence, (now at New York University) relates an interesting Arrow story: when his term paper in Arrow's course had been lost, nervously he brought a new copy to Arrow who read the 12 pages in 2 seconds per page, including the math. Spence, of course, thought that Arrow had just skimmed it until he asked a penetrating question about a result on page 5.

Arrow being the top professor in a very powerful economics department at Stanford felt he should participate in student seminars to help the students so he went frequently. In almost every case he was so much ahead of them they were completely overwhelmed. So they decided to play a trick on him and discuss a paper that they fully expected he would not know anything about. They choose a paper on the economics of anthropology of apes and just when they thought they had tricked him, he pointed out that he had refereed the paper and pointed out some things wrong with it.

My sabbatical went to the summer of 1973 with teaching at UBC to start in September. We planned a great trip starting in January. We went to Germany and bought a new white VW camper bus, again from the factory for US$3,000. Despite a low salary, money lasted well then and we could go to very interesting places many of which one cannot safely return to now.

In Switzerland we almost started an international incident by driving in the park near the zoo in north Zurich where I was giving a lecture at the University of Zurich. Fortunately my host, the late Professor Peter Kall, vouched for me and we were let off with a warning to not drive in the park. This was the first of many visits to the University of Zurich which continue to this day. In the early days I visited operations research speaking about theoretical stochastic programming and in recent years its the Swiss banking institute where I speak on applied investment topics invited by Thorsten Hens. In fall 2017 I am giving a course in portfolio theory and applications.

In Yugoslavia, the high point was the Plitvici Lakes which rival Iguazu Falls on the common border of Brazil and Argentina as fabulous water falls, spreading over a large area with walk ways to enjoy them. Niagara is bigger and spreads into two countries, but these two are more beautiful. Iguazu Falls has shops with semi-precious gems for sale.

We went through the mountains in Macedonia camping on a peak and awakening to a group of boys and men who were very interested in us.

We drove to Italy and spent lovely days there in Florence and drove through Italy taking the ferry from Brindisi to Greece. Our car was hoisted onto the deck of the small ferry with two giant rubber bands and lifted off when we got to Greece.

Driving through the hills with the colorful goats passing by was a lovely scene. Prices were low then, we recall a crayfish dinner with a large plate

A boat with a kilim

Pamukkale and Troy

of crayfish with calamaries and retsina on Mykonos. It was a real feast for $5.

We spent some time in Greece. When we hit Turkey, it was winter so we headed for the south coast staying at places like Mercin, Antalya, etc.

In Ankara, I gave some lectures at the Middle East Technical University. Turkish students and faculty are very good with many at the top US and European universities. In some places, like the Princeton financial engineering department, there is a pipeline to bring very top Turkish students to the US and they have been very successful. Ankara is less interesting than Istanbul but does have a wonderful museum of Anatolian civilizations going back more than 10,000 years. The founder of modern Turkey, Kemal Mustafa Attaturk moved the capital there and there is a monument to him.

We spent some days in Konya having good meals at the restaurant of a former chef for the Russian embassy. After each meal we vowed to leave but were always invited back. We had the best Adana kebabs there. Konya is the center where Mevlana Rumi the 13th century mystic whose belief in the use of poetry, music and dance as a path to god led to the practice of the whirling dervishes.

We traveled around western Anatolia including Troy, Bergamo which had one of the earliest libraries and Pamukkale which has these interesting limestone formations. I fondly recall George Elford whom we met in Cappadocia in the winter of 1973 — that year we got "stuck" in a couple places including Cappadocia and Konya. George was a chess master who could play lightening chess in which moves must be made in 10 minutes or less. George could also play up to 20 games simultaneously blindfolded, so he had a great memory. He had plans to use a metal detector to discover gold.

In eastern Turkey, the young kids would throw rocks at foreign cars but we survived that. We often camped at gas stations. In one, we went in for warmth by the fire inside and a group of them were sitting around drinking tea and playing with knives. It was great that we were married with specially designed gold wedding rings. Some brothers and sisters with no rings had been killed for suspected incest. But we had no real trouble except in Mercin where some kid hit Sandra with a needle. I ran him down to show our displeasure. Fortunately, she was all right. Otherwise there were no incidents. Eastern Turkey was a swamp of mud with interesting places. You could buy good kilims for $20 and we got some. The mistake was not buying the $100 ones which later were worth thousands. But we got some good ones.

Throughout Turkey there are beautiful mosques where the faithful pray five times a day. Here is me in one of them in Eastern Turkey with a few young boys. The nomads with their camels are frequently on the move as we see here. The East has many interesting buildings such as that shown here.

Iran and Afghanistan

Eventually, we decided it was time to cross the border into Iran where I was to lecture in Shiraz. When we hit the Iran border, it was a new world with a lovely paved highway going right up to the border. So the mud was finished and the weather warmed. We drove to Tabriz, the first major city, then to Teheran and saw the Shah's jewels and other sights.

We headed south to Isfahan and its spectacular sights and Shiraz where I gave lectures on my academic work. It was good to meet colleagues there. Iran was safe but, if you did not give them the exact change at gas stations, they would cheat you. Houses had to have high walls with protection because if no one was there thieves might take all the belongings. So someone must always be in the house.

Near Shiraz is Persepolis the city of Cyrus the Great where the Shah had just celebrated the 2,500 year anniversary. The British Museum has examples of the fine carvings that are seen in Persepolis. Besides the great ruins there, they set up nice yurt-type tents with Persian designed fabric on the walls.

Then we worked our way back to eastern Iran or Persia as we preferred to call it. The border town in this Baluchistan was Mashad. Then we went into Afghanistan. All along the route, people were either coming or going

Me with some children, caravans traveling as they frequently do, and a scene from the Turkish east

On the roof of our hosts' house in Shiraz and dinner in Isfahan

The photos shows Sandra on the balcony of the Shah Abbas hotel in Isfahan and Persepolis

to India. In those days India was a standard goal of travels and Sandra who had been studying yoga wanted to go there.

The first town, Herat, was a bargainers paradise — a junk shop full of treasures so heaven for me. But we soon realized that cashing money was difficult. To cash a $20 travelers' check might take 2 to 4 hours (and we had the problem that most of our travel checks were of larger denomination).

Bargaining in Herat   Closing the deal

However, that money would buy a lot in Afghan currency. An 18 inch *naan* (bread) cost two cents. For the equivalent of about $2.25 you could have custom made sandals and for $20 you could get a good six by eight foot rug. We learned that the road to Kandahar was full of bandits — indeed as it still has been in the recent war that George W Bush got the US into. We decided to go no further.

After 5 months off from research work I was keen to get back. The return trip was an adventure in itself as we collected trunks which were full of our purchases. At night we had to take these out so we could open the bed. And at borders they created a problem. We drove back across Iran and Europe and arrived in Zurich. There I sold the camper for 12,000 Swiss francs so I got more than we paid for the car. Such is the beauty of currency changes — if it goes your way. The Swiss franc was then four to the Canadian dollar and we got more than we paid, now in 2017 it's worth more than five times as much.[1]

In the fall, I had a visiting position in the Berkeley business school and I commuted up there from Stanford in the 1970 red VW camper with our dog Shanti, a pure white Samayoed. It was great teaching again in Berkeley and rekindled my great love of Berkeley.

Return to India and Afghanistan

In 1974, we returned to Asia to finally take Sandra to India. We went directly to India expecting to travel around the subcontinent. We began in Bombay visiting the caves Ajanta and Ellora, took a train to Delhi, went to the Taj Mahal, Jaipur, etc. It was hot. Then there was a train strike and we found travel via bus very difficult as the seats were oversold, and people rode on the roof, etc.

So we took a break and went to Kabul. Flying in was interesting as there were no lights at the Kabul airport. Also we were stuck for 27 hours in the Delhi airport before the flight. Sandra always wanted to go places that were difficult to get to. We met a couple (a pilot and a stewardess) who worked for Varig in Miami. Together we rented a jeep and driver for a week (for $100 for each couple total cost for the car, driver and the four of us) and took off via the Solange tunnel to the North. That was a memorable week with visits to Bandi Amir, the five beautiful blue lakes, the valley of Bamiyan and the two giant Buddhas (we walked on the head of one), and Mazari-Sharif known for its Blue Mosque to Ali where the pigeons turn white on arrival. In Mazari we had some fantastic dinners at the Bakti restaurant. I used to say it was so neat that it was worth getting sick to eat there on tables covered with nice Afghan carpets! Actually with fully cooked lamb we had no problem. For six people I recall paying $1.85 in total. They sure had inflation under control by making it difficult for foreigners to exchange funds! We bought some good carpets there.

Turkish Flatweave Book

I found a nice paperback book on Persian tribal carpets published by Scorpion in London. It seemed that we could produce a similar book on Turkish kilims and other flat weaves. So I approached Scorpion and made a deal to co-publish the book *Turkish Flat Weaves* which came out in 1979 just prior to Rachel's birth. We had bought a number of good pieces but the book needed more plus greater rarer pieces. So co-author Abdul Kadir Akatay came from Turkey to Vancouver. Together we visited the textile museum in Washington, DC and some noted collectors and dealers such as Dennis Dodds in Philadelphia and Arky Robbins in San Francisco.

The Taj Mahal

The book was finished and I bought 2,000 copies at $4 each to lower Scorpion's risk and have books for us to sell and give away. These were with our Yoruk carpets and kilims logo. Then Scorpion had the remaining 3,000 printed with their logo in London. We received some royalties on their sales. As a publisher with one book selling was complicated. We got some in various places but the major sales were to Hachet a French book seller with a branch in Turkey. They paid only in Turkish lira so to get the money out I would buy carpets from Lutfu Bayhan, a major dealer in the Istanbul

The photos show the jeep we rented, the yurts we stayed in, the blue Bandi Amir lakes and the Bamyin Valley with the Buddhas that the Taliban destroyed. Sandra with a purchase and our group enjoying dinner at the Bakti restaurant. The fellow in the middle was our Miami companion, and the white pigeons of Mazari.

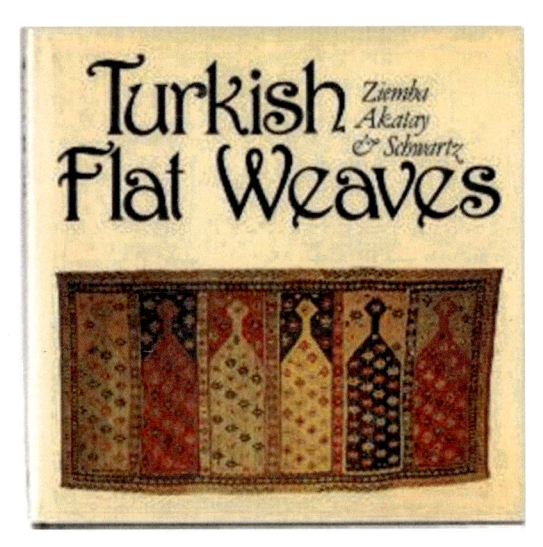

Spinning and weaving in Anatolia. Spun wool is woven into carpets and kilims either on a horizontal or vertical loom. We observed this process in Anatolian villages.

Turkish Flatweave cover

bazaar. I would bargain then about half the cost would be the Hachet sales and half new money. Then I had more carpets to keep or sell.

 Some we kept and some I sold or auctioned off. The plan worked until Hachet would not pay for the last 400 books so we never got paid for those and attempts to contact them failed. But all in all it was a great experience to do the book and it got me into the concept of self publishing which I

In St Petersburg with Elena Tsvara and Zari Rachev 1992

Tiles in the Rustem Pasha

Detail of one of my favorite carpets with a lovely design (15th century anatolian)

would later do successfully with the racing book *Betting at the Racetrack* in 1986 and the lotto 6/49 book (less successfully). In 1986, I had 3,000 copies of BATR printed (6″ by 9″ format) for $9,000 total and sold them all for $24.95 retail. Prior to that, Sandra had produced an 8.5 × 11 version for a mail order racing outlet which sold 4,000 in 1 month at $49.95 giving Don and me a $10,000 fee. The leftover books from them I bought for $1 each and I sold them all.

The Pazyryk Carpet

The study of oriental carpets is interesting and the field has various types of experts and advanced amateur collectors. They have their own literature, commercial and academic, some journals with the best being *Hali*, with great photos and articles. I subscribed early on and have the full collection. The star academics are an odd mix. At the top and still the best is Walter Denny, a University of Massachusetts art history professor. Walter maintains the carpets at Harvard's Fogg museum. He did his Harvard PhD there on the 15th–16th century Iznik tiles in the Rustem Pasha mosque in Istanbul and is an excellent tour guide and writer of significant articles and books. Other stars are Dr Jon Thompson, a London physician and big expert on Turkomen carpets and Dr Elena Tsvara of St Petersburg who curates the ethnographic museum there and its famed Bulbughoff carpets. These were made in 1907 and stored away — they look like they were made last week!

We were the guests of famed fat tailed financial market expert Professor Zari Rachev in 1992 following a keynote at the International Informs Conference in Helsinki. To support herself, Elena was selling tribal jewelry. We were fortunate to return in 2013 to see the vast differences in Moscow and St Petersburg.

Also in St Petersburg is the famous Pazyryk carpet hidden away in the Hermitage in an obscure Siberian section of the museum. The carpet, dating from the 5th century BCE, was found in 1949 in a frozen Siberian burial chamber filled with felts, mummies of people and horses and other items all on display. The exact origin of the carpet is unknown though it is likely Scythian as the horses are nearly identical to horsemen on a frieze in the ancient city of Persepolis.[2]

What makes this carpet famous and important is that the next high quality carpets from Seljuk date to the 13th century. If anything the Pazyryk carpet is of higher quality than the geometric Seljuk carpets. That's fully 18 centuries: so where are the intervening carpets? There are

Rachel in Samarkand April 2016 along with some ceilings

some fragments from Egypt and other bits and pieces but no real carpets. The Seljuk carpets had been in the Turkish and Islamic Arts Museum in Istanbul with some of them now housed in the new carpet museum near the Aya Sofya and the Topkapi Museum in Istanbul.

There were other good scholars and one was David Brown in Vancouver who studied antiques and carpets as a hobby. David and I taught an extension class at UBC twice, which was challenging to sound like an expert on all sorts of areas and evaluate pieces the attendees brought in. Later, I did the course twice with Beth Nobel who is academically trained in art history. Vancouver at the time was still a very simple place but there were a few people who were serious students. To boost my knowledge I went and spoke at some oriental run conferences.

In the winter break in 1982, when we were both visiting professors at UCLA, I went on a trip to Central Asia with a group from Boston who were mostly Harvard University Professors' wives with Walter Denny. That was a real treat. Walter is simply the best at oriental carpets, tiles and related art work which he has written about extensively. He has a photographic memory and tells good stories. We arrived in Moscow. I recall many phone calls to my room which I thought must be the authorities checking up on me but nothing happened. The museums were great and the city a delight. Then it was off the Central Asia to see Samarkand, Bokhara and Shakhrisabz which were right above northern Afghanistan, there the people looked just like the Afghans. It is great now to recall these wonderful 70s and 80s trips that are more difficult if not impossible to make today. Sandra and Rachel went with an Oxford–Cambridge organized tour of Central Asia in April 2016. They went to Uzbekistan and Turkmenistan.

We went on a *Hali* oriental carpet magazine organized trip to Georgia and Armenia with a stop in Istanbul in May of 2016 and Hali has a fall trip to Iran which starts in Shiraz and ends in Teheran. It would be nice to go, maybe next year. Armenia has many museums with beautiful antique

Carpets in Armenian and feast there and a view of the old part of Tblisi

carpets likely made by Armenians living in the Ottoman empire. Many carpets and kilims known as Anatolian likely were woven by Armenians.

Oriental Carpet Conferences

It is fun and interesting to go to the international oriental rug conferences which are held every 3 years in interesting places like Istanbul, Milan, Venice and Florence and San Francisco. It is a separate academic field where everyone has a job somewhere else, except for the dealers who are there to sell their goods. It is a lot like London, Vancouver, etc., where the majority of rich people made their money somewhere else. The conference in Italy was split between Milan, Florence and Venice — all places with great carpets and it was nice to revisit all of them. The conference in Istanbul was organized by Memhet Çetinkaya. It highlighted the collection of Josephine Powell who had traveled extensively and collected a superb set of Anatolian kilims. Some of the bold designs of these kilims are shown below.

Following the conference we took a tour to Eastern Turkey to update ourselves about current conditions there. I was able to buy nice Persian senneh kilims in Erzurum. They were new but well made with good materials.

Memhet and Walter on a panel at the International Oriental Rug Conference, Istanbul and noted Kilim collector, the late Josephine Powell

Designs on Anatolian Kilims

Cathryn Cootner, wife of the late Paul Cootner of efficient market fame and author of one of the most important efficient market books, was one of the organizers of the San Francisco meeting. While Paul was winning big time in commodity futures at MIT, she invested some of the family money into a house full of impeccable oriental rugs and weavings. Her home on Mayfield street at Stanford University, where Paul moved, was simply a gem to see. (By Stanford policy, houses on the campus are reserved for faculty, so when Paul died, she had to move.) She became the curator of the carpet collection at the De Young Museum in San Francisco.

In recent visits we have been impressed by how many entrepreneurs in Istanbul are from the east. Memhet Çetinkaya, the top carpet dealer in Istanbul and one of world's major experts with impeccable taste, now has four shops with beautiful pieces. He grew up in eastern Turkey where many of the top business people in Istanbul originated. Besides the antique pieces, he has top quality new pieces in silk and wool with classic Caucasian designs using the best materials including natural dyes. Some 350 women in Uzbekistan and 400 in Armenia are making the pieces and boosting their family income. His most recent project is beautiful silk scarves made hand woven with material and dyed by Mehmet himself using natural dyes. They

An Armenian embroidery

Me with a yellow Suzani from Uzbekistan

are woven near Hatay, which is close to the Syrian border by originally arab speakers. He is working on a new project, again with his own dyes, that are scarf like veils.

The Armenian embroideries take a woman 1 year in her "spare" time to make one square meter. The one pictured is old but new ones are made by Mehmet's people in Armenia using his dyes made in Istanbul. They are expensive but have true natural colours and historical and new designs. That's, of course, part time but it is a lot of work and it shows in the quality of the pieces. Above is me with a yellow Uzbek suzani.

Travels on a Flying Carpet 51

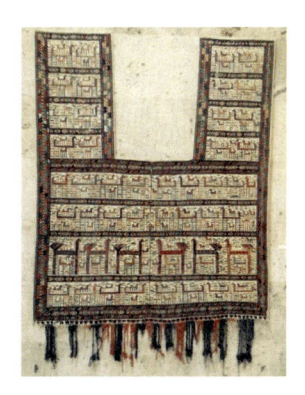

Armenian Horse Cover

Armenian Design

Armenian Embroidery

The Hali editor, Ben Evans in Tiblisi, Georgia

Armernian carpet before 1915, much of today's central and eastern anatolia was Armernian

Golden coat used in a church

Georgian hill in Tblisi

More Travels in 2015

I felt I was back in the 70s as the plane passed over eastern Turkey close to Nemrut Dag. Then it went into Iran just as we did on our 1973 trip and skirted down the west side all the way to Dubai. Along the way it passed Iraq and was not far from Syria when it left Turkey. The Dubai airport, one of the world's busiest is very modern and you go a long long way mostly by moving walkways to get to the immigration and luggage. Our adventure in Dubai, Doha and Abu Dhabi had begun. Rachel had come there many times but it was our first visit to this region.

I was in Dubai to present a paper on stock market crashes predicted and unpredictable to the 56th meeting of the European Working Group on Commodities and Financial Modeling conference held at Zayed University. I had attended a few of these semi-annual conferences which were generally organized by Erasmus finance professor Jaap Spronk. My Rome colleague Rita D'Eclessia has been the president since 2009. The local committee at Zayed University led by Ghulame Rubbaniy with his very able assistant Mary Jahshan were running the conference which was held at a women's only section of the university. Professors there have no tax, fairly good salaries and other benefits.

I had expected Dubai to be a bustling center but never expected it would be 5–10 Hong Kongs placed one after another from south to north with Abu Dhabi fully 90 minutes of fast driving on a straight road north. The city is modern with zillions of big apartment buildings. One of Rachel's friends is an oil/energy correspondent for the Wall Street Journal. Meeting her after a 30 minute extremely fast cab ride showed the extent of the construction boom there as we ended up near the southern boundary. We went up the tallest building in the world the Burj Khalifa. We got the premium tour and went first to floor 148 for a view of all this progress and then down to floor 125 for the normal tour. The structure actually goes up another 20 floors composed of offices. The building is accessed from the Dubai Mall which is a phenomenal collection of many upscale stores and restaurants with a Las Vegas style exploding fountain in the center. One thing is clear this is the fast lane and everything is moving at a rapid pace.

Many of the conference presenters were Zayad University professors but they had come from many parts of the world. The two Dutch keynote speakers gave general talks. Spronk was particularly provocative calling for a rethink of finance to include the social context within which financial decisions are made. Much of his request was for operations research type studies that realistically analyze situations. But for me, I go for the results. I had almost 2 hours to speak and had about 100 slides from the 7 City Fitch presentation on the same topic presented on November 9, namely predictable large crashes and non-predictable mini declines. Since I had a lot of time, and use racetrack wagering bias ideas in my futures and futures/options trading, and to add color to the talk, I showed and discussed four major 2015 races. These were the Met Mile, the Whitney Stakes, the Belmont Stakes and the Breeders' Cup Classic. The first two were won by Honor Code, a horse I co-own with others in a group. He runs from way off the pace and has a tremendous finishing kick. If there's a fast pace then it sets it up perfectly for Honor Code as it did in these two races. In the Whitney Liam's Map went out fast and led the entire way until Honor Code made up many lengths and just beat him at the wire. Both horses were going to have one more race and then go to the Breeders' Cup in Kentucky to possibly face America's top mare Beholder who soundly beat the males in the Pacific Classic at $1\tfrac{1}{4}$ miles and American Pharoah owned by Egyptian–American Ahmed Zayat, the number one rated horse in the world who won wire to wire easily all three of the US triple crown races to be the first horse in 37 years to accomplish this feat. But his times were slow, nothing like Secretariat's breaking the track record in all three races — the Kentucky Derby ($1\tfrac{1}{4}$ miles), the Preakness ($1\tfrac{3}{16}$ miles) and the Belmont Stakes, ($1\tfrac{1}{2}$ miles). However, he won so easily and then easily won the Haskell but was second in the Travers. There he had a speed duel with Frosted all the way down the stretch and another horse, a late runner, Keen Ice beat them both.[3] Liam's Map won a grade I ($1\tfrac{1}{4}$ miles) and Honor Code's trainer put him in a mile race not to wear him out before the $1\tfrac{1}{4}$ mile Classic where he finished third. He was rated seventh best in the world. Our group which owns 4.5 of the 40 shares of Honor Code traded 1/2 share of him for a full share of Liam's Map. Both of them will go to a stud career at Lane's End Farm in Kentucky. Liam's Map stud fee is $25,000 and Honor Code's is $40,000. They breed to about 140–155 mares each year the usual book.

Then the stage was set for the $5 million Breeders' Cup Classic held October 31, 2015 at Kneeland Racetrack in Lexington Kentucky, close by the great farms, several owned by Dubai rulers led by Sheik Mohammed. I enjoy visiting these farms and typically go in May.

It was decided to run Liam's Map in a Breeders Cup race where he was most likely to win. So he ran in and won in record time despite a bad trip, the Las Vegas Dirt Mile on Friday the day before the Classic. Meanwhile,

Beholder had a minor bleeding problem from a workout so was scratched. That left American Pharoah as the lone speed horse in the classic and he put on his usual show wiring the field winning easily with Honor code third. I suppose had Liam's Map or Beholder been in the race challenging American Pharoah, Honor Code might have won. Still with third earning $500,000 putting his career earnings over $2.5 million is a good outcome. Liam's Map won $550,000 for being first in his 1 million race. A number of us have had a friendly debate about how good American Pharoah really is. His times are slow, but, except for his first race fifth and the Travers, he won easily. See Chapter 30 for more discussion.

We had a lovely dinner hosted by the granddaughter of the ruler of the Emirates at a very modern palace. She was a graduate of Zayed University and presented herself well. Another evening, the keynote speakers and their wives were taken for a lovely Arab dinner. I never got to see the Meydan racetrack as it was far away and time got eaten up with other events.

Then we flew to Doha the main city of Qatar. Well we went to the wrong airport but nicely got rebooked on another flight at that airport. That cautioned us in future as the region has lots of airports. As we were doing customs the one bottle of good bordeaux was taken away — you cannot bring any alcohol into Qatar. But after filling out papers we did get it back upon leaving the country.

We stayed at the Movenpick on the corniche. Across the street was the Four Seasons with a nice Italian restaurant right on the water. They had pretty good food and wine rather highly marked up but available. I passed on the Tignanello at 1,450Dirum a bottle about US$400 versus C$100 in the overpriced Vancouver liquor stores. A Puglia wine for 300 about US$85 was good.

The Crossroads of Civilizations museum is a gem. It is in a lovely location in a beautiful building designed by Pritzker Prize laureate I M Pei who found his inspiration in the ablutions fountain of the mosque of Ahmed Ibn Tulun in Cairo. It is housed in the residence of Sheik Hasher al Maktoum and is the private collection of Ahmed Obaid al Mansoori containing brass, pottery, copper, ancient artifacts and manuscripts from the 7th to 19th centuries.

The next day we had a tour. Our guide was from Nepal and a pleasant person that made the day special. We were the only ones on the tour so could keep our luggage in the mini van for drop off at the airport. Our first event, after a nice desert drive seeing many sand houses, was the camel racing center. The races are on a straight track like in the UK but on the specially mixed sand over 6 or 8 or 10 kilometers. Parallel was a road so a driver could control the robot jockey riding the camels. Little boys at the back behind the hump are only for training. Prestige, higher breeding fees and a car are the prizes. The top stallion cost about US$10 million and is owned by a Dubai person.

Our guide filled us in on many of the background information on Doha and Qatar in general. The leader is the Amir and only 15% of the population of 2.2 million are Qataris. The locals receive free tax on their about US$8,000/month salary, subsidized gasoline, other utilities plus co-ownership in the businesses of foreigners. Hence, like Switzerland which is also very smartly organized to benefit the locals, there are two types: rich and super rich. While the government organizes much of ordinary life, the situation is very good for the locals and quite good for the foreigners who receive free tax and other benefits.

On our tour, our first stop was the camels, the dromedary one humped variety, are ridden by robots in actual races. The robots are small devices behind the hump controlled by a person in a car on a parallel road next to the 6, 8 or 10 kilometer straight racetrack. Small boys are jockeys for training but not for racing. Prestige is high and the prizes include cars as shown in the photo. Top camels are worth US$1–10 million just like thoroughbreds. The countryside is desert populated by desert colored buildings that appear periodically. The clean and non-cluttered feeling appeals to me.

Our next stop was Sheikh Faisal Private Museum at Shahaniya, a private museum, that was full of old antique cars, lots of modern uninteresting turkish style kilims and various artifacts. The vast building housed the treasure chest of the owners belongings.

Camels, note the robots on the back

At the Sheikh Faisal Museum

The Sheik Zayed Mosque

Our third visit was to the horse breeding center. Most of the horses are geldings for show jumping not for racing. There were a few stallions. Thoroughbreds are kept elsewhere and Qatar is a force in the worldwide thoroughbred market. I found Qatar and Doha city very pleasant and uncluttered, quite a change from the hectic Dubai and Abu Dhabi.

We then went to Abu Dhabi where we met up with Rachel. On our return to the airport we had a stop at the exquisite Sheik Zayed Mosque.

Spain

After our Gulf visit we returned to London the route backtracking through Iran, across Turkey and Europe into London. That was a short 2 day visit, then it was off to Seville where we had a nice historical hotel in the center of the city, the Donna Maria. The Real Alcazar castle is a main attraction as a top moorish castle. There is a main cathedral in the square near the hotel. Rachel came with us and we trained to the sherry center Jerez. The production of sherry is different from wine. The aging process is much longer and the buildings are not underground but on the street level with giant ceilings called cathedral style. Three levels of aging are in barrels and these are mixed periodically while stored away in old barrels. In contrast to wine, which changes every few years, these are kept for 50+ years after getting the wood scents out. Our tour had 9 sherries ranging in age out to 20, 30 and 40 years Prices are not high and one gets a good appreciation of the drink. We visited the Lustau factory, a sherry which we often purchase in London at Fortnum and Mason. We had a fabulous lunch with sherry pairing which our guide Rachel arranged.

After Rachel returned to London, we had 2 more days at the hotel — one of which we used as a day trip to Cordoba. The great mosque is one of

Sandra in Doha

the worlds architectural wonders, the most striking example of Islamic art in the west. The 856 (1,113 originally) columns are in white and red stone. Embedded in the mosque is a cathedral. The mosque was opened in 785 but was continually expanded over the next 200 years by Hishan (788–796) who finished the work begun by his father Abd al Rahman I. Forty years later Adb al Rahman II (822–852) added new aisles and 100 years later in 951 the Caliph Adb al Rahman III built a new minaret.

We took a 3 hour train to the mountains in Granada to visit the Alhambra. Our hotel, the Alhambra Palace, was spectacular with great views and wonderful food, a dream. The Alhambra represents the height of moorish influence in Spain, reminiscent of the Topkapi Palace in Istanbul filled with beautiful tiles and geometric designs and fountains. It is a vast area and just to get from the ticket office to the building took more than the 15 minutes allotted! On the grounds in the palace built by a student of Michelangelo's was an exhibit of modern art by William J R Curtis which I enjoyed. He used light, shadow and water and space.

Back in London I organized a suckling pig dinner for Rachel and our friends Mark Davis and Jessica Smith that was nice as I fondly recall dinners at Orestes in Vancouver where I occasionally enjoyed suckling pig. They

At the sherry winery with Rachel

take a 6 kg suckling pig, head and all, and roast it. An additional treat is the special ham made from young pigs which are fed acorns.

The LSE Systemic Risk Research Centre where I visit periodically has moved to a place on Aldwich near the Strand. The entire campus was under a massive reconstruction and, for me, it is very easy to get lost in the maze. LSE is issuing my response to the Samuelson letters as a working paper to get more attention to it and some other papers. It was also being published in the *Journal of Portfolio Management* and is reprinted in *Great Investment Ideas* which contains the 12 papers I published in the *Journal of Portfolio Management*. The visits to LSE are pleasant as so much is happening there. It is a good place to have an affiliation. We now have a very good place to stay in Farringdon close to where Rachel lived before moving back to New York. I also qualified for membership in the Oxford Cambridge Club on the Pall Mall close to Trafalgar Square. I joined the club in 2016 and we stayed there for 4 days in May on our way back from Istanbul, Georgia and Armenia. It has the feel of being in a Cambridge or Oxford college with good food and wine in nice surroundings.

Notes

[1] See Lleo and Ziemba (2016) who study the Swiss franc over time, including the January 15, 2015 unpegging against the euro which caused huge losses among many market participants.

[2] The Pazyryk burials are of the Scythian culture, horse-riding pastoral nomads of the steppe. They accumulated great wealth trading with Persia and China over 2,000 years ago and this is evident in the finds in the tombs, which include felt hangings, Chinese silk, the earliest known pile carpet, horses decked out in elaborate trappings, and wooden furniture and other household goods as well as mummified horses and mummified warriors complete with tattoos on their flesh. One of the mummies — the Siberian Ice Maiden was clothed in a silk tunic likely from India. These finds were preserved when water seeped into the tombs in antiquity and froze, encasing the burial goods in ice, which remained frozen in the permafrost until the time of their excavation in 1949.

[3] Consulting in Little Rock, Arkansas for a family that has trainer Bob Baffert for some of their horses I learned that Baffert was furious at an exercise rider who ran A P way too fast just prior to the race so he likely was not at his best in the Travers.

Chapter 6

The Canadian Sports Pool and a New Name, Dr Z, 1982

In my teaching at UBC I had some flexibility in the PhD class. I normally taught the PhD sequence on nonlinear programming and portfolio theory in the fall and then applied stochastic programming and asset-liability management in the winter. Over the years I had between 4–8 students and it was a great class to teach. My 1974 class started the stochastic programming asset-liability modeling work and had Jerry Kallberg and Martin Kusy both of whom wrote major papers with me. There were also other good students. Once in a while the PhD course could be in speculative investments and there I could cover the mathematics of that such as the nice book of Epstein (1977, 2012) plus the applications. Also I could go into interesting topics like blackjack, casino gambling, horse racing, lotteries, etc. The BC Lottery Commission had me as a consultant and that was a lot of fun plus a bit of extra income which was useful for a low paid professor in an expensive city.

In 1981/1982, Sandra and I were visiting professors at UCLA. Richard Roll, a top finance professor, offered me the choice of one of four finance courses which was kind of him as UBC finance would not let me teach any of their courses though I was able to manufacture my own courses in the Management Science division. At UCLA, I chose Finance Theory. For me, at the time, it was easier to teach theory than practice as theory lends itself to more precise exam questions. That class was fine. My other teaching in management science was arranged by star mathematical programmer Arthur Geoffrion.

Rachel was two and went to a local day care.

I had started consulting for the Canadian sports pool in 1981 designing games based on hockey, baseball, basketball, etc. The typical game had three outcomes: home wins, away wins or a tie. So in hockey, if the sports lotto had 13 games, you had to get all 13 right to win the jackpot. Second and third prizes were 12/13 and 11/13. In baseball, a one run game was considered a tie. In basketball ± 3 points was a tie, etc. So all the games could fit into one framework.

I made models to predict games and even though I have only gone to two hockey games in my life, I found a model to predict well. It is simple, kept secret but uses the records of the teams and the home advantage. Being at home is an advantage as the rink is designed for the team, they do not have to travel and the crowd is a big plus. I could pick the games such that the bettors thought there was skill but really there was no skill involved and home, away, ties each had 1/3, 1/3, 1/3 chance of winning. This was easiest in baseball.

One of my hockey games was memorable. In 1982, the Edmonton Oilers were a very good team (47 wins, 12 losses, 12 ties) with Wayne Gretzky at 21 in his prime, arguably as good in his game as anyone in history plus they had a terrific supporting cast including Mark Messier, Glenn Anderson, and Jari Kurri, who all had over 100 points, namely 106, 104 and 104, respectively. Paul Coffey had 96 in their balanced attack. These were some of the top players in the NHL. Gretzky that year had 196 points to lead the whole league.

One way to measure greatness is how good is the star player compared to the average player. For example, in baseball in the early 1900s the average player batted 260 and in each subsequent 20 year period, the average player still hit about 260. What has changed in these 100 years was the distribution of all the players. The standard deviation has become less and less so Ty Cobb, Honus Wagner and others playing in the early part of the century had higher batting averages than the best players in the 40s to 60s like Ted Williams and later players such as George Brett. But all of these and some others were 3 standard deviations about the average. If you look at all sports, one standout 4 standard deviation player was Gretzky in scoring goals and assists in hockey. Besides his skill of knowing where the opposing defender would be going before that defender even knew, Gretzky was simply a tower above all other players in his era. One that's also likely about 4 standard deviations was Babe Ruth who was hitting around 50 home runs a year with the next players at 20 or so. Ruth was also high in batting average but only in home runs is he a 4.

Let's go back to the hockey game. We were visiting professors at UCLA and went to an LA Kings–Edmonton Oilers game. It was loud so you could not even hear the person next to you. Edmonton led 5–0 with not much time remaining in the third period. As the crowd left and the voice subsided, the Kings rallied and won the game 6–5. Even the late Jerry Buss, owner of the Kings and Lakers, had left. It was a historic come back.

Quebec started a hockey pool with 13/13, 12/13 and 11/13 as prizes. The Federal government sued them. The Canadian criminal code said that the provinces could have nonskilled, completely luck, lotteries but not games of skill. So I was asked by the Federal government to be their witness. I needed to show that the Quebec game had skill. My friend, and great thinker, the late Shelby Brumelle, another professor in my UBC department, helped me make a model. I used the prediction model which generated about 1,000–4,000 tickets on each lottery play all with different combinations. I applied the model to 10 lottery games and won $70,000 by getting 13/13 three times plus some other secondary prizes. The bets were computer money, not actually made. But that was good enough to get a lot of publicity. And the Dr Z name came out of this.

In the trial in Montreal it was easy to prove that the Quebec game was skill not luck. But, the Quebec lawyers found a Manitoba case where the Federal government also led by Pierre Trudeau did not block a skill lottery and based on this, Quebec won the case and was allowed to continue their hockey lottery. Shortly after, all of the Canadian provinces and many countries created similar lotteries based on sports often called sports pools. Later, I was invited by the Singapore Pools, their national lottery organization, to help them design sports lotto games. That was a nice visit and I was glad to help them.

Later, the BC Lottery Commission had lotto bets based on sports. They used Las Vegas odds maker Michael (Roxy) Roxborough of the Las Vegas Sports Consultants, a well-known odds maker and line setter to help set the lines. They often made mistakes like betting basketball over under based on preseason games. Well before the season, the defense is not as good and tries less hard but the offensive is sharp. The result is that the scores are higher so when these values were used in regular season games, there was a huge advantage to betting under. I was not involved in that but it is one example of the errors lotto organizations made. Since they make huge fees, approaching 50% in some games, it may not matter much.

I had a very good rapport with BC Lotto Director Guy Simonis. Even though Guy did not know much math or statistics he had a good feel for what was right in lotto games. On numerous occasions his staff would have an error in the game design and I would be called in to fix it. In each case, Simonis grasped the correct analysis right away.

One example I was involved with was studying the hockey line. Hockey was less known as a bet in Las Vegas so they used Roxy with me as a check. This was a sports lottery game with 13 individual games win, lose or tie. My line won 74% of the games that were supposed to be set on a 50–50 basis. Roxy's line was off. What did they do? They averaged Roxy's line with mine 50–50. Of course this is not ideal but it improved their gain. Other lotto games with errors making them bearable are described in my co-authored lotto 6/49 book (Ziemba et al., 1986).

Does it Pay to Buy the Pot?

There have been lotto games in Canada, Australia, Singapore and elsewhere where it was possible to buy all the tickets and be sure to win the jackpot and make a profit. It only pays to do this if there is a large carryover and for some reason sales are not too high. This happened in a small BC lotto game because nobody won the jackpot for a number of weeks and people thought it was unwinnable so avoided it for other lotto games.[1] Moffitt and Ziemba (2016a, b) discuss when and how it's optimal to buy the pot in 6/49 and other lotteries. A good part of the strategy that leads to an edge is to cover combinations not covered by the other players. The idea is that because of quick pick betting and limited budgets of most lotto players many numbers are not played. So it is advantageous to cover those.

We did have a case in BC where a management error through a give away that had a faulty design so that each ticket had a huge advantage and by buying lots of tickets, the risk of losing was essentially zero. So a group of us bought about 15,000 tickets. It took quite a while to actually buy all these tickets and to go through the stacks of tickets to find the winners; but we made a nice gain and had lots of fun doing it. The error (actually it was a giveaway of $10 million of unclaimed prize money not collected by the winners) was to give six tickets for the price of one. Each ticket had a $1 return of $0.385 and with six tickets this gives an edge of 131% with expected value of $2.31. So even with a large take with six tickets there was a huge edge. To get the chance of losing money close to zero, it was optimal to buy a lot of these tickets. Basically as many as you could afford or actually obtain from the lottery retailers.

A German mathematician who was an expert in combinatorial optimization with a famous name, Euler, was visiting my department at UBC.

One question I have been interested in is how do you physically buy the pot with thousands or millions of separate tickets? There are available various combination tickets of varying size so the natural question is "is there a weighting of the individual combination tickets that covers the board with essentially no double tickets?" What Euler and I found was that we could cover the board but we had to have a little bit of excess. We wrote a paper on this but never published it, so it will be put in one of the volumes of my collected works by World Scientific.

Game Design in Lotto, Sports Lotto and Bingo Games

It is a lot of fun to do game design. As a consultant to the Canadian sports pool I was designing various games based on hockey, baseball and other sports. A goal is to design a game so that the players think they have skill but it is really random. For example, in baseball, where the pitcher is a major factor in success, you can have home, way or tie where a tie is a one run game like 6 to 5, such that each of these three outcomes has very close to a one third chance of occurring.

In lotto design, the shape of the ticket is important because of where the popular and unpopular numbers lie. Unpopular numbers are high ones and those ending in 0s and 9s mostly. So in a different game, you can rotate the ticket layout to move the unpopular numbers to popular spots. A factor here is that most of the numbers chosen are in the middle and on the left of the boxes that contain the number because more people are right handed. They start picking numbers mostly on the left and in the corners. Before you know it they have used up their six numbers and created a popular six-tuple.

Consulting for the Singapore pools was a lot of fun because they treated me well, flying me business class, putting me in a top hotel with Singapore's wonderful cuisine plus they paid a good consulting fee. They were ready to add sports lotto games to their offerings so I was to help them think about what to do. It was all very pleasant. The only issue being that by Singapore government rules they pay the fee for each full 8 hour day so I had to recycle ideas and concepts several times during the day to use up the time during day. Each time I recycled the information I retold it in a different way so that by the end of the day they had mastered what I wanted to say. The Singapore pools has been very successful as have most of the lotto organizations around the world. There are plenty of takers even at 50% or less payback because of the large prizes given out.

Lotto players are different than horse players. Horse players want to study everything so buy all the books available in an attempt to beat the difficult game. When we made *Betting at the Racetrack* as a self published book, all the books were sold. Lotto people do not buy many books, they would rather buy more tickets. When the 6/49 Lotto book was nearing completion in 1986, I was interviewed on a Vancouver radio station and asked the interviewer how many books do you think I should print. He said I think you will sell 5,000 in BC in the first month. So I had 5,000 printed. Now in 2017, I still have 2,000 copies in my basement. Looking at amazon.com which lists the book as out of print, the book is still one of the best lotto books around. The BCLC wanted me to design a bingo game with huge top prizes, ample medium prizes and a lot of small prizes, so players feel they can win something plus huge jackpots. We call this a convex payoff structure, shaped like a stretched out capital U or a capital C on its side. So Sandra and I went to a few Vancouver bingo parlors. The rooms were full of women smoking and playing games to win $20, or $50 or $100.

You start with a bingo card with 25 spots on it. There are 5 rows and 5 columns with the center, called the *free spot*, free. There are 75 possible numbers. Standard bingo requires filling in either a column, a row or a diagonal. There were lots of such games. Some involved blackout where the entire board is covered. We needed a different concept and that we found with shapes. So our prizes were based on the number of spots on the card, covered or uncovered. There are tickets that are pure like a 7 or a plus, which is a Swiss flag, or the four corners. Then there are games with what we call garbage such as a 7 filled in but with other spots to be filled from the draws. So the way the games worked was a certain number of the 75 possible numbers would be drawn and various shapes were worth certain amounts of money. Having 1, 2, 3, 4, ... spots gave the various shapes. The probability theory to compute the chances for the various prizes is tough so I enlisted Shelby Brumelle, a UBC colleague, to help me with the calculations. We had the two sets of shapes, pure and garbage, and a rule as to how many draws of the 75 are needed and then the game stops. The top prize could be $10 million with some $1 million second prizes all the way down to a lot of $10 small prizes. Later, a variant was when I was the Gibraltar website lottery expert for Mansion. They wanted a $100 million jackpot with second prize of $10 million plus all the smaller prizes. These games have a huge expected value edge for the management. A problem here is that somebody could hit these huge prizes before the profits from many games came in.

To protect yourself you had to *sell the tails*. That changes the distribution of the winnings from running the bingo game. Some organization such as Buffett's Berkshire Hathaway or Lloyds of London, would buy the tail for half or one third or one fourth of fair expected value. The net result is a bingo game with lower expected value to management but no risk of a huge loss. Then for the buyers of the tail, they on average, double or triple or four-fold their investment. Although the arrangement we made was with Lloyds of London, this is classic Buffett: have lots of capital and take large risky bets with a huge advantage.

Note

[1] The 6/49 Lotto Guidebook, Ziemba *et al.* (1986) discusses these issues.

Chapter 7

Fortune's Formula: How the Pros Wager

Daniel Bernoulli, 1700-1782   Claude Shannon, 1916-2001   John Kelly, 1923-1965

Claude Shannon playing chess with world champion M. Botvinnik[1]

The use of log utility dates to the letters of Daniel Bernoulli in 1738. The idea that additional wealth is worth less and less as it increases and thus utility tails off proportional to the level of wealth is very reasonable. This utility function seems safe for investing. However, I argue that log is the most risky utility function one should ever consider using and it is most dangerous. However, if used properly in situations where it is appropriate, it has wonderful properties. For long-term investors who make many short-term decisions, it usually yields the highest long-run levels of wealth. This is called Kelly betting in honor of Kelly's 1956 paper that introduced this type of betting. In finance, it is called the Capital Growth Theory or *Fortune's Formula*.[2] Kelly was working at Bell Labs and was greatly influenced by Claude Shannon, the father of information theory.

Two great investors who behave like full Kelly bettors are Warren Buffett and George Soros. Evidence of this in their wealth paths which are very violent with many monthly losses but even bigger monthly gains and the most final wealth. Full Kelly investors have large positions in few of the very best investments. Their September 30, 2008 equity portfolios were very concentrated. Soros had a 50.53% position in Petroleo Brasileiro plus 11.58% in the Potash Corporation of Saskatchewan, 5.95% in Walmart, 4.49% in Hess Corporation and 3.28% in Conoco Phillips. Buffett has many close to 10% positions such as 8.17% in Conoco Phillips, 8.00% in Proctor and Gamble, 5.62% in Kraft Foods and 3.55% in Wells Fargo. Both of them, especially Soros, trade futures, options and other derivative positions as well.

The famous economist John Maynard Keynes was another Kelly-type bettor. He ran Kings College Cambridge's Chest Fund from 1927 to his death in 1945. Keynes lost a lot of money, over 50% in the first two years, as did the market index in that depression era. Obviously his academic brilliance and the recognition that he was facing a rather tough market kept him in this job. His geometric mean[3] return over the whole period beat the index by 10.01%. Keynes was an aggressive investor with a capital asset pricing model beta of 1.78 versus the benchmark United Kingdom market return, a Sharpe ratio of 0.385, geometric mean returns of 9.12% per year versus -0.89% for the benchmark. Keynes had a yearly standard deviation of 29.28% versus 12.55% for the benchmark. These returns do not include Keynes' (or the benchmarks) dividends and interest, which he used to pay the college expenses. These were about 3% per year. Kelly cowboys have their great returns and losses and embarrassments. Not covering a grain contract in time led to Keynes taking delivery and filling up the famous chapel. Fortunately it was big enough to fit in the grain and store it safely until it could be sold.[4]

Keynes emphasized three principles of successful investments in his 1933 report:

1. A careful selection of a few investments (or a few types of investment) having regard to their cheapness in relation to their probable actual and

potential intrinsic value over a period of years ahead and in relation to alternative investments at the time;
2. A steadfast holding of these in fairly large units through thick and thin, perhaps for several years until either they have fulfilled their promise or it is evident that they were purchased on a mistake and
3. A balanced investment position, i.e., a variety of risks in spite of individual holdings being large, and if possible, opposed risks.

He really was a lot like Buffett with an emphasis on value, large holdings and patience.

In November 1919, Keynes was appointed second bursar. Up to this time King's College investments were only in fixed income trustee securities plus their own land and buildings. By June 1920, Keynes convinced the college to start a separate fund containing stocks, currency and commodity futures. Keynes became first bursar in 1924 and held this post which had final authority on investment decisions until his death in 1945.

And Keynes did not believe in market timing as he said:

> We have not proved able to take much advantage of a general systematic movement out of and into ordinary shares as a whole at different phases of the trade cycle. As a result of these experiences I am clear that the idea of wholesale shifts is for various reasons impracticable and indeed undesirable. Most of those who attempt to sell too late and buy too late, and do both too often, incurring heavy expenses and developing too unsettled and speculative a state of mind, which, if it is widespread, has besides the grave social disadvantage of aggravating the scale of the fluctuations.

The rest of the chapter discusses three topics: investing using unpopular numbers in lotto games with very low probabilities of success but where the expected returns are very large (this illustrates how bets can be very tiny); good and bad properties of the Kelly log strategy and why this led me to work with Len MacLean on a thorough study of fractional Kelly strategies and futures.[5]

Betting on Unpopular Lotto Numbers Using the Kelly Criterion

Using the Kelly criterion for betting on favorable (unpopular) numbers in lotto games — even with a substantial edge and very large payoffs if we win — the bets are extremely tiny because the chance of losing most or all of our money is high.

Lotteries predate the birth of Jesus. They have been used by various organizations, governments and individuals to make enormous profits because of the greed and hopes of the players who wish to turn dollars into millions. The Sistine Chapel in the Vatican, including Michelangelo's ceiling, was partially funded from lotteries. So was the British Museum. Major Ivy League universities in the US such as Harvard used lotteries to fund themselves in their early years. Former US president Thomas Jefferson used a lottery to pay off his debts when he was 83. Abuses occur from time to time and government control is typically the norm. Lotteries were banned in the US for over a 100 years from the early 1800s and resurfaced in 1964. In the UK, the dark period was 1826–1994. Since then there has been enormous growth in lottery games in the US, Canada, the UK and other countries. Current lottery sales in the UK are about five billion pounds per year. Sales of the main 6/49 lotto game average about 80 million pounds a week. The lottery operator takes about 5% of lotto sales for its remuneration, 5% goes to retailers, 12% goes to the government in taxes, and another 28% goes to various good causes, as do unclaimed prizes.

One might conclude that the expected payback to the Lotto player is 50% of his or her stake. However, the regulations allow a further 5% of regular sales to be diverted to a Super Draw fund. Furthermore we must allow for the probability that the jackpot is not won which is about 15% of the time. This means that the expected payback in a regular draw is not much more than 40%. This is still enough to get people to play. With such low paybacks it is very difficult to win at these games and the chances of winning any prize at all, even the small ones, is low.

There are various types of lottery games in terms of the chance of winning and the payoff if you win. Lottery organizations have machines to pick the numbers that yield random number draws. Those who claim that they can predict the numbers that will occur cannot really do so. There are no such things as hot and cold numbers or numbers that are friends. Schemes to combine numbers to increase your chance of winning are mathematically fallacious.[6] One possible way to beat pari-mutuel lotto games is to wager on unpopular numbers or, more precisely, unpopular combinations.

Another is to look for lottery design errors. As a consultant on lottery design for the past 30+ years, I have seen plenty of these. My work has been largely to get these bugs out before the games go to market and to minimize the damage when one escapes the lottery commissions' analysis. Design errors are often associated with departures from the pure parimutuel method, for example guaranteeing the value of smaller prizes at too high a level and not having the games checked by an expert. In lotto games players select a small set of numbers from a given list. The prizes are shared by those with the same numbers as those selected in the random drawing. The lottery organization bears no risk in a pure pari-mutuel system and takes its profits before the prizes are shared. I have studied the 6/49 game played in Canada and several other countries.

Combinations like 1, 2, 3, 4, 5, 6 tend to be extraordinarily popular: in most lotto games, there would be thousands of jackpot winners if these combinations were drawn. Numbers ending in eight and especially nine and zero as well as high numbers (32+, the non-birthday choices) tend to be unpopular. Harvard Professor Herman Chernoff found that similar numbers were unpopular in a different lotto game in Massachusetts. The game Chernoff studied had four digit numbers from 0000 to 9999. He found advantages from many of those with 8, 9, 0 in them. Random numbers have an expected loss of about 55%. However, six-tuples of unpopular numbers have an edge with expected returns exceeding their cost by about 65%. For example, the combination 10, 29, 30, 32, 39, 40 is worth about $1.507 while the combination 3, 5, 13, 15, 28, 33 of popular numbers is worth only about $0.154. Hence there is a factor of about ten between the best and worst combinations. The expected value rises and approaches $2.25 per dollar wagered when there are carryovers (that is when the jackpot is accumulating because it has not been won). Most sets of unpopular numbers are worth $2 per dollar or more when there is a large carryover. Random numbers, such as those from lucky dip and quick pick, and popular numbers are worth more with carryovers but never have an advantage. However, investors (such as Chernoff's students) may still lose because of mean reversion (the unpopular numbers tend to become less unpopular over time) and gamblers' ruin (the investor has used up his available resources before winning). These same two phenomena show up in the financial markets repeatedly.

The most unpopular numbers in Canada in 1984 were 39, 40, 30, 20, 41, 10, 42, 38, 46, 48, 45, 49 and 1. These were 34.3 down to 8.4% more unpopular than average. In 1986 the advantages were 26.7–8.2%, somewhat lower but the numbers were very similar; they were: 40, 39, 29, 30 and 41 for the top five, the same top five as in 1984. The remaining numbers were 38, 42, 46, 29, 49, 48, 32, 10, 47 and 1. Ten years later in 1996, the top 3 numbers are the only ones that were 10% or more unpopular than average. The best numbers in 1996 were 40, 39, 48, 20, 45, 41, 46, 38, 42, 37, 29 and 30, which is 6.2% more unpopular than average. Similarly, as some stock market anomalies like the January effect or weekend effects have lessened over time. However, the advantages are still good enough to create a mathematical advantage in the Canadian and UK lottos.[7]

Strategy Hint #1: When a new lotto game is offered, the best advantage is usually right at the start. This point applies to any type of bet or financial market.

Strategy Hint #2: Games with more separate events, on each of which you can have an advantage, are more easily beatable. The total advantage is the product of individual advantages. Lotto 6/49 has 6; a game with 9 is easier to beat and one with 3 harder to beat.

But can an investor really win with high confidence by playing these unpopular numbers? And if so, how long will it take? To investigate this, consider the following experiment:

Case A assumes unpopular number six-tuples are chosen and there is a medium-sized carryover. Case B assumes that there is a large carryover and that the numbers played are the most unpopular combinations. Carryovers (called rollovers in the UK) build up the jackpot until it is won. In Canada, carryovers build until the jackpot is won. In the UK 6/49 game, rollovers are capped at three. If there are no jackpot winners then, the jackpot funds not paid out are added to the existing fund for the second-tier prize (bonus) and then shared by the various winners. In all the draws so far, the rollover has never reached this fourth rollover. Betting increases as the carryover builds since the potential jackpot rises.[8] These cases are favorable to the unpopular numbers hypothesis; among other things they correspond to the Canadian and UK games in which the winnings are paid upfront (not over 20 or more years as in the US) and tax free (unlike in the US). The combination of tax free winnings plus being paid in cash makes the Canadian and UK prizes worth about three times those in the US. The optimal Kelly wagers are extremely small. The reason for this is that the bulk of the expected value is from prizes that occur with less than one in a million probability. A wealth level of $1 million is needed in case A to justify $1 ticket. The corresponding wealth in case B is over $150,000.

We can calculate the chance that the investor will double, quadruple or increase tenfold this fortune before it is halved using Kelly and fractional Kelly strategies for Cases A and B, respectively. These chances are in the 40–60% and 55–80% ranges for Cases A and B, respectively. With fractional

Kelly strategies in the range of 0.00000004 and 0.00000025 or less of the investor's initial wealth, the chance of increasing one's initial fortune tenfold before halving it is 95% or more with Cases A and B, respectively. However, it takes an average of 294 and 55 billion years respectively to achieve this goal assuming there are 100 draws per year as there are in the Canadian 6/49 and UK 6–49.

An investor can have a 95% plus probability of achieving the $10 million goal from a reasonable initial wealth level with the quarter Kelly strategy for cases A and B. Unfortunately the mean time to reach this goal is 914 million years for case A and 482 million years for case B. For case A with full Kelly it takes 22 million years on average and 384 million years with half Kelly for case A. For case B it takes 2.5 and 19.3 million years for full and half Kelly, respectively. It takes a lot less time, but still millions of years on average to merely double one's fortune: namely 2.6, 4.6 and 82.3 million years for full, half and quarter Kelly, respectively for case A and 0.792, 2.6 and 12.7 for case B. We may then conclude that millionaires can enhance their dynasties long-run wealth provided their wagers are sufficiently small and made only when carryovers are sufficiently large (in lotto games around the world). There are quite a few that could be played.

What about a non-millionaire wishing to become one? The aspiring investor must pool funds until $150,000 is available for case B and $1 million for case A to optimally justify buying only one $1 ticket per draw. Such a tactic is legal in Canada and in fact is highly encouraged by the lottery corporation which supplies legal forms for such an arrangement. Also in the UK, Camelot will supply model agreement forms for syndicates to use, specifying who must pay what, how much, and when, and how any prizes will be split. This is potentially very important for the treatment of inheritance tax with large prizes. Our aspiring millionaire puts up $100,000 along with nine others for the $1 million bankroll and when they reach $10 million each share is worth $1 million. The syndicate must play full Kelly and has a chance of success of nearly 50% assuming that the members agree to disband if they lose half their stake. Participants do not need to put up the whole $100,000 at the start. The cash outflow is easy to fund, namely 10 cents per draw per participant. To have a 50% chance of reaching the $1 million goal, each participant (and their heirs) must have $50,000 at risk. It will take 22 million years, on average, to achieve the goal.

The situation is improved for case B players. First, the bankroll needed is about $154,000 since 65 tickets are purchased per draw for a $10 million wealth level. Suppose our aspiring *nouveau riche* is satisfied with $500,000 and is willing to put all but $25,000/2 or $12,500 of the $154,000 at risk. With one partner he can play half Kelly strategy and buy one ticket per case B type draw. The probability of success is about 0.95. With initial wealth of $308,000 and full Kelly it would take million years on average to achieve this goal. With half Kelly it would take, on average, 2.7 million years and with quarter Kelly it would take 300 million years.

The conclusion is that except for millionaires and pooled syndicates, it is not possible to use the unpopular numbers in a scientific way to beat the lotto and have high confidence of becoming rich; these aspiring millionaires will also most likely be residing in a cemetery when their distant heirs finally reach the goal.

What did we learn from this exercise?

1. Lotto games are in principle beatable but the Kelly and fractional Kelly wagers are so small that it takes virtually forever to have high confidence of winning. Of course, you could win earlier or even on the first draw and you do have a positive mean on all bets. The largest jackpots contain about 47% of the 19 most unpopular numbers in 1986 versus 17% unpopular numbers in the smallest jackpots. Hence, if you play, emphasizing unpopular numbers is a valuable strategy to employ. But frequently numbers other than the unpopular ones are drawn. So the strategy of focussing on three or four unpopular numbers and then randomly selecting the next two numbers might work. Gadgets to choose such numbers are easy to devise. But you need deep pockets here and even then you might ruin. The best six numbers in our lotto 6/49 book (Ziemba et al., 1986), once won a $10 million unshared jackpot in Florida. Could you bet more? Sorry: log is the most one should ever bet.
2. The Kelly and fractional Kelly wagering schemes are very useful in practice but the size of the wagers will vary from very tiny to enormous bets. My best advice: never over bet; it will eventually lead to trouble unless it is controlled somehow and that is hard to do!

Good and Bad Properties of the Kelly Criterion

What are the good and bad properties of the Kelly expected log capital growth criterion?[9] If your horizon is long enough then the Kelly criterion is the road, however bumpy, to the most wealth at the end and the fastest path to a given rather large fortune.

The great investor Warren Buffett's Berkshire Hathaway actually has had a growth path quite similar to full Kelly betting. Buffett also had a great record from 1977 to 1985 turning 100 into 1429.87 and 65,852.40 in April 2000 and about 216, 278 on April 6, 2015.

The main disadvantages result because the Kelly strategy is very very aggressive with huge bets that become larger and larger as the situations are most attractive. The optimal Kelly bet is the mean edge divided by the odds of winning. As I repeatedly argue, the mean counts by far the most. Good mean estimates are essential in any portfolio decision problem. There is about a 20–2:1 ratio of expected utility loss from similar sized errors of means, variances and covariances, respectively.[10]

Returning to Buffett who gets the mean right, better than almost all, notice that the other funds he outperformed are not shabby ones at all. Indeed they are George Soros' Quantum, John Neff's Windsor, Julian Robertson's Tiger and the Ford Foundation, all of whom had great records as measured by the Sharpe ratio. Buffett made 32.07% per year net from July 1977 to March 2000 versus 16.71% for the S&P500. Those of us who like wealth prefer Warren's path but his higher standard deviation path (mostly winnings) leads to a lower Sharpe (normal distribution based) measure. Chapter 20 proposes a modification of the Sharpe ratio to not penalize gains. This improves Buffet's evaluation. Since Buffett and Keynes are full or close to full Kelly bettors their means must be even more accurate. With their very low risk tolerances, the errors in the mean are 100+ times as important as the covariance errors.

Kelly betting has very low risk aversion, hence it yields very large, risky bets.[11] Hence it never pays to bet more than the Kelly strategy because then risk increases (lower security) and growth decreases so is stochastically dominated. As you bet more and more above the Kelly bet, its properties become worse and worse. When you bet exactly twice the Kelly bet, the growth rate is zero plus the risk free rate. If you bet more than double the Kelly criterion, then you will have a negative growth rate. With derivative positions ones bet changes continuously so a set of positions amounting to a small bet can turn into a large bet very quickly with market moves. Long term capital is a prime example of this overbetting leading to disaster but the phenomenon occurs all the time all over the world. Overbetting plus a bad scenario leads invariably to disaster. Thus you must either bet Kelly or less. We call betting less than Kelly fractional Kelly, which is simply a blend of Kelly and cash. So half Kelly is half the full Kelly wager and half cash.[12]

The good properties

- Maximization of the expected log of final wealth maximizes the asymptotic rate of asset growth and never risks ruin. Ruin means zero wealth.
- The expected time to reach a preassigned asymptotically large goal is minimized with a strategy maximizing the expected log of final wealth.
- The absolute amount bet is monotone in wealth and maximizes the median.
- The Kelly bettor is never behind any other bettor on average in $1, 2, \ldots,$ trials.
- The Kelly bettor has an optimal myopic policy. He does not have to consider prior nor subsequent investment opportunities to obtain the optimal decision. This is a crucially important result for practical use. The myopic policy obtains for dependent investments with the log utility function. For independent investments and power utility a myopic policy is optimal.
- The chance that a Kelly wagerer will be ahead of any other wagerer after the first play is at least 50%.
- Simulation studies show that the Kelly bettors fortune usually pulls way ahead of other strategies wealth for reasonable-sized samples. The key again is risk.
- If you wish to have higher security by trading it off for lower growth, then use a negative power utility function or fractional Kelly strategy. We can compute the correct coefficient to stay above the growth path with given probability.

The bad properties

- False Property: if maximizing the expected log of final wealth almost certainly leads to a better outcome then the expected utility of its outcome exceeds that of any other rule provided the number of periods is sufficiently large.[13]
- If the Kelly bettor wins then loses or loses then wins with coin tosses, he is behind. The order of the wins and losses is immaterial.[14]
- The bets are extremely large when the wager is favorable and the risk is very low. For single investment worlds, the optimal wager is proportional to the edge divided by the odds. Hence, for low risk situations and corresponding low odds, the wager can be extremely large. There, in the inaugural 1984 Breeders Cup Classic $3 million race, the optimal fractional wager on the 3–5 shot Slew of Gold was 64%. (See also the 74% future bet on the January turn of the year effect in Chapter 9. Thorp and

I actually made this place and show bet and won with a low fractional Kelly wager. Slew finished third but the second place horse Gate Dancer was disqualified and placed third. Luck (a good scenario) is also nice to have in betting markets. Wild Again won this race; the first great victory by the masterful jockey Pat Day.

- One overinvests when the problem data is uncertain. Investing more than the optimal capital growth wager is dominated in a growth-security sense. Hence, if the problem data provides probabilities, edges and odds that may be in error, then the suggested wager will be too large.
- The total amount wagered swamps the winnings — that is, there is much churning.
- The unweighted average rate of return converges to half the arithmetic rate of return. As with the above bad property, this indicates that you do not seem to win as much as you expect.
- Betting double the optimal Kelly bet reduces the growth rate of wealth to zero plus the risk free rate.[15]
- Despite its superior long-run growth properties, it is possible to have very poor return outcome. For example, making 700 wagers all of which have a 14% advantage, the least of which had a 19% chance of winning can turn $1,000 into $18. But with full Kelly 16.6% of the time $1,000 turns into at least $100,000. Half Kelly does not help much as $1,000 can become $145 and the growth is much lower with only $100,000 plus final wealth 0.1% of the time.
- It can take a long time for a Kelly bettor to dominate an essentially different strategy. In fact this time may be without limit.[16]

Notes

[1] Photo of Shannon and Botvinnik from Fay Zadeh (1998) *My Life and Travels with the Father of Fuzzy Logic*.

[2] For those who would like a technical survey of capital growth theory, see MacLean, Thorp and Ziemba (2010, 2011).

[3] To measure returns over more than one period, the geometric mean is more accurate than the always at least as high arithmetic mean. Suppose I win 50% and then lose 50%, that turns 100 into 75 which at -13.7% is the geometric mean. The zero arithmetic mean is not correct here.

[4] Keynes' investment behavior, according to Ziemba (2003) was equivalent to 80% Kelly and 20% cash so he would use the negative power utility function $-w^{-0.25}$.

[5] The UMASS *Alternative Investment Analyst Review* has published my paper trying to explain why Kelly strategies should be used more, that is titled "Understanding and using the Kelly capital growth investment strategy." This paper is half of the two part explanation of the Kelly criteria for institutional investors. The other paper responds to Professor Paul A Samuelson's critique of Kelly investing articulated in three letters he sent to me. That one lays out the four basic critiques and argues that they are correct and sharpen the theory but do not affect much the good applications. Samuelson points relate a lot to not overbetting and the fact that Kelly investing provides the most final wealth most but not all of the time. the paper "A response to Professor Paul A Samuelson's objections to Kelly capital growth investing" in the *Journal of Portfolio Management*, 2015.

[6] Ziemba *et al.* (1986), *Dr Zs Lotto 6/49 Guidebook*. shows how these schemes are fallacious. While parts of the guidebook are dated, the concepts, conclusions, and most of the text provide a good treatment of such games. For those who want more theory, see MacLean, Ziemba and Blazenko (1992) and MacLean and Ziemba (1999, 2006).

[7] In Dr Z's 6/49 Lotto Guidebook (1986), the question is asked "how good are the unpopular numbers?" There are six numbers chosen so the expected return is $0.45 F_1 F_2 F_3 F_4 F_5 F_6$ where 0.45 is the payback and the F_is are the individual unpopularity factors. These factors are not the individual unpopularity indices but rather how people pick these numbers in combinations of six numbers. Then the best numbers are 32, 29, 10 and 30. They are not the most unpopular by themselves but in combinations they are better than numbers like 39, 40, 20 and 41 which, although they are more unpopular by themselves are over bet in combinations largely because the lottery organization published the marginal distributions, but, as a consultant, I had access to the six-tuples. Using these factors yields some good combinations with edges despite a 55% take. The most unpopular six-tuples are worth about $1.50 per dollar wagered with no carryover. A table with many such positive edges is in the guidebook, page 49. Also some popular combinations are worth only 15 cent, about a tenth of the best combinations. With carryover the best combinations are worth $2–2.25 per dollar invested. McLean, Ziemba and Blazenko (1992) discuss the chance of actually winning and how long that might take. The experiments in the text, with cases A and B uses this research to compute the statistics stated.

[8] An estimate of the number of tickets sold versus the carryover in millions is proportional to the carryover to the power 0.811. Hence, the growth is close to 1:1 linear. See Ziemba *et al.* (1986).

[9] See MacLean, Thorp and Ziemba (2010, 2011, 2012).

[10] See Chopra and Ziemba (1993).

[11] Kelly betting has essentially zero risk aversion since its Arrow–Pratt absolute risk aversion index is $-u''(w)/u'(w) = 1/w$, which is essentially zero.

[12] Consider the negative power utility function δw^δ for $\delta < 0$. This utility function is concave and when $\delta \to 0$ it converges to log utility. As δ gets more

and more negative, the investor is less aggressive since his Arrow–Pratt risk aversion is also higher. For a given δ and $\alpha = 1/(1-\delta)$ between 0 and 1, will provide the same portfolio when α is invested in the Kelly portfolio and $1-\alpha$ is invested in cash. For example, half Kelly is $\delta = -1$ and quarter Kelly is $\delta = -3$. So if you want a less aggressive path than Kelly pick an appropriate δ. This result is correct for lognormal investments and approximately correct for other distributed assets. See MacLean, Ziemba and Li (2005).

[13] *Counter Example:* $u(x) = x$, $1/2 < p < 1$, Bernoulli trials $f = 1$ maximizes $EU(x)$ but $f = 2p - 1 < 1$ maximizes $E \log X_N$.

[14] The order of the wins and losses is immaterial for one, two, ..., sets of trials since $(1+\gamma)(1-\gamma)X_0 = (1-\gamma^2)X_0 < X_0$. This is not true for favorable games.

[15] See Stutzer (1998) and Janacek (1998). Proof that betting exactly double the Kelly criterion amount leads to a growth rate equal to the risk free rate. This result is due to Thorp (1997), Stutzer (1998) and Janacek (1998) and possibly others. In my 1992 management science paper with Leonard Maclean and George Blazenko, we show the results empirically in graphs, see Maclean, Ziemba and Blazenko (1992). The following simple proof is due to Harry Markowitz.

In continuous time

$$g_p = E_p - \frac{1}{2}V_p,$$

E_p, V_p, g_p are the portfolio expected return, variance and expected log, respectively. In the CAPM

$$E_p = r_o + (E_M - r_0)X,$$
$$V_p = \sigma_M^2 X^2,$$

where X is the portfolio weight and r_0 is the risk free rate. Collecting terms and setting the derivative of g_p to zero yields

$$X = (E_M - r_0)/\sigma_M^2,$$

which is the optimal Kelly bet with optimal growth rate

$$g^* = r_0 + (E_M - r_0)^2 - \frac{1}{2}\big[(E_M r_0)/\sigma_M^2\big]^2 \sigma_M^2$$

$$= r_0 + (E_M - r_0)^2/\sigma_M^2 - \frac{1}{2}(E_M - r_0)^2/\sigma_M^2$$

$$= r_0 + \frac{1}{2}[(E - M - r)/\sigma_M]^2.$$

Substituting double Kelly, namely $Y = 2X$ for X above into

$$g_p = r_0 + (E_M - r_0)Y - \frac{1}{2}\sigma_M^2 Y^2$$

and simplifying yields

$$g_0 - r_0 = 2(E_M - r_0)^2/\sigma_M^2 - \frac{4}{2}(E_M - r_0)^2/\sigma_M^2 = 0.$$

Hence, $g_0 = r_0$ when $Y = 2S$.

The CAPM assumption is not needed. For a more general proof and illustration, see Thorp (2006).

[16] Suppose $\mu_\alpha = 20\%$, $\mu_\beta = 10\%$, $\sigma_\alpha = \sigma_\beta = 10\%$. Then in 5 years A is ahead of B with 95% confidence. But if $\sigma_\alpha = 20, \sigma_\beta = 10\%$ with the same means, it takes 157 years for A to beat B with 95% confidence. In a coin tossing suppose game A has an edge of 1.0% and game B 1.1%. It takes 2 million trials to have an 84% chance that game A dominates game B, see Thorp (2006).

Chapter 8

The Invention of the Place and Show Betting System

The place and show betting system was based on academic papers in *Management Science* in 1981 and 1985 and popularized through the books *Beat the Racetrack* and *Betting at the Racetrack* in 1984–1986, *Efficiency of Racetrack Betting Markets* (1994, 2008), *The Sports and Lotto Handbook* (2008) and my 2017 book *Exotic Betting at the Racetrack*. Using this system people could win at the racetrack not knowing anything about the horses. It was purely based on mispricings which in finance is called weak market efficiency. If prices are not fair then that is referred to as a weak market inefficiency.[1]

The market for win was fairly priced subject to the favorite-longshot bias where long shots are greatly over bet and favorites are somewhat under bet.

At the track in 1982

The Dr Z system then simply used these win probabilities from this simple market to price bets in a more complex market that is to place and show. For place you collect if your horse is first or second so it is more complicated than win. And show is for 1–2–3 finish in any order. If there are 10 horses in the race, there are 720 possible 1–2–3 finishes. Evaluating a particular horse for show is complicated and it is easy to be off. It is these bets that are off that we bet on if they are good enough.

At the track you simply watch four numbers on the toteboard screen, namely, the amount bet to win on the horse in question and the total win bet. The ratio of these two numbers is an estimate of the probability the horse wins. The for a possible place bet, you observe the bet to place on this horse and the total place pool. Then that ratio is the estimate that the horse will come second. So a good bet is if the amount bet to place on the horse is low. You just compare the two ratios and when the place ratio is quite a bit lower than the win ratio, it is a good bet. The idea is to bet as close to the start of the race as possible as these numbers change as the betting proceeds. More detail is later in this chapter and also in the full 1984 Breeders Cup discussed in Chapter 10.

A calculator is available to quickly compute the expected values and amounts to bet using the *Fortune's Formula* Kelly criterion by simply inputting these four numbers. Ziemba (2017) has tables and graphs for this where you can read off how good the bet is and how much to bet, updated from the Ziemba and Hausch 1986 book.

I started going to the races in my teens while in high school in Adams. There were some local racetracks like Pownal, across the Massachusetts border in Vermont and the Great Barrington Fair which had summer racing, but the key place was Saratoga Spa a great racing center dating from the mid 19th century. It was about an hour and a half leisurely drive into New York. The town is very artistic and has a wealthy clientele with beautiful, enormously large houses and very high quality racing. It was there that the idea of working more on racing was born. Later, when I got serious, Donald Hausch and I collected data and experience from the local Hastings Park racetrack in Vancouver. This racetrack is five eighths of a mile and is almost a circle and referred to as a bull ring type track. The tight turns make it dangerous for many horses. Shared Belief, a Candy Ride gelding and the fastest 4 year old in training, was injured in 2015 in such a bullring track in West Virginia. His connections planned a return to racing in 2016, but he died. Also we had the Cloverdale harness racetrack where many Dr Z place and show bets would occur each day.

A young Rachel with Don Hausch

Kazak, our second samoyed, here with Don Hausch, a young Rachel and me

The system evolved from research I was doing with Donald Hausch in Vancouver at a time when I was visiting on sabbatical at the University of California, Berkeley. David Pyle introduced me to Mark Rubinstein who was also working on racing and we started collaborating. Then when

I returned to Vancouver, Donald and I continued and that led to the first paper in 1981 that the three of us co-wrote. Donald and I did a second follow-up paper in 1985 that dealt with different track takes and bet sizes and various practical issues in implementing a betting system. The place and show bets occur because there is relatively less wagered in these markets as would be if the win odds fairly allocated the betting pools to place and show betting. These are considered women's bets rather that manly bets to win.

What we did was formalize the idea that they can be wagers with positive expected value and we determined an optimal Kelly amount to bet depending on the bets of the other investors. Bets are only made when there is an advantage of 10% or more. To be effective you should bet as close to the off as possible. Typically there are two to four such bets each day. Approximations, changing odds and other minor errors reduce the actual edge as do the last minute bettors using the system. In *Dr Z's Beat the Racetrack* (1987), we calculate the number of people who can optimally play the system if they are betting in sequence. This led to our definition of playing the horses where we would consider the pricing of the wager to be our strategy so we would like to price various bets to determine their true value and bet on those that are underpriced. That is fully developed in Ziemba (2017), an update and expansion of the 1986 *Betting at the Racetrack*.

The idea that we introduced in a formal way was to view racing as a stock market. So a good bet is one that has an expected edge, not a good horse *per se*.

Nowadays we have rebates from betting shops which you call up on the phone or email bets. They send the bets to an aggregator who sends them into the track pools. So the money is bet in the pools where the horses are running. The track take is split among the three parties: the track, the betting shop and the bettor. So this in effect makes the track take lower for rebate bettors and higher for other bettors at the track.

If you want to have fun, watch Secretariat win the 1973 Belmont for free on Steve Roman's website[2] www.chef-de-race.com and the wonderful 2010 movie Secretariat starring Diane Lane as the legendary owner Penny Chenery. Hers is one of the gutsiest woman's stories you will ever see. In that mile and a half race, Secretariat ran each $1/4$th of a mile faster than the previous $1/4$ and his 2.24 time is still the record. Penny made a cameo appearance in the movie near the end when her dream was completed. At

96 she is a big hit when she returns to Churchill Downs or Belmont, the scene of Secretariat's great victories.

The great jockey Laffit Pincay Jr was asked: what is the best horse you ever rode, he said "Sham." Sham broke the record in the 1973 Kentucky Derby and Preakness but was beaten by Secretariat who still holds both of these records as well as the Belmont record. There is an asterisk on the Preakness as the official time was not recorded but it is clear that Secretariat did break the record and beat Sham whose record time was recorded. In the Belmont, Sham kept up with Secretariat most of the race, then Secretariat moved to win by 31 lengths. This is all the more impressive because dirt race horses usually run fast at the start and get slower and slower with the horse charging at the finish line not the one accelerating the most but the one decelerating the least. In grass races it is the reverse usually with many horses close at the finish line. They say that great horses win with their hearts. Well, in this case, it was basically true. A normal horse heart weighs 8 pounds but Sham's was 18 and Secretariat's 22!

The bet was a Dr Z bet with the win paying 2.20 at 1–10 per $2 bet and the place $2.40. This was one of the greatest advantage bets ever.

The full Kelly wager on that was huge. There were in the 1980s, 1990s and into 2000 about 2–4 of these bets per day at a typical track. Nowadays (in 2016) it is more complicated with many syndicates betting at the last second, pooled betting where bets simulcast from many racetracks coming into the pools lagged enough, so about half the money does not appear until the horses are actually running, off track betting at places like betfair.com and other places with long and short bets and other features. One must forecast where the win odds and place and show pools will end up making the bets more complicated and risky.

John Swetye, who works with me, has a program using the Dr Z system that searches for bets at 80 racetracks. It is harder to win in 2016 than it was before. But there are good bets occurring. One was on the 2016 Kentucky Derby favorite Nyquist. In the grade I Florida Derby, he paid 4.20 to win, 3.20 to place and 3.60 to show so was a very good Dr Z bet. Also, getting rebates is crucial. These rebates work to provide more betting for the track which shares the track take with the rebate shop and the bettors. So the effective track take becomes about 10–12% rather than 13–30% for bettors at the track. In one experiment, I put up $5,000 and we bet $1.5 million recycling this money. The system lost 7% but we were ahead about 2% or $26,000 because the average rebate was about

9%.[3] One professional syndicate in St Kitts, where one of the rebate shops is, bets about $800,000/day, breaks even but wins the rebate and makes $20–40 million/year.

The Breeders' Cup Distaff, 1990

Race 5 on the program at Belmont Park on October 27, 1990 was the Breeders' Cup Distaff. It was basically a match race between Bayakoa the 6 year old champion from Argentina and the brilliant 3 year old filly Go for Wand. The main competition Gorgeous was scratched the day before and the rest of the field seemed quite outclassed. The two of them were together all the way down the stretch, step by step throughout the entire race. Then the impossible happened. Go for Wand broke her leg and had to be destroyed. I was press for that race and sitting at the rail and the accident occurred right in front of us. It was a devastating and brutal tragedy and

Go for Wand, Beppie Weiss

not much fun cashing the wagers on Bayakoa. However it was one of the greatest Dr Z bets I have ever made.

Go for Wand was the favorite at 3–5 with Bayakoa the second choice at even money. The next lowest odds horse was Colonial Waters at 14–1. I gasped when I saw the toteboard with about 5 minutes to post time. The expected value per dollar bet to show was an astounding 2.62![4] This on the world's best mare. Trainer Ron McAnally made three trips from his base in Santa Anita to Argentina and finally purchased Bayakoa for $300,000.

The optimal Kelly wager, with only $5,939 bet on Bayakoa versus $67,666 for show on Go for Wand, was $533 for a $1,200 bank roll. Obviously, the bridge jumpers who piled all that money for show on Go for Wand assumed that they would collect 2.10 minimum for sure or possibly more. As I watched the board, wondering how many Dr Z bettors would jump on the amazing bet to show on Bayakoa, I was pleased that the wager remained terrific. It showed me that there were many more to be converted to my methods. The toteboard evolved and in the rest of the betting until post time. Near post time, the expected value per dollar to bet on show on Bayakoa was still 1.58 with an optimal Kelly wager of $599. This wager is larger than at 5 minutes because with a larger pool, one depresses the odds less. The payoff to show, 4.80 on an even money shot, was astounding and it reflected too small an amount bet on Bayakoa to show. Bayakoa was also a system to show as well as place at Calder.[5]

As Donald Hausch and I explain in *Dr Z's Beat the Racetrack* (1987), when there are two wagers on the same horse to place and show, one must make a separate calculation to determine the optimal wagers. In this case, the optimal wager was $230 to show and $125 to place. It was a great race to bet on but a sad one to watch. Go for Wand was buried at Belmont as was the famous filly, Ruffian, who had a similar accident in her match race with Kentucky Derby winner Foolish Pleasure in 1976. Famed artist Beppie Weiss, painted a tribute to Go for Wand, highlighting her career.

At the Harness Races in Finland

The system applies to harness races as well as thoroughbreds. One application was in Finland and Sweden where harness races are very popular and essentially the only type of horse races run. The Finnish application was straightforward and the system is used there. The photo shows me and Professor Antti Kanto of the University of Vassa, Finland, applying the Dr Z

Vassa, Finland

place and show system to harness races at the Lahti race course. I was in Finland to give an invited tutorial on world wide security market anomalies to the international meeting of the Institute of Management Sciences at the end of June 1992. There was also a meeting in Vassa called the Midnight Sun Empirical Finance conference and I was one of the speakers for that as well. I spoke there on the turn of the year and turn of the month effects based mostly on ideas for trading US markets. Vassa is about 5 hours north by train from Helsinki and we had a pleasant journey through the many lakes and treed terrain on the way up. Finland is a small but interesting country.

I had many visits to Finland as I was the external examiner for a number of PhD theses such as Matti Koivu, who went on to the European Central Bank. Matti arranged for me to speak on risk management to the ECB. It was a pleasant visit once I got through the n layers of security in Frankfurt.

At Finnish racetracks, the toteboard quotes win odds as in England, that is, odds instead of odds +1 as in North America. So if you bet 50FM and the odds are 2.2, then if the horse wins, you collect 110 for a profit of 60. The breakage, or rounding down of the payoffs, is to the nearest 0.10 as in North America. The Dr Z system is easy to implement in Finland. The first step, using our calculator chip, is to estimate the probability of each horse i winning the race, that is, Q/odds, which for horse i is $0.79/odds_i$ since the track take is a hefty 21%. The place pools are shown as P, the total pool, and P_i, the bet on horse i. This is in contrast to the win pool where you only see the win odds and not the win bet, W_i, and total win pool, W. W_i can be approximated using W and $odds_i$.

So with the Dr Z calculator (HP 41 series, handheld and later a more sophisticated version), you plug in Q = 0.79, W_0 your betting wealth, say 1,000FM (the currency doesn't matter), $odds_i$, p_i, the bet to place, and P, the total place pool. You must use show on the calculator since Finland's place, as in England, is the same as North America's show.

In the seventh race at Lahti on June 28, 1992, our bet was on Meadowbranch Fred, who was the 1.8–1 favorite in this race. He was in post position 9, which is not a favorable position as horses 1–6 have the advantage and 7, 8, 9 start in the second row behind these 6. Fred was a shipper from the US with total winnings of 118,600FM. He was seventh in his next to the last start and won his previous two races and was sixth in the race before that. He was 17.9–1 when he was seventh, but in the races he won he was at short odds, namely, 1.1 and 1.6. His place expected return per FM bet was 1.37 for a 37% edge. The optimal Kelly bet was 288FM out of the 1,000 bankroll. The payoff was 17 so we made 202FM. Fred did not win but came second, so we collected on our bet. The winner and third horse were both also American shippers.

I do not know how many Dr Z bets there will be on typical days at the harness racetracks in Finland. Like harness tracks in North America, the pools are small, but there often are favorable bets. There are larger pools in the quinella, where you have to get the first two horses in any order.

There are other aspects to keep in mind and techniques. The first I learned quickly and it cost me a winning bet. The horses began to go in a circle around and around. Before I knew it they were running the race and it was too late to bet. What happened was the handicap. In some races, a group of the horses actually run a shorter distance than the other horses. They also get to start in front. For example in the first race in Lahti on June 27, the front seven horses ran 2,140 meters, horses 8–11 ran 2,160 meters and horse 12 had to run 2,180. This distance is based on career winning.

I was able to attend the trotters three times during my brief visit and we had a lot of fun and all of us came out winners.

Notes

[1] Roberts (1959, 1967), working at the University of Chicago business school, categorized efficiency as weak — dealing with price inefficiency, semi-strong — dealing with publicly available information inefficiencies and strong — dealing with any information at all, including insider information.

[2] Roman has retired and the site is no longer maintained but I will redo a site that people can use for free.

[3] Racetrack betting record of the place and show system

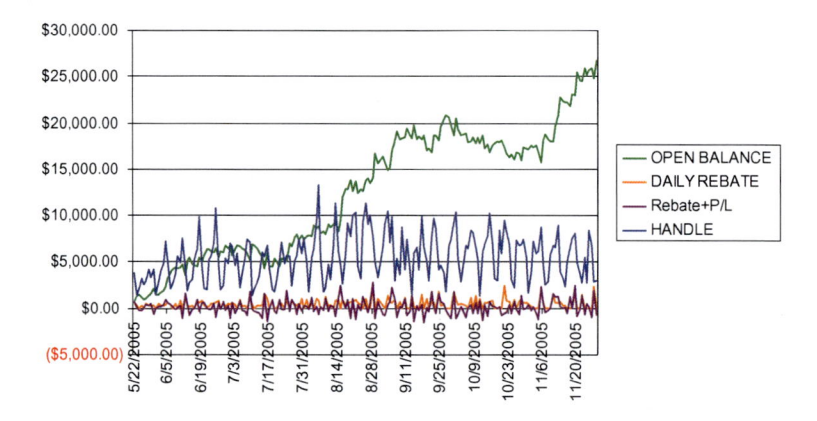

[4] The payoffs were:

	Totals	Go for Wand	Bayakoa	Expected Value/$ Bayakoa for Show	Optimal Wager w/$1200 Bankroll
Odds		3–5	1–1		
Win	201,332	94,722	76,509		
Place	79,402	29,069	37,639		
Show	87,744	68,660	5,939	2.62	$533
Odds		3–5	1–1		
Win	257,180	117,276	97,961		
Place	91,006	34,754	40,347		
Show	106,927	77,027	13,338	1.70	$591
Odds		3–5	1–1		
Win	468,651	222,489	184,965		
Place	139,292	58,132	54,521		
Show	184,236	129,486	25,936	1.58	$599

[5] The payoffs were:

	Totals	Go for Wand	Bayakoa	Expected Value/$ Bayakoa for Show	Optimal Wager w/$1200 Bankroll
Odds		3–5	6–5		
Win	53,991	27,383	19,896		
Place	18,476	10,073	4,786	1.12	$125
Show	10,643	4,713	2,121	1.23	$230

The payoffs there, thanks to Ron Dettero, were:

	Win	Place	Show
Bayakoa	4.40	3.80	3.40
Colonial Waters		7.80	4.60
Valay Maid			8.00

Chapter 9

The Turn-of-the-Year 1982/1983

The S&P500 started trading futures on the index in 1982. That way you could take levered positions long and short on the large cap sector of the US stock market. That can be profitable but it is risky and if the market falls suddenly and you are long, then you can lose a lot of money. Many have done precisely this and I discuss some of that in Chapter 21. I was studying US calendar anomalies and from a teaching visit to UCLA in 1981/1982, I learned about the small cap effect and the January effect and their relationship.

Richard Roll, my host at UCLA's finance department, and others at USC in Los Angeles had a conference on these topics. I did not attend that conference but heard about it. Roll is a brilliant empirical finance professor and an active trader but he looks at the market from an efficient market perspective. And, although he wrote one of the most important early papers on the small firm titled *Vas ist dat?*, he does not really believe in such anomalies in his trading. I suppose he would argue that it is just taking more risk to get a higher return. But I wanted to study and trade this. The historical record is that small cap stocks have had higher returns in January than the large cap stocks. There are a number of reasons for this such as bid-ask spreads pushing prices higher with these generally low price stocks in January after they were tax loss sold in December. Also small caps are favored by smaller ordinary investors as opposed to large institutional investors and new money in January is put to work then. Small caps have had a big advantage in Democratic presidential terms, see the discussion in Chapter 18. Then there are various institutional reasons why the returns in January are higher.[1]

I studied the literature and the facts are that over long periods of time, January returns have been high.[2] And over the 70 years from 1926 to 1995, small cap stocks (that is the smallest stocks by market capitalization) beat the largest cap stocks by 10.6% per year in January! That's 10.6% per year, on average, if you compare the smallest decile with the largest decile — a huge outperformance in 1 month. Also, looking at the results year by year, one sees that in almost all of the years, the small caps outperformed and when they do not, which is not often, they only slightly underperform.

So how can one bet on this? Buying individual stocks in 1982 would not work as you will change the price too much if you buy even a small amount. Of course, in 2016, this could be done using the new financial instruments we now have — small cap ETFs for example. But in 1982, one option was to go long a small cap futures contract and there was one, namely, the Value Line equally weighted about 1700 stock index and short the large cap S&P500 index futures. By being equally weighted, universal widgets has the same weight as IBM, GE and other big companies. So the equal weighting gave more attention to the small caps than a large cap value weighted index would. So the long–short spread picks up the January small firm effect advantage with low cost and low price pressure as it is futures not individual stocks. I established a futures account with a commodity broker, Ross Clark in Vancouver for this and we studied this together. We found that we were not the only ones who knew about this so the futures moved well before January, anticipating the effect. In fact, the effect seemed to start in mid-December and end in mid-January.

There was one other key factor that must be considered and that's how the equal weighting is computed. In that period, it was geometrically weighted. This comes from dynamic returns. Suppose you gain 50% in year one and lost 50% in year two. The arithmetic mean is zero. But $100 become $75. So to do this calculation right you need to use geometric means which are always lower than arithmetic means giving the correct geometric return of -13.7%. The effect of this is that there is a downward drift of the index. So if stocks stay even, that is all of them rise by the same percent, there is a downward drift of a half percent per month. This is lost. So if you gain, say, 3% by the move, you actually gain about 2.5%.

This is tricky and even talented researchers can get this wrong. Ritter (1996) relates how he and three other University of Pennsylvania finance PhD students, all famous professors now, got trapped by buying the spread months is advance and then had many months of this downward drift. The late great academic and investor Fisher Black was on the other side of these trades while at Goldman Sachs.

Ross and I traded this successfully for the 4 years from 1982/1983 to 1985/1986. Then I wrote a paper with Clark based on our work explaining clearly how we did this. We stated the the following trading rule

> buy the spread on the first closing uptick, starting on December 15 and definitely by the 17th, and sell on January 15. Waiting (to enter) until (−1) now seems to be too late: possibly finance professors and their colleagues, as well as other students of the turn-of-the-year/January effect who are in on the strategy, move the VL index. There seems to be a bidding up of the March VL future price relative to the spot price. (Clark and Ziemba, 1987, page 805)

Their idea at that time was that the January small firm effect existed and occurred during the first 2 weeks of January in the cash market (as argued by Ritter, 1988; see also comments by Ziemba, 1988), but that futures anticipation would move the effect in the futures markets into December. Hence, an entrance into the Value Line/S&P500 futures spread trade in mid-December and an exit in mid-January should capture the effect if it actually existed. With data up to the 1985/1986 turn-of-the-year (TOY), their trade rule was successful. They concluded that small cap advantage was mainly in the first half of January, with some anticipation in the final days of December, and with a large cap advantage in the second half of January.

I continued trading this spread for the 14 TOY's (all winners) from 1982/1983 to 1995/1996 and updated the results in Ziemba (1994) and Hensel and Ziemba (2000).

Hensel and Ziemba (2000) analyzed the January effect in the futures markets and concluded that for the 1980s and early 1990s there was a small cap advantage in the futures and cash markets. However, they show that from 1994 to 1998 there was no advantage in the cash market, and that anticipation built up in the last half of December in the futures markets. As a consequence, for the four TOYs during the 1994/1998 period, the January effect only existed in the last half of December, in the futures market. They analyzed small minus large spread trades between the Value Line and the S&P500 futures contracts and concluded that the January effect was exploitable in the futures markets in this period.

Some people might ask why are you not keeping this secret? Well it does not really matter since the paper was published in a top A quality journal but one where the readers would not trade and those who trade would not read this operations research journal. As the years went by I continued to trade this and write updated papers on it.[3] After 14 wins in 14 years — you can find the year by year graphs in the papers and my 2012 anomaly book, *Calendar Anomalies and Arbitrage*.

I stopped trading this for two reasons. First, the trading volume on the Value Line was drying up and although the effect still existed there, it was pretty risky to trade with this low volume and over the years my size got larger and I became fully 7% of the market. Secondly, in an effort to get consulting with Morgan Stanley in New York, I consulted one day with a new group headed by young former Barra researcher Peter Muller, who had a BA in Math from Princeton. Peter invited seven professors to come to New York to discuss trading ideas. I was just there for 1 day but did explain about this and other calendar anomaly trades. Over time the market changed slightly with the effect moving totally into December and the weighting was changed to unweighted — that is just add up the returns on the individual stocks. I do not know if Muller's group did much with my idea. But he became very successful with his group making $5 billion and making him famous. Now in 2017 he has his own fund with billions in it.[4]

I continued to write papers but not trade this. However, I started again for the 2009/2010 turn of the year and have had six more wins through December 2014/January 2015. The great options trader Blair Hull gave me a small consulting contract to study all the US calendar anomalies and Constantine Dzhabarov worked with me helping with the calculations so that prepared me to resume trading in the January small firm effect and other anomalies. This trade dovetails into my research on small cap outperformance with Democratic presidents which is discussed in Chapter 18. The six years to 2015 use the Russell2000 futures contract which is more or less the fourth decile of small cap stocks. Despite all the research, talks, etc, most market participants are not into such trades. And the fact that many textbooks and trade books say that the January effect does not exist make it easier to still trade this successfully. Except for micro stocks which still outperform in January, the general conception is that the January effect does not exist. This is helpful to my trading — little do they know that it does in the month of December![5] So the record to 2015 was 20 wins in 20 plays, but January 2016 started with the worst 5 opening days in more than 50 years. This was a bad signal and is discussed later. The turn-of-the year's trade had finally failed. The reason likely was the fear of greatly higher interest rates plus Chinese slowdown and US growth worries. In December 2015 the FED raised short term rates by $1/4\%$ but suggested many future rises. This led to a six week decline in the stock market and the turn-of-the-year failure.

Notes

[1] A useful source of information on this are the yearly *Stock Trader's Almanac* by Yale Hirsch and now with his son. Hirsch and Hirsch (2016) discuss these reasons.

[2] For the literature on high January returns, see the original paper by Rozoff and Kinney (1976) and Chapter 1 of Ziemba (2012a) which summarizes the literature concerning January returns, small cap versus large cap and trading this effect using the futures markets.

[3] See Clark and Ziemba (1988), Ziemba (2004), Rendon and Ziemba (2007) and Ziemba (2012a). I also have given talks on calendar anomalies where I discuss this trade. The audience is always interested but they are afraid to trade themselves or with me. Two such talks were the keynote in January 2010 to the Battle of the Quants in New York and the Chicago Quantitative Alliance in Las Vegas in April 2012 where I was the first main speaker.

[4] Muller's fund is PDP Partners in New York and London. While giving a master class at the London School of Economics in May 2015, one of the attendees bought my book *Investing in the Modern Age* and arranged for me to speak to the PDP group in September 2015 which has been delayed but might happen later.

[5] See Donald Keim's paper on this in our book, Keim and Ziemba (2000).

Chapter 10

Testing the Dr Z System with Ed Thorp

This chapter recalls a memorable day on November 10, 1984 when Ed Thorp and I attended, with my late Vancouver colleague Bruce Fauman, the first Breeders' Cup day at Hollywood Park. The purpose of the day in addition to fun, was to test my Dr Z system co-developed with Donald Hausch with some early help from Mark Rubinstein. The idea of the system is simple: use the data from a simple market, in this case the win probabilities to fairly price bets in the more complex markets, such as place and show. For example, with 10 horses, there are 720 possible finishes for show. Then one searches for mispriced place and show opportunities. This is a weak form violation of the efficient market hypothesis based solely on prices. How much to bet depends on how much the wager is out of whack and it is a

Don Hausch I had many memorable trips to the Kentucky Derby for research and fun

good application of the Kelly betting system. We use a model that takes our bets into account and are solved with a nonlinear programming algorithm. There is a lot of data here on all the horses and not much time at the track. So a simplified approach is suggested. Don and I solved thousands of such models with real data and estimated approximation regression equations that only involve four numbers, namely, the amounts bet to win in the total pool and the horse under consideration for a bet, plus the total place or show pool and the place or show bet on the horse under consideration.

In our trade books Ziemba and Hausch (1984, 1986, 1987) we study this in various ways, including different track takes, multiple bets for place and show on the same horse and how many can plan the system before the edge is gone.[1] This system revolutionized the way racetrack betting was perceived viewing it as a financial market not just a race. This led to pricing of wagers and the explosion of successful betting by syndicates in the US. Hong Kong and elsewhere; see, for example, see the books Hausch, Lo and Ziemba (1994, 2008) and Hausch and Ziemba (2008).

A race by race analysis of that Breeders' Cup day, plus the previous day when I went by myself, with racing charts, optimal wagers, etc., is in Ziemba and Hausch (1986). Fauman wrote his own version which follows, and was written in 1995 but never published. So I have edited it slightly and updated it in a few places. A few comments appear as a postscript after his paper from Ziemba and Hausch (1986). I did not alter his comments about me which on the whole are correct. Before that begins, you might ask: does the system still work in 2017 and what is changed?

The main new features are:

1. These days we bet at rebate shops by phone or electronically. The rebate is a sharing of the track take by the track, the rebater and the bettor. The effect is to take all bets from a track take of 13–30% for various bets to about 11–13%.
2. Betting exchanges in the UK and elsewhere allow for short as well as long wagers and
3. There is a lot of cross track and last minute betting and this takes time to be sent to the pools at the racetrack. Hence, about 50% of the wagers do not actually appear in the pools until after the horses are running. So one must estimate the final odds (probabilities).

Syndicates exist that break even on their wagers yet make millions on the rebate. One syndicate which bets about $800,000 per day, breaks even but collects the rebate is in the $20–40 million annual range.

Regarding the Dr Z system, John Swetye works with me and we wager with rebate searching for bets at 80 racetrack. Basically the system still works but the task is not easy. One successful 6 month period with a $5,000 bankroll, the system lost 7%, received a 9% rebate. The total wagers were $1.5 million giving a 2% or $26,500 profit. (See Chapter 8, note 2 for a graph of this.)

Three to Beat the Breeders' Cup by Bruce C Fauman

This is the description of our day at the 1984 Breeders Cup by my former colleague Bruce Fauman. Bruce died shortly after the internet stock market crash on December 12, 2002 at age 59. To publish this I have slightly edited and updated his original copy. My own description of that day with more technical discussion, racing charts, etc., appears in the 1986 book *Betting at the Racetrack*.

Three decades ago, at the first Breeders' Cup in 1984, three ordinary jamokes in their forties, among whom one could count a total of three wives, six kids, nine degrees, about 500 IQ points, and a system to beat, the track, set out for Hollywood Park to test their theories and equations on horse racing's biggest day ever.

First Race: The Juvenile, 1 mile, for 2 year old colts and geldings, purse $100,000

The ground growls as I stand at the rail beside the 16th pole. The vibrations travel faster through earth than through air, so I feel the horses before I hear them. The front runners reach the head of the stretch, three wide, a length behind one another. Their hooves sound not a distinct clip clop beat, but a series of overlapping thuds upon the fast track surface.

Number 5, a bay with white stockinged forelegs, has gained steadily on the early leader throughout the back stretch. As they pass me, he pulls even and tries to fend off another bay's late charge between horses. At 35 miles an hour, the horses spew fragments of track soil with each hoofs raising. The warm November morning accentuates the aromas of rich soil, fresh manure, damp straw, saddle leather and horse sweat, which in a more subtle form are often invoked as barnyard bouquet when complimenting a well balanced mature Burgundy.

Watching a horse race from the stands is as different from watching at track side as it is from watching on television. I left our box to see the first race from the rail and became so engrossed in the pre race ritual that I

Ed Thorp

Bruce Fauman

forgot to make the first system bet of the day. The possible opportunity appeared early on the tote, but by the time I remembered to ignore the horses and recheck the odds, the horses were loading, and I was too late to get to the betting window. Some say the first things to go in an ex athlete are the knees. Not true; it's the short-term memory. The grandson of both Northern Dancer and Secretariat holds on to win by nearly a length. Remembering our day's real purpose, I will no longer be so cavalier as to watch a race for pleasure. We're not here to enjoy the races, but to beat the track on what promises to be horse racing's biggest day in history.

Second Race: The Juvenile Fillies, 1 mile, for 2 year old fillies, purse $1,000,000

Dr Z introduces Ed, Jeff and me to the occupants of the box to our right, Lindsay a local newspaper reporter and an English author of handicapping books who mumbles his name, Foofraw or Frew faw, in upper class Brit speak.

Bill Ziemba, is my colleague, sometime co-author and seminal mind behind the system. I am the creator of his Dr Z *nom de plume*, the reality checker of his mathematical manipulations, and one of the few people willing to tolerate his bustling, blustering and occasional boorishness in return for access to the treasures of a polymath's mind.

Our third adventurer is Ed Thorp, who developed the original card counting system for beating blackjack in the 1960s, and since no casino will let him near a 21 table anymore, he has gone on to other things. But Ed is always interested in any system that can actually beat the house, and is here to see for himself whether the system will beat the racetrack.[2]

Ed wears a cocoa heather herringbone jacket and beige slacks. I'm in my I can go anywhere uniform of a navy blazer, gray flannels, button down shirt and sincere necktie. Ed and I remove our ties, which we believed were required in the clubhouse. Jeff's is unchanged from half mast. Bill is in a conservative glen plaid suit adorned with a most unconservative floral tie.

Foofraw asks me which filly I like in the race, but before I can answer, he tells me, "The 3 if she runs true to form, with the 9 right after that. Unless the 6 filly has been laying in the weeds and I'm quite taken with number 8's works, so she could upset."

Bill and Ed made the system bets on Chiefs Crown in the first race. Dr Z tells me at $2.40 to show his $100 wager puts him $20 ahead. Ed doesn't say how much he bet. In addition to disappointment in my forgetfulness, I'm also a little disappointed in the small payoff, while Dr Z is pleased that the horses are running true to form, which means the system should run true to form as well.

We check the tote board with each flash. The favored filly, number 4, has offered a likely system bet since early in the wagering. The show bet underlay fluctuates around 35%, which ought to give me an expected payback of 1.17, or $1.17 for every dollar bet. My usual cutoff is 1.15, which means I'll make a bet only when I have at least a 15% advantage. However, for an event like the Breeders' Cup, with great horses and ideal conditions, I reduce the cutoff to 1.10 as recommended in *Beat the Racetrack*. Throwing darts at the racing program gives an expectation of about 85 cents per dollar wagered, since the track take is 15 cents of each dollar wagered. A fair bet is like tossing a coin, where the expectation is 1.00. Unless a bet is for small sums between friends, fair is for fools.

Just like Wall Street, the racetrack is a financial market, in which people invest money in ventures with uncertain outcomes. The stock market is said to be "efficient", because neither knowing how a stock has performed in the past, nor having public information about the company's activities, provides any prediction about the stock's future price. The current price reflects all available information and is the best predictor of the future. The racetrack is also a financial market, a turf market and efficient as well. The odds offered are the best predictor of any given horse's probability of winning. The tote board odds reflect all available information about each horse's relative speed, stamina, breeding or other factors that predict performance.

Some handicappers rely directly on such historical information about a horse to make betting decisions, while others eyeball the animals being saddled or parading to the post. However, the tote odds already reflect the handicappers' varying opinions. Forty years of research confirms that horses whose post time odds predict a 25% probability of winning do win about 25%, of the time. There is a tendency for the turf market investors to under bet heavy favorites and significantly over bet longshots.[3]

While the win betting market may be efficient, often the market for place or show is not, giving a profitable opportunity to those who can recognize the inefficiency and take a risk arbitrage position in the turf market.

I am not a gambler. However, I have been known to invest money in events with uncertain outcomes, but only if I can expect to take out somewhat more than I put in. When the efficient win pool indicates a horse is two to one, but the show pool offers me a payoff equivalent to that of three to one, I invest.

The system is based on similar reasoning and much more exactitude.[4] Dr Z developed the nonlinear estimation and optimization routines to calibrate the equations which tell us whether and how much to bet. Dr Z and Donald Hausch wrote a book on the system titled Beat the Racetrack. Originally they used the terms "Hausch Ziemba algorithm" and "H Z method" to describe the system. When I reviewed the draft of the 1981 working paper[5] and suggested Dr Z as a better name for title system and a *nom de plume* for Bill's non academic writing. Their manuscript now refers to it as the "Dr Z System". Bill wrote a column for *Gambling Times* on lotteries and horse racing for some time under the Dr Z byline before noticing another sports writer for *Sports Illustrated*, who I don't think is a real doctor of anything, use the same Dr Z moniker. I guess that's what happens when you choose, such a common name; there are 273 John Smiths or J Smiths in my local white pages, but not even one Pocahontas. Later, Bill told me a lawyer checked and he has the rights to the name.

The system has been tested a number of times at our local Vancouver racetrack. It's a small track with a small crowd, in a climate that makes for an iffy track surface, which offers only two or three system bet opportunities in a typical day's ten race, card. Furthermore, a wager of $200 or so is big enough to influence the odds in the parimutuel betting pool in which the bets of the losers are divided among the winners. We needed better controlled conditions to validate the system. Today, Hollywood Park has become our laboratory. The Breeders' Cup is the biggest day, in racing history, offering $10,000,000 in purses for the horse owners. The dirt track is fast so each horse should run true to form; the purses are huge, so no trainer or jockey will hold back; and another 10 million should pass through the betting windows, making the pools big enough in which we will always be small fish whose wagers won't alter the payoff odds.

The tote board flash at 1 minute to post indicates an acceptable 25%,underlay. Dr Z and I each bet $100 on number 4. Again Ed doesn't say how much he bet. The horses are off to a start of thumping and bumping. Our filly breaks stride early and finishes well back.

I feel my chest drop into my stomach as the race ends. I know you can't win them all; nevertheless, I'd like to. The system delivers cashable tickets about 75% of the time. I sure hope that Lindsay and Foofraw hadn't bet the 22–1 or 75–1 fillies that finished one two. They hadn't. A loser loves company, even if they are one time losers. Foofraw tells Dr Z that an exacta bet on the longshots would have paid $8,000, ignoring the fact that this race has no exacta betting. Bill and Don developed an exacta variant of the system, which would almost never consider a bet that includes even one such long odds horse, in their 1986 book Betting at the Racetrack, since it would not price out to have an advantage.

Third Race: The Sprint, 6 furlongs, for 3 year olds and up, purse $1,000,000

En route to the track I picked up Ed Thorp, who lives in a gated community on a Newport Beach hilltop. After passing muster with the gatehouse guard, I drove up to Ed's brand new, old California mansion. He greeted me and offered coffee, pointing to a bigger than a breadbox, brass plated, Italian gizmo and said he'd be ready to go in five. Ed is about as average looking as a rocket scientist can be pushing 50, gray shot walnut hair, but all still there, tortoise shell glasses over blue eyes, an inch or so less than six feet, medium build, probably within 5 pounds of his graduation weight because of the marathons he still runs. I too am within five pounds of my graduation *avoirdupois* of 230, but some of it must have migrated south from my chest and shoulders, since my waistline has grown an inch or four. I no longer run the long distances of my high school and college days, which were seldom more than a furlong on a track and 40 yards on a football or rugby field. I've also lost half an inch of my six three, which my daughter attributes to my hair having been blown away from driving too fast in my convertible. My counter reminds her that until I had children I had a full head of thick black hair; *post hoc ergo propter hoc.*

Mug of world-class coffee in hand, I roamed the main floor and could understand how there was several million in the place at least 10,000 square feet of house, 12 foot ceilings, Architectural Digest kitchen, a view out to China, a sunken tennis court, indoor outdoor pool. The kind of house fit for one of the greatest hedge fund traders of all time.

As I salivated at the stereo and video components in the den, a face Killroyed over the eight foot oatmeal leather sofa. Once standing, he introduced himself as Ed's son Jeff, and said he was coming to Hollywood Park with us. Jeff was 19 or 20, five-ten, with rust brown hair and a few freckles. He wore a dress shirt, a neck tie pulled halfway down, pressed khakis and polished Weejuns.

Ed descended and sent Jeff upstairs to fetch something. When I asked about the curious slot in the kitchen ceiling, Ed said that his wife didn't like to carry packages in from her car. The slot was an industrial conveyor track, leading from the garage, through double hinged doors and into the kitchen. He demonstrated, hanging one of a dozen yellow plastic baskets from a concealed hook and pressed buttons that smoothly carried the basket around the loop. I guess an ex nerd with imagination and money can indulge himself in creative gadgetry, for Ed exuded an inventor's pride in the device. Judging from the house, the gadgets and the cars, Ed spilled more before breakfast than Dr Z or I earned in a year.

In my Hertz hippopotamus on wheels, I told Ed, "I became a decent skier thanks to you. Your book paid for four winters of skiing at Tahoe". Ed is the math professor who developed the card counting technique for beating blackjack. After the casinos banned him from play he wrote *Beat the Dealer*, a book describing the technique. I mastered his method, and before the casinos changed their rules for everyone, I could play blackjack for an hour or two before, dinner at a North Shore casino and pick up the $100 or so that would pay for a week end of skiing, at Squaw Valley 15 years ago. While a grad student, I skied 20 days a winter courtesy of Ed Thorp, and now might have a chance to repay him.

I think Ed's accustomed to such occasional acknowledgments, for he just shrugged. He's now into bigger things. After being banned from blackjack, he worked out the techniques for stock warrant hedging, the precursor of options theory, portfolio insurance and methods of valuing various derivative securities. Ed now runs an investment pool of seven figure amounts from each of a few dozen investors. His fund searches for small discrepancies among the prices of equivalent securities, such as convertibles, warrants, options and the underlying stock, then arbitrages that discrepancy.

Ed played navigator, reaching into the satchel at his feet for an inch thick road atlas of the LA area, and directed me through the back streets of Inglewood, avoiding the heavy track bound traffic.

As the horses begin the parade to the post for the third, with 10 minutes to go, I scan the tote board and see possible place and show system bets on the 3 horse Ellio. Every minute or so Dr Z keys data from the tote board into his gozinto. The calculator Bill holds in the palm of his hand contains a custom chip on which he programmed the system. It has more computing power than the MIT mainframe Ed used for his original blackjack analysis in 1959. At 3 minutes to post time I estimate underlays of about 50% to place and 55% to show. Dr Z confirms my approximation and indicates the optimal bet size. He bets $110 to place and $215 to show; I bet $100 and $25 because I'm lazy. Ed buys tickets on both, but still isn't saying how much he bet.

Our choice leads wire to wire, with just enough stamina to hold off a late closing 35–1 bay, and wins by a nose.

The average margin of victory in a grade I stakes race is only about one length, or 20 feet in a mile and a quarter race, which makes the second best horse 99.7% as fast as the winner. There aren't many second place finishers in business, sports, school or the arts, who the public perceives to be 99.7% as good as the person who finishes first. The winner is remembered but not the runner up. How many of us can name the world's second best cellist or high jumper?

I go to the window to cash my tickets. Ed just hands his to Jeff. While I'm delighted at the $3.80 place and $2.80 show payoffs on a 6–5 horse, when I return I see Dr Z is unhappy. With both place and show bets on the same horse, the system should adjust the optimal wager amount to reflect the joint probabilities. Bill hadn't had time to complete the additional calculations with only 1 minute to post. Afterward he computed that the optimal bets should have been $84 to place and $351 to show, which would have netted him another $31.

Fourth Race: The mile, 1 mile on the grass, for 3 year olds and up, purse $1,000,000

I scan the crowd through Jeff's field glasses. Inside the glass walled VIP dining pavilion to my right, where neckties definitely are required, I see Cary Grant at a table directly in line with the finishing pole. He's on the Hollywood Park board of directors and deserves a prime table. I focus the 10 × 50s on him and think I'd like to look that good when I get to be his age. Actually, I expect that by the time I get to be Cary Grant's age, I will have been dead for 10 years.

Dr Z hasn't eaten in more than, 2 hours, probably a daylight personal best. He has only two paces fast and even faster and needs to refuel every hundred ideas or so. Nevertheless, Bill is finicky about his diet and won't ever eat junk food like most of us. Before the tote odds firm up, he canters to the V.I.P. dining pavilion, where he's able to procure a take out order a club sandwich on whole wheat toast, with no butter, no mayo and no bacon for $18.00, plus tax and tip.

Dr Z is a fortyish dervish with curly graying red hair and a beard to match. Even while wearing a suit that a banker might buy, he frequently sports the bright blue tam o'shanter knit by his wife. Hes written a dozen books in as many years on everything from stochastic optimization in corporate finance, to Turkish weavings, the mathematics of lotteries, and now his system for beating the racetrack. Bill flits around the world, often towing his wife and a beardless 5 year old miniature of himself, to give invited talks at universities and conferences before audiences who bob their heads in understanding. Back home, most of his UBC colleagues are of two types the majority, who cannot understand the depth and range of his work, and therefore resent him, and the few who can understand but not match it, and with quiet envy, resent him even more.

A conversation with Dr Z is like taking a drink of water from a fire hydrant. If I could bottle and sell injections of that energy and intellect, I'd have even more money than Ed and a conveyor track system with a spur line to my wine cellar.

Bill once told me that I was probably his best friend, and appeared somewhat miffed when I didn't reciprocate. But throughout life I've had only one very good friend at a time, and in the 14 years since she was naive enough to marry me, my wife has been that friend. Besides, having Dr Z for a friend isn't all that easy. You've got to accept his occasional grating idiosyncrasies with his brilliant insights, as indivisible as a quark. He talks nearly full time at full speed, even more so than 1, and frequently while his mouth is filled with one of the six meals a day it takes to fuel his mega metabolism. He changes topics in mid sentence, because even at 200 words a minute his mouth is three lengths behind his mind. Yet he's unnecessarily generous with his co-authors, listing each alphabetically. But I think that Bill Ziemba is hoping to find a new protege named Zollen or Zufiuyden.

Having me for a friend or colleague isn't that easy either. I don't suffer fools gladly. I know a bad idea when I see one, and am outspoken enough to say so, believing that keeping silent does no one a service. My outspokenness extends to carrying on my part of an insulting dialogue with the TV news anchor, shouting expletives about his half truths and omissions at the man in the $50 haircut on Channel Two, who doesn't seem to respond to my compelling debating points.

Back in our box, Dr Z alternately punches tote board data into the gozinto and chomps the portion of his $18.00 sandwich that doesn't slop on his tie. "Elizabeth Taylor is eating lunch over there", he mumbles through the turkey and toast in his teeth, and gestures at the dining pavilion, flinging half a tomato slice on my shoe. I'm skeptical, since Dr Z probably hasn't had the patience to sit through a 2 hour movie since Liz was on her third husband.

Dr Z and I each handle the tote information differently. I do approximations in my head. He keys in the data about every third flash and gets precise results. The system's algorithm calculates how much to bet, based upon the advantage offered and the bettor's risk capital. He shouts the exact amount to bet, based on a bankroll updated for the day's income or outgo from earlier races, and even the $18.00 club sandwich. Bill gives numbers like $366.47, which means I'll bet either $350 or $400.[6] Given Ed's bankroll, he ought to bet 10 times as much, but, doesn't say. The earlier computer simulations used exact whole dollar amounts, a technical nicety that isn't practical in the real world. Imagine the patience of a typical bettor behind you in the queue should you request exactly 183 $2.00 show tickets with half a minute to post time.

At each flash the tote's been bouncing on either side of the cutoff point for a system bet on number 1, the only filly in the field. I want to make a bet, but only if I have a healthy edge. Remember, fair is for fools.

We move from the box and stand at our key vantage point, as close to the $100 betting window as we can yet still see the tote board. With 1 minute to post the show bet crosses the 1.10 threshold and Dr Z and I each bet $100. Ed is taciturn as usual, but I see that he keeps a half inch thick stack of $100 bills in the inside left breast pocket of his jacket, fastened shut with a two inch safety pin.

On the backstretch our filly is steadily overtaking horses. She wins the race by more than a length, sets a new American record for a mile on turf, and pays $2.80 to show. A veteran winner now, I eschew walking up to the payoff window and nonchalantly hand my ticket to Jeff to cash.

Fifth Race: The Distaff, 1 1/4 miles, for fillies and mares, 3 year olds and up, purse $1,000,000

I'm getting the bettor's blues. When you lose, you regret losing the money you bet. But when you win, you regret not making a bigger bet. Damon Runyon said that all life was eight to five against. Runyon was an optimist.

After returning with our pelf, Jeff goes to find lunch for the two of us, foraging passable corned beef sandwiches, packets of regular and hot mustard, a bag of Fritos and a couple of Pepsis. Ed pulls a container of yogurt from his satchel.

I open my wallet to give Jeff money for the sandwiches. "Ed, look at this", I say, and pull the Thorp card from between my birth certificate and medical insurance card. It's a chart of Ed's high low blackjack counting system. I've carried it in my wallet since 1964, in case I happen to stumble upon a casino, like on a cruise ship, a Caribbean island or Anytown Nevada.

As I said, I don't gamble, and don't go places just to gamble, but I will invest in opportunities with uncertain outcomes, so long as I am in the neighborhood anyway, and most importantly, have advantage. When we go to Palm Springs each winter, I play in a modest stakes poker game that gives me such an edge. Leo Durocher is a semi regular in the game. The winter before last, when I told him that Elston Howard had died earlier in the day, Leo reminisced fondly about the Yankee catcher and said, "Ellie was a winner in a loser's game." "You too, kid", he added "that's how you stay at this table." Since he's twice my age with half my hair, Leo can call me kid; and he's right about how I play. At our level, poker is a loser's game, in which money is lost by those players who make big mistakes, and then divided up among the other players who don't make the mistakes. Conversely, big money poker is a winner's game, in which the money is made by the players who make brilliant decisions and collected from the other players who don't make such plays. The racetrack is a major loser's game, since the house cuts 15% or more off the top. To win at the races you have to identify enough big mistakes by the crowd to offset that track take. The system can do so for those who have the knowledge, patience and discipline.

Ed focuses thoroughly on one major endeavor at a tune, gets seriously rich by practicing it. Dr Z has several projects underway at a time, each getting his best for several hours or days at a time, but few earning him anything but professional accolades. I am merely a dilettante, a dabbler in many things, few in depth or with passion. I like academic research, and keep up with the literature in several fields, but have little interest in doing much myself. My few publications in big league academic journals aren't sufficient for tenure, and my published recipes and satirical columns on business mid economics don't count. Because I'm an omnivorous reader, and the more meaningless the information, the more likely I retain it, I've amassed at least twice the amount of useless knowledge about more subjects than the two of them combined. I ought to make a good Jeopardy! contestant since I can't get anyone to play Trivial Pursuit against me anymore.

An odds on favorite offers the only possible system bet in the fifth. I check each flash of the tote board. In the last 5 minutes Foofraw has touted four different horses as possible winners in a seven horse field. Should one of them prevail, he'll say, "See, I gave you that winner", or the Brit mumble equivalent. I suspect that Dr Z may be a closet handicapper, because he says he thinks highly of the 4 year old favorite. Foofraw jumps on the bandwagon and cites dosage index numbers, workout times and the filly's recent races. Ed doesn't care about horse lingo, for he knows that the value of dosage is already imputed in the tote odds. Didactically, he explains to Foofraw that since none of us owns a horse in the race, we cannot win any part of the $1,000,000 purse, only a return on our bets. "Buying a hundred shares of General Motors stock isn't the same as buying a Buick."

With 3 minutes to post time, the possible system bet on number I still hasn't materialized. We're here to test the system, but without a horse whose odds meet our criterion we won't wager. Dr Z and I check the tote board at each flash, as if our encouragement will cause the numbers to change and give us the opportunity to bet. I can understand a little of how a compulsive gambler must feel, ever eager to place a bet. At 1 minute to go I guesstimate that the expected payout has across our threshold. Dr Z's computer confirms it. We buy our tickets as the horses are loading at the gate. Ed and I walk down the stairs as the horses break from the gate. Hearing the track announcer calling the race over the P.A., Ed asks, "What's the horse we bet on?"

"What's on second", I respond, on automatic shtick, in a pretty fair Bud Abbott voice. "I think it's Princess something?"

"Bruce, I only hope she has four legs."

Princess Rooney, all four legs intact, romps to win by half a dozen lengths. She pays a disappointing $2.20 to show, which is why this odds on favorite was nevertheless only borderline as a system bet. Foofraw and

Lindsay hold an exacta, wheel with her and each of the other six entrants. So they win their exacta but the bet actually loses money doing so, spending $30.00 for each six ticket wheel on which they'll collect only $28.00.

Sixth Race: The Turf, 1 1/2 miles on the grass, for 3 year olds and up, purse 1,000,000

The Turf attracts several European horses. Foofraw is holding forth beside us, rating the imports against the locals, although all are American bred. He and the newspaper guy are serious handicappers. They pore over past performance charts in the Daily Racing Form, and talk speed ratings and bloodlines. Foofraw mumbles overmuch. Were a Henry Higgins present, I'd offer two to one he'd pronounce Foofraw a non-U fraud.

Lindsay and Foofraw favor the low probability, high payoff exotic bets. Foofraw calls ours, "ladies' bets", saying that wagering on a favorite to show for a $2.60 payoff, isn't really wagering at all. Except for the pyhrric exacta in the fifth, those two haven't cashed a ticket yet, while after each race Jeff returns and deals out $100 bills to Ed, Dr Z and me like it was a card game. It takes a lot more real testosterone to maintain the self discipline to bet our way than his. I don't mind if Foofraw insults my manhood; keep those hundreds coming.

The starting gate is now at the head of the grass turf course. There are 11 horses in the field, but only All Along, the crowd's second choice at 7–2, is a decent Dr Z system bet. She's a 30% underlay.

In addition to keying data into the computer, Dr Z also scrawls information about the win, place and show pools at 5, 3 and 1 minutes before post time. A month earlier I'd hypothesized that a late drop in the win pool odds might be so-called smart money, a predictor that a horse would win. If true, the anomaly would violate our assumptions of an efficient turf market, yet provide us new higher payoff betting opportunities. He was collecting information to test my conjecture. Dr Z isn't really sure the, stock market is efficient either, citing anomalies. Ed, knows it isn't, and has made his fortune arbitraging many small inefficiencies.

The zoom lens on Jeff's camera can't shoot the tote board in a single frame. Ed says we could capture the data quite easily by mounting a camera with a 20 millimeter wide angle lens and motor winder, focussing on the tote board and snapping the shutter every minute. I one up him suggesting a video camera cabled to a digitizer which would not only capture the image but also convert it to numerical data and directly input it to the computer. Ed tops me with a scheme to transmit the computer's betting instructions by radio signal to one of us at the $100 window. That's not too fanciful, for 5 years ago a group of Ed's fans in Silicon Valley constructed a toe operated computer built into a sneaker and programmed it for roulette.[7]

Ed has never been to Hollywood Park before, and I'm not sure he's even been to any racetrack in 20 years. He's here to see the system in action, in the real world, in real time, with real money. When Bill first explained the reasoning behind the system and the basis of the complex optimization calculations, Ed took all of 5 minutes to concur, probably performing the pages of calculus equations in his head as Dr Z spouted them. Ed's experience in the financial markets has made him question any theory's applicability in practice. He's seen what happens to the bid ask spread when he tries to take a big position in a stock. He thinks that in a parimutuel betting system, the payoff offered when we make a decision won't be the same as when we go to cash our tickets if we get cash them at all. Ed also doesn't care for the idea of putting money on humans or animals, because there's too much random error in a one performance of one jockey on one horse in one race. Furthermore, he's discomfited knowing the turf market offers only 10 races a day, and a top horse will typically run in at most a dozen races a year for 2 or 3 years. A small number of investment opportunities, high transaction costs and a fat tailed distribution are an anathema to a man who makes hundreds of individual trades a day in the Wall Street and Chicago financial markets. The few thousand dollars he'll bet today are merely to test whether Dr Z system is valid in practice.[8]

Hearing I too would be in Los Angeles that weekend, Dr Z invited me to join the expedition. The box he'd borrowed had empty seats and, since I was in the neighborhood anyway, why not. When I was Jeffs age, my uncle entered one of his horses in the Kentucky Derby. Since then I've enjoyed horse racing, but in moderation. At home, my trips to the track with Dr Z are purely for research purposes, although on a sunny afternoon we'll each bring a daughter along to enjoy the event and to log a twofer of betting and father bonding. Once or twice a year I go to the track with friends for dinner, and as long as I'm there and I have an advantage, I'll make a few system bets to pay for the wine, and sometimes for the dinner too.

Dr Z is here for all of it. He wants to validate his system on horse racing's biggest day in history. He also wants Ed Thorp to watch him do it, in real time for real money. But Bill really does like horses and racing. He's trying to get a release to use a picture of himself with Secretariat on the dust jacket of Beat the Racetrack, the book he and Don Hausch have in press. If he makes any money on the securities market anomalies project he is beginning, I think he'd like to squander it on owning a racehorse. I do believe Dr Z is a closet handicapper.

The field breaks cleanly from the gate and. Willy Shoemaker rides his roan out to an early lead along the rail. The field is tightly bunched as they cross the patch of dirt track and back onto the grass. On the backstretch All Along steadily gains on the leaders and pulls into the lead before the stretch run. She's nipped by a neck and finishes second to a 50–1 longshot. Since a 12–1 horse finishes third, this should be a big payoff on our system bet. At $4.40 to show, it's huge. Hooray for Hollywood Park!

Seventh Race: The Classic, 1 1/4 miles, for 3 year olds and up, purse $3,000,000

This is a tough race for most other bettors to get excited about. The standout, a son of Seattle Slew, should go off odds on. While the payoff will likely be modest, there'll almost certainly be a system bet available, because the crowd does agree with Foofraw. Back at the office on Monday, there will be no bragging rights in telling how you cashed a $2.20 ticket, so the crowd won't wager heavily on the favorite in the place or show pools.

Super favorites often provide outstanding returns if you bet them with enough conviction. While the system is new and quantitatively sophisticated, some people had been doing the no brainer equivalent for years. There's a likely apocryphal bettor in Kentucky called the Bridge Jumper. Whenever offered a one to five or shorter odds on favorite, the Jumper would bet $20,000 to show, buying several different tickets so he needn't fill out IRS forms when he cashes them in separately. While California requires a payout of $2.10 on a $2.00 bet, the Kentucky minimum is $2.20. At one to five, assuming an efficient turf market and independent sub races, the probability of the favorite finishing out of the money is only one-half of 1% but the track has to payoff as if it were 9%, a huge underlay. Looming above is the one half of 1% risk he's a Joe Bltsftk that day, and the $20K goes kaput; hence the bridge.

If you owned a 1,000″ color TV, it would be the Diamond Vision screen in Hollywood Park's infield that displays close ups and replays of each race. Following each winning system bet, I watch the Diamond Vision replay of the finish line through Jeffs field glasses and zoom in on the efficient market equine benefactor who favored us by running true to form.

Dr Z returns from fetching another $18.00 plus club sandwich, without mentioning anyone famous. There are system bet possibilities for both place and show on Slew O'Gold. Dr Z likes the horse as well as the tote, citing data from the Daily Racing Form. I Groucho my eyebrows and flick an imaginary cigar, letting him know my doubts about his piety toward the system.

The 30% underlay is enough for me to make both bets 3 minutes before post time. Returning to the box I see the tote board flash a big change. In the last minute someone has bet another $50,000 to win, making the respective place and show underlays 40% and 50%. Dr Z punches in the new numbers. The optimization genie in the gozinto still says our $250 place bets are in line, but the show bets should have been $927, not the $500 we'd each bet. I push Jeff aside, mount the stairs in threes and sprint toward the $100 window. I shout to the clerk from 20 feet, "$100 Show, Number One, four times." Midway through my plea, the bell rings. I'm shut out at the window.

Even though the race action isn't supposed to matter, I thrill in watching this outstanding finish. The horses bump and shove on the long Hollywood Park stretch run. Three horses are in contention. Slew O'Gold with Angel Cordero, Jr., up is getting sandwiched between number 2, Wild Again, on the rail and number 5, Gate Dancer with his muffed ear covers, veering in from the outside. The horses finish 2, 5 and 1, no more than an arm span separating first from third, some five lengths ahead of the also rans. Wild Again won at 30–1. He was supplemented at considerable cost by his owners and the win was one of the starting points for the career of the great jockey Pat Day.

The inquiry sign, on the tote board lights, indicating either the stewards' or a jockey's claim, of foul. Dr Z keys in the final betting pool data, and tells us his last prerace estimates were within 3% of the algorithm's optimum bet. Right now I don't care about the algorithm. Will the race result hold up? Will the stewards, take down Slew O'Gold? As the horses finished, we lose our place bets, and don't make enough on the show bets to offset that loss, but if I'd gotten the additional $400 down, it would have. However, if the stewards completely disqualify Slew O'Gold my loss will be that much greater. I ruminate on all the woulda coulda shoulda combinations. The stewards take 4 or 5 minutes, which is geological time for the tenterhooked ticket holders of the maybe in the money horses. The Diamond Vision screen replays the stretch run at full speed, then in slow motion. The inquiry light turns off and the tote displays the official results. The finish order is now 2, 1 and 5; the stewards took Gate Dancer down. Our place and show system bets both pay off, at $3.00 and $2.20.

Dr Z too likes to invest in other uncertain situations, so long has he has an advantage, and we have a few followers who will join us when we spot one. A year ago we each independently found a one shot, one day lottery opportunity which offered an expected payout of $2.31 for each $1.00 ticket. We rounded up the usual suspects from the department. The six of us each descended on a different local retailer at 7 am on a Friday, politely asked to commandeer the lottery terminal, and then spent the morning hours making it spit out 1,000 or 2,000 tickets. All day Sunday we sorted through grocery bags led with lottery tickets gleaning our winners, and collected our predicted payoff.

While my confidence in Dr Z is high, it's less than perfect. He sometimes needs my reality-checking skepticism. Last winter Bill calculated a way to regularly play the lottery that had a payback with an expected value of almost $11.00 for each $1.00 ticket bought. We have each consulted for government lotteries, he on the mathematics of game design and I on marketing and strategy, so once we discussed the logic behind it, I trusted his estimate. Our departmental syndicate bought 100 tickets on each lotto draw. When after 5 months we were so far behind, I asked Dr Z to recheck his calculation of the expectation, and also to look at the higher moments of the probability distribution. The next day we lunched at the Faculty Club, and when he treated me to a Heineken, I knew there was bad news coming. Yes, at 10.7267 the long run expected payout was as he'd previously calculated. Since such a huge chunk of the lottery prize pool goes to a winner who hits all six numbers of the 6/49, a 13.9 million to one shot, it might take some time to achieve that expected value. Even if we bought 1,000 tickets a week, it would be more than 15 years before we could be 90% certain of being ahead of buying government bonds instead. John Maynard Keynes said, "In the long run, we're all dead."

Eighth Race: Fleet Nashrullah Stakes, 6 furlongs, for 2 year olds, purse $60,000 added

Much of the crowd was leaving. Cary Grant's table was empty. Elizabeth Taylor had left, if she'd even been there. The seven Breeders' Cup races were at the start of the day to reach East coast TV audiences, so Hollywood Park slated two more races to fill out the program. The tote board isn't leaving with Cary and the illusory Liz, even though only about one third as much is being bet on this race as on the Classic. None of the entrants are important to Dr Z and Ed still doesn't care to know the horses' names., There are five contenders and two long shots, in the seven horse field. The tote has been pretty steady, offering a show bet on only the fourth favorite, number 3. We make the bet.

Naturally, who was the catcher on Bud Abbott's baseball team, our pick Teddy Naturally, leads the field throughout and wins by nearly ten lengths, to pay $3.40 to show. While Ed still isn't talking about how much he's bet, I see his other inside. breast pocket now holds a second stack of hundreds as thick as the first, without a protective safety pin.

Ninth Race: Seabiscuit Claiming Stakes, 1 1/2 miles on the grass, for 3 year olds and up, purse $100,000 added

Even though this is a claimer, with claiming prices of $500,000 and $1,000,000, there are no ringers in the race.

An early scan of the tote board gives me possible place and show bets on the favorite, number 10. Five minutes before post time I make the underlays 35% to place and 50% to show. Maybe he's another double dipper? Bill's tracking the tote on his gozinto. As the horses are milling before the starting gate, we walk up to bet both to place and to show. I'm approaching the window, when Dr Z shouts to me to come back. Starting at the vantage point, he tells me the system bet to place has disappeared, and the optimum show bet is $219. I put the extra bills back in my pocket and bet $200 to show. This is the day's final race, so Dr Z bets exactly $219.

Our horse starts from the outside post position, runs at the back of the pack for the first half of the race, and then begins to chip away at the field to finish second by a length. He pays $3.00 to show, and $4.00 to place, had we made the place bet.

We cash the last tickets on our way to the parking lot. Dr Z is going north. Ed, Jeff and I are headed south. Ed and his street atlas route us through a new set of one way Inglewood alleys, getting us to the freeway at least two times faster than by driving the rhumb line.

Two days later, before going to the airport, I stopped in to be tested for Jeopardy! and got a passing grade. When the contestant coordinator said they received a late cancellation for the next day's taping, I postponed my flight and stayed over. I postponed it again each of the following days. Just to show that there are some payoffs for being a dilettante, I became an undefeated 5 day champion. For me it was that once in a lifetime experience, winning a year's salary ($43,398) on a TV game show. Assuming he had a typical ho hum time at the office, Ed made more money those few days than I.

Bruce Fauman August, 1995.

Excerpts from the Postscript by Ziemba

The Breeders' Cup was conceived by John Gaines of Gainesway farm on the Paris Pike near Lexington, Kentucky. Its purpose is to promote racing at the highest level both through bonus additions to purses at various race tracks across North America and through a major culmination day of racing. Breeders' Cup Day features seven races of which five have purses of $1 million and the others have purses of $2 and $3 million. The day is meant to bring together a tremendous collection of the top horses. With a 4 hour TV special it's like a World Series of racing. The Breeders' Cup program is paid for by stallion season donations. For a horse to be eligible for Breeders' Cup races, the owner of the horse's sire must donate the equivalent of one breeding season that year, be it worth $500,000 or $1,000. Thus, to have a chance to collect the large purses and fame, breeders have to donate. It's a brilliant idea for breeding and racing and so far it has been quite successful. In 1984 the purses were $1 million for each of the first races with the $1\frac{1}{2}$ mile grass race for $2 million and $3 million for the classic in 1984, a total of $10 million. In 2015, there were 13 races over 2 days with the Breeders' Cup Classic at $5 million and $2 and $1 million purses for the other Breeders' Cup races.

The inaugural Breeders' Cup Day was held on November 10, 1984 at Hollywood Park. Ed Thorp and Bruce Fauman joined me. I pocketed my earlier winnings and again started with a bankroll of $1,500. Again I would bet $100 on horses with expected values above 1.02 but below 1.10 and use 1.10 as my cutoff for Dr Z system bets.

The final Breeders' Cup race was for a purse of $3 million. The classic was for 3 year olds and upwards over 1 1/4 miles. The choice was Slew O'Gold. A win here would probably have sewed up horse of the year honors over John Henry. Slew O'Gold was part of an entry with Mugatea. With 1 minute to go the toteboard was:

	Totals	#1,1a Slew O'Gold and Mugatea	Expected Value Per Dollar Bet	Optimal Kelly Bet
Odds	3–5			
Win	716,354	367,710		
Place	255,600	99,846	1.19	613 → 367
Show	128,746	50,090	1.19	951 → 780

Clearly it was time to load up! The edge for place and show is good but the safety of a 3–5 place horse and even more so a 3–5 show horse plus having an entry leads to a very big Kelly bet. With the huge pools you do not influence the odds much at all. Betting for place by itself indicated a bet of $613 and for show $951. When you consider the effect of both bets using the formulas, the optimal bets become $367 for place and $780 for show. These are gigantic bets with my fortune of $1,785; but recall that is a Kelly property when the chance of losing is small. I bet $250 to place and $500 to show — roughly the 1/2, 1/2 idea I used before.

The race was a classic with Wild Again at the rail, Gate Dancer charging on the outside and Slew O'Gold sandwiched in the middle with Angel Cordero Jr. attempting to bring him in. There was a tremendous amount of bumping among these three horses. In the end Wild Again won the race followed by Gate Dancer and Slew O'Gold. Fortunately for us the stewards took Gate Dancer down and awarded Slew O'Gold second place. Mugatea finished last. Slew O'Gold paid $3.00 to place and only $2.20 to show (breakage cut deeply into this payoff.) I made $125 on my place bet and $50 on my show bet so my bankroll was now $1960. The final toteboard and chart were as follows — so the Dr Z bets on Slew O'Gold to place and show were even better at post time than when I bet.

	Totals	#1,1a Slew O'Gold and Mugatea	Expected Value Per Dollar Bet	Optimal Kelly Bet
Odds	3–5			
Win	809,920	423,222		
Place	269,107	102,480	1.24	694 → 386
Show	151,289	52,467	1.30	1135 → 957

The eighth race was the Fleet Nasrullah Stakes, a $60,000 added event. A bit of a comedown after the Breeders' Cup races but still a high class race. The feature and late races are prime candidates for Dr Z system bets. Late in the day most bettors are behind and do not want to consider low paying bets to place or show. These races also feature excellent horses. The ninth race was the Seabiscuit Claiming Stakes, at $500,000 and up, this was no ordinary claiming race. I bet $35 on Teddy Naturally who won the eighth race (for a profit of $29.50) and I bet $219 to show on Late Act in the ninth. Late Act finished second and paid $3.00. My profit was $109.50. That gave me a final bankroll of $2,094 for a nice profit of $594 on the day.

My colleagues Ed Thorp and Bruce Fauman did well also. Ed was betting heavier than I was, using a $10,000 initial fortune that led to bets in the range $500–$750. He made $1,851 on the day. He did not feel that he needed to look at the Daily Racing Form or a program. This made a great impression on the handicappers in the next box. Here a talented student of betting was able to win big without knowing much about the horses while they, the experts on handicapping, were having a rough go of it. The odds board told the story. Bruce who made bets similar to mine made a tidy $345.

We all had a fun time at the Breeders' Cup and it was very profitable. Except for the mishap on Bessarabian, we had excellent luck that helped us. On average Dr Z system bets win about 60% of the time. The bets with expected values between 1.02 and 1.09 on favorites have similar outcomes. However, these bets will not on average have payoffs as good as the Dr Z system bets. To gain our edge of 10–20% we will have our ups and downs, winning and losing streaks. However, if played properly, the Dr Z system should provide you with an upward drift in your bankroll at a rate of about 10% of the value of your wagers. I wound up losing $143 the day after Breeders' Cup.

Notes

[1] Technical detail is in Ziemba and Hausch (1986).
[2] Ed's story is in his new trade book, Thorp (2017).
[3] Historical and recent graphs are in Hausch and Ziemba (2008).
[4] The 1984 book Beat the Racetrack, which was revised in 1987 into the book *Dr Zs Beat the Racetrack*, has simulated results from Exhibition Park, Aqueduct and Santa Anita plus calculations on how the Dr Z bets affect the odds, how many can play the system, etc.
[5] This was the paper Bill and Don along with Mark Rubinstein of portfolio insurance infamy published in *Management Science* in 1981.
[6] With full Kelly bets, you should never bet more, so $350 is ok but $400 is over betting according to the theory; see MacLean, Ziemba and Blazenko (1992) for graphs that show that betting more than full Kelly has lower growth and has more risk, that is, less security.
[7] Ed Thorp wrote a column about this in Gambling Times. A power function is estimated based on what numbers cross the start and the time of one revolution. One then forecasts where the ball might land. This leads several winning systems. One very simply is to either bet or don't bet on a 40 payoff.
[8] Which he confirmed in the preface to Beat the Racetrack.

Chapter 11

The 2 Minute Sprint

Daniel Siegelman of *Fortune* magazine wrote a short blurb about the Dr Z place and show betting system. He referred to it as the 2 minute sprint and had a lovely cartoon as shown below.

In the book *Beat the Racetrack* (1984 original version and the 1987 updated version), we did calculations concerning how many people could play the system optimally before the edge was taken out. Related to that and consistent with the 2 minute sprint idea is the idea to be rely and grab the edge before others can get it. Of course, in doing this you cannot over bet and we recommend that the bet be at the most full Kelly which in the one-dimensional case is the edge divided by the odds. These books also discuss the effect of differing track takes and all the features were put into a handheld calculator.

To followup and be more thorough, *Fortune* approached me about doing a full story on the betting strategy in the fall of 1986. I responded by saying let's do it at next year's Kentucky Derby Day. I would make place and show system bets and also try to pick the winner of the Kentucky Derby. They agreed and to prepare I gave talks on how to predict the winner of the Derby at Cornell and Stanford universities. Both of these top schools had invited me for an asset, liability stochastic programming talk and I simply asked if I could give my Kentucky Derby talk as well.

The Derby talk was based on something different than the place and show system. Rather than being based on prices measured by odds discrepancies — what finance people call weak market inefficiency. The dosage theory was based on breeding and racetrack performance. The pioneers of the breeding theories that became what we now call dosage theory were studying matchings and the performance of the offspring starting with Vullier.

Steve Roman, a research chemist working for Shell Oil in Houston, Texas, followed racing as a hobby. In 1981, he had written, along with the *Daily Racing Form* columnist Leon Rasmusen, an influential column. There were several parts. Steve, Leon, along with Abraham Hewitt established a list of current chef-de-race stallions. This updated previous lists made in the 1920s, 1930s, 1940s, etc. These were the stallions who essentially made the thoroughbred racing breed. If you looked at pedigrees of current top horses you would see these names showing up all the time. The contribution of Roman especially with help from Rasumssen and Hewitt was to formalize the analysis of the offspring. First, to be a chef, the stallion much produce consistent offspring not noise along a span to stamina axis with five distinct categories. The axis was labeled brilliant (pure speed), intermediate, classic (the ability to run the distance of the triple crown races), solid and professional. The last two categories related more and more to stamina, namely, the ability to run long distances.

The list of chefs was not a quality contest although many great stallions were listed. Rather it was a way to define the breed. Some great runners such as Secretariat were never made chefs. Secretariat never produced a male horse as good as he was. The closest being Risen Star who won the 1988 Preakness and Belmont in 2:26.40 only two plus seconds slower than Secretariat's record 2:24.[1] He also sired General Assembly who won the 1979 Travers Stakes at Saratoga running the $1\frac{1}{4}$ in a flat 2 minutes which was the record for this race until Arrogate at 1:59.2 in 2016. And Secretariat sired 1980 Melbourne Cup winner Kingston Rule who still holds the record for that race. However, Secretariat was the top broodmare sire and produced many outstanding female horses such as Lady's Secret. The greatest horses Secretariat produced were the sons of his daughters such as top sires A. P. Indy, Storm Cat, Gone West and Giants Causeway.

The next element was to evaluate a particular foal. The way this was done was to score up the chefs in the background in the first four generations of the pedigree.

The dosage index was then the left side speed divided by the right side stamina with classic being shared. This is a crude measure that does not weigh the tails higher but it has worked well. Steve Roman found that from 1929 to 1990 no horse with a dosage index above 4.0 had won the Kentucky Derby. So in subsequent years, a filter was used to essentially eliminate horses with two much speed and too little stamina namely those with a dosage index above 4.0. Since 1990, there have been a few exceptions of winners above 4.0 but none up the the year when I was scheduled to take *Fortune* to the Derby. The exceptions also tended to be explained by observing a missing chef. Also in recent years very few Derby entrants have dosage indices above 4.0, however the trend is up for the winners, so the breed is moving more towards speed.

The final piece of the story is the concept of a dual qualifier. Among the horses with dosage indices below 4 which ones have the best chance of winning on the first Saturday in May. A measure was how good were they as 2 year olds. The Jockey Club rates the 2 year old horses with 126 or 128 pounds the highest with a super horse at 130. So the rule is be within 10 pounds of the top horse and have proper dosage and then you are a dual qualifier. Over the years, dual qualifiers have had a remarkable record in the Derby and the Belmont Stakes, the two races where the horses have not run the distance before, $1^1/_4$ and $1^1/_2$ miles, respectively, A list year by year of the winners of these two races plus the Preakness $1^3/_{16}$ mile race is in my 2017 book *Exotic Betting at the Racetrack*.

Now let's go back to the 1997 race. Looking at the dosage values, the ratings had Silver Charm the best, Captain Bodget second and Free House third. So that was my picks announced in the Cornell and Stanford talks and to the *Fortune* magazine reporter who followed me around along with a top photographer whose previous assignment was the Silk Road and next assignment Bo Derek. The photographer was paid $2,000 for the day. The actual bets I made on the place and show system and the luck-skill perfect 1–2–3 Kentucky Derby pick gained $5,000. So it was a very good outcome. While dosage was helpful, getting 1–2–3 was pretty lucky. But I did feel that these were the three best horses and they did run true to form. All this was exciting as I discussed the horses with the reporter.

I went after to Hong Kong where I was consulting on racetrack factor models for the British racetrack bettor Paul Makin. Makin, who had invited me there, was renting suites in a big hotel for US$24,000 a month.

Makin knew of my work and had inside knowledge of much of the methods and strategies of the top Hong Kong racetrack bettor, Bill Benter. Besides my own work in *Beat the Racetrack*, as departmental editor for finance of the journal *Management Science*, I accepted a paper by Bolton and Chapman (1986) that was the key to developing a factor model to predict the probability that each horse would win a race. They did it for North American races. Later, Chapman consulted with Benter regarding Hong Kong races and the outcome was an 85 factor model to predict this probability using the odds at the track as well as other fundamental factors. The Bolton–Chapman paper and its separate application to Hong Kong races along with the only published paper Benter ever wrote, are in Hausch, Lo and Ziemba (HLZ) (1994, 2008). HLZ became a classic cult book and originals sold on eBay and Amazon for $2,000+ and one sold for $12,000. I sold one for $1,400 to an Australian entrepreneur who invited me to come to Sidney for a week to discuss racetrack betting. While he was not technically trained, he had made millions in a computer company and now wanted to try racing. Putting serious resources into it, he developed winning models for Australian racetrack betting. Later, he was bought out by the top racetrack syndicate, Jelko. Our experience helping Benter through correspondence and phone calls did not help Hausch or me. See his letter in Chapter 16 where he says he is a businessman and we are academics so he cannot pay us. I guess he forgot that professors consult! But in 2014 he recommended me as the expert witness in a major Hong Kong court case involving a dispute concerning winning Hong Kong racing models by the developer and the client. The case continues still. Benter also added much to our knowledge concerning professional racetrack betting.

Makin wanted me mostly for the Kelly optimization part, that is the optimal sizing of the bets. He had a very good computer programmer who helped him a lot. Much progress was made on that trip writing computer codes for the various Hong Kong wagers. I returned to Vancouver and continued the work with a very good graduate student Raphael Sangre from Valencia, Spain. Raphael a master's student was the top student in my PhD class on nonlinear programming and portfolio theory in the fall term and applied stochastic programming and asset-liability management in the winter term. Raphael did coding and helped with some of the math I was formulating the various optimization models associated with the different

In Australia with Rafael Sangre

bets. Raphael and I made two trips to the Gold Coast of Australia where Makin rented a nice condo for us. Sandra came on one of the trips.

Makin's assistant, a Hong Kong Chinese super programmer got it all programmed. Then, as often happens to consultants, it was time for us to go before the big money was made. Rumor has it that Makin made about $7 million in Hong Kong and we did not get any of that. Plus he made many more millions in Japan using similar techniques. Raphael and I were not involved with any of the Japan work but of course the models we helped on were very similar. The technique Makin used to get rid of us was to ask me for a consulting invoice for that year's work for Raphael and I including our airfares. I submitted one similar to the previous year which included some money for a number of months Raphael worked part time in Vancouver. Makin objected, saying it was too much. I said we can reduce it and Raphael did work for many months outside Australia. His response was that once an invoice is presented it must be paid. And it was. But thence were banished from his house in the hills and I was accused of stealing his wife's purse! Anyway that was the end of that.

We then spent the final week on the beach waiting for our flights. Makin did resurface some years later with a New Zealand champion horse who shipped to the Breeders' Cup. He was an expensive one but lost. Neither Raphael nor I have had any contacts with Makin since. Makin reneged on the earlier promise of a share of the winnings but we did have some good experiences and learned a lot.

Notes

[1] Other fast Belmont's (thanks to Steve Roman) were: Easy Goer, 2:26; AP Indy, 2:26.13; Point Given, 2:26.56; and Gallant Man, 2:26.60. American Pharoah's Belmont in 2015 was 2:26.65 the second fastest behind Secretriat of those who won the Triple Crown.

Chapter 12

Susquehanna

When you come to a fork in the road, take it.[1]

Beat the Racetrack attracted a lot of attention as it was purely based on mispricings. Because of this work, Jeff Yass, the main partner of Susquehanna in Philadelphia contacted me in 1987. Jeff was one of five partners, all about 28 years old who were friends at The State University of New York at Binghamton. They were betting racetrack pick 6's, etc., successfully and moved to Philadelphia to start a firm market making on the Philadelphia stock exchange. This exchange is known as the home of bandits who nickel and dime on trades to generate fortunes. Jeff's group were clever and hired young smart non-finance students from elite schools in the northeast and trained them to be market makers. They preferred students from philosophy, political science, etc., rather than finance graduates who might be corrupted by efficient market theory. The idea was to make those nickels and dimes and quarters by selling high at the offer and buying low at the bid in various markets. This was a good business.

Jeff wanted an academic who was practical as the director of research so came to Vancouver to discuss this with me and I visited their offices in Philadelphia. It was all very interesting but at 46 I was a lot older than them and Sandra hated Philadelphia having grown up there; UBC was not so bad then, Rachel was in a good school and the opportunity to go to Japan was another option. So I took Japan. Later, the next year, 1988, in Japan, Jeff offered me the chance to sell Susquehanna for $200 million to some rich Japanese person or firm for a 1% fee. I did search around but got no takers. Going to Susquehanna would have made me richer in money as they became a giant multibillion dollar outfit very successful in many areas of investments. But maybe I got to do more interesting things by taking the other path. Anyway both choices were good ones.

I wrote five rather important racing books, plus a number of good research papers with Don Hausch on the right, and Gerry (Jarl Karlberg) and I wrote a number of classic portfolio theory and practice papers that continue to be important

NY Yankees, mid-1950s

In November 2014, it was announced that Susquehanna was sold for US$2.5 billion. So Jeff is a billionaire. At the London school of economics, where I visit once or twice a year to do research and give some talks in London, I was contacted by an old Susquehanna statistician. He had no real academic publishing experience but had produced an interesting applied investment book based on 30 years of experience, starting with a very good PhD in statistics. I edited and gave comments to him and it was a good read and in the end he is doing a two volume set of books in my books in finance series for World Scientific.[2] He related one story typical of these times. Foreign firms were making a lot of money doing index arbitrage in Japan. Japanese firms were propping up the Tokyo stock exchange by buying futures. Then these foreign firms, including Solomon Asia and Morgan Stanley, shorted these futures and bought stock. Held to maturity there is no risk here and the foreign firms grab all the gains. Of course the Japanese well known as the world's best at losing money, had this all wrong. They should have bought stock not futures. Then they would not have transferred funds from Japan to the US firms.

Susquehanna was raking in the money. A story, perhaps apocryphal, has a Susquehanna executive and his wife flying to Japan. Their dog was not allowed to sit with them in first class. They did not want the dog in the luggage area, so they bought all the seats in first class! I am sure this did not sit well with the Japanese at a time when their economic world was falling apart.

Notes

[1] This is one of Yogi Berra's famous sayings, see for example his books *The Yogi Book: "I really didn't say everything I said!"*, *You can observe a lot by watching*, and *Wit and wisdom of Yogi Berra*, all available on Amazon. I had a great visit to Yogi's museum on the campus of Montclair State University. I recall fondly, that as a kid and a Red Sox fan, I understood that Yogi was a great. He would hit anything and in the clutch he was at his best. His ten world series victories are more than any other player. Up to his death at 90 in 2015, he was the most popular baseball player even though he played his last game in 1965.

[2] We are working on lottery research, see Moffitt and Ziemba (2016a, b). Steve wrote the codes for the pick 6 plays and other such advantageous wagers. He took suitcases of money to bet at places far away. He is now part of my racetrack betting syndicate.

Chapter 13

What is Japan Doing Right to Get All that Money? Will they Lose It?

The phone rang. Keizo Nagatani, a University of British Columbia colleague from the economics department called asking if I would be interested in going to Japan. Keizo, from Japan himself, had contact with Tsukuba University, one of the national universities and in the city where all the major Japanese manufacturing firms had research facilities. Yamaichi Securities, the fourth biggest Japanese brokerage firm and sixth biggest in the world had given the university money to support five visiting finance professors over the next 5 years. I had a chance to be the first.

In Japan, there is a status hierarchy with Kabuki dancers, sumo wrestlers, national potters at the top and stock brokers below garbage collectors at the bottom. Also the society is supposedly male dominated as a wife will cook a dinner but not be allowed to dine with the husband's male guests. The women are in charge of the minor things such as where the children go to school, where they live, where they go on vacation and how they spend and invest their money. The men are in charge of the important things like what kind of sandwich they take to work. I found out that the control of money and stock investments by the wives would clue me in on a number of key stock market anomalies such as the turn-of-the-month (TOM) effect.

I jumped at the chance to go to Japan and went for an interview to Tokyo. There were two parts to the job — teaching on Monday to Wednesday in Tsukuba to the students there plus some young people from Yamaichi and then consulting on Thursday and Friday in Tokyo, some 60 kilometers south. I liked the idea to do both and proposed two projects: stock market crashes and stock market anomalies. Also my courses were good ones on investments and options.

It was 1988, at the height of Japanese stock and land prices and right after the October 1987 stock market crash. Going into the crash week, I was managing a portfolio for Charles Ying from Hawaii who had sold Kodak a product for $20 million. During the week before the crash, the Dow Jones Average was very violent with big increases and larger deceases. It quickly became an impossible market to figure out so by late in the week I cashed out. This period was similar to early August 2011 discussed in Chapter 27. It was a time to be out of the market because the violence exceeds the ability of any rational pricing model to give guidance as to what to do.

On Friday night I watched *Wall Street Week* with Louis Rukeyser. He had three guests — the one who made the biggest impression on me was Marty Zweig, a savvy Wall Street veteran who was good at analyzing the market based on past data, trends and the like. The Dow Jones Average stood at 2200. His face, white as a sheet of paper, Zweig said "I don't know how much it is going to fall on Monday, but it is going to be a lot, maybe 250 points or more." Zweig, like me, knew that there was a lot of pent-up selling demand that had not been executed including some by portfolio insurers. Portfolio insurance was invented by my Berkeley friends and colleagues, two star finance professors, Mark Rubinstein and Hayne Leland. Rubinstein had a hand in my racetrack place and show betting system discussed in Chapter 8 and we wrote a key 1981 paper on that. Leland and I used to play tennis together when I was visiting Berkeley and is currently an advisor to a book series for which I am series editor for World Scientific. Both were very talented, Hayne being the aloof brilliant professor and Mark, the explosive emotional one with the added skill of being a first class computer person with tremendous tenacity and stamina. They used a version of the Black Scholes option pricing model to create what seemed to be a superior product. Instead of having a portfolio where you could gain and lose, they take a little bit of the gains and use that money to eliminate all the losses? So you never lose. Now in 2017 you can do this by having a long portfolio such as the S&P500 index fund plus a long dated put on the S&P500 at the break even point. This is actually pretty well fully safe now. But in 1987 the Leland–Rubinstein approach was different. They would create a synthetic put using futures on the S&P500. Professors often get their ideas stolen by others since they like to publish their results in academic papers and give talks. In this case the two professors gave presentations and at least one firm stole the idea. So they brought in a sales person, John O'Brien, and LOR was born with the three of them.

Business was good and they had about $60 billion under management. The service was simple, just adjust the futures so that the portfolio was still protected from losses. This meant buying futures dynamically when the market went up and selling them when it fell but you had to do this continuously. As long as the market was liquid, they were fine. The two of them were named businessmen of the year by *Fortune* magazine in 1987. Even with a small fee of 10 basis points per year, the fees were $60 million, not bad for full time professors with a side business. Some copycat firms entered the business. Just like the LTCM disaster in 1998, when there are too many following the same strategy, it is hard to get out of positions if disaster strikes.

But *buy high, sell low* runs counter to *buy low, sell high* which is what sellers not buyers of portfolio insurance and put sellers would be doing. There was a huge amount of portfolio insurance that had not been executed on the Friday and that was one of the things that bothered Zweig. Also Germany had increased interest rates. The futures opened sharply down at a discount to cash. Theoretical S&P500 December futures should equal the current spot value of the S&P500 cash plus the interest out to the December expiry. And index arbitrage should keep this in balance.

Index arbitrage works as follows: if futures are too high, sell then and buy all the 500 stocks. Then if you hold both positions to expiry, you have an arbitrage where you make a gain for sure. And if futures are too low, they are bought and the 500 stocks are sold. This is also a way to prop up markets as the Japanese big brokerage firms did in 1990. They bought futures so others would buy stocks. I always argue that the Japanese are the best at losing money. In this case, $500 million was transferred from Japan to the US firms. Morgan Stanley, Saloman Asia, etc., which sold the futures and bought the stocks and made huge index arbitrage gains.

So the Monday had futures selling then stock selling, etc. At the end of the day, the futures had fallen 29% and the cash index had fallen 22%.

It was a slaughter and market makers who are supposed to provide liquidity were too scared and left the market so as not to be wiped out. LOR was slow making a mistake in not recognizing that the *correct* price is the futures not the lagging cash. Finally, by the Tuesday, they established the various positions but there was a loss gap. Other firms followed the rules more carefully but all had trouble. According to the *Wall Street* reporter Scott Peterson in his interesting book *Quants on Wall Street* on five major quant players, Rubinstein still thinks the drop was a one in 10^{140} chance — that's by assuming the efficient market idea that all days are the same and the crash was a random event. I, of course, think the chance is much less, maybe 1 in 5 or even higher. The signals were there and there is daily serial correlation especially in violent markets. My colleague and friend, legendary *between the wall paper and the wall* option trader Blair Hull bought at the bottom and helped stop the crash. This was a brilliant move by an exceptionally great trader.

We will see later that LTCM, the hedge fund that was too smart to lose, made the same mistake assuming perfect liquid markets in their 1998 demise as discussed in Chapter 19. The result was a big blow to efficient market theory as some have said *the efficient market theory also crashed on October 19, 1987.* LOR was finished. This was hard personally for the two professors but they have survived and continue to be top academics at the University of California, Berkeley. Futures based portfolio insurance was then replaced by long-term puts which are much safer.

My proposals to have a study group on stock market crashes was accepted as was the second study group on stock market anomalies. So we had a deal with me and my wife teaching at Tsukuba, me going to Tokyo by train or bus on Thursday morning and returning Friday night. And our red-head daughter, Rachel, now a managing director focusing on emerging markets, oil markets and other areas at Nouriel Roubini's firm Roubini Global Economics in New York and London, at nine entered a sea of black haired children in Japanese public school. We were especially proud that she fit in and learned Japanese largely from playing after school with other children and from the helpful mothers and studying the BC curriculum until she got up to speed with her Japanese and could fully join the class. She continues this creativity to this day being an expert on sovereign wealth funds, China, oil, the Middle East and other economic areas.

Learning about Japan during their Salad Days: September 1988–September 1989

Our year in Japan was a most interesting one and, for me, a tremendous learning experience. My classes were fine and I could teach material that I was not able to in Vancouver such as options and futures and anomalies to a finance audience. About 10 of the Yamichi Research Institute's young staff came to the lectures plus the students enrolled in the Tsukuba National University. We bought a car for local transportation but you could not drive outside the city as you would be a maze of unrecognizable Japanese signage and be totally lost (it was easier driving around Iran). On one trip

Kats Sawaki, Vice President of Nanzan University with us there

Rachel guided us to Nara, which is filled with 2,000 deer wandering around, and other places.

My former student Kats Sawaki shown in the photo was then a vice president at Nanzan University in Nagoya so we went there. Walking around the campus we saw the wife of famed Professor Ito of Ito's lemma of the Black Scholes formula fame passed us reminding me of the small world of finance. Japan was exciting then and we were treated well and the learning of the culture was very exciting.

Yamaichi invited me for four big lectures with 100+ attendees which I always enjoy. When my wife's birthday came, there were orchids — they had simply found from her resumé at the university.

I was invited for fugu — the fish delicacy that if you don't cut it right you can die and about 200 per year suffer this fate at the hands of non-licensed chefs. I learned why it is so expensive — about US$100 for a plate of about six inches across. Two or three fishermen will go out all night and catch about two small fugo. It is simply rare as well as deadly. It was OK but not wonderful, Alaska black cod in Vancouver is a much superior dish.

I was invited for golf. As a foreigner, the etiquette was to finish last but not be far below the others.

My Berkeley PhD advisor, Bill Zangwill, now at the University of Chicago, was there visiting and researching Japanese manufacturing efficiency. Bill was a dynamo showing up at Berkeley as an acting associate professor which meant that he had to get tenure in 2 years or lose his position. He was the first PhD student of the late Arthur (Pete) Veinott, Jr. Pete was perhaps the most brilliant in the Stanford Operations Research department which was #1 with Berkeley a close #2. Pete had 28 PhDs and Zangwill 1 — me! Bill and I practiced golf and he was friendly to Rachel who would later go to the University of Chicago for her BA in Medieval History.

I managed to come in last and make a decent showing. At that time, golf courses in Japan were a major traded commodity through memberships. Zari Rachev, a noted researcher in fat tailed stable distributions and I studied their pricing. We found that the tails of their price distributions were even much fatter than US or Japanese stock prices. This meant that the prices could change fast and furious and these markets did collapse.

Later Mikhail Zhitlukhin and I studied exit strategies from bubble type markets. This is when to get out of expensive markets hopefully before they crash although the models do not require an actual crash occurring. In Shiryaev, Zhitlukhin and Ziemba (2014) we studied Apple Computer in 2012 and the Nasdaq100 in 2000. The model sold Apple around 680 and then it later fell to about 380 and subsequently has had a rise to the 800 area. The model also exited the Nasdaq near its peak and it subsequently fell to one fifth of the peak. Then in Shiryaev, Zhitlukhin and Ziemba (2015) we studied the Japanese golf course membership index markets and the Nikkei stock average (NSA) in the 1989–1990 area and in 2013.[1] The world's greatest bubble trader is George Soros who has made tens of billions trading various markets but he got two of them wrong by shorting too soon. These were the NSA in 1988 where the BSEYD model (see Chapter 14) did not have a danger signal until April of 1989 with an eventual fall starting on the first day of January 1990 and the Nasdaq100 in 2000. The BSEYD applies to the S&P500 and not necessarily to the Nasdaq but they are highly correlated.

The anomalies project was very interesting and proceeded with me explaining the US evidence and the study group of about 10 of them providing Japan feedback and doing calculations. YRI was loaded with data. Anomalies are of at least two types: fundamental based on stock information such as price–earnings (PE) and book to price, and size effects and seasonal or calendar based on cash flows as particular times and institutional practices such as the TOM and turn-of-the-year effects. We studied both. Paul Samuelson, the world's top economist of the last century and an astute judge of markets, had written me "the Japanese stock market is held together with chewing gum." It certainly was expensive with PE ratios about 60. Some companies even had PEs over 1,000. This included the stock of the Japan's richest person whose stock was at 1,200. But it was hard to tell where all the assets were. I quickly clued in that land was the key plus cross holdings. The cross stock holdings were A had stock of B and C who both had A were for relationships. When I tried to take companies apart and I saw land and stocks which owned more land. Nippon Steel started out at 105 PE and ended up at 5. But the land, the world's most expensive was really at high prices. Choice land in central Tokyo was worth nearly \$300,000 per square meter.[2] But little traded — only 2% per year. The companies cash rich from their massive exports were able and willing to scoop up parcels that were for sale. Some was for more factories. Some, like owning golf course memberships, was for relationships. In the end in 1990+, the key mistake was apparent, only 3% of their assets were in foreign assets despite overpaying for Pebble Beach golf courses and many other expensive properties.[3] They simply invested their manufacturing profits in two things they already owned: their land and their stocks. After the crash in 1990, a 50% fall, they lost \$5 trillion in stocks and \$5 trillion in land or about \$10 trillion in all.

My wife, a Berkeley trained economist, quickly said "they are going to lose all this money." She was trained and knew real economics not the stuff hidden behind the math that dominates PhD programs these days and creates people who do not really know how economies work. Gerald Debreu, a fabulous teacher of clear mind, devised elegant mathematical economics Nobel Prize winning theories which were enjoyable to study but have in the end supported some of our environmental problems with assumptions required for closed form solutions such *as assume free disposal*.

Besides the interaction with the students at Tsukuba and the young YRI employees who were both in my Tsukuba classes and the study groups, I had many long talks with one of YRI's top executives, Mr Okada. We would sit facing each other. He talking in Japanese and me in English with a translator. We discussed world wide financial markets as well as the US and Japan. Besides learning some things from him, especially some particularly Japanese traits and policies, my part helped me clarify my thinking. While explaining ideas, I had to couch them in a way he could grasp and respond to. Four large lectures with more than 100 in the audience including employees of Yamaichi Securities, the parent company and YRI also helped me clarify and understand the US research better.

The fundamental anomaly project followed various ideas plus the influential 1988 *Financial Analysts Journal* US factor model by Bruce Jacobs and Kenneth Levy. They actually wrote three papers that year in the FAJ but the key one was on the fundamental anomalies and the resulting factor model. It has 25 variables and came in two versions. There was a January model and a rest of the year model. January in the US, as we saw before in Chapter 9, is a special month and Jacobs and Levy realized that in this model. They were PhD students at Wharton and started their business rather than finishing their doctorates. And it paid off. After a slow start, a *Wall Street Journal* article got them moving and now in 2017, they manage over 8 billion using various models. They recently gave $12 million to Wharton to establish a quantitative investment management research centre headed by Professor Donald Keim, with whom I did an anomalies book for Cambridge University Press (CUP) in 2000 based on sessions on anomalies I organized for the 1995 Isaac Newton 6 month institute on financial mathematics. Various people organized specific weeks. I organized 2 weeks with the other on asset-liability management, which led to another CUP volume with Professor John Mulvey of Princeton. CUP is a top publisher but is rather greedy as are many publishers. Despite two very successful books, the three of us received zero royalties as these were "scooped up for the Newton Trust." The university was more generous, hosting us nicely during that most enjoyable conference. I keep in contact with Bruce Jacobs who I met at several investment conferences over the years. But just as a colleague having no input to their business although I do send Bruce some papers.[4]

I wanted to make a similar model for Japan. The Jacobs–Levy model had monthly revisions of data and used 25 factors that they thought are the best to predict these monthly stock price changes. The idea is to rank all the stocks from best to worst. So you could then do all sorts of things like long–short investing going long the good and short the bad or go long the best stocks. They actually made four models. You can think of it as horses pulling your cart. You can use one at a time finding out who is the best horse. Or as in Ben Hur's chariot race, add a good one to the exiting ones. Sometimes a new horse (factor) improves the performance but not always. Back in 1967, when I was a graduate student at Berkeley Barr Rosenberg isolated small cap and low price to book value as key variables. Later in 1992, Euguene Fama and Ken French took the credit for this idea with a famous thorough study of these factors in a *Journal of Finance* article. Rosenberg only had a paper in 1985 with co-workers Ron Lanstein and Kenneth Reid. This grabbing of credit by those who publish in certain academic journals considered superior by those running them when someone else did it before but published in a less prestigious journal is rampant in modern academic finance. It also happens to me all the time.

The Jacobs–Levy factors that worked the best were the usual favorites: low PE plus small cap (another typical outperformer) plus high sales relative to stock price, positive trends in earnings estimates lagged 1, 2 or 3 months. Not surprisingly, the fresher the news the better the predictions so 1 month lagged is the best. Another factor that adds value was earnings surprise, that is higher earnings than expected but only if it is fresh, that is in the last month. The 1967 Barr Rosenberg factor, price to book, popularized by Fama and French who rediscovered this in 1992 added value but high sales to price was more powerful. Finally, various mean reversion factors and value were used.

Japan is, of course, different than the US so one would expect the factors that predict stock prices to be a bit different. I discussed all this with the study group after presenting the Jacobs–Levy paper and other US market-based literature. Then we discussed which factors might be good in Japan and I discussed this with Mr Okada. I then put in a request for the data using 30 factors over many years. The idea was to test the model out of sample to see how it really works. So you estimate the model using monthly data for a number of years and then test it on the new data. The model we developed was re-estimated yearly with new monthly data fed in as it becomes known. Then after a year when we had all that year's data, we added that to the other past data and re-estimated the model. Month by month we had the best stocks and then we bought good new ones and sold short old bad ones paying a transactions cost which had three parts: commission, bid-ask spread and price pressure. If we buy or sell a lot we move the bid-ask spread.

After waiting 2 months, the word came, the data had arrived. Asaji Komatsu, one of the anomaly study group members who had a masters degree in statistics from New York University helped me with the calculations.

The academic finance community does not believe in full blown factor models but I, like other practitioners as well as some theorists, do. Why not have 30 horses pulling your cart? They can have one, the capital asset pricing model's beta, or use the Fama–French–Rosenberg two or three, but I will take the 30. Of course, if some horses (factors) are not improving the predictions we can return them to the stable. Some fancy statistics to deal with correlations across factors could be used but a straight forward multiple regression model worked fine out of sample.

The very best factor — future expected earnings divided by current price that is the future price earnings ratio was the best variable. Just this variable provided about 10% excess return per year when updated monthly, which is a huge contribution to returns. We used an average of three forecasting systems which worked better as it usually does than any one forecaster. The ordinary trailing PE ratio based on actual reported earnings was also one of the best seven. So was the perennial favorite small cap and two mean reversion variables, namely last month's excess return and the weighted sum of several months' excess returns. (By mean reversion: if these factors are trending positive, then the stock price, on average, falls in the next month.) The other two were book value relative to stock price (a negative effect) and current price relative to the high over the last 2 years.

The other 23 variables mostly added value but were less valuable. Ordered by multivariate rank, they were:

> number of shares outstanding, standard deviation volatility, acceleration of dividends relative to current price, dividend acceleration over the past two years, acceleration of the dividend percent payout, acceleration of relative strength, sales acceleration relative to current price, beta (yes beta is way down here, it's fourth best if you just do one predictor at a time but it's 16th best when you consider all of these 30 variables), two year acceleration of dividend payout ratios, sales growth relative to current price, percent of shares held by individuals, zero dividend effect (a 0–1 variable), sales relative to price, next to last month's excess return, acceleration of book value relative to current price, earnings change relative to current price, dividends relative to price, low price, excess returns, acceleration of earnings relative to price, a par variable, and dividends relative to earnings

For the coefficients for univariate and multivariate, January and other seasonal effects and those for the US Jacobs–Levy model, see Ziemba (2012a).

Once the model was developed we turned it over to Yamaichi. I never heard if they used it. But I got some good use out of it. After returning to Vancouver, I co-wrote three books based on the Japanese research plus a number of research papers. In the book *Invest Japan* published in 1991 that I wrote with my wife Sandra, I discussed the factor model along with other factor models developed by Ned Elton and Marty Gruber of NYU and Richard Roll and Stephen Ross for their Roll and Ross business.

Buchannan

The phone rang. It was a call from London. The hedge fund Buchanan Partners was in the business of buying cheap Japanese warrants and hedging by shorting more expensive Japanese stocks. They had their own models but saw quickly that my model for ranking the best to the worst stocks, revising monthly, was better. So they offered me a job in London which I changed into consulting. This period in the early 1990s was one of declining stock prices in Japan but the model estimated during a period of rising stock prices still worked with minus signs replacing positive signs.

Working with Buchanan was fun. There were three partners. One, Perigrine Moncrief was descended from Scottish royalty. In his house on his extensive farm near Moncrief Hill in Perth, Scotland, is a photo of his parents' wedding with a young Queen Elizabeth and Prince Philip in attendance. My days consulting with Buchanan were enjoyable and I was with them for several years with some visits to London and activities from Vancouver. They eventually cashed out of a very successful operation and went their separate ways and I lost contact with them.

The seasonal anomalies part of the project went well too. We studied various US anomalies and found that essentially all of them existed in Japan lists Those who would like details, can find them in Ziemba (2012a) where all the papers are reprinted. One of the most interesting anomalies is the TOM effect. It is caused by cash flows entering the market then and institutional practice of buying them by pension funds and others who invest monies they receive right away. In the US markets, the TOM was then −1 to +4. This means the last trading day of the previous month and the first four trading days of the current month. The futures move first and then, by index arbitrage, the cash stocks then move. This works fine for the liquid 500 stock S&P500 large cap value weighted index. But for the small cap Value Line index with about 1,500 stocks that is equally weighted (meaning that Microsoft counts the same as universal widgets), it is too hard to trade all 1,500 stocks so there is no index arbitrage. The same is true in 2016 with the 2,000 stock Russell2000 value weighted index which replaced more or less the Value Line when the latter's volume dried up.

In fact −1 to +4 historically got most of the month's gains with some in the second week and essentially nothing in the rest of the month.[5]

So when does the TOM exist in Japan assuming it exists? The wife receives the salaryman's wages on −5 and the brokerage firms know this so they are at the door asking for investments. This led to a strong −5 to +2 TOM in the cash equity market. Could you trade this in the futures markets? You could but not in Japan where there were no derivatives traded then. But you could on the SIMEX exchange in Singapore. I did not trade this but those who did should have had good gains as the TOM was anticipated on trading days −8 to −5 with mean gains of 2.8%. Later, there were derivatives trading in Japan and they led to a large transfer, about US$500 million from the Japanese brokerage firms who pushed up the futures to the US traders at Morgan Stanley and Saloman Asia which scooped up this money with index arbitrage.[6]

Visit to Taiwan from Japan was also Good for the Family

At Christmas time we went from Japan to Taipei, Taiwan for a conference. Sandra gave a series of lectures on "The debt and the debtors, parts I and II" and "Creativity, innovation and growth: A craft approach". Rachel

The family heading to a conference in Taiwan

attended and absorbed economics. At nine she had some good conversations with James Tobin, economics Nobel Prize winning Yale professor, at the conference. Little did we know then that she would become a star in the world of economics. I learned that two papers in management science where I was still Departmental editor for Finance counts for full professor in economics at the best university, National Tsing Hua University, in Taiwan.

Notes

[1] In Ziemba, Ileo and Zhitlutkin (2017), we study stock market crashes big and small and in Chapter 9 we present a model to exit at a good time and price from bubble like markets including the crashes in 1929 and 1987.

[2] See D. J. Stone and W. T. Ziemba (1993), Land and stock prices in Japan, *Journal of Economic Perspectives* and W. T. Ziemba (1991b), The chicken or the egg: Land and stock prices in Japan, in W. T. Ziemba, W. Bailey and Y. Hameo (Eds.), *Japanese Financial Market Research*, pp. 45–68. New York: North Holland.

[3] For a list of such properties, see W. T. Ziemba and S. L. Schwartz (1992), *Power Japan: How and why the Japanese economy works*, Chicago: Probus Publishing.

[4] The two Cambridge University Press Newton Institute books from the conference were D. J. Keim and W. T. Ziemba (Eds.) (2000), *Security Market Imperfections in Worldwide Equity Markets*, Cambridge, UK and W. T. Ziemba and J. M. Mulvey (Eds.) (1998), *Worldwide Asset and Liability Modeling*, Cambridge, UK. Lists of the set of Jacobs-Levy factors for the US in non-January and January and the best Japanese factors are in Ziemba (2012) along with t-statistics and discussion.

[5] See R. Ariel (1987), A monthly effect in stocks returns. *Journal of Financial Economics 18*, 161–174.

[6] For more on the TOM in Japan, see Ziemba (1991, 1994, 2012a) for details.

Chapter 14

The Bond–Stock Earnings Yield Crash Prediction Model

The crash model prediction project worked well. There was no US literature on the topic, just data on crashes. In looking at the 1987 stock market crash, I quickly came up with the bond–stock earnings yield model (BSEYD). The idea is simple: bonds and stocks compete for the money. When interest rates are high, the money goes to bonds and when they are low it goes to stocks. Of course, no simple or even complex model works all the time, but I have found over the years 1948–2016 that this BSEYD model is very useful for at least two things. First, it is very good at predicting stock market crashes. Secondly, it is good at indicating when to be in and when to be out of the stock market for long-term investors.

The BSEYD model is defined as the most liquid long-term government bond rate minus the stock earnings yield, namely the reciprocal of the trailing report earnings price-earnings ratio. In looking at the October 1987 US stock market crash I found that the BSEYD was about 1.00 to 2.00% throughout 1996 up to April 1997. It then leapt to 3.39% which is in the *danger zone*. By danger zone I mean an area where almost for sure a crash of at least 10% or more will occur usually within 4 to 12 months. It is an upper confidence limit violation, that is a rare event. Usually the market rallies from the initial danger zone penetration but then falls so that it is at least 10% below the initial signal.

The long bond, 30 years then, in April 1987 was 9.56% versus 7.65% the previous month. So with earnings about the same and stock prices increasing the earnings price ratio was about the same, 6.17% versus 6.09%. The market stayed in the danger zone during April, May, June, July, August and September with the S&P500 stock index rising from 282.47 (March) to 318.06 (September). Meanwhile, the stock market moved further into the danger zone. My late colleague, famed University of Chicago Professor

Merton Miller remarked to me that the crash actually needed only a twig to get it started. Remember we want here to predict that a crash will occur but we do not know when. The twig was very high stock market volatility the previous week plus an increase in German interest rates, plus a lot of unexecuted futures based portfolio insurance. The crash on October 19, 1987 was a 22% fall in the cash S&P500 futures index and a 29% fall in the December futures. That moved the November S&P500 to 245.01 and the BSEYD was out of the danger zone, falling as low as 0.59% in January 1988.

So we had a model! Now we needed to test it on new data out of sample. We looked at Japan's Nikkei stock average (NSA), some 225 stocks price weighted like the US Dow Jones Average. In Japan the TOPIX, like the S&P500 is value weighted, this just means that stocks with high value count more, just like Apple now in 2017.

From 1949, when the Japanese stock market reopened after World War II to 1988, the stock market had gone up 222 times in yen and fully 550 times in US dollars. So US$10,000 invested in Japan in 1949 at 360 yen per dollar was worth US$5.5 million with the yen much higher at 118.99¥/$. But despite this huge rally in stock valuations, the move up was very bumpy. There were in fact 20 of these 10% plus declines.

So how did the model do in predicting them? It turned out that the BSEYD model went into the danger zone 12 times and in each case there was one of these 20 crashes. So the model looks good being 12 for 12. Eight of the 20 crashes were caused by reasons other than the BSEYD which relates interest to earnings and reflects too high interest rates relative to earnings.

In late 1988 the great bubble trader George Soros shorted the Japanese market. He was right, it was very expensive and possibly overpriced but when would it crash? He lost $1 billion by shorting too soon. His funds, run by Stanley Druckenmiller lost a reputed $5 billion shorting the Nasdaq too soon in 2000. But don't worry about Soros, with $25+ billion he is doing fine in all sorts of areas and he usually wins on these bubble trades.

I am very interested in predictions of how to exit these bubble-like markets. It is not easy to get these correct. In 2000, the internet index fell 17% in 1 day and then preceded to reach new highs later. The BSEYD model predicted that the S&P500 would fall in that period. The related index for the Nasdaq 100 that Soros shorted too early and lost a reputed $5 billion, was exited by the model Mikhail and his thesis advisor Albert Shiryaev built that we were applying. The second paper dealt with circa 1990 Japan and we studied the golf course membership market which had a market cap

Bubble investor Soros

larger than the Australian stock market of A$250 billion. That was a much bigger bubble than the Nikkei and Topix stock exchanges and the model was very good at providing exit strategies. Professor Shiryaev, who was the top student of the legendary probability theorist A N Kolmogorov, invited me to speak at a conference in Moscow in the summer of 2013. So I got to see first hand all sorts of papers on optimal stopping rules. Moscow is expensive and has top sights and very good restaurants. We returned to St Petersburg to revisit the Hermitage and other museums and sights. As in our 1992 visit, we searched out the famed Parzyryk carpet. It was still hard to find but well worth the effort, see page 31 for a discussion.

In July 2015, Soros seems to be shorting too soon again. He has been buying puts for more than a year now. As these have gone to zero, expiring worthless he has bought more. All of my crash measures are not in the danger zone. But Warren Buffett's value of the economy it value of the economy might be signaling trouble. Sebastien Lleo and I studied this (Lleo and Ziemba, 2015a). We found that straightforward use of the model does not work but using a modification borrowed from the BSEYD model does then provide statistically significant predictive value.[1]

What was the Buffett measure predicting in mid 2015? Using the last official GNP release for 2015Q1 the Buffett measure was at 123%. That's in the danger zone based on Buffet's fixed 120% rule; but not in the danger zone using our confidence level rule. Our estimate for 2015Q2 (June 30th) was 124%. To get this estimate, we considered the latest GDPNow forecast for Q2 GDP, which is 2.4% annualized, and used it as proxy for the growth in the GNP.

Well, *unexplained* crash number 6 in Chapter 27 bailed Soros out. But let's give him credit for predicting it. The several day crash on Wednesday, Thursday and Friday August 19–21, continuing into Monday and Tuesday August 24 and 25, was a most violent one. Mohammed El Erian viewed it as repricing lower growth, little policy response and less available fed tools. Continuing drops in the Shanghai and other stock exchanges, another 8.5% during the night of Sunday August 23, commodity drops, much higher VIX, a continuing Greek saga and other worries finally took their toll. At the end, many stocks like AAPL and country indices were in 20%+ bear market declines. The puts sky-rocketed, so Soros cleaned up.

The BSEYD model finally went into the danger zone in April 1989. In 1988, the Japanese diet parliament) in discussion with the Bank of Japan wanted to try to deflate the stock and property bubbles by increasing short-term and hence long-term interest rates. Indeed they continued increasing these rates until August 1990. The stock market continued its climb during the rest of 1989.

In August 1989, we left Japan for Vancouver although I was still working from Vancouer on the factor model to rank monthly all the stocks on the Tokyo stock exchange first section. Shegeri Ishi had worked with me in the crash study group and on the BSEYD model. He had a masters degree in finance from Yale. At that time, Yale was the top finance school in the world if you use a Harry Markowitz mean-variance model. Actually they only had one finance Professor, Stephen Ross, a very top researcher. With only one professor there was zero variance and he had a high mean. See how misleading models can be with limited data. Chicago and other places were, of course, better than Yale but Ishi took Ross's courses so learned a lot. He spoke perfect English too. So I asked Ishi to tell the YRI bosses in Japanese — I knew them all from golf, etc., but it seemed cleaner to inform them through one of their own that the stock market was way in the danger zone. Indeed it was further into the zone than at any time since 1949. They did not believe the results. They assumed that a *gaijin* (foreign) professor could not possibly understand their complex market. So they did not act. The interest rates and stock markets continued to rise in the fall of 1989 with the BSEYD going further and further into the danger zone. The Miller twig was a surprise additional interest rate rise at Christmas time plus the start of the year. The stock market peaked at 39,916 at the end of December

1989. It began to fall on the first trading day in 1990. It actually fell 56% during that crash. In 2016, despite rallies over those 25 years, the NSA is still less than half its end of 1989 value. Fully 75% has been lost and that is in nominal terms. In real terms, accounting for inflation, it is much more. That continued increase in interest rates throughout 1990 when the stock market was falling into August had a lot to do with this 20+ year decline. The inability to let businesses go bankrupt because of Japanese politics was a major factor in this period. Within 5 years Yamaichi Securities was basically bankrupt and, as of 1999, no longer exists. The other big brokerage firms have survived so obviously took some steps to avoid what happened to Yamaichi.

I received a letter from German colleagues asking is I could take one of their students and help him with a thesis. The student who came was Klaus Berge from Dresden. I suggested that he test the BSEYD model as a prediction measure for long-term investing. He did a nice thesis on this and later Giorgio Consigli of the University of Bergamo, who I had worked with in the past and was interested in a version of this topic which was to find the theoretical fair price of the S&P500 as a function of the value of the BSEYD index. He joined the team and we wrote a paper about analyzing the use of this measure for long-term market timing in five equity markets (US, Japan, UK, Germany and Canada) from 1980–2005 and 1975–2005. They found that the rule, stay out of the stock market when the BSEYD measure is in the danger zone and move to cash and otherwise be in the stock market index has about double, with less standard deviation risk, than being in the stock market buy and hold all the time. The BSEYD model was in the danger about 20% of the time. Similarly, the short-term confidential T-measure WTZIMI, a Canadian investment company, uses in trading has good short-term predictability (3–6 months). Since 1985, the T-measure has had $T < 0$, that is, in the danger zone, for the S&P500, six times. The net result was that the sum of the returns in the next quarter were minus 41.7%.[2]

T is negative when the market is over confident as measured by relative put and call option prices. Then it is very dangerous since there are few sellers and many buyers but sellers will usually appear soon to drive the market down. Of these six $T < 0$ occurrences, we have the October 1987 crash and the 3Q2002 crash when the S&P500 fell -22% in this quarter. My S&P bias trade is not done when $T < 0$. Otherwise the S&P bias trade of WTZIMI is very successful when $T > 0$. From 1985, there were no losses for $T > 100$, as it has been since 3Q2003.

In the six quarters when $T < 0$, there were four losses and two times the measure did not predict correctly. Still the sum of the six returns yielded a combined arithmetic loss of -41.7%. Hence, these two measures are useful but they do not predict all 10%+ crashes nor do they predict some small declines. For these two declines under 10% and the September 11, 2001 14% decline, other reasons must be found, which we will consider below. There have been no $T < 0$ signals since the third quarter of 2003, even though the VIX has hit the 10 area a few times.

My T crash measure is based on overconfidence. I measure that by the relative prices of calls (long positions) to puts (short positions). High call prices yield the crash signal. Another measure along these lines is the price of Sotheby's stock. Being just one stock versus an entire index is potentially more problematic, but the signal called the Japan (1989), US tech (2000) and US housing (2006) bubbles.[3] On August 13, 2015 Sotheby's stock was $38.10. On July 11, 2016 it was $27.89. It would take a price of about $75 (double) to trigger a signal. Sotheby's has high end auctions for wealthy people. The idea is that these high-end wealthy people sell some items at the top of the market that they have accumulated in the recent boom years. Sotheby's auction volume and stock performance soars right at the top only to collapse once the market implodes.

A survey of application and predictions of the BSEYD model is in Lleo and Ziemba (2015a). In my AIMR monograph Ziemba (2003) I study the 2000–2002 period in the US. The model went into the danger zone in April 1999. The market fell in April 2000 then rallied back to the old high (1527 in March 2000) and had a final drop on September 17, 2000 to a low of 1085. Then there was a second danger signal that led to a 12% fall in July 2002 and had a low close of 768.63 on October 10, 2002. Lleo and Ziemba (2012) study the 2006–2009 period and show that the BSEYD model did predict correctly the declines in China, Iceland and the US. China was a strange one with danger signals on December 12, 2006 (95% confidence) at 2218.85 and December 25, 2006 (99% confidence) at 2435.76, a rally to 6029.26 on October 16, 2007 and then a fall to 1706.70 on November 4, 2008. So it rallied, was up then fell so the model worked but would have been difficult to profit from it until the end.[4]

Iceland was interesting as a place to visit with fascinating financial markets. I was there speaking at an International INFORMS conference, giving a keynote on Kelly investing strategies. All the signals were for an overheated market ready to crash. My wife referred to the 300,000 person country as an over leveraged hedge fund. That was in 2006 and the small cap stocks were in the danger zone by the BSEYD model. But the index with six banks amounting to about two thirds of the index were not. That was because the large earnings from the hedge fund trading made the price–earnings (PE) ratio only 10. But when the long bond went way up in the period around the Lehman Brothers collapse in October 2008, the index fell fully 95%. On February 11, 1998 the index was 977.58. It peaked at 6287.29 on February 2, 2006 and fell to 581.76 as of December 31, 2008. Since then, the market has not been able to recover and as of December 31, 2013 it was 864.93.

How Accurate is the BSEYD as a Crash Prediction Model for Long Periods in the US

I showed the 2006–2009 study to Harry Markowitz and he liked the results. He then suggested that we do a much longer study in the US over 50 or so years and compare the results with Professor Robert Shiller's high price earnings ratio model. I have argued that to actually predict crashes you need the interplay of high PERs and high interest rates. The first thing we observed, and it's from a table in my pension retirement book with Marida and Sandra (Bertocchi, Schwartz and Ziemba, 2010, 2015), is that bull runs start with low PERs and end with high PERs.[5]

We tested the predictive ability of the BSEYD model on a 51 year period starting January 1, 1962 and ending December 31, 2012 (12,846 daily data). The methodology is based on a standard likelihood ratio test conducted on a 'hit sequence' derived from the time series of signal. This approach is similar to the run tests used to determine whether a coin is fair. The methodology is complemented with a Monte Carlo study for small sample bias and by an analysis of the robustness of the measure. Between January 1, 1962 and December 31, 2012 the S&P500 Index had 18 crashes, defined as a decline of at least 10% from the previous peak in less than 1 year. The three largest crashes were, respectively, a 52% decline from peak to trough in 2007–2008, a 37% decline in 2000–2001 and a 36% decline in 1968–1970. Overall, seven crashes exceeded 20% and 13 exceeded 15%.[6]

What is the track record of the BSEYD model? The BSEYD model based on a standard confidence interval went into the danger zone 39 times in these 51 years. The prediction proved correct on 28 instances, giving a 72% accuracy. The number of predictions is higher than the number of actual crashes because several distinct crash signals may precede the same crash. This was the case for example in 1969, when the BSEYD model produced four distinct signals on June 6, 1967, May 31, 1968, November 18, 1968 and May 25, 1969. The local peak was reached on November 29, 1968. But by June 20, 1969 the market had declined 10% within a year. The trough was eventually reached on May 26, 1970. The observations for the BSEYD model based on Cantelli's inequality are similar: the model had 26 correct predictions out of 37 signals, a 70% accuracy.

The maximum likelihood estimate of the signal $\hat{p}$ equals the historical accuracy of the model. The likelihood ratio of the likelihood of the chance under the null hypothesis that the BSEYD predictions are random, to the likelihood using the estimated probability $\hat{p}$. The p-value is the probability of obtaining a test statistic higher than the one actually observed, assuming that the null hypothesis is true. The degree of significance and the p-value are both based on the χ^2-distribution with 1 degree of freedom. The critical values at the 95%, 99% and 99% level are, respectively, 3.8415, 6.6349 and 7.8794.

The BSEYD measure based on a standard confidence interval is significant at a 99% confidence level and the BSEYD model based on Cantelli's inequality is not far from the 99% mark. The null hypothesis that the BSEYD predictions are purely random can be rejected: the BSEYD has an ability to predict crashes over a 1 to 2 year horizon.

In addition to testing 8 choices of parameters for the BSEYD model, Lleo and Ziemba also tested the predictive ability of the logarithm of the BSEYD, the P/E ratio and the logarithm of the P/E ratio. Historically the original BSEYD model and its logarithmic version have shown a higher predictive ability than the P/E ratio. Among the models tested, the logarithm of the P/E ratio showed the least consistency and robustness.[7]

Notes

[1] From Wilson (2015) on Bloomberg Business: The value of Warren Buffetts favorite stock-market gauge has little use as an indicator of share-price declines, according to a new study. The chart tracks the indicator: the market value of all US companies as a percentage of gross national product before inflation, which Buffett mentioned in a 2001 article for Fortune magazine. The Wilshire 5000 Full Cap Price Index is used to represent market value, as it was in the study. GNP figures are compiled quarterly by the Commerce Department. Stocks capitalization exceeded 120% of GNP in each of the past three quarters, as it did when a bull market peaked in 1998–2000. The figure was

studied as a harbinger of market losses by Sebastien Lleo, an Associate Professor at France's Neoma Business School, and William T Ziemba, an alumni Professor at the University of British Columbia. The level does not provide sufficient evidence to forecast most equity market downturns, Lleo and Ziemba wrote. The conclusion was drawn by analyzing 19 declines of 10% or more in the Standard & Poors 500 Index between October 1970 and March 2015. Buffetts indicator is more useful when the 120% threshold is replaced by one determined through a statistical analysis, they wrote. Their favored approach pointed to losses 11 times in the 45-year study period, and proved accurate on eight occasions. The results dispel the theory that absolute value matters for the market value-to-GNP ratio, Lleo and Ziemba wrote. They published the data July 12 on the Social Science Research Network, an online repository.

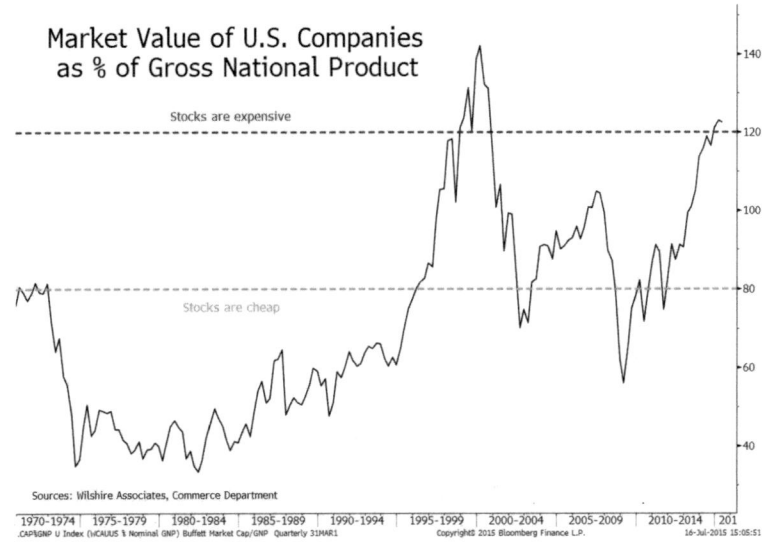

Market Value of U.S. Companies as % of Gross National Product

Sources: Wilshire Associates, Commerce Department

[2] The results of the six times out of 85 quarters the T-measure was negative for the S&P500, Tompkins, Ziemba and Hodges (2008). The sum of the S&P500 changes in the next quarter was −41.7%.

Quarter	3Q 1986	4Q 1986	4Q 1987	4Q 1990	3Q2002	3Q2003
T	−3.20	−0.95	−3.50	−1.9	−142.8	−50.4
Strategy						
Return	2.278%	26.42%	−123.49%	−0.123%	−34.94%	−4.415%
	Profit	Large profit	Bond/stock measure in danger zone	Small Loss	T-measure worked well extreme danger zone	small loss
S&P Return in Quarter	−8.20%	+3.70%	−24.50%	+4.80%	−12.00%	−4.5%

[3] Sotheby's Stock Price,
Source: floatingpath.com.

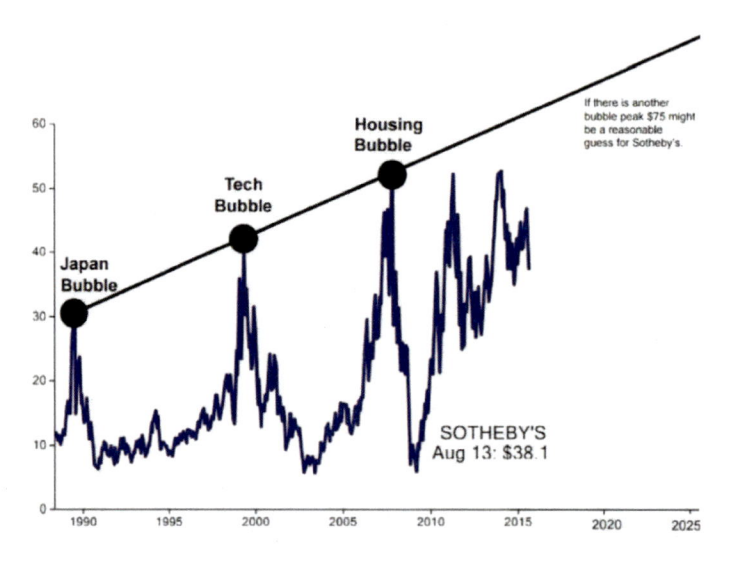

[4] Lleo and Ziemba (2012) analyzed the crash of the Shanghai Stock Exchange in early 2008.

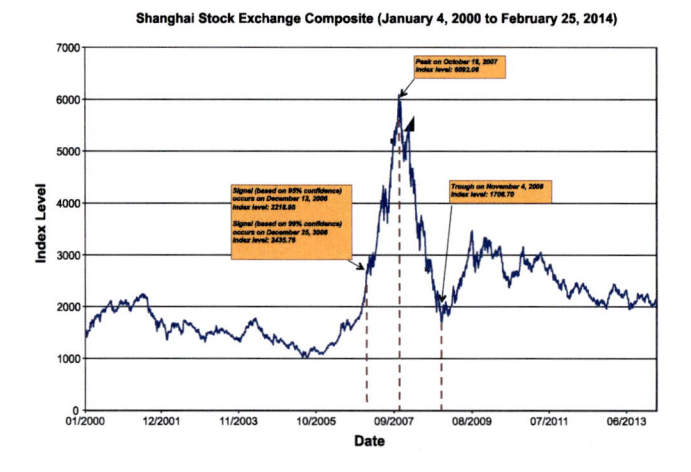

The graph shows the rise of the Shanghai stock index from January 4, 2000, to February 25, 2014. The market bottomed at 1011 on July 11, 2005, then rose six-fold to peak at 6092 on October 16, 2007. Next, there was a crash of 11.98% from 5180 to 4560 on January 21–22, followed by another 7.19% fall from 4762 to 4419 on January 28, 2008.

The graphs show that the BSEYD model succeeded in predicting the crash. The signal goes into the danger zone and the market continues to rise, before crashing less than 12 months after the initial signal. The first two use a 95% confidence one-sided moving average interval using prior data out-of-sample. The danger signal occurs on November 12, 2006, some 11 months before the stock market peaked on October 16, 2007. The second two use a 99% one-sided confidence interval and gives the first danger signal on June 29, 2007, with the index at 3821. The market reached its peak less than 4 months later, on October 16, 2007.

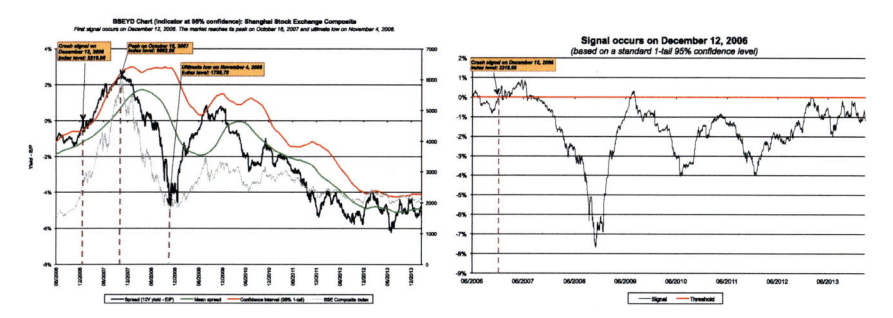

BSEYD crash indicator (95% one-sided moving average confidence interval): Shanghai Stock Exchange Composite.

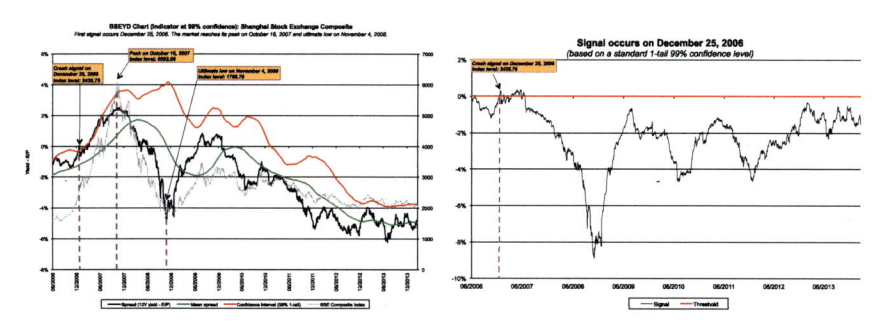

The first signal occurs on December 25, 2006. The market reaches its peak on October 16, 2007. BSEYD crash indicator (99% one-sided moving average confidence interval): Shanghai Stock Exchange Composite.

[5] Evolution of the P/E over selected 20-year periods with high annualized returns.

Columns 1 and 2 report respectively the beginning and ending year of the 20-year period. Column 3 shows the annualized returns over the period, ranked from loses to highest. Columns 4 and 5 report respectively the Price-to-Earnings (P/E) ratio for the beginning year and the ending year. *Source*: Bertocchi *et al.* (2010, 2015).

Beginning Year	Ending Year	Annual Rate of Return	Beginning P/E	Ending P/E
1975	1994	9.6%	10.9	20.5
1977	1996	9.7%	11.5	25.9
1942	1961	9.9%	12.2	20.5
1983	2002	10.9%	7.3	25.9
1978	1997	11.9%	10.4	31.0
1981	2000	12.8%	8.8	41.7
1979	1998	12.9%	9.4	36.0
1982	2001	13.0%	8.5	32.1
1980	1999	14.0%	8.9	42.1

[6] The S&P500 Index had 18 crashes between January 1, 1962 and December 31, 2012. *Source*: Lleo and Ziemba (2017).

	Peak Date	S&P Index at Peak	Trough date	S&P Level at trough	Peak-to-trough decline (%)	Peak-to-trough duration (days)
1	1966-02-09	94.06	1966-10-07	73.20	22.2	240
2	1968-11-29	108.37	1970-05-26	69.29	36.1	543
3	1971-04-28	104.77	1971-11-23	90.16	13.9	209
4	1973-01-11	120.24	1974-04-25	89.57	25.5	469
5	1975-07-15	95.61	1975-09-16	82.09	14.1	63
6	1976-09-21	107.83	1978-03-06	86.90	19.4	531
7	1978-09-12	106.99	1978-11-14	92.49	13.6	63
8	1980-02-13	118.44	1980-03-27	98.22	17.1	43
9	1980-11-28	140.52	1982-08-12	102.42	27.1	622
10	1983-10-10	172.65	1984-07-24	147.82	14.4	288
11	1987-08-25	336.77	1987-12-04	223.92	33.5	101
12	1990-07-16	368.95	1990-10-11	295.46	19.9	87
13	1998-07-17	1186.75	1998-08-31	957.28	19.3	45
14	1999-07-16	1418.78	1999-10-18	1254.13	11.6	94
15	2000-03-24	1527.46	2001-09-21	965.80	36.8	546
16	2007-10-09	1565.15	2008-11-20	752.44	51.9	408
17	2010-04-23	1217.28	2010-07-02	1022.58	16.0	70
18	2011-04-29	1363.61	2011-10-03	1099.23	19.4	157

[7] Maximum Likelihood Estimate and Likelihood Ratio Test

Signal Model	ML Estimate $\hat{p}$	$L(\hat{p})$	Likelihood ratio Λ	Test statistics $-2\ln\Lambda$	p-value
Standard	71.79%	8.3989E-11	0.0217	7.6648**	0.56%
Cantelli	70.27%	1.6640E-10	0.0437	6.2597*	1.24%

*significant at the 95% level; ** significant at the 99% level.

Chapter 15

Arbitrage and Risk Arbitrage

Arbitrage is when you construct a sure bet so that no matter the outcome, you either break even or turn a profit. Most observers say that arbitrage does not exist but actually it does in many instances because there are different financial markets for the same sports betting or financial security situation. This is because different people have different sets of information and beliefs. Lets take the simplest case: either A or B wins. Let, O_{ah} be the British odds given on the event that A wins from betting source h and O_{bi} that for B winning from betting source i. With these UK odds, the odds are the total return per 1 unit bet. In comparison, US odds are UK odds -1 and their payoffs are US odds $+1 =$ UK odds.

Arbitrage exists when $(O_{ah} - 1)(O_{bi} - 1) \geq 1$. This holds for all utility functions. Arbitrage involves two bets made at the same time so you cannot lose. For example, you might have different prices for the same event at different places or can construct an arbitrage. Risk arbitrage is when one attempts to create both sides of a betting situation at different times so the equation holds. But the match might never exist or there could be a sequence of risk arbitrages. Betfair odds and US track odds in racing frequently are sufficiently different to create risk arbitrages and, sometimes, arbitrages.[1]

I do a lot of betting on Betfair in London where they use British odds. Betfair is blocked in the US and some other countries but in the UK. It had been legal in Canada but unfortunately, Canadian accounts, even in pounds were shut down in January 2016. On Betfair you could wager on NFL games, NCAA and NBA basketball, major league baseball, US and UK politics including the US presidency, Fed interest rate announcements — these are all ones I trade. There are also a myriad of other situations that are on Betfair.[2] As an example of political events I shorted Howard Dean at 4 to 5 US odds and covered at 16 to 1 once he had his rant on TV that ruined his changes of getting the Democratic presidential nomination in 2004. In 2014, I went long Mitt Romney to get the 2016 Republican nomination at 38 to 1, then, when it looked like he was going to run again, I hedged him at much lower prices, around 8 to 1. Thus, I had a sequence of bets so that I win no matter who wins the nomination. Later in 2015, I went long Donald Trump at 36–1 then reduced the bet when he was 6–1 to lock in some gains. The Republican nomination is very interesting with about 15 candidates with many long shots to short. Scott Walker and Rick Perry had already dropped out guaranteeing a win on my short bets on them. On the Democratic side, Hillary Clinton was a 1–2 odds on favorite. Before her email and Benaghi troubles (trumped up by unfair Republicans and the FBI director), she was 1–5. Joe Biden, who was most likely not to run, was an attractive short at 6–1. Bernie Sanders, at 8–1, was leading Hillary in some states but the odds still favored her. The actual scoring of the money did not happen until the event was settled on November 8, 2016. So the wager stake was tied up till then. In my own betting I try to use rebate shops for racing and Betfair for other wagers. In the end Trump won and is dramatically changing the U.S. and the world. My bets settled favorably with a gain. Now I can bet at Pinnacle in the Caribbean for the NFL and others wagers on various events and the rebate shops for racing.

Two advantages of Betfair are that you can go long or short and the odds are changing as the game or other situation evolves. I regularly do this in NFL football games where the prices, namely the odds, are going up and down as the scores go up and down. This movement is what we call *mean reversion* which originated in the 1983 Poterba and Summers paper on the US stock market. I take advantage of this in the S&P500 futures markets. A classic example of mean reversion risk arbitrage was an NFL playoff game between New Orleans and San Francisco in 2012 when there were four lead changes in the last 3 minutes. It was mean reversion heaven.[3] In my money management of client and personal accounts and a futures fund, I use various strategies based on anomalies, institutional practices and investor behavior and mean reversion trades in the S&P500 and Russell2000 small cap index.

A Risk Arbitrage Convergence Trade: The Nikkei Put Warrant Market of 1989–1990

Ed Thorp and I, with assistance from Julian Shaw (then of Gordon Capital, Toronto, now the risk control manager for Barclays trading in London), did a convergence trade based on differing put warrant prices on the Toronto and American stock exchanges (ASEs). The trade was successful and Thorp won the over $1 million risk adjusted hedge fund contest run by Barron's in 1990. There were risks involved and careful risk management was needed. This edge was based on the fact that the Japanese stock and land prices were astronomical and very intertwined.[4]

First let me describe the historical development leading up to the NSA put warrants.

- Tsukamoto Sozan Building in Ginza 2-Chome in central Tokyo was the most expensive land in the country with one square meter priced at ¥37.7 million or about $279,000 US at the (December 1990) exchange rate of about ¥135 per US dollar.
- Downtown Tokyo land values are the highest in the world, about $800 million an acre.
- Office rents in Tokyo are twice those in London yet land costs 40 times as much.
- The Japanese stock market, as measured by the Nikkei stock average (NSA), was up 221 times in yen and 553 in dollars from 1949 to the end of 1989.
- Despite this huge rise, there had been 20 declines of 10% or more in the NSA from 1949 to 1989. The market was particularly volatile with two more in 1990 and two more in 1991. Stocks, bonds and land were highly levered with debt.
- There was a tremendous feeling in the West that the Japanese stock market was overpriced as was the land market. For example, the Emperor's palace was reputed to be worth all of California or Canada. Japanese land was about 23% of world's non-human capital. Japanese Price–Earning (PE) ratios were 60+.
- Various studies by academics and brokerage researchers argued that the high prices of stocks and land were justified by higher long run growth rates and lower interest rates in Japan versus the US. However, similar models predicted a large fall in prices once interest rates rose from late 1998 to August 1990.[5]
- Hence, both must crash!
- There was a tremendous feeling in Japan that their economy and products were the best in the world.
- There was a natural trade in 1989 and early 1990

    — Westerners bet Japanese market will fall.
    — Japanese bet Japanese market will not fall.

Various Nikkei put warrants which were 3 year American options were offered to the market to fill the demand by speculators who wanted to bet that the NSA would fall.

NSA Puts and Calls on the Toronto and ASEs, 1989–1992

The various NSA puts and calls were of three basic types: I's were ordinary puts traded in yen. II's were currency protected puts (often called quantos). III's were the Nikkei in Canadian or US dollars. The latter were marketed with comments like: you can win if the Nikkei falls, the yen falls or both fall. The payoffs were in yen, US or Canadian dollars. A simulation showed us that for similar parameter values, I's were worth more than II's, which were worth more than III's. But investors preferred the currency protected aspect of the II's and overpaid (relative to hedging that risk separately in the currency futures markets) for them relative to the I's.

At the peak, the puts were selling for more than three times their fair price.

Our convergence trades in late 1989 to early 1990 involved:

1. Selling expensive Canadian currency Bankers Trust I's and II's and buying cheaper US currency BT's on the ASE; and
2. Selling expensive Kingdom of Denmark and Salomon I puts on the ASE and buying the same BT I's also on the ASE both in US dollars. This convergence trade was especially interesting because the price discrepancy was based mainly on the unit size and used instruments on the same exchange.

Basically we shorted expensive puts and bought cheap puts that were very similar and waited for the prices to convergence and then we exited the trades. We preformed a complex pricing of all the warrants which was useful in the optimization of the position sizes. However, comparing options premiums simply provides the trades that were good to make. For example, 9.8% premium year means that if you buy the option, the NSA must fall 9.8% each year to break even. So selling these at 9.8% and BT-II's at 6.9% and buying BT-US at 2.6% looks like a good trade, which is what we did.

Some of the reasons for the different prices were:

- Large price discrepancy across the Canada/US border.
- Canadians trade in Canada, Americans trade in the US.
- Different credit risk.

- Different currency risk.
- Difficulties with borrowing for short sales.
- Blind emotions versus reality.
- An inability of speculators to properly price the warrants.

The BT-I's did not trade until January 1990 and in about a month the Canadian BT-I's and BT-II's collapsed to fair value and then the trade was unwound. The Toronto newspapers inadvertently helped the trade by pointing out that the Canadian puts were overpriced relative to the US puts so eventually there was selling of the Canadians, which led to the convergence to efficiency. To hedge before January 1990 one needed to buy an over the counter put from a brokerage firm such as Salomon who made a market in these puts. Additional risks of such trades is being bought in and shorting the puts too soon and having the market price of them go higher. We had only minor problems with these risks.

For the second trade, the price discrepancy lasted about a month. The market prices were about $18 and $9 where they theoretically should have had a 5 to 2 ratio since one put was worth 20% and the other 50% and trade at $20 and $8. These puts were not identical so this is risk arbitrage not arbitrage. The discrepancy here is similar to the small firm, low price effect (see Ziemba, 2012a). Both puts were trading on the ASE.

The brokerage firms in the US which made a lot of money in Japan on the way down wanted to cash in on the expected rebound. There was a similar inefficiency in the call market where the currency protected options traded for higher than fair prices. There was a successful trade here but this was a low volume market. This market never took off as investors lost interest when the NSA did not rally. US traders preferred Type II (Salomon's SXZ calls) denominated in dollars rather than the Paine Webber (PXA) which were in yen.

The Canadian speculators, who had little knowledge of options pricing and *overpaid* for the put warrants that our trade was based on, made $500 million Canadian since the NSA's fall was so great. This is a great example of the mean dominating! That's a lot more than we scientists made but we did ok. The issuers of the puts also did well and hedged their positions with futures in Osaka and Singapore. The losers were the holders of Japanese stocks. We did a similar trade with Canadian dollar puts traded in Canada and hedged in the US. The difference in price (measured by implied volatility) between the Canadian and US puts stayed relatively constant over an entire year (a gross violation of efficient markets).

The trade was also successful but again like the Nikkei calls, the volume was low.

Notes

[1] Hausch and Ziemba (1990a) discusses arbitrage across different venues. Hausch and Ziemba (1990b) discusses construction of arbitrages. Ziemba (2015) has examples of arbitrages using Betfair odds versus track odds.

[2] The last six to 2017 playoffs and Superbowl wagers are in *Wilmott* columns with three of them in the book Ziemba and Ziemba (2013).

[3] See Ziemba and Ziemba (2013) for a discussion of the mean reversion heaven.

[4] Additional discussion and technical details of the trade appears in Shaw, Thorp and Ziemba (1995). See Stone and Ziemba (1993) for more on the relationship between the Japanese stock and land prices.

[5] The relationship between interest rates and growth is discussed in Ziemba and Schwartz (1991) and French and Poterba (1991) and Chapters 14 and 23.

Chapter 16

Bill Benter Letter

The world's most famous and successful race track better has been Bill Benter. Bill, like many successful hedge fund and other traders such as Ed Thorp, Blair Hull, Harry McPike and Bill Gross, started out their mathematics of gambling careers by becoming professional blackjack players. This training, involving fast-moving market play, taught them about risk and return and the preservation of capital and its growth over time.

Turning professional race track betting into a workable computerized model that is reliable takes about 2 years of research plus a large investment in manpower, data and computers that can exceed $1 million. But the rewards can be very high and in the case of Benter giving total gains in the US$1 billion area. The wealth graph from his Hong Kong betting shows essentially no gains for a period of time then steady gains.[1] He also has betting in the US and other countries plus later Hong Kong betting.

Donald Hausch and I completed our academic papers Hausch, Ziemba and Rubinstein (1981) and Hausch and Ziemba (1985) and our three trade books Ziemba and Hausch (1984, 1986, 1987) on our place and show and other pricing systems by the time of Benter's letter to us dated October 12, 1989. Benter was with familiar with our work and he related that to the Hong Kong situation. Some contributions of Benter were:

- He observed that Hong Kong did not have a favorite-longshot bias as US and UK markets did. Nor did it have a reversed bias as Busche (1994) found in some other Asian markets.
- He observed that the Harville formulas are not accurate for estimating the second or third place probabilities and need adjustment. He suggested in the letter and later in his paper in our 1994 book to use discounted Harville formulas. These lower the second and third probabilities for favorites and raise them for longer price horses compared to the data which indicates that horses that do not win finish second or third less

than the Harville formulas suggest. Lo, Henry and Stern and others have researched this issue. See their papers in Hausch, Lo and Ziemba (1994, 2008).
- Hausch and I knew in our 1981 paper and elsewhere that for our place and show system we did not have to adjust for this second and third probability bias because the favorite longshot bias for win bets cancels with these biases. But the second and third biases are important for other wager such as quinella, exacta and trifecta.

Hausch and I had phone calls with Benter in 1989 and I met him during the INFORMS meetings in Phoenix in 1993. He was giving his paper that was later published in Hausch, Lo and Ziemba (1994, 2008) in a cluster of racing research papers. I advised on that group of racing session and organized and chaired the finance cluster. I had no other contact with Benter until he recommended me as an expert witness in the Hong Kong court case which continues. The case involves professional race track betting in Hong Kong where one party paid for a Benter-type model then had it stolen and used by the consultant professor. It's a tricky case but with the help of a UBC computer science colleague we were able to show that the original owner's bets and those of the offending professor were in fact the same by a variety of circumstantial and statistical tests.

Mr. William Benter
1 King's Road
Park Towers 1
Flat 21-D
Hong Kong
(tel) 852-5-716587

12 October 1989

Dear Donald and Bill,

Here are the Hong Kong win and place pool files from Sep. 1981 through 1st October 1989. As you know, there is no "place" pool in Hong Kong and the show pool is called the place pool. (That is, the Hong Kong place pool is equivalent to the American show pool.) I believe the accuracy of this file is very good, it has all been manually checked at least once. However, there is some possibility of a large error in one or more of the pool sizes. I would recommend that you put error traps in your analysis programs to detect grossly out of line win versus place pools. If you find any suspicious looking pool sizes, please contact me for verification. I have included a file called "read.me" on the diskette containing more technical information on the data file. A subset of these files were given to Busche and Hall, and were used for their research.

I have been an avid follower of your place and show pool betting research for some time. However, as I have mentioned in our telephone conversations I believe that your use of the Harville formula for determining conditional second and third place probabilities is not correct. The contest for second and third is significantly more random than the contest for first. Imagine the contest for last place and next-to-last place. Obviously, this would not be proportional to the win pool percentages of the horses involved. That is, a Harville formula esimation would drastically overestimate the probability of the more favored horse beating the less favored horse. I believe that the win pool "favorite versus long-shot" bias that is present in most horse racing markets compensates to some extent for your ignoring the greater randomness of the contest for second and third. The fact that favorites are underbet to finish first makes their Harville-formula determined probabilities of finishing second and third more correct, and the overbetting of long-shots makes their Harville-formula determined probabilities of finishing of second and third more correct also.

A technique that I propose for determining second and third place probabilities is as follows:

First, adjust the win percentages so that they accurately reflect the true win probabilities, i.e. compensate for the long-shot favorite bias. (In Hong Kong this is not necessary as the win betting accurately reflects true win probabilities with only small biases.)

Second, use a multinomial logit model approach for determining the proper weighting of "win percentage" as an independent variable in deciding the contest for second and third. I have achieved the best results using the natural log of win percentage as the independent variable.

The results of logit model runs I have performed here result in (approximately) the following formula, presented here as a BASIC computer subroutine. The array Q1(MAX) is assumed to contain the unbiased win probabilities from the win pool. The arrays Q2 and Q3 are returned with the non-normalized probabilities or finishing second and third. They are only correct as conditional probabilities when they are normalized using a Harville type formula.

```
DIM Q1(MAX),Q2(MAX),Q3(MAX)
Q2SUM = 0
Q3SUM = 0
COEF2 = .78
COEF3 = .66
FOR I = 1 TO #HORSES
    Q2(I) = EXP(COEF2 * LN(Q1(I)))
    Q3(I) = EXP(COEF3 * LN(Q1(I)))
    Q2SUM = Q2SUM + Q2(I)
    Q3SUM = Q3SUM + Q3(I)
NEXT I
FOR I = 1 TO #HORSES
    Q2(I) = Q2(I)/Q2SUM
    Q3(I) = Q3(I)/Q3SUM
NEXT I
```

As an example, the trifecta probability of the horses finishing in the order 6,8,3 would be:

PROB = Q1(6) * (Q2(8)/(1-Q2(6)) * (Q3(3)/(1-Q3(6)-Q3(8))

The coefficients of .78 for second and .66 for third are approximately correct for the Hong Kong betting market, they have been derived from multinomial logit runs on this data set. I do not have any other data, so I cannot comment on the applicability of these coefficients to North American betting markets. Appropriate coefficients would have to be determined by logit studies on the local pools.

In effect the Q2 and Q3 arrays are randomized versions of the original Q1 win percentage array. Note that the coefficients of .78 for second and .66 for third would both be 1.00 if the Harville formula was correct. The logit model with one independent variable seems to do a reasonable job of creating accurate 2nd and 3rd place probability estimates. It can be made to adjust for nonlinear biases by adding more terms in addition to just log of win percentage.

This formula has proved to be quite accurate in practice here in Hong Kong for estimating probabilities as well as for predicting quinella and trifecta dividends. That is, it seems that the public bets according to these probabilities. Utilizing this formula for show pool betting results in significantly less bets than using the Harville formula, but the results are far more accurate. I have included a crude histogram of the probabilities versus actual frequency of finishing first, second and third based on the data I am sending you, and calculated using the above formula. The second and third place probabilities are the conditional probabilities given that another horse has finished first. To show the dramatic difference between the logit based formula and the straight Harville formula I have included another version of the same histogram made using the Harville formula.

Another problem which interests me greatly is the question of deriving win probabilities from the full set of quinella odds. As I have mentioned to Donald in our phone conversations I have about 450 quinella dividend grids. I have been experimenting with various methods of deriving 1st and 2nd place probabilities from these grids. I have achieved some spectacular results with some of these methods, but I am concerned about backfitting a rather small sample. In Hong Kong the quinella pool is more than twice the size of the win pool, and indications are that it is very smart. Some interesting correlations have appeared, for instance, when a horse is underbet in the place pool compared to its win percentage it also tends to be underbet in the quinella pool. This could either be caused by someone making large bets in the win pool, or more likely by a smart public which realizes that the horse in question is of the 'Silky Sullivan' type. My research seems to point toward the latter explanation. I am very interested in any thoughts that you might have on the quinella grid problem.

As you know, I am a professional player, and you are in the business of disseminating information to educate the horseplaying public. This fact unfortunately puts us on somewhat opposite sides of the fence. However, I do feel a debt to the two of you for the very useful research and analysis that you have published. Also, I am very grateful for the information that Donald has sent me. Hopefully, we can continue to exchange information and I look forward to meeting the two of you in person some day.

Sincerely,

William Benter

Note

[1] See Figure 6.6 in Ziemba and Ziemba (2013).

Chapter 17

Scenario Optimization in Action — The Russell–Yasuda Kasai Financial Planning Model

It was the fall of 1989 and we had just returned to Vancouver from Japan. The phone rang with a call from the Frank Russell Corporation in Tacoma, Washington about helping them with a financial planning model for Yasuda Kasai, a major Japanese insurance company. Russell was run by George Russell, the son of Frank and George had turned the business into a tremendous consulting operation. The basic business had just 40 clients such as IBM, Shell and the like but they all had huge company pensions. What Russell did was to recommend to those companies organizations to manage their monies for a small percentage fee. But the size was huge so this was very profitable. Other businesses included running their own portfolios and some specific projects. One of the latter was the model for Yasuda Kasai. They had worked on this for 9 months with little success.

The Tokyo client wanted a model better than static mean-variance analysis. Since the problem at Yasuda Kasai was to manage their assets, some US$26 billion, against their liabilities which consisted largely of insurance claims. Many of the policies were over several years and had a large investment component as well as the insurance. So what they really needed was a dynamic multiperiod model to allocate resources and to pay liabilities that included uncertainty. They tried dynamic programming models and they were hopeless to implement. One of the team members was David Cariño who did his PhD at the Stanford Engineering Economic Systems Department and David knew about me. So that was the contact.

I met with them in Tacoma and suggested a multiperiod stochastic linear programming model approach. That was an extension of models I started discussing in my 1974 stochastic programming course at UBC. Two students in these classes did their PhDs under my direction and we wrote two papers on these models — one in *Management Science* with student Jarl Kallberg and UBC finance professor Robert White. White was not into stochastic optimization but knew about asset-liability models so worked with Kallberg and me. Jarl was a very good student and we did seven very good papers together and he landed a job an NYU's very strong finance department and has since moved to the Thunderbird business school in Phoenix, Arizona and then to the Washington State University. He was a strong and hard worker and we clicked together while he was in Vancouver. The second paper was with Martin Kusy and that model was developed for the Van City Credit Union and had even more of the elements I needed to get ready for the Russell–Yasuda Kasai project. Kusy was more of an administrative type and parlayed his one good paper, our 1986 *Operations Research* paper into a position as director of research at Concordia University in Montreal. Last I heard, he took early retirement at 53 and became Dean of the Brock University business school. He was a great example of the huge flaw in Canadian universities while saying in the faculty handbook that professors are to be evaluated on research and teaching, the fact is that administrators get the largest share of the financial pie with dubious contributions. But in 2017 this practice is also true in the US with huge salary gains for administrators and modest gains for research faculty.[1] So Kusy took a good path if you want these rewards. My work with him pushing him to finish his thesis in 1978 did payoff. It took me until 1986 to get the paper published but it is still a classic as it introduced stochastic programming to asset-liability management.

Andy Turner, the head of the Russell research group, treated me well and the group, several with PhDs, listened and together we had a great time making the model. There was an 18 month period to do this and we had a very good intellectual experience making the model which at the time was the largest computer application of dynamic asset-liability management. Cariño was a good optimization model formulator and David Luenberger, his Stanford advisor, told me he was the tops there at setting up models. I became the main consultant to the research department which I liked a lot. Among others things, replacing my old friend Bill Sharpe who had moved on, gave me a good level of prestige in many circles. Sharpe had taught them mean-variance CAPM type portfolio allocation. Of course, the pure UBC finance types took no notice, all they were interested in was efficient market pure theory from some idealized model. I was more

Wilt Chamberlain in the 4th grade already a stand out as an extreme event

interested in real markets. We formulated the model and it had 10 periods and 2,048 scenarios. The scenarios are intended to cover the possible future evolution of the problem situation. This includes some tail scenarios to represent extreme events. The picture shows one such tail outcome, namely, basketball's great Wilt Chamberlain in the 4th grade.

Then there was the question how we might solve this. To our pleasure, many top academics learned from the grapevine about the model but not its details which were kept secret. We had offers to help solve the model for free from the best professors in the world such as Stanford's George Dantzig who wanted to test their algorithms and computer codes. I suggested that we discuss this with Roger Wets, my teacher of stochastic programming at Berkeley and the top person in the field. Wets is extremely brilliant and besides his math skills, he is very strong in computer implementations. Roger had contacts at IBM and arranged for us to use the top super computer in the world to attack the problem. We did not actually discuss the meaning of the model, rather we just provided the raw equations with data numbers.

The super computer almost solved the model in 27 hours. At Russell we had IBM RISK6000 workstations costing $90,000 each and, despite this power, in 1991 there was no way they could solve the problem especially with repeated runs with different data. The exercise convinced us that a ten period model with this many scenarios was too hard to solve and even if we did, too difficult to interpret. So we moved to a much simpler five period model with a lot less scenarios. To deal with the future, we used a modification of an end effects model of Richard Grinold to let the model's time horizon go to infinity. So there was the first quarter, the rest of the first year, the second year, years three to five and then five and forever. The end effects I knew about as Richard, an old friend from Berkeley student days, was at an energy conference we organized in Vancouver and had a paper on this applied to energy planning. The end effects added one more period to the model so it was a five period model.[2]

We now had the model formulated and could solve it. All the data was collected. David Myers, who worked with us, was responsible for penalty costs and insurance product details. The Japanese colleagues tested the model and a simulation model was built to see how the model operated under normal and severe conditions. Finally, in April 1991, the model was unveiled in a big ceremony in Tokyo attended by some Tacoma people and those from Tokyo. The results were good and over the first 2 years, the model provided good advice and gained US$95 million over what the competing mean-variance model would have produced over a 2 year period. So it was a big commercial and academic success to actually implement the model. Sharpe when asked responded that he thought making it would be impossible; later he praised the model's success. We entered the model in the 1993 Edelmann Prize competition sponsored by the INFORMS society for the best application of operations research.

The Edelman prize was established to honor Franz Edelman an early operations research applications pioneer at RCA. About 50 submissions are made and of these, 6 are chosen to be in a competition. The usual application is brainstormed by a professor and implemented together with a company so we fit well. We had practice sessions and prepared our presentation with many parts. I did the part on the previous literature. We had a good case and performed well in the 1993 competition, but Bell Labs beat us for the $10,000 first prize but we received second prize and a $3,000 bonus which the Yamaichi people took. I suppose they deserved it as they paid Russell for the model and in turn gave me prestigious and well paid consulting and began a 9 year consulting relationship. Bell Labs won because their model, while not as innovative as ours, saved more money and they had professional presenters who were very slick. Our paper on this was published in the January–February 1994 issue of *Interfaces* along with the other five contestants and the video of our presentation was available and a useful teaching tool.

The project established me as an expert in asset-liability modeling and I continued research in this area that led to a number of good papers and books. At Russell, there was politics and the group wanted to basically go it alone so they wanted to do the models without me and they did make a few more models that were basically clones of the Russell–Yamaichi Kasai model that I advised on.

There was also the issue of publishing the technical papers based on the model. At first, they wanted to exclude me but I talked Andy Turner into keeping my name on that along with David Cariño and in the second paper with Cariño and David Myers. They knew I was much more skilled than they about publishing in top journals. So after a long sequence of revisions which I did, the two papers were published in the top journal, *Operations Research* in 1998 where the paper with Kusy had been published in 1986. Getting papers in the top journals is important for careers and can be time consuming. The model was delivered in 1991, with the major papers published in 1998.

I was more interested in staying on the payroll then worried about who did the next model. And the Russell people did a good job on the subsequent models. I got the slides and used them in courses and lectures but they were never published. They did not want me to be involved with these models, nor did they want me to work with anyone else. So there was a simple solution, namely, to keep me on the payroll and have me do other things. Despite my wife's view to expand ALM elsewhere, I was happy to move into anomalies and Japanese stock market studies. While the model builders were PhDs, the ones I then worked with were MBAs. Since I was good at publishing, they were keen to work with me. One colleague, Doug Stone, later left Russell to join the San Diego money management firm Nicholas Applegate. Another colleague was Chris Hensel and we worked on anomalies as discussed in Chapter 18.

After the big success of the Russell Yasuda Kasai model, I proposed a company Russell–Mulvey–Ziemba with them to make similar and other models. John Mulvey at Princeton University who I had known for a long time was also making asset-liability management models. They were quite different from the ones I was doing and proposing but also successful. John's models had decision rules embedded in them like fixed mix. Fixed mix is essentially a strategy of the volatility pumping variety. Stanford Engineering Economic Systems Professor David Luenberger in his very nice book

Investment Science has also studied these types of strategies that attempt to profit form volatility of asset prices. For fixed mix, one balances the portfolio in each period to the same weighting. For example if it is 60% stock and 40% bonds, then one keeps this same weighting in each period. So assets that rise in value are sold and assets that fall are bought to maintain the 60–40 mix. This strategy has the advantage of selling high and buying low. John then had smaller but more complicated to solve models but he had ways to do this and had some successful implementations. We thought that combining our research and hooking up with Russell would be good for them to lock in the two top North American asset-liability professors and good for us to have the resources and contacts of Russell. Before we even got going, John jumped the gun by having a lawyer to determine a legal deal. Russell liked the proposal and basically stole it by starting a new division called Russell Business Engineering. That was to be run by other Russell people so John and I were out of that. But Russell wanted to keep me on the payroll and not be in competition with them so I switched to the study of anomalies, another favorite topic of mine.

I enjoyed the work at Russell and although I designed the Russell–Yasuda Kasai model and bailed them out of a big problem of not begin able to deliver a model, the client in Tokyo wanted, politics reared its ugly head and I was basically kept out of future models the Russell team made. In fact I even had to battle to co-author the three papers written on the Russell–Yasuda Kasai model even though I basically wrote the vast majority of those papers.

It is often corporate policy to dump consultants once you learn what they know. But I was important and ahead in this field so the best thing was to eliminate me as competition by keeping me on the payroll but doing other things. So I worked on anomalies, Japanese markets, etc with Chris Hensel, Douglass Stone and others. That was fine as I enjoyed that and the consulting money helped the family in various ways. In 1998, Russell was sold to the insurance company Northwest Life and the 9 years of consulting ended. But I was keen from the research in my various books in the 1990s to make a new and better model.

I was able to continue ALM research at UBC and do consulting at Russell on anomalies. Staying on the Russell payroll was very helpful financially and I enjoyed the anomalies work as discussed in Chapter 19 where I discuss my chance to build a better model.

Notes

[1] I recommended my top student, Chanaka Edirisinghe for a chair in financial engineering at RPI, a well known engineering and technical school in Troy New York. He got the chair and a very good salary with favorable teaching and other terms but his terms don't come close to those of the new president who got $7 million twice and lives in New Jersey!
One of the RPI professors, Arpana Gupta, a Stanford PhD graduate who did her PhD thesis with Bill Sharpe, invited me to give a talk there and proposed that I teach a course while at Saratoga close by around the racing season. Despite high pay to the permanent faculty, for a visitor all they would pay was $\frac{1}{6}$th of one student's yearly tuition per course. So I am not teaching there despite how much I would have been able to help them. Visiting MIT 11 years earlier was more favorable. They gave visitors half the pay of regular faculty, which was quite favorable, to pay expenses and have a little left over, and a much better university. Such is the strange policies of many schools to older, distinguished part time faculty. Most shocking is the RPI presidents' outrageous salary.

[2] See Grinold's paper and other papers in Ziemba., Schwartz and Koenigsberg (Eds.), *Energy Policy Modeling: United States and Canadian Experiences*; Vol. I: *Specialized Energy Policy Models* and Ziemba and Schwartz (Eds.), (1980). *Energy Policy Modeling: United States and Canadian Experiences*; Vol. II: *Integrative Energy Policy Models*. Martinus Nijhoff Publishing, Boston.

Chapter 18

Anomalies Research at Frank Russell, 1989–1998

The anomalies work was excellent. Russell had sharp well-trained MBA level people from the top schools like the University of Chicago but none were at my level of creativity and knowledge so I had many people wanting to work with me. Russell had very good data sources and the people there were skilled at the computer and statistical work needed to carry out good applied investment studies. What they needed was research creativity and how to generate good applied investment papers and get them published. I could supply that.

Doug Stone and I worked on Japanese stock and land prices and their relationship. This was a continuation of research I had done in Tokyo at the Yamaichi Research Institute in 1988–1989. That earlier work is described in Chapters 14 and 17 and resulted in three books and a number of research papers one of which I wrote for a 1991 academic book was called "The Chicken or the Egg: Land and Stock Prices in Japan." The aim was to try to determine who leads who in price changes. I found that basically stock prices moved first, then golf course membership prices move about 3 months later and finally regular land moves about 6 months later.

Doug and I wrote a paper called "Land and Stock Prices in Japan" in 1993 in the *Journal of Economic Perspectives*, a very good place to publish that has the wide readership of the American Economic Association. The editor was Joseph Stiglitz, one of Paul Samuelson's top MIT students and later a Nobel Prize winner in Economics. Stiglitz was born in Gary, Indiana and Samuelson used to say that he (Samuelson) was the second best economist born in Gary. Samuelson thought enough of Stiglitz to entrust him to edit his 1966 collected works. Other top students edited other parts of Samuelson's great contributions to all sorts of areas in theoretical and applied economics and public policy.

Stiglitz was the same, super good at everything. Once in a while his outspoken way got him into trouble but he certainly has had a great career which continues in 2017. We were pleased when Joe liked our paper and took the time to write out 9 pages single spaced comments on a 20-page paper. We revised and the paper was published and is widely cited. Doug was thrilled when it got accepted and published in a top quality journal.

Chris Hensel and I had a very good working relationship. Like Doug Stone, he was a University of Chicago MBA with good statistical training. Chris was seriously into health foods and exercise so was always drinking carrot juice or going to the gym but we got a lot done. Our topics were mostly US stock market anomalies and we produced seven good published papers in applied investment journals like the *Financial Analysts Journal*, the *Journal of Portfolio Management* and the *Journal of Investing* plus some reports and papers in books and conference proceedings.

The turn-of-the-month (TOM) work continued what I had done in Japan. There I studied the US literature then researched Japan. Now it was focused mostly on the US as that was closest to Russell's business. But the Russell management gave me free reign to work on what I thought was important. The work was then presented to Russell clients through talks and research reports and later we published in the journals. For the TOM effect we studied the cash and futures markets and found strong effects around the -1 to $+4$ days, namely, the last trading day of the ending month plus the first four of the current month. (Recall from Japan, their TOM was -5 to $+2$ because that's when the wives get the money to invest in the financial markets.)

The month end is when salaries are paid, pension investments are made, etc., so its not surprising that -1 to $+1$ are strong up days on average. This is a tradable anomaly most of the time and I and others trade this on a regular basis.

We found that in virtually every anomaly the small cap effect exceeded the large cap effect and often by huge margins. For those interested in US and other anomalies with details current to 2012, see my book, *Calendar Anomalies and Arbitrage*, World Scientific. While I cannot tell everything there, readers will find many good ideas with lots of data, tables and graphs.

In our work on the January barometer, we found that when January was positive then the rest of the year was positive about 85% of the time plus if it was not positive the mean return was not much negative. But if January was negative then the rest of the year was noisy, namely 50–50 chance of gaining or losing. And if it gained it was not much on average and if it lost the average loss was large. We found similar results across most of the world. These results with updates to 2012 confirm that these effects still exist, see Ziemba (2012a).

A third important area is the presidential election effect. Russell's businesses are varied but much is to recommend managers and they often use 60–40 strategies (60% stocks and 40% bonds). The reason being that when stocks fall, bonds tend to rise hence standard deviation risk is lowered. All well, but Chris and I found that the simple strategy invest only in small cap stocks with a Democratic president and intermediate term bonds or large cap stocks with a Republican president gave about 20 times more final wealth than 60–40 during the period 1940–1995. Well, that is a long period but 20 times! Democrats have policies that favor small cap stocks and Republican policies favor bonds and large cap stocks. You might ask does it still work with Clinton, Bush and Obama and the answer is yes; see Ziemba and Ziemba (2013) for details. It is still about 20–1.

The best anomaly of all is discussed in Chapter 9. It is related to the presidential election effect, namely the higher small cap returns compared to the large cap returns around the turn of the year. The effect is there in Republican as well as Democratic administrations, but is stronger with the Democrats. In trading this in the futures markets, I had all winners from 1982/1983 to 1995/1996 with the Value Line and S&P500 and 2008/2009 to 2014/2015 with the Russell2000 and the S&P500 only 2015/2016 failed. I think because of the fear of great higher interest rate which did not actually occur.

When I finished my 9 years at Russell in 1998 because they sold the company to Nationwide Life Insurance, I lost contact with my Russell colleagues. Then the phone rang. Chris had died at 45. He was on a bike tour with other Russell colleagues when he fell and bloodied up one of his knees. He bandaged it and continued the tour. A week later he had a heart attack while driving in Seattle. This was very sad for his family and for me. My other Russell colleagues I lost touch except for a 2003 occasion where I was the dinner speaker for Professor John Campbell of Harvard for his Arrowstreet Capital client conference in Seattle (coming from Oxford where I was teaching) and at the April 2012 at the Chicago quantitative alliance group conference in Las Vegas where I spoke on US calendar anomalies.

Some Say *Sell in May and Go Away*

We found that the period May 1 to the TOM of November, that's five trading days before November in late October has historically produced virtually zero returns. Meanwhile, the rest of the year has essentially all the year's gains in the better months, November to the end of April. There is a huge difference here and the strategy go to cash in the weak period and go long in the strong period has about double the returns of buy and hold and triple for the small cap Russell index over the period 1993–2015. Alexandre Ziegler and I have studied the effect of weather on the sell in May research. When the weather is good, the returns are high on average.[1]

For the S&P500 a buy and hold strategy turns $1 on February 4, 1993, into $3.13 on October 24, 2016; whereas, sell in May and move into cash, counting interest (Fed funds effective monthly rate for sell in May.) and dividends for the buy and hold, had a final wealth of $5.76, some 84.2% higher. For the Russell2000, the final wealths were $2.83 and $6.99, respectively, some 147.1% higher. So the Sell in May and Go Away strategy has been working to produce much higher final wealth with lower risk and, as with most anomalies, the small cap results are the best.[2]

The Various Efficient/Inefficient Market Camps: Can You Beat the Stock Market?

Trading and using calendar and fundamental anomalies in investment strategies can be very beneficial. In trading, winning has two parts: getting an edge and then betting well. The former simply means that investments have an advantage so $1 invested returns on average more than $1. The latter involves not over betting, and truly diversifying in all scenarios in a disciplined, wealth enhancing way.

Market camps can be categorized by the ideas which inform how various people try to get an edge. Some feel that one cannot get an edge. This becomes then a self fulfilling prophecy and they, of course, are not in our list of great or even good investors. Many great investors are Kelly or fractional Kelly bettors who focus on not losing. Market participants can be divided into five groups. There are other ways to do such a categorization but this way is useful for my purpose of isolating and studying great investors and naturally evolves from the academic study of the efficiency of financial markets.

The Five Groups are:

1. Efficient markets (E)
2. Risk premium (RP)
3. Genius (G)

4. Hog wash (H)
5. Markets are beatable (A)

The first group are those who believe in efficient markets (E). They believe that current prices are fair and correct except possibly for transactions costs. These transaction costs, which include commissions, bid-ask spread and price pressures, can be very large.[3]

The leader of this school which had dominated academic journals, jobs, fame, etc., in the 1960s to the 1980s was Gene Fama of the University of Chicago. A brilliant researcher, Fama is also a tape recorder: you can turn him on or off, you can fast forward or rewind him or change his volume, but you cannot change his views no matter what evidence you provide; he will refute it forcibly.

This group provided many useful concepts such as the capital asset pricing model of Sharpe (1964), Lintner (1965) and Mossin (1966) which provided a theoretical justification for index funds which are the efficient market camp's favored investment mode. They still beat about 75% of active managers. Since all the managers comprise the market, that's 50% of them beaten by the index. Transactions and other costs eliminate another 25%.

Over time the hard efficient market line has softened into a Risk Premium (RP) camp. They feel that markets are basically efficient but one can realize extra return by bearing additional risk. They strongly argue that, if returns are above average, the risk must be there somewhere; you simply cannot get higher returns without bearing additional risk they argue. For example, beating the market index S&P500 is possible but not risk adjusted by the CAPM. They measure risk by Beta, which must be greater than one to receive higher than market returns. That is, the portfolio risk is higher than the market risk. But they allow other risk factors such as small cap and low book to price. But they do not believe in full blown 20–30 factor models such as described in Chapter 13. Fama and his disciples moved here in the 1990s. This camp now dominates the top US academic journals and the jobs in academic finance departments at the best schools in the US and Europe.

The third camp is called Genius (G). These are superior investors who are brilliant or geniuses but you cannot determine in advance who they are. The late MIT Professor Paul Samuelson has championed this argument.[4] He feels that these investors do exist but it is useless to try to find them as in the search for them you will find 19 duds for every star. This view is very close to the Merton–Samuelson criticism of the Kelly criterion: that is, even with an advantage, it is possible to lose a lot of your wealth. Some simulations on this appear in MacLean *et al.* (2011).

The evidence though is that you can determine them *ex ante* and to some extent they have persistent superior performance, see Fung *et al.* (2006) and Jagannathan *et al.* (2006). Soros did this with futures with superior picking of futures to bet on; this is the traders are made not born philosophy. This camp will isolate members of other camps such as in (A) or (H).

Two great investors: Warren Buffett and Paul Samuelson

The fourth camp is as strict in its views as camps (E) and (RP). This group feels that efficient markets which originated in and is perpetuated by the academic world is hogwash (H). In fact the leading proponent of this view and one with whom it is hard to argue as he is right at the top of the list of the world's richest persons is Warren Buffett, who wants to give university chairs in efficient markets to further improve his own very successful trading. An early member of this group, the great economist John Maynard Keynes was an academic. We see also that although they may never have heard of the Kelly criterion, this camp does seem to use it implicitly with large bets on favorable investments.

This group feels that by evaluating companies and buying them when their value is greater than their price, you can easily beat the market by taking a long-term view. They find these stocks and hold them forever. They find a few such stocks that they understand well and get involved in managing them or they simply buy them and make them subsidiaries with the previous owners running the business. They forget about diversification because they try to buy only winners. They also bet on insurance when the odds are greatly in their favor. They well understand tail risk which they only take at huge advantages to themselves when the bet is small relative to their wealth levels.

The last group are those who think that markets are beatable (A) through behavioral biases, security market anomalies using computerized superior betting techniques. They construct risk arbitrage situations with positive expectation. They research the strategy well and follow it for long periods of time repeating the advantage many times. They feel that factor models are useful most but not all of the time and show that beta is not one of the most important variables to predict stock prices. They use very focused, disciplined, well-researched strategies with superior execution and risk control. Many of them use Kelly or fractional Kelly strategies. All of them extensively use computers. They focus on not losing, and they rarely have blowouts. Members of (A) include Ed Thorp (Princeton Newport and later funds), Bill Benter (the Hong Kong racing guru), John Henry (trend follower and the Red Sox owner), Blair Hull (mirpriced options trader), Harry McPike (trend follower), Jim Simons (Renaissance hedge fund), Jeff Yass (Susquehanna Group) and David Swensen (Yale endowment). Blowouts occur more in hedge funds that do not focus on not losing and true diversification and over bet; when a bad scenario hits them, they get wiped out, such as LTCM, Niederhofer and Amaranth; see Chapter 21. My idea of using scenario dependent correlation matrices is very important here, see Chapter 19.

How do investors and consultants do in all these cases?

All investors can be multimillionaires but the centimillionaires are in (G), (H) and (A) like the seven listed before me in (A) and Buffett. These people make more money for their clients than themselves but the amount they make for themselves is a huge amount: of course these people eat their own cooking that is they are clients themselves with a large amount of their money in the funds they manage). An exception is someone who founded an (RP) or (E) company kept most of the shares and made an enormous amount of fees for themselves irrespective of the investment performance given to the clients because the sheer volume of assets they have gathered under management is so large. I was fortunate to work/consult with about ten A, G or H's and was also the main consultant to the Frank Russell Research Department for 9 years which is perhaps the leading conservative RP implementor. (A) people earn money by winning and taking a percent of the profits, Thorp returned 15.8% net with $200 million under management; fees $8 million/year (1969–1988). (E) and (RP) people earn money from fees by collecting assets through superior marketing and sticky investment decisions.

Many great investors use Kelly betting including most in camp (A). There are compelling reasons for this discussed in previous chapters.[5] But there are critics and chief among them are Nobel Prize winners Robert Merton and Paul Samuelson. Their argument is that successful investing requires a lot of luck and it is hard to separate luck from skill. Therefore, while many Kelly investors will make huge gains, a few will have huge losses. Indeed they are correct. A good way to explain this is via the simulation Donald Hausch and I did. A simulation of 700 bets, all with a 14% edge, was performed 1,000 times.[6] In support of Kelly, 166 times out of the 1,000 simulated wealth paths, the investor has more than 100 times initial wealth with full Kelly. But this great outcome occurs only once with half Kelly. However, the probability of being ahead is higher with half Kelly, 87.0 versus 95.4. A negative observation, and related to the Merton–Samuelson criticism, is that the minimum wealth is only 18. So you can make 700 bets all independent each with a 14% edge and the result is that you still lose over 98% of your fortune with bad scenarios. Half Kelly is not much help here. It is still possible to turn $1,000 into $145! The conclusion is that the Kelly strategies usually, but not for sure, provide more final wealth than any other strategy.

The Effect of the Fed Meetings[7] See Lucca and Moemish (2011, 2015) with Data up to 2011. Dzahabrov and I Updated the Data to 2016 Here

Former Federal Chairman Alan Greenspan wrote in his 2007 memoir:

> People would stop me on the street and thank me for their 401(k); I'd be cordial in response, though I admit I occasionally felt tempted to say, 'Madam, I had nothing to do with your 401(k)'. It's a very uncomfortable feeling to be complimented for something you didn't do.

This is naive — his policies created a stock market bubble which burst and then created a bubble in real estate which also crashed.

A study by David Lucca and Emanuel Moench (2011, 2015) of the Fed shows the influence of the Fed Open Market meetings since they were publicized and announced in 1994 through mid 2011. Since then the S&P500 has risen from 450 to 1,300. More than 80% of the equity premium on US stocks was earned over the 24 hours preceding scheduled FOMC meetings. And virtually all in the 3 day window around these meetings.[8]

The returns are uncertain with a positive bias but considerable variation. So the Fed effect does seem to work but there is risk in it in a particular meeting. Given the confidence intervals, one sees the returns are not straight up. Also some tests Constantine Dzhabarov ran for me indicate that the effect is less pronounced in recent data ending September 30, 2012.

Matt Koppenheffer of Motley Fool used market data going back to 1994. He randomly removed 136 days (8 per year for 17 years, or 1 for every FOMC meeting) He ran the simulation several hundred times, removing different sets of random days. The difference was trivial. Nothing came within a third of the skew caused by removing the days shortly before FOMC meetings. Over the long haul, stocks are driven by fundamentals, in the short term they are impacted by headlines including waiting for the FMOC announcements which add to volatility.

To study this further we updated this research to July 2015 using the S&P500 mini futures as well as the Russell2000 mini futures plus we investigated the 5 day period adding 1 day before and 1 day after the 3-day Fed meeting. The results are best shown in two graphs which are in the notes and summarized here.[9] The gain in points per S&P500 mini futures contract from September 1997 to July 2015 peaked at slightly above 700 (that is $35,000 per contract, a huge gain) in September 2007 and was lower, about $425 at the end of the Lucca and Moench (2011, 2015) study. The drop coincided with the S&P500 drop from a peak of 1522.50 on July 14, 2007 (see Lleo and Ziemba (2012) for the June 14, 2007 signal exiting the S&P500 based on the BSEYD model being in the danger zone). The March 9, 2009 low was 676.53. Since then there have been gains back to the peak level. The Russell2000 small cap index had a similar pattern but with a much lower low and a much lower total gain which peaked at 215 in June 2015 versus a local high of 205 in September 2003. According to Hensel and Ziemba (1995) and Ziemba (2012a), small stocks are supposed to outperform large caps with Democratic presidents and handily beat a 60–40 stock-bond mix. In fact, during Obama's two terms, small caps did outperform but not during these Fed meeting periods.[10]

Finally, there are the 5 day stock movements surrounding Fed meetings.[11] The Fed announcement and statement is at 1 pm eastern time on day 4. Days 3 and 4 prior to the announcement have had high gains but neither closed in July 2015 at the peak. Days 2, 3, 4 and 5 all had gains that were similar in total up to July 2015. Day 1 had losses that have accelerated since September 2012. The Fed anomaly is a powerful one which I watch carefully. The large cap minus small cap advantage in this period is another trading opportunity. We see that the effect during the Fed meetings is mainly in the large cap stocks with the small cap stocks hardly moving.[12] This Fed trade did not play a major role in the next section's contest.

Winning the Battle of the Quants Trading Competition, May 2015

My own trading has gone well and I was pleased to win first prize in the Battle of the Quants trading competition for futures funds and beating the equity winner in May 2015. My daughter, Rachel presented my acceptance speech and accepted the prize for me in New York as I was lecturing PhD students at the University of Bergamo on portfolio theory and asset-liability management at the time of the awards ceremony.

Acceptance speech

First, many thanks for the organizers for having my futures fund Alpha Z Futures Fund LLC, in their Battle of the Quants trading competition. Thanks also to my daughter Rachel Ziemba, Director of Emerging Markets, Roubini Global Economics here in New York for accepting the award for her father while I am in Europe.

This is a victory for the anomaly approach to investing based on extensive research by others and myself. Anomalies always draw interest when I speak about them, but they are poorly understood and not used much except by a few great traders. Most people seem to believe that they either do not exist or go away quickly or have limited possibilities for gain. A prime example is the January turn of the year effect where small cap stocks out preform large cap stocks. Most finance books say the effect does not exist anymore. But the reality is that it often does in the latter half of December in the futures markets. I have now traded this 20 times with positive results. Fourteen were from the 1982–1983 start through 1995–1996. I stopped because of low volume on the value line contract. Then, after a consulting job to study anomalies in the US of the calendar variety as opposed to the fundamental type, I started trading again using the Russell2000 versus the S&P500 futures contract. The last 6 years have been successful.

My background from my PhD at Berkeley with a lot of Stanford involvement was in stochastic optimization. This was a great help in portfolio theory and practice and I became a leading theorist in the 1970s and 1980s.

Rachel with Battle of Quants award

In 1988, I went to Japan for a year as the first Yamaichi Visiting Professor at the University of Tsukuba and consultant to the Yamaichi Research Institute in Tokyo on anomalies and crash prediction models. I had been working on racetrack anomalies and my book Beat the Racetrack with Donald Hausch changed the way people looked at racing. We viewed it as a financial market so then we could study biases and profit from them. That book and our later book, Efficiency of Racetrack Betting Markets, which became the bible for racetrack syndicates, especially in Hong Kong, prepared me for US and Japanese calendar and fundamental anomalies through factor models.

After Japan, I helped the Frank Russell company make asset-liability management models and they allowed me to study practical implications of anomalies. While there, I wrote papers with Chris Hensel and Doug Stone. We discovered that the small caps, when held with Democrat presidents and bonds, when held during Republican administrations, gave 20 times more wealth at the end of the 1940–1995 period than the 60/40 stock bond mix that Russell was then recommending. Updating to account for three more presidents administrations — Clinton, Bush and Obama — in 2012 gave the same 20 times result. So in my trading in the Alpha Z Fund, this is a useful strategy in the futures markets. One other strategy employed is mean reversion in the S&P500 — see my *Calendar Anomalies and Arbitrage* book for examples in NFL playoff and Superbowl betting which is also effective. The idea here is similar to NFL football on Betfair in London where one might bet on team A to beat team B, but because of various mean reversion moves, one may win overall even though team B ultimately wins the game. Mispriced options can be traded with a similar bias as the racetrack favorite-longshot bias.

That's similar to Kahanemann–Tversky's observation that in real situations low probability events are observed to be overestimated and high probability events are observed to be underestimated. This leads to about multiple versions of an options selling strategy with different deltas and different levels of hedging depending on projected market conditions. Other anomaly strategies that are used are TOM and options expiry effects.

This collection of strategies, along with risk management models and the use of prediction models to monitor for potential market corrections, is the core of the Alpha Z Fund portfolios performance. I always have an exit strategy for each new position and corrective action to modify a trade that is not working so that there are gains in the end.

Alpha Z Advisors LLC is my entity that trades S&P 500 and Russell 2000 futures and futures options for a futures fund and private accounts. It is registered and audited in the US based in Chicago. I can be reached at wtzimi@mac.com and my books and papers, etc., are on the website www.williamtziemba.com as well as on www.amazon.com The track record of this fund (from July 2013 to June 17, 2017) is displayed here. I have been pretty good recovering from problems and getting the Feb 12 2016, the Trump election, Brexit, French election and the current Trump-Comey bad scenario right. More hedging and constant attention and experience hopefully avoids kinks like the one in the fall of 2015. Writing the companion book Ziemba, Lleo and Zhitlukhin (2017) on *Stock Market Crashes: Predictable and Unpredictable and what to do about them* helps too.

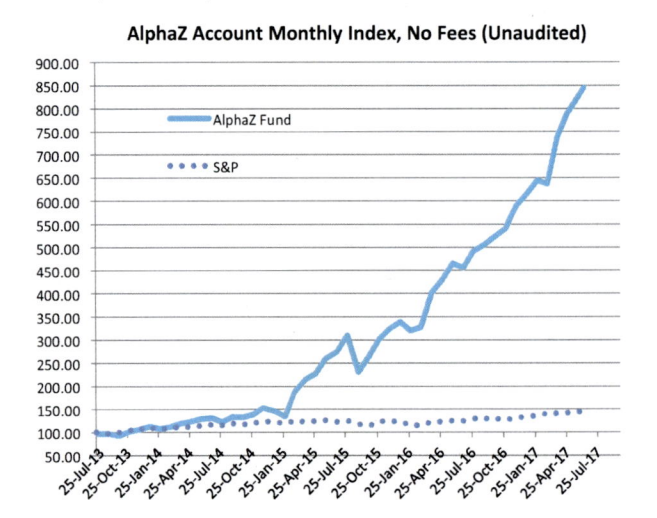

AlphaZ Account Monthly Index, No Fees (Unaudited)

Notes

[1] See Ziegler and Ziemba (2015), "Sell in May and go away and the weather", Working Paper, University of Zurich.

[2] The gains are a bit jagged and larger for the small caps as the graphs show.

S&P500 Futures Sell in May (SIM) and B&H Cumulative Returns Comparison. 1993-2016.
(Entry at Close on 6th Day before End of October. Exit 1st Day of May.)

Russell 2000 Futures Sell in May (SIM) and B&H Cumulative Returns Comparison. 1993-2016.
(Entry at Close on 6th Day before End of October. Exit 1st Day of May.)

[3] A BARRA study by Andy Rudd some years ago showed that these costs averaged 4.6% one-way for a $50,000 institutional investor sale. This is if you use a naive market order for the full transaction rather than limit orders or smaller market orders. Thorp, in a private communication, told me that he traded about $60 billion in statistical arbitrage from 1992 to 2002 in lot sizes

192 *The Adventures of a Modern Renaissance Academic*

of 20 K to 100 K and found that the mean transaction cost was about 1 cent per share and the market impact was about 4.5 cents per share for shares averaging about $30. So the one-way costs were about $0.18.

[4] Despite what he argues here, Samuelson was a co-founder of the very successful trading operation Commodity Corporation in Princeton, NJ which used various anomalies successfully. Many great traders evolved out of the Commodity Corporation.

[5] For long and mathematical survey papers, see the MacLean, Thorp and Ziemba (2010, 2011) handbook.

[6] See also the empirical paper by Bicksler and Thorp (1973) where they calculate the probability that investors will be ahead after given numbers of favorable bets and the simulations in MacLean *et al.* (2011). Their conclusions are consistent with those in the Hausch and Ziemba study. A response to the Samuelson critique using Samuelson's private letters to Ziemba and Samuelson's papers, many of which are reprinted in MacLean, Thorp and Ziemba (2010, 2011) is in Ziemba (2016).

[7] This section adapts Housel (2012).

[8] (a) The S&P500 index with and without the 24 hour preFOMC returns and (b) Average cumulative returns on S&P500 on days before, on and after FOMC announcements.

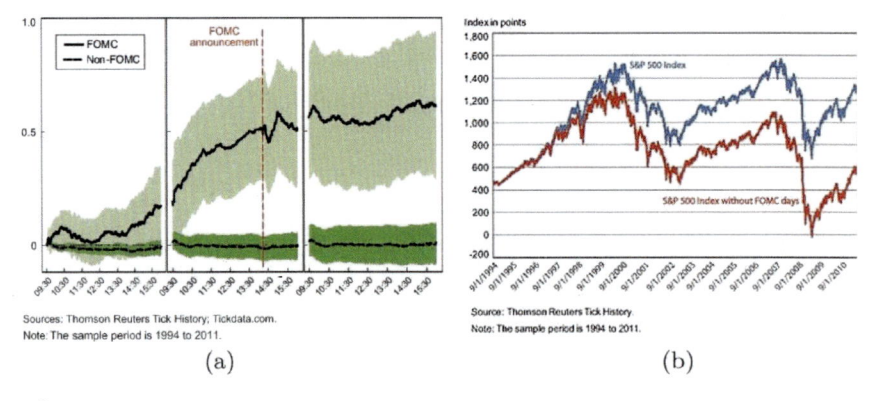

(a)

(b)

[9] Graphs summarizing the impact of the 5 day period around the Fed meetings.

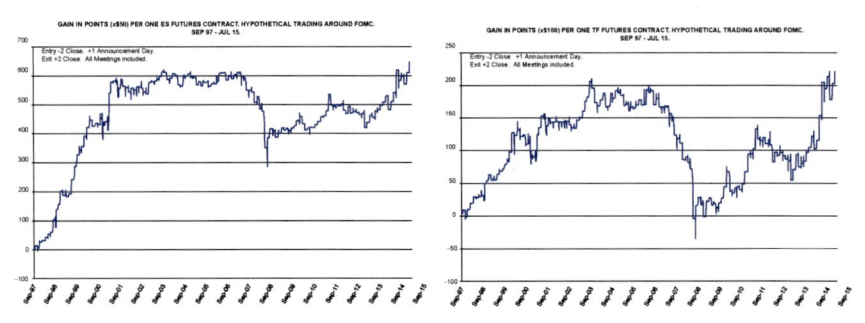

[10] Small cap is still beating the S&P500 which is still beating 60–40

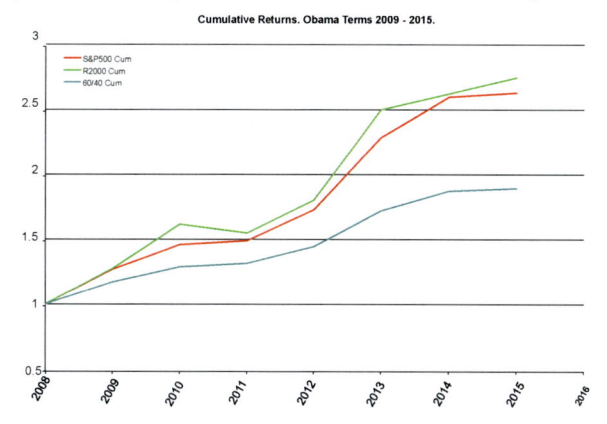

Cumulative Returns. Obama Terms 2009 - 2015.

[11] Graphs showing the day by day impact of the 5 day period around the Fed meetings.

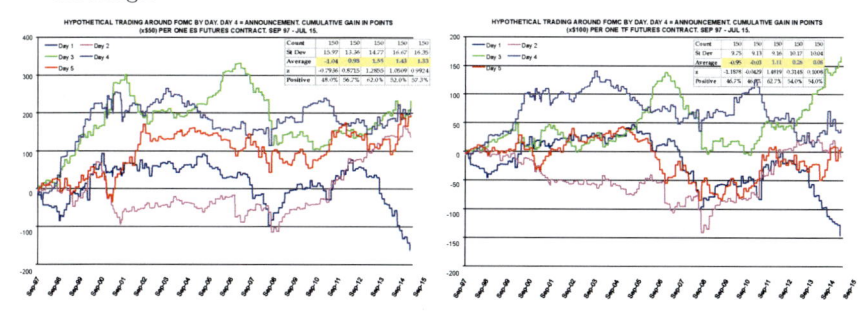

[12] Not every FED meeting provides positive returns and those where the large caps beat the small caps. But most do.

Usually after the 2pm New York time announcement there is a lot of volatility as people adjust positions. This period is usually good in trading and then the market usually rallies. FED Chairman Janet Yellen is doing a good job steering the FED into helping the economy with their dual mandate of dealing with inflation and employment. Her dovish policy has been very beneficial to those of us trading during FED meetings and other times. Eventually the interest rate rises will cool the stock market rally. The forecast are for three rate increases in 2017 and three to four in 2018. If there are these increases then the short-term rate will be in the 2%+ area. Thats not high. For example my colleague, Ed Thorp had a great record in his fund during 1968–88. In my Journal of Portfolio Management papers reprinted in my Great Investment Ideas book on my DSSR modified Sharpe ratio designed to show the brilliance of the best managers, I show that Thorp and Renaissance Medallion stand out as having outstanding trading records. During 1968–88 the S&P 500 averaged 10% but T-bills were not far behind at 8%. Thorp's Princeton-Newport fund earned about 16% after fees with a very smooth record and very few monthly losses. Obviously the high T-bill rate helped in the smooth-no loss months. The situation is more difficult now with many bigger computerized players, much talent and low interest rates. In the latest FED meeting with the announcement on Wednesday March 15, 2017 which occurred on the -3 day of the Friday options expiry another positive effect co-incided with the expected $1/4$ point interest rise of the FED. I, of course went strongly long taking off my hedges on Tuesday which conveniently had a decline to help me. Then on Wednesday the market was straight up all day with small caps dominating. In mid-session I hedged back partly in case of the usual reversal volatility. That never occurred so I left some on the table which was still a very good outcome for my Alpha-z futures fund and private accounts. One attempts to follow Maverick's pappy's saying you only quit when you have won it all. We can't do that but some is pretty good.

Chapter 19

Risk Management and Planning in the Vienna Siemens Pension Model, InnoALM

The Russell–Yasuda Kasai model was a great success and it was wonderful to implement a very good asset-liability planning model. After this model was implemented in 1991 and we won second prize in the Edelmann practice of management science contest in 1993, I kept on this line of research. In 1995, there was a 6 month workshop at the Isaac Newton Institute at the University of Cambridge. The facility is beautifully laid out with open spaces for research contact. These programs were very prestigious and people like Stephen Hawking were involved in other similar programs. Ours was called *financial mathematics* and the organizers invited me to put together 2 weeks of the program. They had known me from a workshop I was involved with in 1993 organized by Paul Wilmott and Sam Howison of Oxford University and Frank Kelly of the University of Cambridge. That earlier workshop led to a special issue of the *Philosophical Transactions of the Royal Society* in London. I wrote a paper on calendar anomalies with my Frank Russell colleague Chris Hensel.

The 2 weeks were pertinent: one on asset-liability management (ALM) and one on anomalies. Cambridge is delightful and the colleges have a special charm. The Newton Institute had excellent facilities and was laid out with offices with no doors on several levels with an atrium in the middle to encourage interaction among the participants. The library had a row about 6 feet long of Newton's publications from his 1643–1726 life. Newton made many discoveries including receiving credit along with Leibnitz for calculus, gravity, low of motion, classical mechanics and optics. Newton built the first practical reflecting telescope and developed a theory of color using a prism that decomposes white light into many colors. He formulated an empirical law of cooking, studied the speed of sound and introduced Newtonian fluid. The Newton trust was important and connected with the top Cambridge college, the famed Trinity, where many Nobel Prize winners and other stars were members. It was just like Berkeley, wall to wall talent. So it was a great honor to be involved.

My 2 weeks had a lot of strong people speaking and went well. Plus it was great to be in Cambridge a very delightful place to walk around. As usual, I was the lead idea person and I planned books based on each week. David Tranah of the Cambridge University Press, arranged the publishing contracts with the Newton Trust which took all our royalties. That's standard for many academic publishers, let the professors do the work and get the prestige but keep the money from the sales to the press. Complaining did not help as it got me a bit blacklisted. I guess they feel that prestige is enough. But the two books came out strong and became important ones in the profession. The 1998 ALM volume was edited with Professor John Mulvey of Princeton and the 2000 anomalies volume with Professor Donald Keim of the University of Pennsylvania's Wharton business school. The Ziemba–Mulvey volume has become a standard in ALM research and well referenced and had a lot of sales for this type of book. It had very good case studies of stochastic programming applications in various areas around the world.

It is still an important reference although it is in some sense overshadowed by the 2005 SIAM-Mathematical programming society book, Wallace and Ziemba, *Applications of Stochastic Programming* which has newer case studies plus descriptions of computer does to solve these large ALM problems. And even more so, by Zenios and Ziemba, 2006 and 2007, North Holland *Handbooks on Asset Liability Management.* Volume I has theory including great papers on mean-variance and extensions by Nobel Prize winner Harry Markowitz and perhaps the greatest single paper on the Kelly capital growth criterion by Ed Thorp. Volume II has case studies including a 101-page ALM paper I wrote describing all the models I have been involved with. I also wrote in 2003 while in Oxford, a monograph for AIMR on the *Stochastic Programming Approach to Asset-Liability and Wealth Management.* This monograph is distributed these days free from the AIMR website. In contrast to the cheap academic publishers, AIMR was generous and gave me a US$31,250 fee for writing the monograph for their institutional members. My editor, Mark Kritzman of Windam Capital in Boston and MIT/Sloan, helped push this book through.

The anomalies book with Keim was a gem. He was great to work with and contributed five new papers. including ones on holidays and small firm

Stavros Zenios and Leonard MacLean

effects in the cash markets, the later with David Booth of Dimension Fund Advisors. The world's best finance department in my opinion is Chicago Booth — named for David who gave $300 million from DFI to bolster their endowment. David was a PhD student at Chicago like Keim was. One day Booth went into Professor Gene Fama's office and said "I am not sure I am good enough to get a PhD." Fama replied," You are right, your are not good enough." But Fama got Booth a job[1] and later when Booth and fellow Chicago former student Rex Sinquefield founded DFI, Fama was made an advisor. His shares from his contribution to DFI are worth more than $50 million. The result was a great success story as DFI now manages more than $250 billion, mostly in various types of index funds.

While the Keim–Ziemba 2000 book was a gem, it was a sales bust. For some reason anomaly books just don't sell much. There is a 1988 anomalies book by Elroy Dimson also from Cambridge University Press. And I have a (2012a) World Scientific book *Calendar Anomalies and Arbitrage*. We will see how this one loaded with good trading ideas including many I successfully use in personal and private accounts sells. For several reasons people have trouble integrating anomalies into their investment strategies. Some think despite the evidence that they don't exist, are not reliable or are too small. My evidence in both of these books counters this but it is a hard sell — although many of the great investors use anomalies all the time.

The chance to make a new ALM model came in 2000 from Seimens Austria. John Mulvey's ALM company in Princeton was hired to make ALM models for the home branch in Munich and other Siemens subsidiaries but not Vienna. John got a lucrative contract and his company made these models. I was not involved and knew little about the details. But Siemens–Austria in Vienna wanted a model as well. They hired Alois Geyer, an operations research professor in Vienna, to make a model. It was supposed to be a dynamic ALM model but when I was consulted on it, I discovered that it was a static model in disguise. I then asked the management if I could design a model on a limited budget. They agreed and I was pleased that Geyer was happy to work with me. Indeed we were a good team. I was the idea person and he did the computer modeling with data assistance from Wolfgang Herold and Konrad Kontriner who were working for Innovest, the pension arm of Siemens Austria.

The model had one major new feature plus better refinements of the ideas in previous models. The new idea was scenario dependent correlation matrices. The LTCM disaster has just occurred in 1998 and they had used value at risk (VaR) and one correlation matrix which they subjected to stress tests. I knew since 1974 that VaR is not safe. It is simple to see why: if you lose $10 million you are penalized A, if you lose $20 million its still A and if you lose $1 or $5 billion it is still A. With convex shortfall penalties, losing $20 million is more than 2A and a $30 million loss is more than 1.5 times the $20 million penalty. That is, the more you lose, the more and more is the penalty. From the early days at Russell, our clients were able to grasp this and agree that it is better and VaR or C-VaR which is double the penalty with double the shortfall. So convex risk measures were in the model.

The multiple correlation matrices add the following important feature: you assign the future scenarios to three groups: good, bad and ugly — thanks Clint. *Good* is what happens most of the time, about 70% when the markets are calm and stocks rise and bonds rise and volatility is not high. In *bad*, volatility is higher, markets are more choppy, bonds and stocks have positive correlation but lower than in good — so they begin to decouple and stocks in various areas measured by indices become more correlated. Finally, in *ugly* or crash, the stocks are falling, bonds are rising so the correlations are negative, a feature other models cannot capture and the correlation between different stock indices gets close to one, that is, they are all falling. This feature is a good one in models and I hope it is used more. But VaR is hard to dislodge as it is in too many regulatory rules. Additional features were the targets; Wealth growing about 7.5% per year to account for inflation and the increase in retirees, a stochastic target of measuring whether or not the managers in the various parts of the portfolio were beating their benchmark indices and the *save for a rainy day* aspect where payments to retirees were increased slightly in good years so a reserve was kept for bad years.

The model was implemented with simple asset classes of bonds and stocks and has been used since 2000.

Since I had published Kusy–Ziemba in 1986 and Cariño–Ziemba and Cariño, Myers and Ziemba in 1998 in *Operations Research*, I wanted Geyer–Ziemba to be there too. It was a long process with a number of revisions but finally in 2008 the paper appeared. The following discussion and the quote from Konrad Kontriner (member of the board) and Wolfgang Herold (senior risk strategist) emphasized the practical importance of InnoALM and helped a lot as the paper was in the practice section of the journal.

> The model InnoALM provides an easy-to-use tool to help Austrian pension funds investment allocation committees evaluate the effect of various policy choices in light of changing economic conditions and various goals, constraints, and liability commitments. The model includes features that reflect real investment practices. These include multiple scenarios, non-normal distributions and different volatility and correlation regimes. The model provides a systematic way to estimate in advance the likely results of particular policy changes and asset return realizations. This provides more confidence and justification to policy changes that might be controversial, such as a higher weight in equity and less in bonds than has traditionally been the case in Austria.
>
> The model is an advance on previous models and includes new features such as state-dependent correlation matrices. Crucial to the success of the results are the scenario inputs and especially the mean return assumptions. The model has a number of ways to estimate such scenarios. Given good inputs, the policy recommendations can improve current investment practice and provide greater confidence to the asset allocation process.
>
> *The InnoALM model has been in use by Innovest, an Austrian Siemens subsidiary, since its first draft versions in 2000. Meanwhile it has become the only consistently implemented and fully integrated proprietary tool for assessing pension allocation issues within Siemens AG worldwide. Apart from this, consulting projects for various European corporations and pensions funds outside of Siemens have been performed on the basis of the concepts of InnoALM. The key elements that make InnoALM superior to other consulting models are the flexibility to adopt individual constraints and target functions in combination with the broad and deep array of results, which allows to investigate individual, path-dependent behavior of assets and liabilities as well as scenario based and Monte-Carlo like risk assessment of both sides.*
>
> *In light of recent changes in Austrian pension regulation the latter even gained additional importance, as the rather rigid*

asset-based limits were relaxed for institutions that could prove sufficient risk management expertise for both assets and liabilities of the plan. Thus, the implementation of a scenario-based asset allocation model will lead to more flexible allocation restraints that will allow for more risk tolerance and will ultimately result in better long-term investment performance.

Furthermore, some results of the model have been used by the Austrian regulatory authorities to assess the potential risk stemming from less-constraint pension plans.

Note

[1] It was with John McKnown of Wells Fargo an early index fund pioneer. While I was a PhD student in Berkeley I gave an econometrics course to John's group. John is also famous in wine having been part of the opening up of Napa valley wines to the world by winning a famous tasting contest in Paris called the Judgement of Paris. Go to the Montelena winery for the facinating story including asking passengers on a flight to Paris to carry wine for the contest.

Chapter 20

Evaluating the Greatest Investors

Sometimes new research comes from unusual encounters.

John Maynard Keynes, a famous Kelly investor

In the winter term of 2005, I was a visiting professor at the MIT Sloan School of Management. I had always wanted to teach at MIT, ever since as a UMass chemical engineering student, we took a trip there. As I walked down the corridor every book I was using was a name on a door. On this visit, I taught a course in investment management, the second term of a year long sequence for engineering, robotics and other non-finance majors, largely PhD students who wanted to learn about investments. The first term term was taught by Andy Lo who arranged to provide me with his notes from the previous time he taught the second semester. I was thrilled to teach at MIT and put more effort into that course than any other I have taught in a long time. MIT has very good terms for visitors, basically they are paid half that of the regular professors, this argues that research and administration count half and teaching the other half. In the course I had three parts: my slides on practical investments, Lo's notes and the text book by Bodie, Kane and Marcus (2005). My TA was helpful and I packed in a lot of material in each lecture. I expected top future stars to challenge me in the lectures but that never happened. In the midterm exam, I had a mixture of the book's test problems and used their answers which were multiple choice, Lo's notes and my lecture material. According to the book, there was one unique correct answer. Unfortunately, some of the students argued with the TA that some of their other answers were also correct. Being a visitor I deferred to my TA who was a PhD student, sticking to the one correct answer. I learned that the students were of two types: (1) those who loved the course and my teaching and were keen on learning several of whom went to hedge funds or Goldman Sachs or similar firms and I helped them with that transition; and (2) the other group who were worried about getting a top grade and were threatened given that we were strict on the midterm, so they marked me down in the ratings which I never looked at (according to my wife who looked at them). It was UBC basic statistics all over again: students uninterested but stronger students. All the MIT students had distinguished records coming into that great university so their fear of not being at the top is understandable. A couple years later, John Cox the MIT finance chair called me about teaching again. I had been very social and took all the seminar speakers to lunch and had been a good visitor colleague. Unfortunately, for John and me, a dean blocked the visit after consulting the ratings: one third terrific and two thirds luke-warm or worse, killed the idea.

In the class, besides the extensive material I had a few guest speakers. One was Lawrence Siegel who was the strategic head of the Ford Foundation endowment discussed their strategy and returns. To maintain their tax free status, they have a mandate to return 5% in real returns plus 0.3% in expenses. I was surprised to see that they had a higher Sharpe ratio than Berkshire Hathaway though Berkshire Hathaway was the best performing stock or mutual fund over a 30 year period. It used the simple strategy: sell insurance to collect money and then invest that in low beta, high performing stocks, essentially borrowing at zero cost from insurees. So Berkshire is about 1.6 levered. Ed Thorp, who bought Buffett stock in 1983, later encouraged me to invest in Buffett's Berkshire Hathaway.[1]

Buffett prefers to measure his performance by the increase in book value. Doing it that way, in the 50 years[2] from 1965 to 2014, the gain was 19.4%

per year or 751,113% in total. In terms of a share price, the gain was 21.6% per year or 1,826,163% in total. This is after tax. Meanwhile, the before tax S&P500 gained 9.9% per year or 11,196% in total. In 11 of the 50 years, Buffett's shares fell in price but in only 2 years, 2001 and 2008 did the book value fall. The S&P500 had 11 losing years.

Berkshire returned 32.07% per year from July 1977 to March 2000 which was a tremendous accomplishment. That led Buffett on his way to enormous personal wealth and fame. I wanted to find a measure to demonstrate that Buffett was in fact a superior investor to the Ford Foundation. The Sharpe ratio is the mean return net of the risk free rate divided by the standard deviation of all the returns. In the calculation of the standard deviation there are contribution from all returns: low, medium and high. To modify this I simply use only the negative returns and change the standard deviation to only count these negative returns. To get the full standard deviation, I calculate the loss side and an equal phony gain side. I call this modified ratio the downside symmetric Sharpe ratio or DSSR. My idea to do this dates to the 1991 book *Invest Japan*. My measure is related to the Sortino ratio which was developed around 1994 which stands on its own. The DSSR is simply a modification of the ordinary Sharpe ratio designed to evaluate the greatest investors by not penalizing them for high positive returns.

When I applied the DSSR and compared it to a sample of funds Siegel gave me with 172 months data from 1985 to 2000. It turned out that only Buffett's Berkshire Hathaway was improved from an ordinary Sharpe of 0.773 to a DSSR of 0.917. His rating was about equal to the Ford Foundation's 0.920 DSSR versus 0.970 Sharpe or the Harvard Endowment but not better, also around 0.9–1.0. Soros's Quantum Fund was lower. Why was Buffett not better? The reason is that Buffett has huge monthly gains for which he is not penalized but he also has many monthly losses that are more negative than any of the other funds. They were the Tiger Fund with Sharpe 0.879 and DSSR 0.865, the S&P500 with 0.797 and 0.696, Soros's Quantum 0.622 and 0.458 and Windsor 0.543 and 0.495, respectively. I then applied the DSSR to Ed Thorp's 1968–1988 Princeton–Newport record. Ed had only 3 monthly losses in 20 years which compares with Buffett and Soros losing about one third of the months. Ed's DSSR was 13.8, a tremendous accomplishment. Ed focused on risk arbitrage trades including situations including mispriced options or warrants. I was pleased to do a Thorp-like convergence with Ed which is described in Chapter 15. Ed was helped by T-bills which averaged a hefty 8% or 0.667% per month to not have many losses.

Average Mutual Funds and Why Most of the Time They Do Not Beat the Market Averages

On average, the typical mutual fund does not beat the market. The evidence is that professional managers all over the world have a hard time beating the market averages. In a given year, only about 25% to 40% of managers actually beat a buy-and-hold strategy of holding the index. Over longer periods, say 5–10 years, the percentage is even lower. There are a number of reasons for this.

- The market averages stay fully invested at all times, never missing market moves nor paying commissions for stock changes and market timing.
- When funds get behind the index, they often make hasty moves to try to catch up and, more often than not, this puts them further behind.
- Portfolio managers have a tendency to window dress at reporting times, adding to turnover and commissions.
- Since the managers collectively more or less are the market (with individual investors forming less and less of the market each year) the indices, on average, beat half of the fund managers. Then with commissions, fees, and these other reasons, only 25% to 40% typically beat the market averages (which does quite well with a lot less work).
- The fund managers take fees; the averages work for free.
- The fund managers' goals may get in the way of the fund's best interests which creates an agency problem.
- Portfolio managers tend to follow each other's moves. They tend to move the market which gains the full amount, and they can easily be a little behind.

We have the following four reasons the high commissions of active trading often lead to poorer performance than the market indices.

1. Commissions are higher in active portfolios because the turnover is greater.
2. The bid-ask spreads are larger for many smaller international securities that an active manager would buy.
3. Exchange taxes can be as large as 1% on both buys and sells.
4. Active managers usually hold a small number of large positions so they have market impact on getting in and out.

Index funds have grown and grown. Dimension Fund Advisors formed by University of Chicago Professor Eugene Fama's students David Booth and

Rex Sinquefield manage about $450 billion and others such as Barclays in San Francisco manage over $100 billion. This is done with low fees in an efficient manner. The indices for these passive funds have grown to include small cap, foreign investments and a variety of exchange traded funds as well as the traditional market index, the S&P500. Despite very low fees, profits are large because the volume under management is so large.

The World's Greatest Hedge Fund

The Renaissance Medallion Hedge Fund was the pioneer in high frequency trading giving them high transactions costs and expenses as well as high profits. For them, it is said, a long trade was 8 seconds. One of their algorithms determines whether a very large order is executed and taking advantage of the inefficiencies of large trades, front runs it.

The head, James Simons, himself a famous mathematics professor, surrounded himself with other top technical brain power. I had a small hand by teaching Simons about the advantages and disadvantages of Kelly betting. Our meeting was in a New York restaurant set up by Jim Fix who was one of Simon's prize winning mathematicians. Fix was trading for the fund through Axcom Trading Advisors but was not successful. Simons grasped the Kelly ideas and the approach is ideal for his type of trading, namely the optimal amounts to wager when you have an essentially unlimited sequence of similar betting opportunities. Mathematically, the Kelly strategy leads to the most long run wealth most of the time.

Another important partner was Elywn Berlekamp, a distinguished MIT trained electrical engineer and mathematician who had worked with John Kelly at Bell Labs 1966–1971 after which he returned to Berkeley as a math professor. Berlekamp bought the largest interest in Axcom Trading Advisors in 1989. Together they devised trades with a mathematical advantage through short term prediction and other models. After the firm's futures trading algorithms were rewritten Axcom's Medallion Fund had a return in 1990 of 55% net of all management and transactions costs. This fund evolved into Jim Simons's Renaissance Medallion.

The entire setup is brilliant and has made Simons a multi-billionaire. First, the fees are very high, namely a 5% management fee plus an incentive fee of 44% of the net new profits by the high water mark system. This means that no more incentive is due until it is really deserved and higher total net profits have been made. If the total profits are X and the fund falls below X,

Jim Simons   Elwyn Berlekamp

then incentives are only due when profits total more than X. Losses that make the fund below X plus gains not exceeding X do not give any more incentive fee. Before 2000, the incentive fee was 20% which is standard, but then, based on the superior performance it was raised to 36% and then 44%. The 5 + 44 means that the management takes about half the profits. Despite these huge fees, the net gain after these fees of the $5–8 billion fund have been spectacular. The yearly fees are paid out so the fund does not grow much in size. In data from January 1993 to April 2005, a period when I had monthly data, the yearly net returns in percent were +39.06, +70.69, +38.33, +31.49, +21.21, +41.50, +41.50, +24.54, +98.53, +29.13 and +27.77, and in 2005 to April, +8.30. There were only 17 monthly losses in these 148 months, 3 quarterly losses in 49 months and no yearly losses. The wealth path is very smooth and the DSSR is 26.4 versus an ordinary Sharpe ratio of 1.68. The DSSR or some other measure is needed to show their true brilliance. Simons, who has the 80 or so employees in the fund paying fees, made $1.4 billion is 2005. Very few others were in the fund and they were essentially told to leave around 2005, as a current client was one of them. So the about 80 employees devise and execute the trades (for which they are paid), invest in the fund, receive very good returns and help make Simons more billions as the major owner of the fund with a 25–50% stake. He has been giving some of these monies to UC Berkeley, the Stony

Brook mathematics department and the Cold Spring Harbor Laboratory for Quantitative Research in Fundamental Biology.

Since 2005, I have, despite considerable efforts, been unable to obtain the monthly returns, but the yearly returns were 44.3% (2006), 73.0% (2007), 80.0% (2008) and 39.0% (2009).[3]

Outstanding Funds in the UMass Hedge Fund Database

I wanted to study the DSSR more and see if there were any funds with records better than Renaissance Medallion. Thomas Schneeweis, who has organized the very important hedge fund data and research center at the University of Massachusetts, Amherst, gave me access to data on their 4,000 funds. I met a French econometrician Olivier Gergaud while visiting at the University of Reims in the Champagne district, slightly northeast of Paris. I discussed the problem with DSSR with Olivier and we wrote a nice paper that editor Frank Fabozzi published in the *Journal of Portfolio Management*, a very good applied journal for academics and industry professionals.[4]

We found some funds with very high DSSRs, above Renaissance Medallion's. For example, Logos Trading Inc., a commodity trading advisor, at a mean return of 8.5% per month from its inception in June 1984 to its close, 157 months later, in June 1997. There were 29 losing months and the Sharpe ratio was 2.77 and the DSSR was 64.4. They had $57 million under management.

An even higher DSSR of 491.8 was obtained by GJ Investment Fund of Flemington, New Jersey managed by Jeeva Ramaswamy. The Sharpe ration was 3.22. There were very high mean returns of 15.5% per month and only one monthly loss versus 12 positive months, yield this huge DSSR. The stated objective of the Fund is to, over the long term, outperform all three major US stock market indices and over 90% of all US mutual fund and hedge fund managers using a non-levered Warren Buffett style value investing approach. The assumption is that the market over reacts to good and bad news resulting in volatile stock price movements that do not correspond to the company's long-term fundamentals, hence undervalued stocks can be purchased. Special situations investing is also used and there are investments in India and China. Fees are just for performance at 25% above a 6% hurdle rate. To date, the Fund has consistently outperformed the Dow30, the S&P500 and the Nasdaq100. They manage only $1.25 million in the time the fund was operating for only the 13 months from November 1, 2008 to January 31, 2010. Funds close for various reasons, such as: too bad performance, too good performance so the manager wants to retire, too many costs for administrative hassles, illness, age, etc.

In Chapter 28, I discuss swindles and Ponzi schemes, we found one in the UMass database, that was the FMG Fund in the Federated MGT Group of funds plus the assets under management and the ordered monthly losses and gains. This CPO reported results from January 1987 to July 2003, some 199 months. It had a geometric mean of +2.3% per month and a Sharpe ratio of 12.35, higher than any other fund in the UMASS DHF database. Apparently there were no monthly losses so the $DSSR = DISR = \infty$! This sounds too good to be true and indeed the CFTC on December 7, 2010 announced that the principals were ordered to pay $26 million for running a Ponzi scheme with 140 participants with $420,720,000 under management. So FMG is suspect and had Madoff made up elements in its reporting and misuse of funds. My point here is to discuss the use of the DSSR measure and an infinity measure is suspect!

Summary statistics on various types of funds such as commodity pool operators, commodity trading advisors, fund of funds and hedge funds that had at least 100 months in operation with mean returns of at least 1.5% per month, had average DSSRs of 4.903, 5.436, 14.542 and 6.772 respectively. So there were many funds with good records.

Olivier got me involved in the economics of wine conferences and I am co-editing a 900, page handbook on the economics of wine in my series at World Scientific. The other editors are Professor Orley Ashenfelter of Princeton, who is the editor of *Liquid Assets* a wine newsletter and former editor of the *American Economic Review*, Karl Storchmann of NYU and Olivier. We went to one of their conferences in Walla Walla, Washington, a top wine center. Olivier has since moved to the Hedge Business School in Bordeaux the site of the 2016 economics of wine conference which my wife and I attended (the 2015 conference was in Mendoza, Argentina). That was a lovely visit in the very nice city, Bordeaux. The wine areas are an hour away and are more spread out than Burgundy which is a compact linear wine area with the best whites south of Beaune and the best reds north of Beaune. The 2017 conference is scheduled to be in Padua just outside Venice, preceded by a workshop in Bolzano.

What are the Effects of Manager Investment in the Fund on Performance and Risk Taking?

Roy Kouwenberg, a post doc with me from the powerful Erasmus University of the Netherlands, and I made a theoretical and empirical study of hedge funds. Our idea was to determine if the amount of the fund owned by the manager affects performance and risk taking behavior. We used a continuous time framework considering management fees and the manager's stake in the fund. Our utility function was one based on behavioral finance inspired by economic Nobel Prize winning prospect theory of Daniel Kahneman, a former UBC psychology professor, and the late Amos Tversky, a Stanford mathematical psychologist. I had meetings with both of them. Together they made a great team, with Dan devising clever behavioral experiments and Amos the theory person. Many of the ideas of prospect theory are similar to the favorite-longshot bias in racing where favorites are under bet and longer odds horses are over bet. In prospect theory, the manager likes gains but hates losses even more. This loss aversion explains the non normally distributed hedge fund returns.

Our main conclusions were:

1. In the theoretical study:

    (a) The performance related component encourages funds managers to take excessive risk.
    (b) However, risk taking due to incentive fees is greatly reduced if a substantial amount of the managers own money (30%+) is in the fund. When the manager has 30%+ in the fund, the call option on other people's money drops dramatically from 18% with on manager money in the fund to less than 1%.

2. In the empirical study of 2078 hedge funds and 536 funds of funds; January 1995–November 2000, Zurich hedge fund universe:

    (a) Average returns though, both absolute and risk-adjusted, are significantly lower in the presence of incentive fees.
    (b) Even after adjusting for style differences, the average hedge fund does not make back their fees, which average 2 + 20.
    (c) Fund of funds have better performance than individual funds.

The management fee covers expenses and provides business income. These fees should moderate risk taking, as negative investment returns reduce the future stream of income from management fees. Most fund managers invest their own money in the fund. This eating your own cooking, helps to realign the motivation of the fund manager with the objectives of the other investors in the fund. The fact that hedge fund managers typically risk both their career and their own money while managing a fund is a positive sign to outside investors. The personal involvement of the manager, combined with a good and verifiable track record, could explain why outside investors are willing to invest their money in hedge funds, even though investors typically receive very limited information about hedge fund investment strategies and also possibly face poor liquidity due to lock-up periods in some funds. The loss averse hedge fund managers increase risk taking in response to the incentive fees, regardless of whether the fund value is above or below the benchmark. One would expect that the hedge fund managers own stake in the fund is an essential factor influencing the relationship between incentives and risk taking, and they find that the model predicts this.[5]

Our model indicates the hedge fund manager has a great incentive to increase risk if they do not have much of their won money in the fund and that can easily lead to large losses. An especially dangerous situation is the multibillion dollar fund with a hot fund manager who has huge bets in a narrow area with little in the fund getting high fees stored away. Since the penalties for a blowup are very low, this manager's incentive is to shoot for the fences and if fired after a blowup, walk away with the previous fees and get another hedge fund job. Examples include Victor Niederhoffer, John Merriwether, Brian Hunter and others. Some examples are discussed in Chapter 21.

Notes

[1] Thorp told me the following story: in 1968 when he was first entering the hedge fund business, he attended a meeting at the University of California at Irvine where Warren Buffett was speaking. Walking out, Ed remarked to his wife Vivian that someday that man will be the richest person in the world. He was that impressed. But he did not buy the Berkshire Hathaway stock until 1983, and it's been a terrific investment for him ever since. He gave some A shares to fund a chair in the Irvine Mathematics Department.

[2] The 2017 annual report with up to 2016 years results shows Buffett keeps winning. For those who like index funds (even me), he is essentially one with about double the S&P 500 returns.

[3] Insider Monkey (December 31, 2010) "Seeking Alpha: Best Hedge Fund Jim Simons Medallion Fund." The data and further analysis is in Ziemba and Ziemba (2007). A stony brook colleague who left that University saying they had no money told me Simon's will gives $1 billion to the University.

[4] It is also reprinted in my 2016 book, *Great Investment Ideas*.

[5] For more on this, including the math and graphs and related literature, see Kouwenberg and Ziemba (2007) and chapters in Ziemba and Ziemba (2013).

Chapter 21

How to Lose Money in Derivatives and Some Who Did

What makes futures and other hedge funds and bank trading departments fail? The common ingredient is over betting and not being diversified in some bad scenarios that can lead to disaster. Once troubles arise, it is difficult to take the necessary actions that eliminate the problem. Moreover, many hedge fund operators tend not to make decisions to minimize losses but rather tend to bet more doubling up hoping to exit the problem with a profit. Incentives, including large fees on gains and minimal penalties for losses, push managers into such risky and reckless behavior. I discuss some specific ways losses occur. To illustrate, I discuss the specific cases of Long-term capital management (LTCM), Niederhoffer's hedge fund, Amaranth and Société Generalé and list some other similar disasters. In some cases, the failures lead to contagion in other hedge funds and financial institutions. I also list other hedge fund and bank trading failures with brief comments on them.

Understanding How to Lose Helps One Avoid Losses!

I begin by discussing how to lose money in derivatives which leads to our discussion of hedge fund disasters and how to prevent them. The derivative futures industry deals with products in which one party gains what the other party loses. These are zero sum games situations. Hence, there will be large winners and large losers. The size of the gains and losses are magnified by the leverage and over betting, leading invariably to large losses when a bad scenario occurs. This industry now totals over $700 trillion of which the majority is in interest and bond derivatives with a smaller, but substantial, amount in equity derivatives. Figlewski (1994) attempted to categorize derivative disasters and this chapter discusses and expands on that:

1. *Hedge*

   In an ordinary hedge, one loses money on one side of the transaction in an effort to reduce risk. To evaluate the performance of a hedge one must consider all aspects of the transaction. In hedges where one delta hedges but is a net seller of options, there is volatility (gamma) risk which could lead to losses if there is a large price move up or down and the volatility rises. Also accounting problems can lead to losses if gains and losses on both sides of a derivatives hedge are recorded in the firm's financial statements at the same time.

2. *Counterparty default*

   Credit risk is the fastest growing area of derivatives and a common hedge fund strategy is to be short overpriced credit default derivatives. There are many ways to lose money on these shorts if they are not hedged correctly, even if they have a mathematical advantage. In addition, one may lose more if the counterpart defaults because of fraud or following the theft of funds, as was the case with the MF Global (2012) disaster.

3. *Speculation*

   Derivatives have many purposes including transferring risk from those who do not wish it (hedgers) to those who do (speculators). Speculators who take naked unhedged positions take the purest bet and win or lose monies related to the size of the move of the underlying security. Bets on currencies, interest rates, bonds and stock market index moves are common futures and futures options trades.

   Human agency problems frequently lead to larger losses for traders who are holding losing positions that if cashed out would lead to lost jobs or bonus. Some traders increase exposure exactly when they should reduce it in the hopes that a market turnaround will allow them to cash out with a small gain before their superiors find out about the true situation and force them to liquidate. Since the job or bonus may have already been lost, the trader's interests are in conflict with objectives of the firm and huge losses may occur. Writing options, and more generally selling volatility or insurance, which typically gain small profits most of the time but can lead to large losses, is a common vehicle for this problem because the size of the position accelerates quickly when the underlying security moves in the wrong direction as in the Niederhoffer disaster discussed below. Since trades between large institutions frequently are not collateralized mark-to-market large paper losses can accumulate without visible signs such as a margin call. Nick Leeson's loss betting on short puts and calls on the Nikkei is one of many such examples. The Kobe earthquake was the bad scenario that bankrupted Barings.

A proper accounting of trading success evaluates all gains and losses so that the extent of some current loss is weighed against previous gains. Derivative losses should also be compared to losses on underlying securities. For example, from January 3 to June 30, 1994, the 30-year T-bonds fell 13.6%. Hence, holders of bonds lost considerable sums as well since interest rates rose quickly and significantly.

4. *Forced liquidation at unfavorable prices*

Gap moves through stops are one example of forced liquidation. Portfolio insurance strategies based on selling futures during the October 18, 1987 stock market crash were unable to keep up with the rapidly declining market. The futures were at a large discount and fell 29% that day compared to −22% for the S&P500 cash market. Forced liquidation due to margin problems is made more difficult when others have similar positions and predicaments and this leads to contagion. The August 1998 problems of LTCM in bond and other markets were more difficult because others had followed their lead with similar positions. When trouble arose, buyers were scarce and sellers were everywhere. Another example is Metallgellschaft's (1993) crude oil futures hedging losses of over $1.3 billion. They had long-term contracts to supply oil at fixed prices for several years. These commitments were hedged with long oil futures. But when spot oil prices fell rapidly, the contracts to sell oil at high prices rose in value but did not provide current cash to cover the mark to the market futures losses. A management error led to the unwinding of the hedge near the bottom of the oil market and the disaster.

Potential problems are greater in illiquid markets. Such positions are typically long term and liquidation must be done matching sales with available buyers. Hence, forced liquidation can lead to large bid-ask spreads. Askin Capital's failure in the bond market in 1994 was exacerbated because they held very sophisticated securities which were only traded by very few counterparties so contagion occurred. Once they learned of Askin's liquidity problems and weak bargaining position, they lowered their bids even more and were then able to gain large liquidity premiums.

5. *Misunderstanding the risk exposure*

   As derivative securities have become more complex, so has their full understanding. The Nikkei put warrant trade (discussed in Chapter 15) was successful because we did a careful analysis to fairly price the securities. In many cases, losses are the result of trading in high-risk financial instruments by unsophisticated investors. Lawsuits have arisen by such investors attempting to recover some of their losses with claims that they were misled or not properly briefed on the risks of the positions taken. Since the general public and thus judges and juries find derivatives confusing and risky, even when they are used to reduce risk, such cases or their threat may be successful.

   A great risk exposure is the extreme scenario which often investors assume has zero probability when in fact they have low but positive probability. Investors are frequently unprepared for interest rate, currency or stock price changes so large and so fast that they are considered to be impossible to occur. The move of some bond interest rate spreads from 3% a year earlier to 17% in August/September 1998 led even savvy investors and very sophisticated LTCM researchers and traders down this road. The key for staying out of trouble especially with highly levered positions is to fully consider the possible futures and have enough capital or access to capital to weather bad scenario storms so that any required liquidation can be done orderly.

   Figlewski (1994) observes that the risk in mortgage backed securities is especially difficult to understand. Interest only (IO) securities, which provide only the interest part of the underlying mortgage pool's payment stream, are a good example. When interest rates rise, IO's rise since payments are reduced and the stream of interest payments is larger. But when rates rise sharply, the IO falls in value like other fixed-income instruments because the future interest payments are more heavily discounted. This signal of changing interest rate exposure was one of the difficulties in Askin's losses in 1994. Similarly, the sign change between stocks and bonds during stock market crashes as in 2000 to 2003 has caused other similar losses. Scenario dependent matrices are especially useful and needed in such situations.

6. *Forgetting that high returns involve high risk*

   If investors seek high returns, then they will usually have some large losses. The Kelly criterion strategy and its variants provide a theory to achieve very high long term returns but large losses will also occur. These losses are magnified with derivative securities and especially

with large derivative positions relative to the investor's available capital.
7. *How over betting occurs*
   Betting more than full Kelly gives more risk measured by the probability of reaching a high goal before a lower level. Virtually all of the disasters occur because of the over betting. It is easy to over bet with derivative positions as the size depends on the volatility and other parameters and is always changing. So a position safe one day can become very risky very fast.

Stochastic programming models provide a good way to try to avoid problems 1–6 by carefully modeling the situation at hand and considering the possible economic futures in an organized way.

Hedge fund and bank trading disasters almost always occur because traders over bet, the portfolio is not truly diversified and then trouble arises when a bad scenario occurs. I now list and discuss a number of sensational failures including Metalgesllshaft (1993), LTCM (1998), Niederhoffer (1997), Amaranth Advisors (2006), Merrill Lynch (2007), Société Generalé (2008), Lehman (2008), AIG (2008), Citigroup (2008), MF Global (2012) and Monti Pashi (2013). Stochastic programming models provide a way to deal with the risk control of such portfolios using an overall approach to position size, taking into account various possible scenarios that may be beyond the range of previous historical data. Since correlations are scenario dependent, this approach is useful to model the overall position size. The model will not allow the hedge fund to maintain positions so large and so under diversified that a major disaster can occur. Also the model will force consideration of how the fund will attempt to deal with the bad scenario because once there is a derivative disaster, it is very difficult to resolve the problem. More cash is immediately needed and there are liquidity and other considerations.[1]

The Failure of LTCM (1998)

There have been many hedge fund failures but LTCM stands out as a particularly public one. The firm started with the talents of the core bond traders from John Merriwether's group at the Salomon Brothers who were very successful for a number of years. When Warren Buffett came on board at Salomon the culture of this group clashed with Buffett's apparently more conservative style. In truth, Buffett's record is Kelly like and not all that different from Merriwether's group in terms of position size but Buffett's risk control is superior. He always has lots of cash to bail out any troubling trades. A new group was formed with an all star cast of top academics including two future Nobel Laureates and many top professors and students, many linked to MIT. In addition, top government officials were involved. The team was dubbed *too smart to lose* and several billion was raised even though there was no real track record, fees were very high (a 3% management expense fee plus 25% of profits) and entry investment was high $100 million minimum. The idea, according to Myron Scholes, was to be a big vacuum cleaner sucking up nickels all over the world. There were many trades, but the essence of the bond risk arbitrage was to buy underpriced bonds in various locales, sell overpriced bonds in other locales, wait for the prices to revert to their theoretical efficient market prices and then unwind the position.

These trades are similar to the Nikkei put warrant risk arbitrage discussed in Chapter 15 except that the leverage they used was much much greater. I call these bond trades *buy Italy and sell Florence*. Suppose the interest rate implied by the bond prices is higher in Italy than in Florence. But the theory is that Florence, a smaller place, would have more risk and thus higher interest rates. Hence, the trade should have an advantage and be unwound when the prices reverted to their true risk priced values. LTCM analysts made many such trades, most much more complex than this, all across the world. They also had many other complex and innovative trades. Their belief was that markets were efficient and, when temporarily out of whack, would snap back quickly. The continuous lognormal assumptions of option pricing hedging led them to take very large positions which according to their theory were close to riskless.

The plan worked and net returns for the part of the year 1994 that the fund operated were 19.9% net. The years 1995 and 1996 had similar high returns of 42.8% and 40.8% net, respectively. Indeed for the principals whose money grew fee-less, the net returns were 63% and 57%, respectively, with taxes deferred. There was so much demand for investment in the fund, which in 1997 was effectively closed to new investors, that a grey market arose with a 10% premium. By 1997, it became harder to find profitable trades and the gains fell to 17.1%. This was a good record for most but not satisfactory to LTCM's principals; among other things the S&P500 returned 31% excluding dividends. Their action was to return $2.7 billion of the $6.7 billion to the investors, a huge mistake! The principals then put in an additional $100 million raised by personal bank loans, another mistake. The banks were happy to lend this money basically unsecured. Banks and others were quite keen to loan to or invest with this group and the investors were not happy to be forced out of the fund. Still, at the start, $1 on February 24, 1994, was $2.40 net at the end of 1997. The year 1998 was difficult for the fund and then turned into a disaster following the August 17 Russian ruble devaluation and sovereign bond default. Bonds denominated in rubles trading for say 60 fell rapidly to 3 whereas Russian bonds denominated in marks or dollars only fell a few percent as they were not subject to the effects of the ruble devaluation. So long 60 short 95 say became long 3 short 92 say. Also there were defaults in currency hedging contracts which added to the losses because that hedge failed.

Such losses occur from time to time in various markets and hedge funds which over bet can be particularly vulnerable to it. The problem for LTCM was that they had $1.25 trillion of positions in notional value (that was over 2% of the world's derivatives in 1998) with a market value of $129 billion financed by $125 billion of borrowed money. They had $4 billion in equity with a leverage ratio of 32. Although the trades were all over the world and hence it seemed they were diversified, they in fact were not. What happened was a scenario dependent correlation situation like that modeled in the Innovest pension fund application described in Chapter 19. There was an underlying variable that frequently lurks its ugly head in disasters, that being *investor confidence*. All the bond rates increased for non-high quality debt. For example, emerging market debt was trading for 3.3% above US T-bonds in October 1997, then 6% in July 1998 was an astounding 17% in September 1998.

LTCM was unable to weather the storm of this enormous crisis of confidence and lost about 95% of their capital, some $4.6 billion including most of the principals' and employees' considerable accumulated fees. The $100 million loan actually put some of them into bankruptcy, although others came out better financially. It did not help that they unwound liquid positions first rather than across all liquidity levels as the two Nobel Prize winners Robert Merton and Myron Scholes recommended, nor that many other copy-cat firms had similar positions, nor that LTCM had created enemies by being so skilled and so brash, nor that the lack of monitoring of margin by brokers eager for their business allowed the positions to grow to over bet levels. A pivotal decision was returning the $2.7 billion to investors. They could have kept the funds in liquid low-risk assets to buffer their mounting losses. However, had they kept the funds they might have made even more risky plays. Returning this money reflected their greediness. They simply wanted to make a higher rate of return with similar positions on a smaller capital base.[2] Smart people bounce back and possibly learn from their mistakes. Various ex-LTCM members joined new hedge funds and other ventures. The lessons are:

- Do not over bet, it is too dangerous.
- VaR type systems are inadequate to measure true risk but see Jorion's (2007) excellent book on VaR and Dunbar's (2000) discussion of the VaR calculations used by LTCM. LTCM analysts did a very careful analysis but the problem was that the risk control method of VaR which is used in regulations does not really protect hedge funds that are so highly levered because you are not penalized enough for large losses. Indeed if you lose $10 million it is penalized the same as losing $100 million if the VaR number is $9 million of losses. CVaR partially addresses this limitation but what you really need are convex penalties so that penalties are more than proportional to losses.
- You really do need to use scenario dependent correlation matrices and consider extreme scenarios. LTCM was not subject to VaR regulation but still used it.
- Be aware of and consider extreme scenarios.
- Allow for extra illiquidity and contract defaults. LTCM also suffered because of the copycat firms which put on similar positions and unwound them at the same time in August/September 1998.
- Really diversify (to quote Soros from the Quantum Funds, "we risked 10% of our funds in Russia and lost it, $2 billion, but we are still up 21% in 1998").
- Historical correlations work when you do not need them and fail when you need them in a crisis when they approach one. Real correlations are scenario dependent. Sorry to be repetitive, but this is crucial.

Good information on the demise of LTCM and the subsequent $3.5 billion bailout by major brokerage firms organized by the FED are in a Harvard Business School case by André Perold (1998), and articles by Philippe Jorion (2000) and Franklin Edwards (1999). Eventually the positions converged and the bailout team was able to emerge with a profit on their investment.

The currency devaluation of some two thirds was no surprise to me. In 1992, we were the guests in St Petersburg of Professor Zari Rachev, an expert in stable and heavy-tail distributions and editor of the first handbook

Exchanging currencies in St Petersburg

in North Holland's Series on Finance (Rachev, 2003) of which I was the series editor. On arrival I gave him a $100 bill and he gave me four inches of 25 Ruble notes. Our dinner out cost two inches for the four of us; and drinks were extra in hard currency. So we are in the Soros camp; make bets in Russia (or similar risky markets) if you have an edge without risking too much of your wealth. Where was the money lost? The score card according to Dunbar (2000) was a loss of $4.6 billion. Emerging market trades such as those similar to the *buy Italy, sell Florence* lost $430 million. Directional, macro trades lost $371 million. Equity pairs trading lost 306 million. Short long-term equity options, long short term equity lost $1.314 billion. Fixed income arbitrage lost $1.628 billion.

The bad scenario of investor confidence that led to much higher interest rates for lower quality debt and much higher implied equity volatility had a serious effect on all the trades. The long–short equity options trades, largely in the CAC40 and Dax equity indices, were based on a historical volatility of about 15% versus implieds of about 22%. Unfortunately, in the bad scenario, the implieds reached 30% and then 40%. With smaller positions, the fund could have waited it out but with such huge levered positions, it could not. Equity implieds can reach 70% or higher as Japan's Nikkei did in 1990/1991 and stay there for many months.

Niederhoffer's Hedge Fund Disaster and the Imported Crash of October 27 and 28, 1997

The Asian Financial crises was a series of banking and currency crises that developed in various Asian countries beginning in mid-1997. Many East and Southeast Asian countries had currency pegs to the US dollar which made it easy for them to attract financing but lacked adequate foreign reserves to cover the outstanding debt. Their pegs to the US dollar and low interest rates encouraged mismatches in currency (debts were in US dollars, loans in local currency) and maturities. Spending and expectations that led to borrowing were too high and Japan, the main driver of these economies, was facing a consumer slowdown, so its imports dropped. So effectively these countries were long yen and short dollars. A large increase in the US currency in yen terms exacerbated the crisis, which began after speculators challenged the Thai Baht and spread through the region. The countries had to devalue their currencies, interest rates rose and stock prices fell. Also, several hedge funds took significant losses. Most notably, Victor Niederhoffer's fund, which had an excellent previous record with only modest drawdowns, but his large long bet on cheap Thai stocks that became cheaper and cheaper quickly turned $120 million into $70 million. Further buying on dips added to losses. Finally, the fund created a large short position in out-of-the-money S&P futures index puts including the November 830's trading for about $4–6 at various times around August–September 1997.

The crisis devastated the economies of Malaysia, Singapore, Indonesia, etc. Finally, it spread to Hong Kong, where the currency was pegged to the US dollar at 7.8. The peg supported Hong Kong's trade and investment hub and was to be defended at all costs. In this case, the weapon used was higher interest rates which almost always lead to a stock market crash after a lag; see Chapter 14. The US S&P500 was not in the danger zone in October 1997 by my models nor, I presume, by those of others. Also, trade with Hong Kong and Asia, though substantial, was only a small part of the US trade. Many US investors thought that this Asian currency crisis was a small problem because it did not affect Japan very much. In fact, Japan caused a lot of it.

A Wild Week, October 20–25, 1997

The week of October 20–25, 1997 was difficult for equity markets with the Hang Seng dropping sharply. The S&P was also shaky. The November 830 puts were 60 cents on Monday, Tuesday and Wednesday but rose to 1.20 on Thursday and 2.40 on Friday. The Hang Seng dropped over 20% in a short period including a 10% drop on Friday, October 25th. The S&P500 was at 976 substantially above 830 as of Friday's close. A further 5% drop in Hong Kong on Monday, October 27 led to a panic in the S&P500 futures later on Monday in the US. They fell 7% from 976 to 906 which was still considerably above 830. On Tuesday morning there was a further fall of 3% to 876 still keeping the 830 puts out of the money. The full fall in the S&P500 was then 10%.

But the volatility exploded and the 830s climbed to the $16 area. Refco called in Niederhoffer's puts mid morning on Tuesday, resulting in the fund losing about $20 million. So Niederhoffer's $70 million fund was bankrupt and actually in the red as the large position in these puts and other instruments turned the $70 million into −$20 million. The S&P500 bottomed out around 876, moving violently in a narrow range then settling. By the end of the week, it returned to the 976 area. So it really was a tempest in a teapot. Investors who were short equity November 830 puts (SPXs) were required to put up so much margin that they had small positions so they weathered the storm. Their $4–6, while temporarily behind at $16 did

Cartoon from the *Economist*

eventually go to zero. So did the futures puts, but futures shorters are not required to post as much margin. If they did not have adequate margin because they had too many positions, they could have easily been forced to cover at a large loss. Futures margins, at least for equity index products, do not fully capture the real risk inherent in these positions. I follow closely the academic studies on risk measures and none of the papers I know address this issue properly. When in doubt, always bet less. Niederhoffer is back in business having profited by this experience. (Whoops — maybe not, see the postscript!)

One of my Vancouver neighbors lost $16 million in one account and $4 million in another account. The difference being the time given to cash out and cover the short puts. I was in this market also and won in the equity market and lost in futures. I did learn how much margin you actually need in futures which I now use in such trading which has been very profitable with a few proprietary wrinkles to protect oneself that I need to keep confidential.

The lessons for hedge funds are much as with LTCM. Do not over bet, do diversify, watch out for extreme scenarios. Even the BSEYD measure to keep one out of potentially large falls mentioned above did not work in October 1997. That was an imported fear-induced stock market crash which was not really based on the US economy or investor sentiment. Most crashes occur when the most liquid long bond interest rates relative to the earnings measures by the reciprocal of price earnings ratios are too high. Almost always when that happens there is a crash (a 10% plus fall in equity prices from the current price level within one year), see Chapter 14 for the 1987 US, the 1990 Japan, the US in 2000, the US in 2001, which predicted the 22% fall in the S&P500 in 2002 and China, Iceland and the US in 2006–2009 are leading examples. Interestingly the BSEYD measure moved out of the danger zone following the 2000 crash. Then, in mid-2001, it was even more in the danger zone than in 1999 because stock prices fell but earnings fell more, In 2003, the measure then moved into the buy zone and predicted the rise in the S&P500 in 2003. No measure is perfect but this measure adds value and tends to keep you out of extreme trouble.

Ziemba–Schwartz (1991) used a difference method and the results of that are in Ziemba (2003). I started using these measures in 1988 in my study group at Yamaichi Research, Japan. The study predicted the 1987 crash. It also predicted the 1990 Japan crash. I told Yamaichi executives about this in 1989, but they would not listen. Yamaichi went bankrupt in

1995; they would have survived if they had listened.[3] From 1948 to 1988 that every time the measure was in the danger zone there was a fall of 10% or more with no misses. This was 12 of 12 with 8 other 10%+ crashes occurring for reasons other than high interest rates relative to earnings. In late 1989, the model had the highest reading ever in the danger zone and predicted the January 1990 start of the Japanese stock market crash.

A mini crash caused by some extraneous event can occur any time. So to protect oneself positions must *never* be too large. Those who had too many positions had to cash out and suffer large losses because they had to satisfy the increased margin required due to of the drop in price and the increase in implied volatility.[4]

Over betting Yields Frequent Trading Disasters

The best way to achieve victory is to master all the rules for disaster, and then concentrate on avoiding them.
In America, people get a second chance ... they don't get a third.

Victor Niederhoffer

After Niederhoffer's failure in 1997, his fund was closed and he lost much of his personal fortune, reputation and happiness. He had failed in 1997 because he greatly over bet, did not diversify and a bad scenario wiped him out. Was this a one time occurrence from which he learned or is it just one of a sequence of similar outcomes? Niederhoffer is a multitalented individual graduating with a PhD in 1969 from the Graduate School of Business, at the University of Chicago where Professor Gene Fama, Merton Miller and other great finance theorists and practitioners are on the faculty. Since his work was against the prevailing efficient markets theory and highly data dependent, he was more comfortable with the statisticians and was supervised by perhaps the world's top Bayesian statistician, Professor Arnold Zellner. Earlier at Harvard, his senior thesis "non randomness in stock prices: a new model of price movements" challenged random walk theory. He argued that stocks followed patterns such as Monday falls if Friday fell.

In 1967, with his PhD thesis unfinished and the title "top US squash player", he headed to the finance department of the University of California, Berkeley business school. I was there then as well but never met Niederhoffer, being a graduate student. Victor was also a whiz at chess and tennis, dating back to his Harvard undergraduate days. I was friendly with one finance legend Professor Barr Rosenberg who went on to greatness in a number of investment areas such as founding the Berkeley Program in Finance, the firm BARRA and later Rosenberg Investments. Both Barr and Victor, like I, were looking for anomalies to beat markets. In 1967, Barr discovered that small caps and low price to book stocks out performed the broad market. This observation forms the basis of the famous Fama–French (1992) factors 25 years later; see Rosenberg, Reid and Lanstein (1985). While Barr stuck to institutional investing with low or no leverage, Victor was a high stakes futures trader using lots of leverage. Hence, if he was right, then the gains were very high but if he was wrong and his risk control was faulty, then there could be substantial losses.

While teaching at Berkeley, Victor co-founded a small investment bank, Niederhoffer, Cross and Zeckhauser (NCZ). Frank Cross was a former Merrill Lynch executive and Richard Zeckhauser, a friend from his Harvard days. Zeckhauser went on to become a well-known economist at the Kennedy School of Government and an avid bridge player. NCZ started with just $400, did mail-order mergers, and sold small private companies to buyers. In 1979, Niederhoffer went into commodities and had great success, averaging 35% net for 15 years through the mid-1990s. George Soros gave him a private $100 million account in 1981 and Niederhoffer traded that until 1993. This account was shut down because, as Soros said, "he temporarily lost his edge... he made money while the markets were sloshing along aimlessly. Then he started losing money and had the integrity to close out the account. We came out ahead." Earlier in 1983, Zeckhauser quit NCZ to return to full time teaching and research partially because of Niederhoffer's high level of risk taking, saying that "no matter what your edge, you can lose everything. You hope and believe he will learn his lesson." Cross died and NCZ became Niederhoffer Henkel and was then run by Lee Henkel, the former general council for the IRS.

After the 1997 blowout, it was hard for Niederhoffer to start again as there was fear of another large drawdown despite his long superior track record. So he began trading for his own account after mortgaging his house. In 2000, he started writing investment columns on websites with Laurel Kenner and in 2001 it paid off. Mustafa Zaida, a Middle East investor set up the offshore hedge fund Matador with $2 million and recruited Niederhoffer as the trading advisor. To reign in Niederhoffer's exuberance for risk, the fund would invest only in US based S&P500 futures and options. The claim was that Niederhoffer had learned his lesson not to invest in markets he did not understand like Thailand which got him on the road to destruction in 1997. A management fee of 2.5% + 22% of the net new profits was substantial. Yet, with good performance, Matador grew to $350 million from non-US investors. Zaida said that "He's definitely learned his lesson." Recall that it was the S&P500 November largely 830 puts that turned $70 million into −$20 million in 1997 after $50 million was lost in Thai equities. Niederhoffer always thinks big and bold so Matador was not enough. In April 2005, Niederhoffer started Manchester Partners, LLC for US investors, named for the Silver Cup given to the winner of the Manchester Cup Steeplechase in 1904. This trophy was one of the many art objects Niederhoffer has collected over the years and hung onto. Manchester's fees were 1% + 20%, and could trade other than the S&P500 market such as fixed income and currencies. Steve "Mr Wiz" Wisdom was Niederhoffer's risk control aide, hoping to have consistent 25%+ returns with maximum losses of 15–20% in 1 month. The bond–stock crash measure flagged a red signal at the end of 2001 because earnings dropped more than stock prices. My confidential investor sentiment model based on relative put/call option prices flashed red in Q4 of 2002. And indeed there was a substantial fall in the S&P500 in July 2002; Matador lost 30.22% in that month.

Still the February 2002 to April 2006 Matador record was a +338% gain, 41% net annualized, $350 million in assets and only 5 losses in 51 months, with a 2.81 Sharpe ratio. This record earned Matador the #1 ranking in 2004, 2005 and 2006 for funds managing $50+ million.

Manchester had only 3 monthly losses in the 13 months from its start in April 2005 to April 2006, a cumulative gain of 89.9%. The approach had the following elements (from Manchester Trading, 2006):

Scientific Rigorous statistical methodologies form the foundation of our proprietary pattern recognition process.
Empirical 'What can be tested, must be tested'. Validation through testing is the basis for all trade recommendations, impact planning and margin assessment.
Innovative Multidisciplinary inquiry draws from such diverse fields as speech processing, information theory and data compression to provide insight and inspiration.
Contrarian Crowd behavior tends to create profitable opportunities. I am more often than not counter trend traders.
Focused Undiluted application of our edge leaves the critical diversification decision in the hands of our investors.

For short-term discretionary day trading:

- Systematic identification of high probability trades.
- Analysis across multiple markets and multiple timeframes.
- Flexible analytical methodology sensitive to changing cycles.
- Tactical execution reduces friction and slippage.

And for the option trading:

- Empirical option pricing versus implied volatility method.
- Strategic/opportunistic seller of expensive premium.
- Forecasting techniques applied to margin pathways enhances risk modeling.
- Flexible position across multiple strikes and timeframes.
- Highly sensitive ongoing measurement of overall liquidity and margin pathway forecasting refines leverage assessment.

And what did they learn from the 1997 blowout:

- We learned our lesson and got back on our feet **fast**.
- We stick with markets and instruments we know.
- We focus on liquidity.
- We are alert to the increasing probability of extreme events, measure their potential impact and prepare for them.
- We implement safeguards and continue to refine trading and risk assessment procedures to ensure survival.

They say it cannot happen again because:

- We tailor our risk profile at all times cognizant of the impact and opportunity extreme events can bring about.
- We are constantly innovating but remain focused on what works empirically. We don't stray from our core strategy.
- Substantial co-investment by the principals of the firm is the most powerful statement we can possibly make with regard to our long-term commitment to our partners.

Manchester does not like to diversify and their literature says that:

> We choose not to diversify or manage the volatility of our fund to a benchmark or index as we believe our clients and their asset allocation advisors are in a far better position to make accurate and economical diversification decisions than we are (Manchester, 2006).

Niederhofer has historically had a long bias in his trades which frequently have 3–6 times leverage with borrowed money.

On May 10, 2006 the Russian New Europe (RNE) fund, was trading at a 37% premium to net asset value according the *Barron's*. RNE treated me well over the years with high returns and generous capital gains and dividends. But a 37% premium was extraordinary. The bond–stock model and the short-term investor sentiment option models I use were both way out of the danger zone and did not predict the subsequent decline. That weekend was a local peak and the S&P500 fell about 7% in the next month with many emerging markets falling 20%+. RNE fell more about 40% to a no premium level. The twig that got the equity markets going on the downside was the threat of higher Japanese interest rates. This caused some hedge funds with yen carry trades to unwind their positions which meant selling the S&P500 and emerging market equities. It also caused them to look closer at high-yielding emerging market currencies and bonds such as Turkey, South Africa and Iceland. Although these have high yields, thus making them attractive for carry trades, they also have high current account deficits. Investors feared both higher interest rates and a higher yen in which they had short positions.

The Matador fund lost 30.22% in May turning a 2006 gain of 31% to −6% at the end of May. The market was down 3% but Niederhoffer was so leveraged that the loss was magnified 10 times to some $100 million. This hedge ratio of 10 means that Niederhoffer must have been massively net long S&P500 futures and/or short S&P500 equity and/or futures puts. This is a huge long position that is not risk control safe and subject to large losses with a modest drop in the S&P500. A medium S&P500 drop, see below, would likely have led to losses in the 50% area and a large 10%+ drop to losses of 75%+. Niederhoffer said "I had a bad May. I made some mistakes, that's regrettable ... but one sparrow does not make a spring; and nor does one bad month." June 2006 continued badly with the Matador fund down 12% for 2006. When the May to July debacle in the S&P500 ended it was down about 7% but Matador lost 67% and Manchester 45%. Both funds are still trading and the saga continues, see below. I maintain the two rules: do not over bet and do diversify in **all** scenarios. One can still make good gains in the S&P500 futures and options and other markets. But somewhat smaller than 30–40% gains are most likely but presumable without blowouts if one has position sizes such that the fund or account will weather a 3–7% decline in 1–4 days or a 10–15% decline over a month.

My experience is that with proper risk control in the S&P500 market, which is not diversified, can yield net gains in the 15–30% to perhaps 25% range but 60+% is usually attainable only with substantial risk that likely will cause a large loss if a bad scenario occurs. Of course, other strategies could yield such higher returns as shown by Blair Hull, Jim Simons, Harry McPike and others and even with me in the AlphaZ Futures Fund, up more than 100% in less than 2 years during 2016 and more later. As of mid July 2017, my original $300,000 investor with reduced friend fees has about $1,900,000 net.

Niederhoffer was given a third chance after all! The May to July blowout is seen in the 8.4% returns in the last 12 months down from 89.9% as of April 2006. But the fund gained 20.44% in January 2007 and the April 5, 2005 to end January 2007 net returns are back to 83.72%, well above the S&P500. So Niederhoffer is back in business once again ... perhaps till the next time.

The Amaranth Advisors Natural Gas Hedge Fund Disaster (2006)

On September 19, 2006 the hedge fund Amaranth Advisors of Greenwich, Connecticut announced that it had lost $6 billion, about two thirds of the $9.25 billion fund, in less than 2 weeks, largely because it was overexposed in the natural gas market. Amaranth's experience shows how a series of trades can undermine the strategy of such a hedge fund and investors' assets. The Greenwich, Connecticut fund which was founded in 2000, employed hundreds in a large investment space with other offices in Toronto, London and Singapore. I analyze how Amaranth became so overexposed, whether risk control strategies could have prevented the liquidation and how these trends reflect the current state of the financial industry. I have argued that the recipe for hedge fund disaster almost always has three parts: A trader:

1. Over bets relative to one's capital and the volatility of the trading instruments used;
2. Is not diversified in all scenarios that could occur; and
3. A negative scenario occurs that is plausible *ex post* and likely *ex ante* although the negative outcome may have never occurred before in the particular markets the fund is trading.

One might expect that these two interrelated risk factors (1) and (2) would be part of the risk control assessment of hedge funds. These risks become more pronounced as the total amount trading grows — especially when trading billions. But are risks assessed in this way?

A knowledgeable risk control expert, realizing that the position is not fully diversified and you need scenario dependent correlation matrices, would simply tell the traders that they cannot hold positions (1) and (2) since in some scenarios they will have large losses. Efficient market types have a lot to learn about real risk control. Hedges are not essentially risk free. Even a simple model would say that bets should not be made under conditions (1) and (2) because they are far too dangerous. Medium-sized hedge funds are likely reasonably diversified. Some type of risk control process is now standard but these systems are mostly based on the industry standard value at risk (VaR) and that is usually not enough protection in (3) as the penalty for large losses is not great enough.

On occasion, even at a large fund, a rogue trader will have such a successful trading run that careful risk control is no longer applied. Instead, people focus on the returns generated, the utility function of the trader and that of the partners of the fund, rather than the longer-term utility function of the investors in the fund. Rogue trades — those that violate (1) and (2) — can be made as long as (3) never occurs. In the case of Amaranth's natural gas bets, their leverage was about 8:1 so $7 was borrowed for every $1 the fund had from its clients. Positions were on exchanges and over the counter and were thus very vulnerable. Those not skilled in risk control can argue that situation (3) which is great enough to wipe them out, simply would not occur because it is far too improbable, that is too far in the tails of the distribution of the underlying asset. They would typically assign zero to the probability of such rare events.

Even skilled risk control experts such as Jorion (2007) and Till (2006) refer to LTCM as an 8-sigma event and Amaranth as a 9-sigma event. The problem is that even modified VaR gives erroneous results and is not safe. Such wipeouts occur with events far more frequent than 8 or 9 sigma: 3-sigma is more like it. Till (2006) argues that daily volatility of Amaranth's portfolio was 2% making the September losses 9-sigma, but the possible losses are not stationary. I argue that this analysis is misleading; the 2% is with normal not negative low probability disaster scenarios. Furthermore, diversification can easily fail, if, as is typical, it is based on simply averaging the past data rather than with scenario dependent correlation matrices. It is the diversification or lack thereof according to the given scenario that is crucially important, not the average past correlation across the assets in the portfolio.

The Nature of the Oil and Natural Gas Market

The crude oil market from November 1, 2005 to November 28, 2006 experienced much price volatility usually above $60 and at times exceeding the August 30, 2005 post Katrina high of $70+. The oil prices peaked at $77 in July 2006 then declined to around $60 for much of the fall. This decline coincided with the decline in the price of natural gas in September 2006. At that time widely watched weather-forecasting centers predicted that the hurricane season would not have major storms and that the winter would be mild. Previously on August 29, September natural gas suddenly rose sharply in the last half hour of trading. Why is not known — but manipulation might have been involved. For Brian Hunter, who was short September and long spring months, both events caused massive losses.[5]

Starting from over $11/million BTU, the futures prices fell to about $5. The event that triggered the Amaranth crisis was the drop in the price of natural gas from $8 in mid-July to around $5 in September. Since gas prices have climbed to $15 and fallen to $2 in recent years, such a drop is plausible in one's scenario set and should have been considered. There are fat tails in these markets. There is a large difference between the daily and long term moving average price of natural gas, making it a very volatile commodity. Thus, such a drop is not a 8–9 sigma event. In the 1990s, natural gas traded for $2–3 per million BTUs. However, by the end of 2000 it reached $10 and then by September 2001 fell back to under $2.

The NYMEX natural gas futures prices from November 1, 2005 to November 22, 2006 which shows much price volatility. The November 22 price of $7.718 had recovered 50% from the September lows.

A chronology of the collapse presents a day-by-day recreation of Amaranth's possible losses including the disastrous last 2 months and final collapse (a loss of $560 million on September 14, 2006) by Till (2006). Davis (2006) and Davis et al. (2006, 2007) discuss the bailout saga and some of the winners and losers. They describe how Amaranth scrambled to unload their positions that were losing more and more day by day:

September 16 Agreed to pay Merrill Lynch approximately $250 million to take over some positions.
September 17 Agreed to pay Goldman $185 million.
September 18 Gave up on Goldman deal when clearing agent JP Morgan would not release collateral.

September 20 Paid JP Morgan and Citadel $2.15 billion to take remaining trades after Amaranth absorbed a further $800 million in trading losses.

Valuing a Fund

Actually the statement that Amaranth had $9.25 billion on September 1 is a bit of a stretch because that was the mark-to-the-market value of their portfolio, the value on which fees were charged. But, in fact, with an estimated 250,000+ natural gas contracts (about 30% of the market), an enormous position built up over the previous 2 years, the liquidating value of the portfolio was lower even before (3), the crisis. As a comparison, in his heyday in the 1990s, a large position for legendary hedge fund trader George Soros of the Quantum Fund was 5,000 contracts. Even with one contract you can lose a lot of money: up to $20,000 in a few days. Indeed much of the previous profits were derived by pushing up of long natural gas prices in an illiquid market. I once had 7% of the ValueLine/S&P500 spread futures market. Even at that level it is very difficult to get out should the market turn on you. With those January effect trades, one has a fairly well defined exit point and the futures cannot deviate too much from the cash spread but even that level is too high and risky.

So the real profits were actually much lower. Those who liquidated Amaranth's positions bought them at a substantial discount. JP Morgan Chase, Amaranth's natural gas clearing broker made at least $725 million after taking over most of Amaranth's positions [Davis (2006), Davis et al. (2006, 2007)]. Of course, with different data forecasts such discrepancies might still occur occasionally but if they are consistently there, assumptions or risk assessments may be questioned.

The trigger for the crisis was a substantial drop in natural prices largely because of high levels of stored gas, coupled with a perceived drop in demand due to changing weather, altering the seasonal pattern of trade. The trading theory was based on the dubious assumption that the natural gas market would underprice winter from summer natural gas prices.

Background, Adapted from Till (2006)

The natural gas market has two main seasons: high demand in winter and generally lower demand in spring and fall. Storage facilitates provide some smoothing of the price. However, in the US, there is inadequate storage capacity for the peak winter demand. Therefore, the winter natural gas contracts trade at ever increasing premiums to summer and fall months to both encourage storage and the creation of more production and storage capacity. Basically the market tries to lock in the value of storage by buying summer and fall natural gas and selling winter natural gas forward.

The prices of summer and fall futures contracts typically trade at a discount to the winter contracts (*contango*) thus providing a return for storing natural gas. An owner of a storage facility can buy summer natural gas and simultaneously sell winter natural gas via the futures markets. This difference is the operators return for storage.

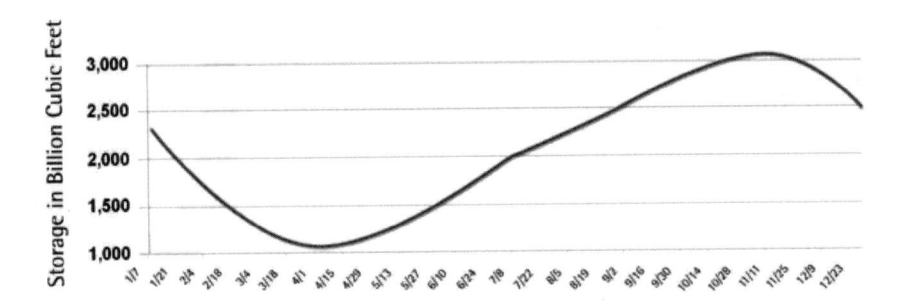

When the summer futures contract matures, the storage operator can take delivery of the natural gas, and inject it into storage. Later when the winter futures contract matures, the operator can make delivery of the natural gas by drawing it out of storage. The figure below shows the average natural gas inventory level in BCF during the year from 1994 to 2005. As long as the operators financing and physical outlay costs are under the spread locked in through the futures market, this will be profitable. This is a simplified version of how storage operators can choose to monetize their physical assets. Sophisticated storage operators actually value their storage facilities as an option on calendar-spreads. Storage is worth more if the calendar spreads in natural gas are volatile. As a calendar spread trades in steep contango, storage operators can buy the near-month contracts and sell the further-out month contracts, knowing that they can ultimately realize the value of this spread through storage. But a preferable scenario would be for the spread to then tighten, which means that they can trade out of the spread at a profit. Later, if the spread trades in wide contango again, they can reinitiate a purchase of the near-month versus far-month natural gas spread. As long as the spread is volatile, the operator/trader can continually lock in profits, and if they cannot trade out of the spread at a profit, they can then take physical delivery and realize the value of their storage facility that way. Till (2006) believes that both storage operators and natural gas producers were the ultimate counterparties to Amaranth's spread trading.

In the winter, natural gas demand is inelastic. If cold weather comes early then there is fear that existing storage will not be sufficient so prices are bid up. The fear of inadequate supplies lasts for the entire heating season. Winter 2005 was an example. At the end of the winter, storage could be completely depleted. For example during February to March 2003, prices had moved up intraday $5.00/MMBtu, but settled only $2.50 higher, which is why Amaranth hoped for a long winter. As a weak hedge they short the summer (April to October). Demand for injection gas is spread throughout the summer and peak usage for electricity demand occurs in July/August. Being more elastic, this part of the curve does not rise as fast as the winter in a upward moving market. This was their hedge.

The National Weather Service issued an *el niño* forecast for the 2006–2007 winter so gas storage was at an all-time record and the spreads were out very wide. This plus the fact that the market basically knew about Amaranth's positions, led to their downfall, which was a result of their faulty risk control.

The Trade and the Rogue Trader

Lets take a closer look at the trade that destabilized Amaranth. Brian Hunter, a 32 year old Canadian from Calgary, had fairly simple trades but of enormous size. He had a series of successful returns. As a youth in Alberta he could not afford ski tickets but at 24, with training as an instant expert on derivatives from courses at the University of Alberta (including two colleagues of mine), he headed to a trading career. He was bold and innovative with nerves of steel while holding enormous positions. Typically he was net long with long positions in natural gas in the winter months (November to March) and short positions in the summer months (April to October).

Amaranth Advisors was a multi-strategy fund, which is quite fashionable these days since they only have one layer of fees rather than the two layers in a fund of funds. On their website it states: "Amaranth's investment professionals deploy capital in a broad spectrum of alternative investment and trading strategies in a highly disciplined, risk controlled manner." They provide a false sense of security from the assumed diversification across strategies. The problem is that diversification strategies can be correlated rather than hedged or independent, especially in extreme scenario cases. As a result, too much can be invested in any one strategy negating diversification. In the case of Amaranth, some 58% of assets were tied up in Hunter's gas trades but risk adjusted, these trades made up 70–90% of Amaranth's capital allocation.

Hunter made huge profits for Amaranth by placing bullish bets on natural gas prices in 2005, the year Hurricane Katrina shocked natural gas refining and production. Hoping to repeat the gains, Amaranth wagered with a 8:1 leverage that the difference between the March and April futures price of natural gas for 2007 and 2008 would widen. Instead it narrowed. The spread between April and March 2007 contracts went from $2.49 at the end of August 2006 to $0.58 by the end of September 2006. Historically, the spread in future prices for the March and April contracts have not been easily predictable. The spread is dependent on meteorological and political events whose uncertainty makes the placing of such large bets a precarious matter.

Jack Doueck of Stillwater Capital pointed out that while a good hedge fund investor has to pick good funds to invest in, the key to success in this business, is not to choose the best performing managers, but actually to avoid the frauds and blowups. Frauds can take on various forms including a misappropriation of funds, as in the case of Cambridge, run by John Natale out of Red Bank, NJ, or a mis-reporting of returns as in the case of Lipper, Beacon Hill or the Manhattan Fund. Blowups usually occur when a single person at the hedge fund has the power to become desperate and *bet the ranch* with leverage. With both frauds and blowups, contrary to public opinion (and myth), size does *not* seem matter: examples include Beacon Hill ($2 billion), Lipper ($5 billion) and Amaranth ($9 billion).

Amaranth's investors will be seeking answers to questions including: to what extent did leverage and concentration play a role in recent outsized losses? I think the latter; (1) and (2) are the main causes here of the setup before the bad scenario caused the massive losses.

Is Learning Possible?

Do traders and researchers really learn from their trading errors? Some do but many do not. Or more precisely, do they care? What lessons are taken from the experience? Hunter previously worked for Deutsche Bank. In December 2003, his natural gas trading group was up $76 million for the year. Then it lost $51.2 million in a single week leading to Hunter's departure from the Deutsche Bank. Then Hunter blamed "an unprecedented and unforeseeable run-up in gas prices." At least he thought about extreme scenarios. Later, in a lawsuit, he argued that while Deutsche Bank had losses, his group did not.

Later in July 2006, after having billion dollar swings in his portfolio (January to April +$2B, −$1B in May when prices for autumn delivery fell, +$1B in June), he said that "the cycles that play out in the oil market can take several years, whereas in natural gas, cycles are several months." The markets are unpredictable but, most successful traders would lower their bets in such markets. My experience is that when you start losing, you are better off taking money off the table, not doubling up in the hope of recouping the losses. It is better to lose some resources and be able to survive than to risk being fully wiped out. However, instead they increased the bets.

Amaranth was a favorite of hedge funds of funds, investment pools that buy into various portfolios to try to minimize risk. Funds of funds operated by well known and successful investment firms Morgan Stanley, Credit Suisse, Bank of New York, Deutsche Bank and Man Investments all had stakes in Amaranth as of June 30, 2006. From September 2000 to November 30, 2005, the compound annual return to investors, net of all costs was a decent, but not impressive, 14.72%. This is net of their 1.5% management fee and 20% of the net new profits. Amaranth had liquidated a significant part of its positions in relatively easy to sell securities like convertible bonds, leveraged loans and blank check companies or special purpose acquisition companies. Liquid investments were sold at a small discount while others, like portfolios of mortgage-backed securities, commanded a steeper discount.

As is common among hedge funds, Amaranth severely restricts the ability of investors to cash in their holdings. For example, investors can withdraw money only on the anniversary of their investments and then, only with 90 day's notice. If they try to withdraw at any point outside that time frame there is a 2.5% penalty. If investors redeem more than 7.5% of the fund's assets, Amaranth can refuse further withdrawals.

My experience is that if you lose 50% of a $2 million fund, you will have a hard time relocating to a new fund or raising new money, but if you lose 50% of $2 billion the job fund prospects are much better. So Hunter moved on to Amaranth whose founder and chief executive, Nick Maounis, said on August 11, 2006, that more than a dozen members of his risk management team served as a check on his star gas trader "what Brian is really, really good at is taking controlled and measured risk." Nick will forever eat these words.

Amaranth said they had careful risk control but they did not really use it. Some 50% of assets in one volatile market is not really very diversified at any time and is especially vulnerable in a crash and doubly so if one's bets make up a large percent of the market. Such a large position is especially dangerous when the other traders in the market know a fund is overextended in this way and many hedge funds such as Citadel and JP Morgan were on the other side of the market. Then, when the crisis occurred, spreads widened, adding to the losses. Hunter's response was to bet more and more (in effect doubling up) until these trades lost so much they had to be liquidated. That is exactly what one should not do based on risk control considerations, but, as discussed below, it makes some sense with traders' utility functions.

Successful traders make a large number of hopefully independent favorable bets which, although they may involve a lot of capital, are not a large percent of the capital nor are they in an illiquid market should one need to liquidate. Warren Buffett's Berkshire Hathaway closed-end hedge fund frequently makes $1 billion risky bets but these have a substantial edge (positive expected value) and about 1% or less of Berkshire Hathaway's more than 140 billion capital. The insurance business brings in a constant flow of billions of dollars in premiums. So Berkshire always has a lot of cash to invest with Buffett keeping billions in cash equivalent reserves for security and good opportunities. A typical Buffett trade was a loan of some $945 million to the Williams pipeline company of Oklahoma at some 34% interest in 2002 during the stock market crash, when the oil price was low and the pipeline company was in deep financial trouble. Banks refused to bail them out. But Buffett knew he had good collateral with the land, pipeline and buildings. Williams recovered largely due to this investment and better markets and paid off the loan early. Berkshire Hathaway made a large profit. In the 2007–2009 stock market crisis and decline, Buffett made $5–10 billion loans to GE and Goldman Sachs which were both in deep financial trouble. In return he got preferred shares paying a 10% dividend plus free warrant options on the stock of GE and GS. Later, when those were cashed in, Berkshire made billions in profits.

The problem is that rogue traders are grown in particular organizations and are allowed by the industry. While they are winning, they are called great traders, then they become rogue traders when they blow up their funds. The Hunter case is similar to those of Nick Leeson and Victor Niedorhoffer but different than LTCM. In the first three cases, there was a major emphasis on trade in one basic commodity. The trouble was the risk control, namely our (1) and (2) and combined with the bad scenario (3). As discussed below the firm's and rogue trader's utility function likely caused this problem by making it optimal for these utility functions to over bet. LTCM is much more subtle. The confidence scenario that hit them was the result of faulty risk control based on VaR and historical data. They needed scenario dependent correlation matrices.

Possible Utility Functions of Hedge Fund Traders

One way to rank investors is by my symmetric downside Sharpe ratio (DSSR). By that measure, investors with few and small losses and good sized gains have large DSSRs. Berkshire Hathaway has a DSSR of about 0.917 for the period 1985–2000. The DSSR of both the Harvard and Ford Foundations endowments were about 1.0. Thorp's Princeton Newport's 1969–1988 DSSR is 13.8. Renaissance Medallion, possibly the world's most successful hedge fund, had a DSSR of 26.4 during the period January 1993 to April 2005.

The results come from the choices made using a utility function. Those who want high DSSRs are investors trying to have smooth and good returns with low volatility and very few monthly losses. Thorp only 3 monthly losses in 20 years; the Harvard and Ford endowments and Berkshire Hathaway had 2-3-4 per year, about one third of the time.

Consider a rogue trader's utility function.[6] The outcome probabilities are:

1. $x\%$ of the time the fund blows up and loses 40%+ of its value at some time; the trader is fired and gets another trading job keeping most past bonuses',
2. $y\%$ of the time the fund has modest returns of 15% or less; then the trader receives a salary but little or no bonus,
3. $z\%$ of the time the fund has large returns of 25% to 100%; then the trader gathers more assets to trade and receives large bonuses.

At all times the rogue trader is in (1) and (2), that is, the total positions are over bet and not diversified and move markets. There is no plan to exit the strategy since it is assumed that trades can continually be made. Then in a multiperiod or continuous time model, it may well be that for the fund managers and traders specific utility functions it is optimal to take bets that provide enormous gains in some scenarios and huge losses in other scenarios. In a theoretical continuous time model with incentives, risk taking behavior is greatly moderated if the hedge fund manager's stake in the fund is 30% or more, see Chapter 20.

In the case of Amaranth and similar rogue trading situations, there are additional complications such as the fund manager's utility function and his wealth stake inside this fund and outside it. Then there is the rogue trader's utility function and his wealth inside and outside the fund. According to Aumann (2005) in his Nobel lecture: a person's behavior is rational if it is in his best interests given his information. Aumann further endorses the late Yale Nobel James Tobin's belief that economics is all about incentives. In the case of Hunter, his share of $1B plus gains (real or booked) was in the $100 million range. What's interesting, and this is similar to LTCM, is that these traders continue and increase bets when so much is already in the bank. Recall in LTCM, that they had a $100 million unsecured loan to invest in their fund. Finally, in such analyses, one must consider the utility functions and constraints of the other investors' money. In the case of Amaranth, Deutsche Bank who had first-hand knowledge of Hunter's previous trading blowups, was an investor along with other well-known firms.

Winners and Losers

Who are the winners and losers here? Hunter is a winner and will get relocated soon. He has hundreds of millions, having made about $75 million in 2005 (out of his team's $1.26 billion profit), and will likely make more later. Of course, his reputation is tarnished but $100+ million in fees over the years helps. Like many others, Hunter had to leave 30% of this in the fund so some of the $75 million was lost. There might be some lawsuits but he likely will not be hurt much. At 32, he is set for life financially, despite the losses. He is likely to begin again. An executive recruiter has offered to help introduce Hunter to investors. He sees opportunities for Hunter to make a fresh start with high-net-worth investors, possibly in Russia and the Middle East.[7] Betting on fallen hedge-fund stars is not all that uncommon. John Meriwether, who led LTCM until its 1998 implosion, now runs another hedge fund. Nicholas Maounis, Amaranth's founder and CEO, was exploring starting a new hedge fund. Instead of being ahead 27% for 2005 his fund had to be liquidated. He lost much of his previous fees by leaving much of it in the fund. Since 2005 there were $70 million in management fees and $200 million in incentive fees, his cut was substantial but like LTCM, he should have diversified his wealth.

Other winners were those on the other side of the trade if they followed proper risk control and could weather the storm created by Amaranth's plays, and those like Citadel Investment Group, Merrill Lynch and JP Morgan Chase, who took over Amaranth's portfolio and the Fortress Investment group, which helped liquidate assets. JP Morgan was named "Energy Derivatives House of the Year, 2006" by *Risk* magazine.

The losers were mainly the investors in Amaranth including various pension funds which sought higher returns to make up for 2000–2003 equity investment mistakes. As of January 30, 2007, they had received about $1.6 billion which is less than 20% of their investment value in August 2006. They will receive a bit more but their losses will exceed 75%. Those who invested in mid-2005 received about 27% of their original investment or about 18% of the peak August value. Other losers are hedge funds like Mother Rock LP which were swept up by the Amaranth debacle including those that lost even though they bet on the right (short) direction because Hunter moved the market long on the way up and those who lost along with Amaranth on the way down. They were long October and short September futures. According to Till (2006), they likely were forced out of their short position August 2, 2006 when the spread rallied briefly but sharply. Another loser was Man Alternative Investments Ltd., a fund of hedge funds listed on the London Stock Exchange in 2001 by the Man Group PLC, which shut down after recent losses tied to Amaranth's collapse and persistently poor liquidity in the shares. It is a small fund with little active trading interest, a concentrated shareholder base and positions that were both difficult to build up and unwind. It had about £31.5 million invested in a portfolio selected by Man Group's Chicago-based Glenwood Capital Investments LLC unit, which is part of Man Group PLC, and has $58 billion in assets under management. The fund lost about one fifth of its gains during the year from the collapse of Amaranth though it was up 6.5% through October.

Archeus Capital, a hedge fund that in October 2005 had assets of $3 billion, announced on October 31, 2006, that it would close, returning $700 million to their investors. The fund, founded and run by two former Salomon Brothers bond traders, Gary K Kilberg and Peter G Hirsch, was like Amaranth, a multi-strategy fund. However, it had a more conservative approach that focused on exploiting arbitrage opportunities in convertible bonds. Archeus began experiencing redemptions last year after its main investment strategy fell out of favor. The fund's founders blamed its administrator for failing to maintain accurate records. Their subsequent inability to properly reconcile the fund's records, led to a series of investor withdrawals from which they were not able to recover. Also, Archeus's 2006 performance did little to inspire its clients. Through the first week of October 2006, Archeus's main fund was down 1.9% for the year. However, the fund had returned 18.5% since July 2005. Still, during a period when hedge fund returns have come under increased scrutiny and have, on average, lagged the returns of the major stock market indexes, such a return was insufficient to keep investors on board.

The $7.7 billion San Diego County Employees Retirement Association has retained the class-action firm Bernstein Litowitz Berger and Grossmann to investigate the Amaranth implosion. Its $175 million investment in Amaranth, which was valued at $234 million in June 2006, is now estimated to be worth only $70 million, thus a $150+ million loss. They should have done better due diligence in advance. Those who bet the ranch on every trade eventually lose it. Investors should have known that was what they were investing in with Amaranth.

Following Amaranth's collapse, investors were seeking someone to blame. Some argued that these bets showed the need for greater or a different sort of regulation of hedge funds, or at least of the sort of over the counter trades in the natural gas market. Others including Gretchen Morgenson of the New York Times, pointed to the persistence of what many of have called the *Enron loophole*, created in 1993, when the Commodity Futures Trading Commission (CFTC) exempted bilateral energy futures transactions from its regulatory authority. This exemption was extended in 2000 in the commodity futures modernization act to include electronic facilities. Many have argued that Enron used such trades to increase the value of long-term contracts. In the run-up of gas prices in 2005/2006, some analysts and politicians pointed to the role of speculators in changing the demand structure, leading a congressional subcommittee to release a report urging that such trades all be the concern of US regulators. Amaranth's collapse brings a different aspect to this debate, as it shows the limits to such self-regulation by market actors. While it is unclear what policy actions might be taken in this matter, this concern is likely to continue and may change the environment in which such trades are made in the future. However, there are limits to the role that can be played by such regulation.

Other small losers are funds of funds of Morgan Stanley and Goldman Sachs who lost 2.5% to 5% from their Amaranth holdings. However, as they helped unwind the trades they may well have recouped their losses when the energy market prices subsequently increased.

There is little impact from this on the world economy. The hedge fund industry now has a bit more pressure to regulate position sizes but most regulators steer away from risk control. When you mention risk control, you are usually encouraged to change the subject. What regulators are interested in is operational risk. The exchanges have limits but rogue traders are able to get around these rules. In any event, if VaR were to be used it would most likely not work unless one is blessed with no bad scenarios. As long as risk control is so poorly understood, misapplied and disregarded and pension funds and others are desperate for high returns, such disasters will occur from time to time; and this is fully expected. It is simply part of the hedge fund zero sum gain. For every Jim Simons or Blair Hull eaking out steady profits using a lot of careful research, excellent execution, position sizing and strict risk control, there is a rogue trader trying to make it by over betting with very little research and a firm which improperly applies risk control. Improper regulation may well hurt more than help.

Mettallgeselschaft Refining and Marketing Inc (1993)

The story of the Mettallgeselschaft Refining and Marketing (MGRM) disaster is still highly relevant today because it is a complex and passionately debated case. Even 20+ years later, several questions remain open:

- Was MGRM's strategy legitimate hedging or speculation?
- Could and should the parent company, Mettallgeselschaft AG, have withstood the liquidity pressure?
- Was the decision to unwind the strategy in early 1994 the right one?

In December 1991, MGRM, the US-based oil marketing subsidiary of German industrial group Mettallgeselschaft AG, sold forward contracts guaranteeing its customers certain prices for 5 or 10 years. By 1993, the total amount of contracts outstanding was equivalent to 150 million barrels of oil-related products. If oil prices increased, this strategy would have left MGRM vulnerable. To hedge this risk, MGRM entered into a series of long positions mostly in the very liquid short-term futures (some for just 1 month). This practice, known as "stack hedging", involves periodically rolling over the contracts as they near maturity to maintain the hedge. Stack hedging helps address the maturity gap between the long-term exposure and the short-term hedging instrument.

In theory, maintaining the hedged positions through the life of the long-term forward contracts eliminates all risk. But intermediate cash flows may not match because of the daily settlement of futures. This could result in liquidity risk. As long as oil prices kept rising or remained stable, MGRM would be able to roll over its short-term futures without incurring significant cash flow problems. In effect, the rollover of the futures would create positive cash flows that MGRM would be able invest until the maturate of the forward. However, if oil prices declined, MGRM would have to make large cash infusions in its hedging strategy to finance margin calls and roll over its futures.

In reality, oil prices fell through 1993, resulting in a total loss of $1.3 billion on the short-term futures by the end of the year. All of the losses related to the cash inflow required by the mechanics of the stack hedging.

Mettallgeselschaft, AG's supervisory board took decisive actions: they replaced MGRM's senior management and unwound the strategy at an enormous cost. In the end, Mettallgeselschaft AG was only saved by a $1.9 billion rescue package organized early 1994 by 150 German and international banks.

MGRM is one of the best studied financial disasters, mostly because it was the stage of a passionate debate. Mello and Parsons (1995) analyzed the disaster shortly after Mettallgeselschaft's rescue. They generally supported the initial reports in the press that equated the Mettallgeselschaft strategy with speculation and mentioned funding risk as the leading cause of the company's meltdown. The same year, Culp and Miller (1995a,b) took a very different view, asserting that the real culprit in the debacle was not the funding risk inherent in the strategy, but the lack of understanding of Mettallgeselschaft AG's supervisory board. Culp and Miller further pointed out that the losses incurred were only paper losses that could be compensated for in the long term. By choosing to liquidate the strategy, the supervisory board crystallized the paper losses into actual losses and nearly bankrupted their industrial group. Edwards and Canter (1995) broadly agreed with Culp and Miller's analysis: the near collapse of Mettallgeselschaft was the result of disagreement between the supervisory board and MGRM senior management on the soundness and appropriateness of the strategy. The key difference between Culp and Miller (1995a,b) and Edwards and Canter (1995) is Culp and Miller's assertion that MGRM's strategy was self-financing, which Edwards and Canter reject.[8]

Société Generalé (2008)

A major event in January 2008 was the rogue trader losses at Société Generalé. One thing to observe is that in times of uncertainty, there are more rogue traders. Besides this loss, some $1.4 billion was lost on wheat in 2 days by a rouge trader at MF Global causing them to lose one fourth of their worth.

On January 21 (a US holiday) and 22, 2008 (Monday and Tuesday) nights, the S&P500 futures was some 60 points lower on Globex trading (1265 area) well below previous lows (1406 on August 16, 2007, 1364 on October 17, 2006 and 1273 on March 10, 2008). On both days, the day market recovered, but much damage was done.

Jérome Kerviel and SG lost 4.9 billion euro trading index futures in the DAX, FTSE and CAC. By correlation, the S&P500 fell to new lows. Many were hurt. How could a junior trader hold $50 billion euro in positions?

What is a Subprime Loan and Why Have They Caused So Much Trouble in So Many Places?

Subprime loans: loans to borrowers who do not qualify for best interest or with terms that make the borrower eventually unqualified as with zero down payment, zero interest.

In general: lending institutions inherently get it wrong. When times are good, they tend to be greedy and try to maximize loan profits but then they are very lax in their evaluation of borrowers' ability to pay current and future mortgage payments.

- Japan in the late 1980s: real estate and stocks, eventually the 10 trillion was lost.
- US mortgages: in the run up of real estate — after the internet bubble and Greenspan, interest rates approached 1%. The assumption was that house prices had to rise as they have year by year.

The lending organizations sell off the mortgages and they are cut and diced and bundled into packages like CMOs and CDOs and sold to others who have trouble figuring out what is in them but look at the rating agency's stamp of approval.

As I have argued, one must be diversified and not over bet in all scenarios to avoid trouble. But the CMOs, CDOs and other instruments were extremely leveraged by banks and others.

- The rating agencies with conflicts of interest are also at fault because they failed to point out the potential risks. Many risky derivative products were rated AAA even though they would implode as they did if only one variable — housing prices — declined.
- So it was easy and cheap money.

Recall, the recipe for disaster is

- Over bet.
- Do not diversify in all scenarios.

Then if you are lucky you can be ok but if a bad scenario hits, you can be wiped out. Since US mortgages are in the range US$17 trillion, it is an enormous amount of money so a small change makes big impact. The bad scenario in 2005+ in real estate was not a small but a large change so the total losses could easily exceed 1 trillion using data Professor Shiller compiled from 1890 to the peak in 2004–2005. This is 1/10 of Japanese losses in the 1990s. In 2008, it is widely recognized as a crisis. Early warnings of a large real estate decline came from Nouriel Roubini and Robert Shiller in 2006.

Once trouble hits, no one wants to lend, even to good risks. The pendulum has swung to too tight and too high rates. The Fed and other injections were helpful in the first few months of 2008. Japan in the early 1990s was similar: expensive money and you could not get it. Canadian banks get it right more often than US institutions but then the structure is different. Among other things, mortgage interest is not deductible except for that portion of a house that's an office. Also there are fewer exotic mortgages and higher down payments are required to obtain a mortgage. US foreclosures in 2008 were for mortgages written in 2006 and this continued. The following figure is a chronology of the subprime saga from June 2007 to January 2008.

A Brief Chronology of Financial Disasters Since The 1980s

Crises of various kinds for earlier periods of time going back many centuries are discussed in Kindleberger and Aliber (2011) and Reinhart and Rogoff (2011). Harvard Economics Professor Joseph Schumpeter had suggested that recurrent mania is simply a normal feature of business life. Notable blowups include Goldman Sachs Trading Company with late 1928 stock price of $104 rising to $222.50 and down to $1.75 by 1932. Irving Fisher (Yale Economics Professor) in 1929 stated "stock prices have reached what looks like a permanently high plateau" just prior to the big crash. He lost millions but Yale rescued him.

Harvard Economics Professor John Kenneth Galbraith (1994, 2009), an astute observer of economic crises from his research and government service had some general comments regarding these crises:

1. A notoriously short financial memory of 20 years or less creates the conditions for a market collapse.
2. The critic must wait until after the crash for any approval not to say applause.
3. Common features of great speculative episodes include specious association of money and intelligence; money is the measure of capitalist achievement, financial genius is before the fall.
4. Something new: reinvention of the wheel over and over again, often in a slightly more unstable version.
5. Debt is secured by real assets.
6. Leverage is extreme.
7. After the crash there is anger towards those previously most admired and scrutiny of the previously much praised financial instruments and practices talk of regulation and reform.
8. Not discussed is the speculation itself or the optimization behind it.
9. The reality is all but ignored.

Bad judgment, difficult times and various levels of secrecy bordering on or being fraud are also rampant. Examples include Enron (2001), MF Global (2012), a futures and options financial brokerage which offers over the counter products, foreign exchange and spread betting and Monti di Paschi di Siena (2013), a bank founded in 1472, are recent examples.

I present in this section a chronology of the major financial and trading disasters that took place since the 1980s.

- Hunt Brothers (1979–1980): Herbert and Nelson Hunt, the two sons of oil tycoon HL Hunt, took the view that silver would greatly appreciate in price in the high inflation environment of the late 1970s. The two brothers used the futures market to physically buy large quantities of silver. Using their family's assets as collateral, Herbert and Nelson made the most out of the leverage afforded by the futures contracts, building their silver position to $4.5 billion and controlling up to two thirds of the silver market. Silver price topped $50 per ounce Eventually, the US commodities regulators introduced futures trading curbs, effectively stopping the Hunt Brother form adding to their position. As demand dried up, silver market stalled and the Hunt brothers faced mounted margin calls. At first, the brothers met their margin calls by borrowing against their family's assets. However, the Federal Reserve intervened, persuading banks

no to lend money to speculators. Having lost the ability to borrow, the Hunt brothers eventually missed a margin call on March 27, 1980. The silver market collapsed from $48.70 per ounce to a low of $11 per ounce.
- US Savings and Loan Crisis (1970s–1995): US savings and loans (S&L) institutions or 'thrifts' originate in the British concept of 'building societies.' They are regional institutions, whose primary purpose is to originate mortgages. From the 1930s onward, Regulation Q had prevented S&L institutions from merging across states and from holding risk investments. By the late 1970s, S&L institutions were under threat. Money market funds, which were not subject to Regulation Q, were able to take advantage of interest rate volatility to provide higher returns than S&L institutions. S&Ls began to lose their customer base. To keep competitive, S&Ls made the case that they should be allowed to invest in a broader range of assets. Key parts of the regulatory framework were repealed, and S&L institutions began investing in riskier activities, making forays into commercial real estate loans and investing in junk bonds. However, many S&L institutions neither had the expertise nor the manpower required to deal with these new types of risks.

  Up to a third of the 3,234 S&L institutions failed over the period 1986–1995: 296 were closed by the Federal Savings and Loan Insurance Corporation (FSLIC) between 1986 and 1989 and a further 747 were closed by the Resolution Trust Corporation between 1989 and 1995. The general Accounting Office estimated that the total cost of the cleanup reached $160 billion, including $132 billion paid directly by taxpayers.
- Mexican Default and Latin America Debt Crisis (starting 1982): during most of the 1970, Latin American borrowed heavily on international capital markets in a bid to speed up the industrialization of the economy. It is reported that Latin American debt to commercial banks increased at a cumulative annual rate of 20.4% between 1975 and 1982, leading to a quadrupling of external debt in the region from $75 billion to $315 billion over the same period.

  The 1979 oil shock and resulting recession prompted the US and European central banks to increase interest rates. This led to a sharp increase in interest payments and refinancing costs for developing countries. By August 1982, Mexico declared that it would default on its debt. As a result, commercial banks reduced drastically their loans to Latin America, triggering a liquidity crisis in the region. The International Monetary Fund intervened, organizing new loans in exchange for the implementation of strict economic measures.

- Continental Illinois National Bank and Trust Company (1984): Continental was born out of the 1910 merger of two Chicago-based banks: the Commercial National Bank and the Continental National Bank. At the time of its collapse in 1984, Continental was the seventh largest bank by deposit in the US with $40 billion in assets. A large part of the blame for Continental's insolvency went to the bad loans it had purchased from Penn Square Bank, which specialized in loans for oil and gas producers and service companies and investors in the Oklahoma, after Penn Square's failure in July 1982. Continental's woes were compounded by frauds committed by a number of lending officers led by John Lyte. By May 1984, rumors of an impeding failure had reached large depositors. Withdrawals topped $10 billion (a quarter of all deposits) by early May. Fearing a generalized bank run, Federal Reserve and Federal Deposit Insurance Corporation (FDIC) intervened, injecting $4.5 billion of new capital. Continental, the original 'Too Big Too Fail', remained the country's largest banking failure until Washington Mutual collapsed in 2008.
- Bank of New York (1985): in November 1985, a computer glitch resulted in a $23.6 billion overdraft at the Bank of New York. The bank required a $24 billion overnight loan from the Federal Reserve Bank of New York, costing $5 billion in interest.
- Black Monday (1987): world markets plunged on Monday, October 19, 1987. The Dow Jones Industrial Average fell by 508 points to 1738.74 (a 22.61% drop). The BSEYD model predicted this in April 1987 based on high interest rates relative to stock earnings.
- Equity and land Crash in Japan (1990–1991): Land fell a year after the stock market. The BSEYD model predicted this in April 1989; see Ziemba and Schwartz (1991) and Shirayev, Zhitukhin and Ziemba (2015). The latter paper discusses the golf course membership market, a bigger bubble than the stock market plus the land and stock market declines.
- Drexel, Burnham and Lambert (1990): Drexel, Burnham and Lambert was the largest and most influential institution on the junk bond market. Several of its leading members are convicted in a massive fraud case involving insider trading, stock manipulation and tax law violations.
- Salomon Brothers Scandal (1991): between December 1990 and May 1991, Paul Mozer, a trader at Salomon Brothers, submitted illegal bids for U.S. Treasuries with the objective of cornering the market.
- Orange County (1994): interest rate derivative losses. When asset market returns are low, it is often tempting to enter into speculative strategies

or untested investment products in a bid to push returns up. Orange County in California did both, with devastating consequences.

At the beginning of 1994, Robert Citron, Orange County's long-time Treasurer, was managing the Orange County Investment Pool with equity valued at $7.5 billion. To increase the fund's return, Citron decided to use leverage by borrowing an additional $12.5 billion through reverse repos, pushing the debt-to-equity ratio up to 1.67 and the financial leverage to 2.67. The assets under management, then worth $20 billion, were mostly invested in Agency notes with an average maturity of 4 to 5 years.

Citron's leveraged strategy can be viewed as an interest rate spread strategy on the difference between the 4-year fixed investment rate and the floating borrowing rate.

This strategy is akin to an invest floating note, or reverse floater. The underlying bet is that the floating rate will not rise above the investment rate. As long as the borrowing rate remains below the investment rate, the combination of spread and leverage would generate an appreciable return for the investment pool. But if the cost of borrowing rises above the investment rate, the fund would incur a loss that leverage would magnify.

Unfortunately, for Orange County, its borrowing cost rose sharply in 1994 as the US Federal Reserve Board tightened its Federal Funds rate. As a result, the Orange County Investment Pool accumulated losses rapidly. By December 1994, Orange County had lost $1.64 billion. This loss amounts to some 8% of the investment pool's assets and 21% of its equity. On December 6, 1994, the county declared Chapter 9 bankruptcy and began liquidating its portfolio.

Jorion (1997) points out that Citron benefited from the support of Orange County officials while his strategy was profitable — it earned up to $750 million (a 10% return on equity) at one point. But he lost their support and was promptly replaced after the full scale of the problem became apparent, which subsequently resulted in the decisions to declare bankruptcy and liquidate the portfolio.

The opinion of Miller and Ross (1997), however, was that Orange County should neither have declared bankruptcy nor liquidated its portfolio. If the county had held on to the portfolio, Miller and Ross estimated that Orange County would have erased their losses and possibly even have made some gains in 1995.

- Mexican Tequilla Crisis (1994): sudden devaluation of the Mexican peso in December 1994 following policies that led to a shortage of foreign reserves. There was a sudden reversal of tight currency controls when a new government took over. Banks over lent with low interest rates to not necessarily the most qualified investors. Prior to this there were two decades of increased spending, hyper inflation from 1985 to 1993, high debt, low oil prices for their exports and large commitments to finance spending by the previous government. Commitments to finance past spending by the previous government. To finance the debt, outgoing President Salinas issued 7% Tesebonas bonds denominated in pesos but indexed to the US dollar. So that was *defacto* a US dollar peso peg. They ran out of US dollars which were used to keep interest rates low in their foreign reserves to maintain the fixed exchange rate, hence the devaluation and scaring away foreign investors. When the government tried to roll over the debt, investors were unwilling to buy hence there was a default. President Bill Clinton, on the advice of Treasury Secretary Robert Rubin, arranged a loan of $50 billion with the IMF, the Bank for International Settlements and the Bank of Canada. In the end, the US made $500 million on their $20 billion part of this. By 1996, the economy was growing and the crisis was over.
- Barings (1995): Nicholas "Nick" Leeson scandal: Leeson went to prison in Singapore and now lectures for about £10,000 per talk.

  Nick Leeson incurred a $1.3 billion loss that bankrupted the 233-year old Barings PLC bank. While based in Singapore, Leeson had accumulated long positions in Japanese Nikkei 225 futures with a notional value totaling $7 billion. As the Nikkei declined, Leeson hid his losses in a "loss account" while increasing his long positions and hoping that a market recovery would return his overall position to profitability.

  But in the first 2 months of 1995, Japan suffered the Kobe earthquake and the Nikkei declined by around 15%. Barings suffered a GBP860 million loss, twice the bank's capital. Barrings went bankrupt and was bought by ING for GBP1.

  Leeson's control over both the front and back office of the futures section for Barings Singapore was a leading contributor to this disaster because it allowed him to take very large positions and hide his losses. Another main factor was the blurry matrix-based organization charts adopted by Barings. Roles, responsibilities and supervision duties were not clearly assigned.

This created a situation in which regional desks were essentially left to their own devices.
- Daiwa Trading Scandal (1995): a New York-based trader for Daiwa Securities Group, Toshihide Igushi accumulated $1.1 billion of losses during an 11-year time period. As in Leeson's case, Igushi had control over both the front and back offices, which made it easier to conceal his losses.
- Sumitomo (1996): copper trading losses. London-based copper trader, Yasuo 'Mr Copper' Hamanaka, entered into a series of unauthorized speculative trades in a bid to boost his section's profits. But the trades resulted in the accumulation of approximately $2.6 billion in losses during 13 years.
- Enron (2001): energy trade failures compounded by fraud and corruption, see Douglass, Yu and Ziemba (2004) which discusses the pension losses of employees.

Enron's calendar year 2000 Form 10K, filed in early April 2001 displayed important warning signs:

— Concerns related to cash flow disclosures: a need for heavy financing as investing cash flow exceeds operating cash flow by a wide margin in 1998 and 1999.
— Enron's management was under pressure to support both the stock price and debt rating: maintaining the investment grade status was critical to the success of its wholesale business and its ability to maintain adequate liquidity.
— Use of mark-to-market method for other types of contracts (other than permitted by US GAAP for its inventory as commodities) was unusual.
— Engaged in securitization of assets in its so-called price-risk-management business: report assets sales to SPEs with inflated values, reported a gain on sale of a portion of a JV when the technology for the venture did not exist.
— Extended its mark-to-market accounting to equity-method investments (the equity method enables companies to keep assets and liabilities off the BS). Under the equity method of accounting, Enron should report its percentage share of GAAP income on its IS, not market-value method.
— The allowance for doubtful accounts grew significantly in the last 2 years, which calls into question the quality of the receivables and underlying revenues.
— Barter transaction recorded.

— Related party transactions: Enron entered into transactions including receivables, derivatives, sales of assets with limited partnership (the Related Party) whose general partner and managing director is a senior officer of Enron.

This type of self-dealing amounting to billions of dollars is what ultimately led to the collapse of Enron when potential write-down related to these activities were announced in October 2001.There were also ample red flags outside of SEC filings:

— In May 2001, Enron's vice chairman resigned.
— In August 2001, the president resigned.
— The proxy statement shows that top management pay was largely from bonus and stock awards (e.g. the chairman of the board received more than 90% of his compensation from bonus and stock awards).

- Stock market drop following 9/11 (2001): markets fell 6% limit after the attack on September 11 then the market was closed for a week and the total fall for the week was about 14%; market was already falling and fell more after.
- Allied Irish Bank (2002): trading losses. Currency trader John Rusnak, working for a small subsidiary in Maryland, USA, accumulated losses of $691 million between 1997 and late 2001. He hid the losses by entering fake hedging trades and setting up prime brokerage accounts, which gave him the ability to conduct trades through other banks.
- Subprime, credit liquidity and quantitative equity crises (2007–2009).
- Bear Stearns (2007): from 2005 to the end of 2007, Bear Sterns pursued an aggressive strategy, relying heavily on leverage to increase its profit,[9] holding large quantities of derivatives, and launching a number of credit-linked 'hedge funds.' By the end of 2007, Bear Stearns had become the US' seventh largest securities firm by capital and ranked among the most admired firms in America. By March 2008, Bear Stearns had joined the vastly less prestigious list of failed financial institutions.

In fact, the first cracks in the building had appeared in the first half of 2007, when rumors spreads that two of Bear Stern's 'hedge funds', the Bear Stearns High-Grade Structured Credit Fund and the Bear Stearns High-Grade Structured Credit Enhanced Leveraged Fund, faced serve losses. On June 22, 2007, Bear Sterns effectively bailed out the Bear Stearns High-Grade Structured Credit Fund with a $3.2 billion loan, an amount 100 times larger than Bear Stern's initial investment in the fund. Simultaneously, the firm started negotiations with other financial institutions on a series of collateralized loans to the Bear Stearns High-Grade Structured Credit Enhanced Leveraged Fund. By mid-July 2007, Bear Sterns was forced to admit that the two funds had lost almost of their value by betting too heavily on highly illiquid CDOs. Shortly after, investors launched a law suit against the two funds and the firm.

The collapse of the two hedge funds also triggered a loss of confidence in Bear Sterns. This made it more difficult for the the firm to finance its highly leveraged balance sheet and ultimately led to its failure. Bear Stearns was acquired by JP Morgan Chase on March 16, 2008 in a deal brokered an partly financed by the Federal Reserve Bank of New York.

- Merrill Lynch (2007): Merrill Lynch Wealth Management currently is the wealth management division of the Bank of America. Based in New York City, it has about 15,000 financial advisors, $13.8 billion (2012) in revenue and $2.2 trillion in client assets and is the world's largest brokerage firm. Prior to 2009, it was Merrill Lynch and Co., and it was merged into the Bank of America on September 14, 2008. The firm goes back to 1914 when Charles Merrill and Edmond Lynch joined forces. In 1919,Winthrop Smith joined and in 1930 they spun off to EA Pierce. In 1941, they merged into Merrill Lynch, Pierce, Fenner and Beane; see Wigmore (1985). Smith was running the firm since 1940, leading to Merrill Lynch, Pierce, Fenner and Smith in 1958. The firm moved into the government securities market which gave them the leverage to develop money market and government fund products that led to large growth in the 1970s and 1980s; and Merrill's large brokerage network named the *thundering herd* allowed it to sell securities it underwrote directly. This gave them an edge on other Wall Street firms. *Fortune* magazine called Merrill's Cash Management Account, where credit cards, check writing and money market mutual fund, the most important innovation in years. Merrill had a hand in the Orange County disaster. They and others were accused of selling risky ill-advised securities to the Orange County treasurer, Robert Citron, thus losing the county $1.69 billion and leading to its bankruptcy. The county sued over 10 advisors, accountants and securities companies. They collected $600 million back of which $400 million was from Merrill which settled without admitting liability in June 1998.

The subprime mortgage crisis hit Merrill hard and in November 2007 they wrote down $8 billion in losses and removed E Stanley O'Neal as its head and replaced him with John Thain. Thain raised $6 billion from selling the commercial finance business to General Electric and shares in

Singapore's Temasek holdings. In July 2008 he announced an additional $4.9 billion in losses in Q4. That made the July 2007–July 2008 losses of $19.2 billion. To try to lighten up their over betting on mortgages, they sold securities and hedge funds to Temasek for $3.4 billion.

In August 2008, Andrew Cuomo, New York Attorney General, threatened to sue Merrill Lynch suggesting that they misrepresented the risk of mortgage backed securities. They responded by offering to buy back $12 billion at auction. They then cut costs, froze hiring and charged $30 billion in losses to their UK operations thus avoiding tax there. They bought back various securities on deposit with the firm from Massachusetts clients under $100 million. According to Miller and Ho (2008), total losses were $51.8 billion. All the trouble started in 2003 when they bought the collateralized debt obligations team from Credit Suisse First Boston. They became the top underwriter in 2004. In 2006, they bought First Franklin Financial, a large subprime lender to supply mortgages for the CDOs. They were the lead underwriter on 136 CDOs worth $93 billion in 2006–2007. The CDOs were declining in value in late 2007 but Merrill did not dump them but just held most of then which led to the losses. By mid-2008, they sold one traunch originally worth $30.6 billion for $1.7 billion cash plus a $5.1 billion loan to Lone Star Funds.

The troubles continued and MBIA a bond insurance company sued for fraud and other violations. The essence being the complicated nature of CDOs with exotic hard to price risky features such as CDOs "squared or cubed" that were supposedly "hidden." But the court ruled otherwise and threw out the claim that AAA rated securities were really AAA quality. So MBIA had to pay. This all led to a September 14, 2008 sale to Bank of America for $38.25 billion in stock. The price was a premium to current mark-to-the-market values but well below the September 2008 value. In March 2009, Merrill reported that they received billions from insurance with AIG and $6.8 billion of AIGs government bailout. There were a number of regulatory actions of various kinds form 2002. Especially troublesome to us is that 36.2% of the TARP money received for their bailout, some $3.6 billion, went to executive bonuses. The bonuses were announced on December 8, 2008 after Bank of America approved the merger but before Q4s financial results were announced. This money went to employees already with salaries of $300,000 plus. Wow! Outrageous actions like this have led to somewhat better approach to executive compensation including performance related pay, deferred compensation and roll backs.

- Lehman (2008): Lehman Brothers, a famed bond operation and financial services firm, filed for Chapter 11 bankruptcy protection on September 15, 2008. The filing is still the largest bankruptcy filing in US history with Lehman holding over $600 billion in assets, including large accounts of various hedge funds and other financial institutions. The systemic risk with much interconnections and a refusal of the US government to bail them out was a major factor pushing the stock market much lower. The Dow Jones Average fell 4.4% on September 15 and another 7.0% on September 29. Meanwhile, the S&P500 futures fell 9.74% in September, 20.11% in October, 9.22% in November and 44.2% for the year 2008. Henry Paulson, the then Treasury secretary, said it was not possible to bail them out. Since Paulson was a former CEO of Goldman and a vicious competitor to Lehman, one wonders if politics might have been a factor here.

  The Lehman bankruptcy is yet another example of over betting, not being diversified and being hit by a bad scenario. They had a huge amount of debt, 31-1 leverage. As they were way over bet, a 3-4% decline in the value of its assets would and did wipe them out. There were over 100 hedge funds which used Lehman as their prime broker, that is to raise funds and hold positions. These positions of value over $400 billion were frozen. Lehman, like others, got sucked into the subprime mortgage market. They securitized low rated mortgages of poorly financed homebuyers including some Ninja (no income, no job, no assets) loans to those with no money no job no assets. For those only rising real estate would work, but as I know, the real estate market peaked in 2005–2006 and then fell sharply in most areas of the US. By the second quarter of 2008, Lehman reported losses of $2.8 billion and raised $6 billion in new capital. Their stock fell 73% in Q1 and Q2 of 2008. They initially released 1,500 people (6%) just before Q3 reporting period in September.

  There were some possible bailouts. One was the Korean Development Bank whose low offer of $6.40 per share was rejected by Lehman and it was not clear if the regulators would accept the purchase. On September 9, 2008, Lehman's shares fell 45% to $7.79 when the Korea Bank dropped out. This led to a fall of 3.4% in the S&P500. On September 10, they announced a $3.9 billion loss. The New York Fed, led by Timothy Geithner, considered a bailout with Barclays and Bank of America involved. But the Bank of England and the FSA in London were against this. Bank of America dropped out when Paulson refused to insure part of the losses.

After the bankruptcy, JP Morgan, backed by the Fed, put up $87 billion on September 15 and $51 billion on September 16. On September 22, there was a revised proposal to sell the brokerage part including Lehman's midtown Manhattan office building valued at $960 million for $1.29 billion. With Barclays back in the game, with no alternative, the deal went through. Barclays received $43 billion in securities and $45.5 billion in liabilities. Barclays had Lehman's employee liabilities of up to $2.5 billion depending upon how long they stayed with them. Finally, on November 22, 2008, Nomura purchased Lehman's Asian holdings.

There were many institutions and individuals who lost the investments they had held by Lehman. For example, 43,700 people in Hong Kong invested HK$15 billion in guaranteed mini bonds. These were supposedly low risk. The Hong Kong government partially bailed out these and other derivative positions at their now deflated value so that these investors got a small part of their investment back. And the final straw: Richard Fuld, head of Lehman Brothers, walked away with $480 million and other top executives were given high pay just before the bankruptcy filing.

The Fed minutes dated 6 weeks after Lehman filed for bankruptcy on September 15, 2008 were released in February 2014. Fed chair Bernanke is recorded saying "What in the heck were you guys doing letting Lehman fail?" The Fed had a meeting on September 16, the day after Lehman failed and did nothing. There was a lot of dissent. For example Christine Lagarde who was France's finance minister at the time, said "For the equilibrium of the world financial system, this was a genuine error."

Both Bernanke and Paulson have since said they could not save Lehman as "their hands were legally tied". Harvey Miller, a lawyer representing Lehman, recently noted that in March 2008 the Fed was able to bailout Bear Stearns and helped bailout AIG the day after Lehman filed for bankruptcy so this was a later rationalization. The real reason why Lehman was not bailed out could be that Bernanke and Paulson expected other Wall Street firms to bail them out and they wanted to avoid other taxpayer bailouts. Of course, we come back to the rivalry of Goldman and Lehman and supposedly Paulson's hatred of Fuld. However, the Fed did try to get a group of Wall Street banks to organize a bailout of Lehman but that failed.

While Lehman collapsed with litigation continuing to this day, Lehman Futures survived during the dark days of September 2008. This is a good case to illustrate that Futures exchanges unlike banks and shadow banks have remained financially stable. Lehman Futures was a shadow bank.

- AIG (2008): the US government made a $85 billion bailout when the American International Group, a multinational insurance company with 63,000 employees in more than 130 countries, failed. The company started in 1919 when American Cornelius Van der Starr established a general insurance agency in Shanghai, China. The business expanded and in 1939 moved the headquarters to New York City. In 1960, Starr hired Maurice R "Hank" Greenberg to develop an international accident and wealth business. Greenberg organized selling insurance through independent brokers rather than agents to avoid their salaries. Then they could price insurance better. AIG was organized in 1967 to include all of Starr's businesses. Then in 1968, Starr made Greenberg the head. They sold credit protection in its London office as credit default swaps on collateralized debt obligations that declined in value. Most were backed by subprime housing loans. The 1970s had many political issues in the Middle East and Southeast Asia. As of April 21, 2013 it had a $57.5 billion market capitalization.

The 1980s led to new special products such as pollution liability and political risk. In the 1990s, they added diversifying investments. In the 2000s, there were a number of legal troubles and finally amid an accounting scandal, Hank Greenberg was ousted and replaced by Martin Sullivan. After Greenberg left, AIG obtained tens of billions of mortgages which were risky and bought mortgage backed securities. When losses occurred in 2007, they had to pay insurance claims and collateral account losses. AIG purchased the remaining 39% to get full ownership of 21st Century Insurance then merged into them in 2008. On June 15, 2008, Sullivan resigned amid the losses and stock price decline.

In late 2008, AIG suffered in the financial crisis and their own over betting on the toxic levered assets including subprime loans. The credit default swaps lost a lot of money. Their credit rating was downgraded so they had to put up more margin money. Then by September 16, 2008, AIG was essentially bankrupt. The US Fed bailed them out with the $85 billions so they could continue with 70% of the stock going to the government. This was the largest bailout of a company in US history. Sjostrom (2009) describes this. See also Greenberg and Cunningham (2013) for the whole story summarized here. But the troubles continued. Huge executive bonuses in 2009 of $165 million to executives and total bonuses of some $1.2 billion led to bad PR. Losses continued. In 2011, and on November 3, 2011, the shares had fallen 49% and had a $1 billion share buy back program. There were more government loans

and stock offerings totaling $182.3 billion but eventually AIG paid back $205 billion so they made a profit.
- Citigroup Inc. (2008) known as Citi, the multinational financial services corporation is headquartered in New York City. The company dates from 1812 and in 2012 was the third largest bank in the US with the largest shareholders including funds from Singapore and the Middle East. They currently have about 16,000 offices in some 140 countries with about 260,000 employees counting the Citicorp and Travelers parts of the business. Before the 2008 financial crisis, they were the largest bank worldwide, a place now held by JP Morgan Chase. They had enormous losses in 2008 from subprime mortgages and CDOs and poor risk management and were bailed out in November 2008 by the US government TARP which later took a 36% equity stake paid with $25 billion of the bailout money along with a $45 billion line of credit (Citigroup, 2008). The government guaranteed losses on more than $300 billion of underwater assets and gave them $20 billion but there were conditions. For example, the CEO had his salary reduced to $1/year and other executives were capped at $500,000 cash plus restricted stock only exercisable when the bailout was paid back. By December 2010, Citi repaid the bailout loans and the government made $12 billion profit from the sale of shares. Citi recovered from the crisis and became one of the best capitalized banks in the world, although along the way in 2012 they failed the Fed's stress test. They, like many others, had their share of legal difficulties over the years such as having a hand in the 2001 Enron crisis and being fined for taking funds from clients credit cards.
- UBS (2008): subprime losses. At the end of 2007, UBS announced that it would write off $18 billion of failed investments involving the subprime housing market in the United States. In 2008, the write-offs increased to more than $50 billion. In April 2008, at the request of the Swiss Federal Banking Commission, UBS published a report detailing the reasons for its losses. In October 2008, the Swiss central bank announced its intention to take $60 billion of toxic assets off UBSs balance sheet and to inject $6 billion of equity capital. Shefrin (2009) uses the 2008 as a base to develop a behavioral analysis of the UBS crisis.
- Madoff fraud (2009): Bernie Madoff ran a ponzi scheme where results were made-up to look good. Some observers like Ed Thorp who investigated it in 1991 for a private client knew about the fraud when he could not find the trades; see his column in *Wilmott* magazine. Many lost money, a list was in the *Wall Street Journal*.

- UBS (2011): rogue trader. Kweku Adeboli was arrested on September 14, 2011 and later sentenced to 7 years in jail in relation with a GBP2.3 billion trading loss. While working at one of UBS' London offices, Adeboli had set up and hidden speculative on S&P 500, DAX and EuroStoxx Futures. When in the summer of 2011 these positions began to incur losses, Adeboli increased his bets in the hope of returning to profitability. This decision further fueled his losses.
- MF Global (2012) had many large fines and penalties for risk supervision failures in 2008 and 2009 during the financial crisis. In March 2008, the stock price fell dramatically due to fears regarding their liquidity among investors, advisors and analysts. In March 2010, Jon Corzine was named CEO. Corzine was a former Goldman, former governor of New Jersey and former US senator. His involvement in the troubles to come is uncertain but could have been a force in the $6.3 over bet on eurobonds. He resigned in November 2011 and was not charged with anything.

  In 2011, they had a liquidity problem and it was thought that they had to use customer money to cover margin on mark-to-market losing positions. The customer money was legally supposed to be in segregated accounts. MF Global took repo agreements off the books. Again, a violation of the rules. Then they made a $6.3 billion bet on European weak country bonds. These led to massive losses as the euro debt crisis worsened. In October 2011, they had a meltdown caused by improper transfers of $891 million from customer accounts to cover trading losses. Then on October 31, 2011 they declared bankruptcy and faced liquidation. Employees were fired without any severance pay or bonuses or deferred compensation. The customer losses as of April 2012 were $1.6 billion. In January 2013, a judge approved a 93% return of customer investments. So most people will get most of their investment funds.
- Monti Pashi (2013): the largest bank in Siena Italy fails. Banca Monti dei Paschi di Siena founded in 1472 is the oldest surviving bank in the world and Italy's third largest bank with about 3,000 branches and 4.5 million customers. Rising yields and declining valuations on Italian government debt in 2008 during the European sovereign debt crisis led to a loss of $2 billion. They were recapitalized by the government. Then in 2009, the Santorini and Alessandria branches had large losses. To hide them, the top management entered into 500–700 million euro derivative contracts with Deutsche Bank and Nomura. The auditors and Banca d'Italia did not know about these positions. But in November 2012, the new board discovered the situation and informed the Banca. The shareholders and

analysts did not know about these derivative losses. On January 22, 23 and 24, the bank's shares fell 5.6%, 8.43% and 8%, respectively. Massari resigned on the 22nd. On January 25, the shareholders gave the board of directors the power to recapitalize, replacing the Tremonti bonds with new Monti bonds and they did receive a 4.1 billion euro government bailout. So they continue but are scarred. The headquarters is in the main plaza where the Palio is run. They sponsored that plus other historic building renovations and other cultural activities which they can no longer support.

Final Remarks

There seems to be no end to a long string of hedge fund and bank trading disasters. The reasons are basically always the same: over betting, lack of diversification and vulnerability to a bad scenario. The lack of severe penalties for losses and the incentives associated with possible massive fees leads to this behavior. Here, I have discussed hedge fund type behavior in hedge fund and other financial institutions such as bank trading departments. I only briefly discuss other types of financial crises. For more on these over many centuries, see Kindleberger and Aliber (2011) and Reinhart and Rogoff (2011). See also Roubini (2011) regarding the European debt crisis of 2011–2014, which in 2017 is still acute in Spain, Italy, Greece and other countries.

Countries fearing contagion when banks and other large investment vehicles fail, continue to bail them out. There have been suggestions that they be recapitalized and follow better risk control but they resist regulation. Sometimes these bailouts even make a profit for the government even though excessive bonuses to executives should have been avoided. The big hedge funds seem to be able to raise new money after big losses. Hence, more blowouts will occur.

There was much debate concerning the true necessity and value of the US 2008 bailouts, irrespective of whether or not in total they made a profit. It is hard to estimate the higher economic value that would have accrued if the institutions that were bailed out would have been required to readjust the mortgages. The 56% drop in the S&P500 from the 2007 peak to the March 2009 bottom, indicates that action was needed, however, actions like Merrill Lynch giving 1/3 of their TARP money to executive compensation was unwise, and a backlash since then will prevent this next time.

Notes

[1] Litzenberger and Modest (2009), who were on the firing line for the LTCM failure, propose a modification of standard finance CAPM type theory modified for fat tails and C-VaR or expected tail losses for the losses. Ziemba (2003, 2007, 2013) presents his approach using convex risk measures and three scenario dependent correlation matrices depending upon volatility using stochastic programming scenario optimization. Both of these approaches would mitigate such losses. The key is not to over bet and have access to capital once a crisis occurs and to plan in advance for such events.

[2] Using the Kelly criterion, you should never bet more than the log optimal amount and betting more (as LTCM did) is dominated as it has lower growth rates *and* higher risk. This point is **not** understood by even the top academic financial economists who insist on using positive power as well as negative power and log utility functions. The positive power utility functions are dominated and reflect over betting.

[3] They could have paid me a million dollars for an hour's consulting and still made more than 1,000 times profit from the advice. It was more important for them to be nice to my family, as they were than to listen to the results of a *gaijin* professor. How could he possibly understand the Japanese stock market? In fact all the economics ideas were there; see Ziemba and Schwartz (1991). I did enjoy these lectures, dinners and golf but being listened to dominates.

[4] But the manager's personal share of the fund may decline in percentage term as the fund grows!

[5] The oil and gas market is discussed in Ziemba and Ziemba (2013, Chapter 32).

[6] An academic treatment of a rogue trader is in Lleo and Ziemba (2015c). Here I sketch some ideas.

[7] Indeed in late March 2007 it was widely reported that Hunter was soliciting money for a series of commodity funds with the name Solengo Capital. It is believed that cash rich investors in the Middle East and Europe are likely to invest. To assuage fears of another meltdown, investors will be able to pick specific managers and commodities. The new fund will impose margin and other restrictions on managers and will eliminate all lock-in restrictions if these controls are violated. The prices of the natural gas contracts Mr Hunter is known to favor had been increasing in anticipation of his return to the market.

[8] This discussion expands on description in Lleo (2010).

[9] By the end of 2007, Bear Stern's leverage ratio reached 35.6 times and held derivatives with a notational value of about $13.4 trillion.

Chapter 22

Trend Following in the Bahamas

It was 1995 and the phone rang. Two colleagues were in Las Vegas and wanted to come up to Vancouver to see me. They had their own airplane — always a good sign. They were working in Nassau with one of them living in South Florida close by. They were looking for professors knowledgeable in the mathematics of gambling who wanted to work with them. Apparently others were not interested but I immediately was. They were already successful using trend following techniques and were looking for ways to improve their investment performance.

Trend following strategies are basically simple but there are tricks as to when to enter trades and especially when to exit trades. I have found over the years that the decision to exit is much more important and complex than when to enter. The main person who was trading on his own money with some investment by friends and employers was Harold McPike. Harry had taken his wife's last name because his name was known in the Blackjack community. The two met in Vienna where Harry was born and lived. A restless person, he did not like university life and from ages 17–21 he studied blackjack strategies. Finally, at 21 with his passport, he was allowed into a Vienna casino and had a stake of $4,000 from various summer jobs. Successful blackjack systems have small edges of about $\frac{1}{2}\%$ up to 6% some of the time and may average about 1%. So if you play 50 hands an hour, you have to play 2 hours to be one hand ahead on average. If the average bet is $500, then you make $250 per hour. Of course, if you get the edge up to 2% then it is $500 per hour. But there is a lot of variance here, even if one plays perfectly with no errors. So it is easy to be behind, depending on how the cards fall. Harry lost $2,000 of his $4,000 stake and noticed that another person was betting similar to him. He quizzed this person, who later became his junior partner, as to how he could play similarly when he, Harry, had invented the systems. He replied, "you dummy,

Ed Thorp wrote a famous blackjack book that introduced card counting into blackjack." Ed also used Kelly betting in which you bet more in favorable and high probability of winning situations and the minimum or zero when there is no edge. Thus *Fortune's Formula* had the first serious application. In the simplest case, with one bet, the amount to bet is simply the edge over the odds so if the edge if 5%, and the odds are 1-1, meaning for each dollar bet you win or lose $1, he bet 5% of your fortune.[1] After some discussions, the two became friends. They proceeded over the next few years to play in 100 countries and be banned in 40. That gave Harry a stake of about $1 million and he returned to Vienna and started a computer business.

Then an opportunity arose. Richard Dennis, a very famous and successful trend follower in the Chicago trading pits announced a contest. He bet his partner that he could train new traders in his methods and they would be successful. The idea was that great traders can be trained and the winning touch was not from inherent skill but from good training and discipline to follow certain rules. That is traders could be generated. They were called turtles. Dennis's methods involved a lot of graphical lines on paper such as new year long highs, moving averages, golden crosses, indicating likely rises, death crosses indicating likely declines, etc. His exact formulas were kept secret but Harry programmed them for one of the turtles into a coherent betting package. Harry did not know about Kelly betting then or later except that it existed. And later I taught it to him. But he knew that the higher the probability of winning was the more he should bet, which was on the right track. Gradually, Harry moved around the world and settled in Nassau on Paradise Island where he has remained. The relationship with me was a lot of fun and I enjoyed going there. We would have lunch at the Ocean Club, a famous hotel featured in the first of the Daniel Craig James Bond movies. A plus for going to Nassau was beautiful beaches, nice weather and occasionally having dinner with John Templeton or Sean Connery at a nearby table. Harry was very successful with the formula — put 75 million into the betting pool. Then, when it doubled, restart at 75 million and put the rest in a safe place. Harry's fees were simple — if they win, he would take one third of the profits with no management fee and, of course, there were no fees for losses.

The trend following systems usually work but have occasionally periods where there are substantial losses. As time went by, more and more of the betting stake was Harry's. Favorable Bahamas taxation helped and outside investors, except for employees, were phased out. So Harry had $300 million plus in various bank accounts. He was the type to not invest a penny until a new system was fully researched. And that might take a year or more. Harry was interested but not knowledgeable about the stock market so discussing that with him was one of my jobs. After a while, he gave me $5 million to manage with very good fees. It was his way of keeping me on a consulting salary more or less similar to the other employees in Nassau and Vienna. I would go there from Vancouver a few times a year and have occasional contact otherwise. He was a control type so preferred to do things in Nassau even if they cost more.

One of my jobs we to help Harry recruit and evaluate employees. A brilliant thinker and executor, Harry had a hard time with employees and was continually dissatisfied with them. But one he liked was a young Cal Tech educated physics graduate Andrew Mart who accepted a job with Harry *in lieu* of going for a PhD at MIT. It was a wise choice as he has had a rewarding and highly lucrative job with Harry. One thing he did was to make a complete Kelly optimization computerized system. I designed it and led the analysis but he did all the data analysis and computer programming. Missing data and new contracts added complexity and Andrew spent about 18 months working on this — part time as he had other duties as well. In my opinion, a Bachelor's degree in physics from Cal Tech is a great predictor of a top student. They are always top notch. Working with Andrew was a pleasure and we showed that adding good Kelly betting would add significantly to profits.

The relationship was a good one and the equity account management fees plus small fees for each visit to Nassau was very welcome. I suggested employees from my academic network and evaluated his. One he hired was a young brash Czech student Karel Janecek. I was giving a lecture at Charles University in Prague on multiperiod portfolio theory including Kelly wagering with some examples which included one on blackjack from my 1992 paper in *Management Science* with Leonard MacLean and George Blazenko. The Charles University statistics department was Berkeley–Stanford quality and their students were top notch. Karel did not attend my lecture but we spoke after. He said I heard you gave a lecture on blackjack. I said I used it as an example. I immediately determined that Karel was brilliant and he had just finished his master's thesis on Kelly wagering. He had the best blackjack website in the world selling various products including complex optimal strategies for various rules changes. Since Harry was looking for people, this looked like a good match. The arrangement was for Karel to come to Vancouver so I could *train him* prior to starting work in Nassau a month later. That was a lot of fun for me as I have always enjoyed great students. I did have quite a few in Vancouver while at the University of British Columbia. I got him housing on campus and we discussed various things. Vancouver had a lot of small casinos so we would go to play blackjack. I understand the theory but am a lousy card counter and although I am decent on the rules, some complex situations eluded me. But Karel knew every rule effect in his head as well as from his computer programs. We made an arrangement. He would bet and I would bet and we would split the profits. It was a good deal for me as I would win $100–$200 and he $3,000. After a while, one of the casinos hired him as a consultant. The month went by fast.

Karel became a good employee of Harry's showing brilliance. He was working on bonds, a most dangerous area that I have always avoided. While I was there I was asked to suggest a bond consultant. The choice was simple, Professor David Heath of Carnegie Mellon's Mathematical Finance Department. I had known David from some talks at Cornell where he had previously taught and did research. David was a co-author of the famous Heath, Jarrow and Morton based pricing model published in the prestigious journal *Econometrica* and was interested in gambling and blackjack. So it was a good match. For 3 days I watched the two of them devising models with current interest rates, future interest rates, expectations, expectations on futures, etc. It is very complicated. Smoke was coming out of the pages of the mathematics. Later, I suggested to Harry from Vancouver not to let Karel trade any money until Heath checked every formula. The usually careful Harry did not listen and gave Karel a $15 million stake. The trading was up and down with high volatility and then a bad scenario occurred. Treasury secretary Larry Summers basically shut down trading on 30-year US treasury bonds which were very liquid. The 10-year Treasury bonds then became the most liquid instrument. But Karel's account lost over half its value and Harry fired him. Karel had amassed some monies and was interested in getting his PhD at Carnegie Mellon in Heath's department. My strong recommendation helped him get accepted and he went there, finished a PhD and is now a successful trader back in the Czech Republic. That was in 2000 when he left Nassau for Pittsburgh. Some unfair blame came to me since I had recommended Karel but that was part of Harry's personality.

Around the same time, Harry asked me to evaluate all the Nassau and Vienna employees and projects. Also, since Harry and his wife Joanne, a great photographer from New Zealand, were always cleaning the office, making coffee, picking people up at 2 am who flew in from Miami, etc., I suggested that he hire an office manager. That turned out to be a good suggestion with a bad outcome. The manager hired, Jim Cone from Chicago, was actually more interested in being involved with all the money. So I, as a valued consultant, was a threat. So the way to get rid of me was to stop the trading account. The reasons were somewhat legitimate — I was trailing the S&P500 which was flying in 1999 with the internet bubble. My own BSEYD model had gone into the danger zone in April 1999. Cone argued that although the account was doing all right, I was ahead after Harry's fees of 12% per year for $3\frac{1}{4}$ years from 1997–2000 and the $5 million was now $7.2 million, but it was underperforming and they felt, correctly, that danger was on the horizon. So the account was closed and I do not know how it would have fared since 2000. I did ask for a small settlement like the other fired employees which was refused. I suppose I could have stayed on as only that account was canceled but it was clear that the good relationship was over. After a bit of complaining, I gave up on that, preferring to remember good days from 1995 to 2000 and a pleasant consulting relationship in an interesting place. I have had no contact since but understand that Harry is up to $3 billion in 2017.[2] This is a great financial success.

He pals around with another billionaire who hired me to devise strategies and trade them in an offshore hedge fund and devise a racetrack syndicate. Some of Harry's money is invested in this billionaire's hedge funds and on other racing syndicates that partially use my racetrack betting strategies. This billionaire claims that Harry was worried that I would reverse engineer and steal the trend following formulas so closing the account that was a small part of Harry's wealth was an excuse to get me out. I had no interest in having these formulas but lots in continuing with Harry as it was a fun consulting job that I miss.

My trading was good and I had fees plus an investment in the fund. Unfortunately, the billionaire stopped paying the fees so I had to ask for my investment back. Meanwhile, his empire was crumbling. He had fraud and poor investments in other parts of his business including some with Madoff. The entire array of assets are now being sorted out by a team of lawyers. I do not expect much from this. Since there has been novel progress in four years with 30 lawyers involved, it is clear those lawyers will get the money and we will likely get nothing. But I learned some things. Sadly my strategies were working well during this period and have continued in the golden era we have had in the S&P500 and other equity markets since the bottom in March 2009. More on this in Chapter 28.

Note

[1] I discuss Kelly strategies in Chapter 7 including its use by many great investors and how to use it with multiple possible investments, transactions costs and other practical details.

[2] Later Cone was fired for suggesting Harry invest with Madoff where he lost many millions — according to Baltoo $79 million.

Chapter 23

The Internet Bubble Crash, 2000–2002

The US stock market had a big run from 1995 to 1999. The low interest rate policy of Fed chief Alan Greenspan with the attendant the so-called Greenspan put helped feed the rally. That put was the belief that if the stock market declined, Greenspan would initiate policies to prop it back up. In 2016, there seemed to be a Yellen put with very different, virtually zero interest rates. The January 1995 S&P500 as 470.42 with a price earnings ratio of 17.10, a long 30-year bond had a high 8.02% and an earnings yield of 5.85% so the BSEYD model was at 2.17, well below the 3.00 needed to be in the danger zone. By April 1999 the S&P500 had ballooned to 1335.18, a tripling of its value. The long bond had dropped by the Greenspan policies to 5.82%. The BSEYD was then just into the danger zone at 3.03. So the stage was set for a crash. The internet crash was on. Stocks with no earnings were trading with huge market values. Naive professors were trying to use faulty models to justify the high prices.[1] So, unfortunately, their conclusion was disproved when the internet crash occurred.

The market rallied throughout the rest of 1999 to close the year at 1459.25 with the BSEYD model remaining in the danger zone. Robert Shiller's book on irrational exuberance came out in April 2000. He had been bearish for years but had the great fortune to bring out the book at a perfect time when the market started falling. This book became the best seller ever for the Princeton University Press.

But the April decline was reversed and the stock market rallied into an August double top similar to the April top. Then it cracked so the BSEYD model had the right call again but some 16 months in the future. The stock market fell but was led down by very few stocks. The high cap stocks, telecoms and high priced technology led the decline. In Canada, the market was up 31% in 1999 but only 3% when three stocks eliminated and one of them had mostly stock in one of the other two. Nortel Networks fell from $120 to almost nothing. I recall buying shares at $1.20 and selling them at $6. The US market was similar with most stocks falling 10% or less. But the S&P500 index bottomed at 666 around March 6, 2009 and by the end of October 2016 has tripled to the 2125 area. Late in 2001 there was a second crash signal because although stock prices had declined, earnings had fallen even more. The S&P500 fell 22% in 2002 with a large fall in the third quarter which was down 12%, especially in July.

As a trader, I need to keep some things confidential. One was a second crash model based on relative options prices. The idea is a simple behavioral finance concept that when there is too much overconfidence, the buyers will stop buying and the market will fall. It is implemented by comparing call options prices with put prices. Usually the puts are worth more as pension funds, insurance companies and the like must buy them to portfolio insure their portfolios. On average, they over pay a lot. But once in a while the calls become worth more. Then it is likely that the market will crash. I found that from the initial S&P500 trading in 1995 when the options market first became liquid, there have been six such signals. One was for the third quarter of 2002 and it worked as the market fell 12%. Another was for the October 1987 crash. Of the six calls, four actually worked and the result was a total loss of -41.7% So that sounds good. But it is not too useful now as the last call was in 2003. The signal may occur again but it has not been there during 2004–2017.

After the 2000–2002 crash, the world hated stocks so went to another asset class — land and housing! I saw this crash coming so sold stocks to payoff three mortgages. But had I thought it through better and realized that stocks were out and real estate was in, I would have bought three more properties instead of getting these three out of debt. No debt does have its charms though! Real estate in the US peaked in 2005–2006 then declined sharply; see the Case Shiller housing indices. But in Vancouver, where I live, prices have continued a step rise into at least 2016. The market is on fire with many properties selling for more than their asking price. An example was a nice house on Bellevue, a very good but not the top street near the university. In 1986 it sold for C$460,000, in 2016 it was listed at C$6,880,000. It received 11 offers, all with no conditions and sold for C$9 million. One of our friends, with a decent but ordinary house on a 50 foot lot, put her house for sale for $3.1 million. In 1 day there were 6 offers, all from Chinese, and the property sold for half a million over asking. My old street where we lived before the 1984 Stanford visit has

10 houses worth $20 million plus. Finally in mid 2016 after the tax evaluations were sent out, the British Columbia government acted with some new real estate transaction rules. In my view it was too late but it has made it more difficult for Chinese and other offshore buyers. The measures were: 1) an additional 15% transfer tax for foreign buyers of Vancouver properties — this is in addition to the regular transfer tax of 1% on the first $200,000 and 2% above that; 2) a luxury tax of an additional 3% for properties above $2 million for all buyers: 3) more stringent mortgage lending rules — the idea is that even though up to 5 year mortgages are available for under 3% people must be able to carry mortgages at rates in the mid 4% area; 4) the usual 5% GST — the goods and services tax payable if the property is newly constructed or on older properties such as condos where the GST has not been paid because the owner before rented the property but the new owner wants to live in it; and 5) a new tax that is supposed to start in 2018 for properties bought but kept empty — the tax is modest and aiming at the problem that a large percent of the Vancouver condos are empty foreign owned units. The result is a lot less sales and a forecast of an about 8% fall in 2017 prices. But the decline did not last long as the foreigners adjusted to the increases and just paid more. I am interested in horseracing betting and horse ownership. So for about one tenth of a vancouver house I was able to buy a big beautifully restored house with 20 acres close to the major horse farms and the Kentucky horse park.

Note

[1] See E. Schwartz and M. Moon (2000) for a model with 30 parameters so you can get any result you want.

Chapter 24

The US Housing Bubble, Credit Crisis, Crash and Recovery 2006 to 2015

President George W Bush pushed the case that all Americans should own their own homes. A low interest rate policy of Fed Chair Alan Greenspan fueled a bond rally with the rates declining from the mid-1990s through to the 2005/2006 peak in real estate prices. Real estate in the US overall has had its ups and downs since the 1700s.[1] However, since the 1940s, the overall US real estate has increased dramatically and the latter part was up each year.[2] The real estate rise in the period up to 2005 was very large and made people feel that the only direction for future real estate prices was up. Many were burned in the 2000–2002 stock market decline so went to a new asset class namely real estate.

Much trouble was created from the concepts of subprime mortgages, ninga loans and securitization[3]: Subprime loans were those made to basically anyone whose assets and ability to pay were loosely checked if they were considered at all. Ninja loans were to those with no assets, no job and no income. So their only hope to carry the mortgage was increasing prices and the ability to take money out of the house like a charge card. Securitization was the concept of bundling up a group of subprime loans and then getting the package rated AAA and then sold to other parties in the US, Europe and elsewhere. Norvik, Norway, a special case, was a city above the Arctic circle that lost most of its assets when the US real estate market collapsed. The extent of the subprime loans was extensive in the US but not in other countries such as Canada where loans are only made to genuine qualified borrowers. All this led to a big mess and eventually the 2007–2009 stock market crash.

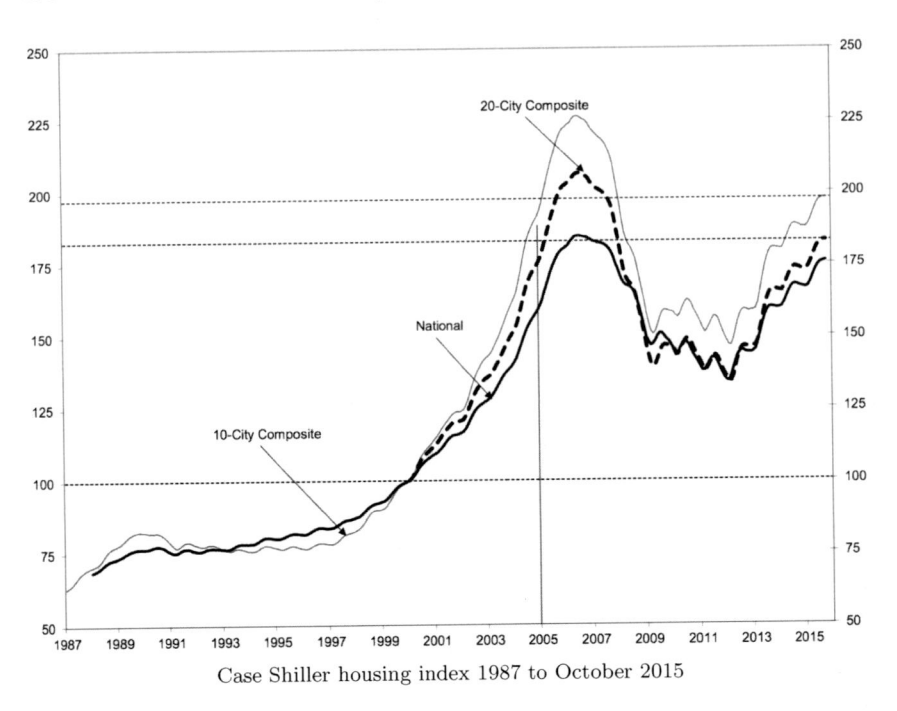

Case Shiller housing index 1987 to October 2015

A 2010–2015 consequence of all this is very weak second home markets in Canada and elsewhere. Finally, in 2015 we have had a bit of a rebound in Canadian dollars in Whistler where I have a ski condo, bought largely for visits by relatives. Real estate prices there doubled in 2002 when the 2010 Olympics was awarded to Whistler/Vancouver. Then they fell while the Canadian dollar rose. Then Canadian dollar collapsed from close to par with the US dollar gradually moving to the 90s then after the Swiss currency unpegging against the euro on January 15, 2015, it fell to about 80 cents so one US dollar was worth about C$1.235 in late June 2015 with a peak in the 1.44 area and about 1.35 at the end of October 2016 when we went to press. So the real estate rise is in Canadian dollars, not US dollars. This has led to an about 20% rise in prices in Canadian dollars. The buyers are not from the US, eastern Canada, Europe or Asia, rather they are Vancouver area people cashing in on large gains in property there. In 2017, I was able to finally sell the Whistler condo at a good price similar to the 2002's peak to a London, UK area person.

The US dollar is strong and with Europe decreasing interest rates as they move into their own QE program, along with US interest rates to be increased in December 2015 or later from the current 0 to 0.24% area to about the 3.5% area in 2 to 3 years. There will be much turbulence along the way with Greece and other European problems forming a major difficulty. Traders like me have a good friend running the FED, namely the calm, collected, very wise Janet Yellen. She tends to be a dove helping fuel equity and other asset prices. My feeling is that the enormous balance sheet of the FED, some $4 trillion, will simply expire away over time, but we shall see! In 2017, the FED is adding positions as theirs mature so the balance sheet remains large.

Notes

[1] See Glaeser, Gottlieb and Tobio (2012) for a tour through these last two centuries. The Case–Shiller indices are useful for current trends.

[2] There was a crash and many foreclosures in the early 60s. The summer Sandra worked for Fanny Mae, there were many foreclosures in Arizona. Also I recall my cousin bought US many properties in the late 60s after a big decline.

[3] The lax lending was completely fueled by the ability of the lending institutions to package the loans and sell them off like hot potatoes, so why bother with standards?!!

Chapter 25

The Flash Crash and High Frequency Trading

In the fall of 2014, I was visiting the London School of Economics, which I do once or twice a year for a month or so. Besides having great resident academics they have an extraordinary strong connection to the very sophisticated London financial and political world. This combination is the best of all the universities I have visited. Though I have had extraordinary experiences at other universities as well, a few are standouts: Chicago Booth has the best research atmosphere, Berkeley and Stanford are the most pleasant, MIT has its fame but brutal weather and Oxford students were the best. Possibly the best single class was at the University of Zurich in 2003 where I had 10 really top students from across the country including the neighboring powerhouse ETH in an asset-liability management course.

There are lots of great lectures at LSE. The public ones are oversubscribed so you have to reserve even in large rooms (and even with a ticket you have to show up early as they give out more tickets than seats!). As a visitor I can get that arranged. Michael Lewis, author of many best sellers such as *Money Ball, Liars Poker, The Big Short* and *The Blind Side*, was invited to discuss his new book, *Flash Boys*.

Lewis is a masters graduate of the LSE and was exceptionally well treated. The interviewer was another writer. The room was filled to capacity plus there were people in adjoining rooms watching on TV, so the crowd was about 1,000 people for the talk and question period. Lewis gave a nice careful, non-arrogant talk which was enjoyable. He puts on a good show. The questions were all badminton style, very easy; no hard questions appeared.

Lewis' main point is that the high frequency traders (HFTs) cheat the rest of the investors and traders in the market. They have tricks to cancel trades, front run, trade among themselves, creating no volume, trading in Black Pools and other shady operations. Then there is the speed. Regardless of the trading or investment strategy, at any given speed level, somebody is going to be trading at the exchange first. The overriding message of *Flash Boys* is that trading speeds have gotten out of hand and need to be reined in through rule making or IEX type speed bumps. The book brought attention to the IEX platform and its order-handling methods designed to level out the advantages of ultra low latency algorithms. IEX predated *Flash Boys* and it likely would have gained prominence anyway because it offered something that institutional traders were open to and willing to pay for. Aequitas Neo Exchange, a similarly motivated venture in Canada, was launched on March 27, 2015. But *Flash Boys* did not take note of more nuanced and responsible attitudes in the industry toward the ever accelerating technology.[1] Later, others came into the high frequency market, and now in 2017 they are everywhere. The game now has changed from careful research by distinguished researchers to a search for speed of execution. What is key is to be as close as possible to the trading exchange. Large sums of money are spent on such systems.[2]

What's the truth and the bottom line? Well that depends on your point of view. Some will feel cheated. For me, the speed is all right and it helps liquidity, but it would be best if the authorities clean up some of the unfair tactics. I trade a lot all the time in equities, futures and futures options. These effects do not hurt me much. I have my own strategies and almost always buy and sell with limit orders so I must be aware of moves that HFT players and others might make. One example where I lost money in two accounts was an options expiry where trading stops on Thursday at the close but the settlement is based on Friday's open prices. I was short some futures which were hedging some options that were going to zero the next morning. The Thursday close of S&P500 was 2072. When I got the settlement the next morning it was 2092 and the futures at that time were trading for 2072. What they did was push the settlement price up 20 full S&P500 points by some sort of manipulation. I have said in lectures that maybe one of the tactics to do this is to offer Microsoft stock $2 above its fair value and sell 100 shares as the first trade Friday morning. The settlement is based on the first trade, not at the same moment in time, on each of the 500 stocks in the S&P500. Since the index if value weighted manipulation is likely in the most valuable stocks. I learned a lesson this time that what you do is you do not go short futures or long futures into that type of options expiry. What you need to do is exit positions on Thursday or before of anything where you could be hurt with a 20–30 point S&P move. Almost always the settlement is moved somehow to a round amount like 80 or 75 or 90 which I have assumed is because those manipulating the market are short options at those round number strikes.

Lewis sold a lot of books and made a big impact in the media but did not change the industry much. HFT continues on. If there is another flash crash there might be more serious changes but even that seems not so much to be caused by HFT but by an imbalance of orders in a short period. HFT then spreads it like a wild fire.

The Flash Crash

We all expected at some stage that there would be a crisis of some sort with all the computerized trading. I was in Victoria on Thursday May 6, 2010 when the flash crash occurred. In a 20 minute period the DJIA fell 10% as did other indices such as the S&P500. I watched the decline and then it hit bottom and recovered about two thirds of the drop. The VIX volatility index increased to 28%, meanwhile, there were many trades at funny prices like 1 cent or $10,000. Most of these were later canceled. On Friday the volatility index rose to 43% and I was an options seller in that market assuming that in the next week the prices would come down and they did. This was another example of mean reversion.

Why the VIX was much higher on Friday than Thursday is related to the transmission of fear. By Friday it was known what had happened but not why.

The culprit that caused the Flash Crash

Stock markets in 2010 were up and down all year with fear and greed alternating. The month of September had a gain of 8.76% and that lifted the year's return on the S&P500 to a slightly positive 2.34%.

The S&P500's gyrations including the May 6 Thursday flash crash in which the stock market fell 10% in a few minutes and then recovered two-thirds of the losses that day. The time line that day had a vicious drop and a fast recovery.[3] We were in Victoria as I needed an AV Node ablation and we were able to watch it all unfold at the hospital. Special thanks once again to the BC medical system. You pay for parking the rest is covered by Stanford harvard quality doctors — a good system.

A joint SEC–CFTC report on the flash crash points to a large fundamental mutual fund trader at Waddell & Reed Financial of Overland Park, Kansas who executed a large sell order using an automated algorithm at a time in the afternoon during which the markets were already stressed.

The report said that

> "the temporary crash resulted from a confluence of forces after a single fund company tried to hedge its stock market investment position legitimately, albeit in an aggressive and abrupt manner".

The computer algorithm accelerating selling as the prices plunged. Some 80 SEC people disallowed trades that were way out of line. We will see what the SEC–CFTC officials devise as new rules. There are already individual trading halts for 5 minutes if some stocks move 10% in 5 minutes. Devising fair rules is complex.

The 6,438 trades totaling 75,000 mini S&P futures contracts had a face value of $4.1 billion.[4] The trading on May 6 was 5.7 million mini S&P500 contracts so 75,000 is 1.3% of that day's volume and less than 9% of the volume during the time period of the sales. W&R's algorithm was to sell at most 9% of the total volume so they accomplished that. In 20 minutes the futures were down 5% and triggered the 1000 point decline in the Dow Jones average in about 10 minutes. Between 14:32 and 14:52, some 20 minutes, there were 147,577 trades totaling 844,513 contracts. The large selloff began at 14:44:20. The bulk of W & R's trades were made after the market bottomed and was rallying back.[5]

According to the CME:

> ...fundamentally negative financial, economic and political events in Europe and elsewhere contributed to investor uncertainty and impacted participation and liquidity in all market segments at certain times that day. Throughout the day on May 6, CME Group markets functioned properly.
>
> ...The prevailing market sentiment was evident well before these orders were placed, and the orders, as well as the manner in which they were entered, were both legitimate and consistent with market practices. These hedging orders were entered in relatively small quantities and in a manner designed to dynamically adapt to market liquidity by participating in a target percentage of 9% of the volume executed in the market. As a result of the significant volumes traded in the market, the hedge was completed in approximately twenty minutes, with more than half of the participant's volume executed as the market rallied not as the market declined.
>
> ...the $3^1/_2$ minute period immediately preceding the market bottom that was established at 13:45:28. During that period, the participant hedging its portfolio represented less than 5% of the total volume of sales in the market.
>
> Source: CME (2010)

According to Zero Hedge led by Tyler Durden and the CME, there was more to the Flash Crash than the $4.1 billion hedge trade. By their research it seems that HFTs began to quickly buy and then resell contracts to each other generating large volume but no real trading. Between 2:45:13 and 2:45:27, these HTFs traded over 27,000 contracts, which was 49% of the volume. Yet the net buying was only 200 contracts. So the ratio of volume to liquidity was 135 to 1. So the HFTs do not provide liquidity but volume at least in this case.

Finally, after 5 years there was someone to blame for the flash crash. Well, maybe, but he possibly had a small hand in it. Navinder Singh Sarao, 36, was arrested in London in late April 2015 and charged with separate civil and criminal charges in the US. It is likely a whistle blower was involved to get the case against him moving.[6] Bail was set at GBP5,050,000 but his assets were frozen by US order. He is trying to avoid extradition to the US. The civil complaint is by the US Commodity Futures Trading Commission and the criminal is by the US Department of Justice. The 2010 Dodd–Frank law makes it easier to prove market manipulation and Sarao has boasted about his prowess as a *spoofer*. He regularly puts in phantom trades to push the market in a given direction, then cancels the trades and profits from the reversal of direction.[7] One approach is to place large sell orders at prices slightly above the current best offer. The goal is to create a sense of heavy selling pressure to try to drive prices lower. Then Sarao would buy at the lower prices only to sell soon after once the original sell orders have been canceled and prices recovered. There is a false appearance of increased supply. He claims to have made $40 million by being a *good trader* during 2010–2014. Actually he is just a bluffer, playing a game of chicken. He operated out of a UK trading *arcade* where is rents desk space and computers and learned this spooking from a training course. He is a CME member for faster execution. This is in the S&P500 futures where I trade minis which are one fifth of a full S&P500 futures contract. They are more liquid and preferred by most traders. The CME contacted Sarao in March 2009 but did nothing. Indeed, his arrogance is as good as his manipulation. On the day of the flash crash wrote to him saying orders are "expected to be entered in good faith for the purpose of executing bona fide transactions." His response a few weeks later was "kiss my ass." He continued spoofing until 2014. The CME is self regulated with members, which include Sarao, enforcing the rules, so there are conflicts of interest everywhere you look.

There are many such trading arcades which are training shops in the UK such as amplify and Futex where Sarao was trained. There are some

1,000 or more traders trying to become "legal crooks." Fortunately, these point-and-click traders who use partially modified off the shelf software are being wiped out by faster computerized high frequency algorithmic traders and competition that makes this business less lucrative.

Sarao was able to place and then cancel orders at a rapid pace using software designed for this purpose. The software would automatically cancel orders as the price of the S&P500 futures shifted closer to the price where he had made his orders. This practice suggests to authorities that Sarao never had intention to fill these orders and instead was trying to manipulate the contract price. Sarao's explanation in emails in the court documents was that he changed his mind a lot. According to Terrance Hendershott, a UC Berkeley professor, Sarao canceled more than 99% of his orders. This compares with other traders who cancel only 48% of the time. Wow, 48%, that's a lot!

Sarao was busy moving money around the world in the International Guarantee Corporation and Security Ltd., in Anguilla. Sarao was billed GBP375,000 for helping save him GBP7 million in tax as a result of transferring money to the Federation of St Christopher and Nevis. In 2012, he had $17 million in the Swiss bank Hinduja. He then wanted to transfer money to the United Arab Bank Dubai. It was clear that the prosecution of Mr Sarao was arbitrary and his contribution to the flash crash negligible. With tens of thousands trading billions in the S&P500 futures contract it seems hard to manipulate, but we have seen that it can be manipulated such as on options expiry days. Sethi argues that HFTs have plenty of bogus orders using algorithms to implement complex strategies that are involved with market making and speculation. HTFs are on one or both sides of 75% of all S&P500 futures contracts, so why was Sarao singled out. Maybe it is because of his transparency, the whistle blower, the arrogance and the medium sided firm. Larger firms are less transparent. Sethi thinks that focus on the largest firms is wisest here, but it sure looks like Sarao is in deep trouble. The size and complexity of the US derivative market plus the limited staff to study such markets is likely behind the 5 year delay here. Sarao's boss says "he is honest and did not cause the turmoil." Well 40 million *stolen* is enough to pursue the case here. Sarao make $879,000 on the flash crash day.

Michael Lewis was surprised that Sarao did not head for the hills after the flash crash with his money in place. That may well be good advise but Sarao made most of his money *after* the flash crash.

Notes

[1] Jeffrey Kutler in *Institutional Investor*, February 19, 2015, A year after *Flash Boys*., high frequency trading lives on.
[2] See Mack (2015) for more on this.
[3] The Stock market action on May 6   The Timeline on May 6

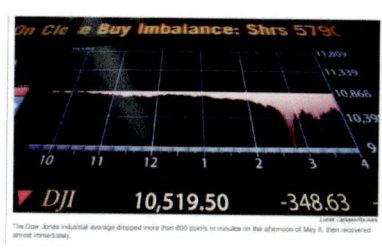

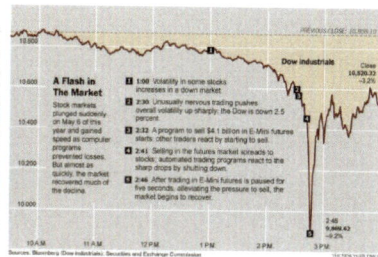

[4] Minis are more liquid than full contracts at $50 versus $250 per point, therefore they are more extensively used by most traders.
[5] Durden (2010).
[6] These whistle blowers get high fees up to $10 million plus. They operate in secret and have computer models to spot spoofing and other illegal tactics.
[7] From Hope, Albanese and Viswanatha (2015), these pictures tell the story:

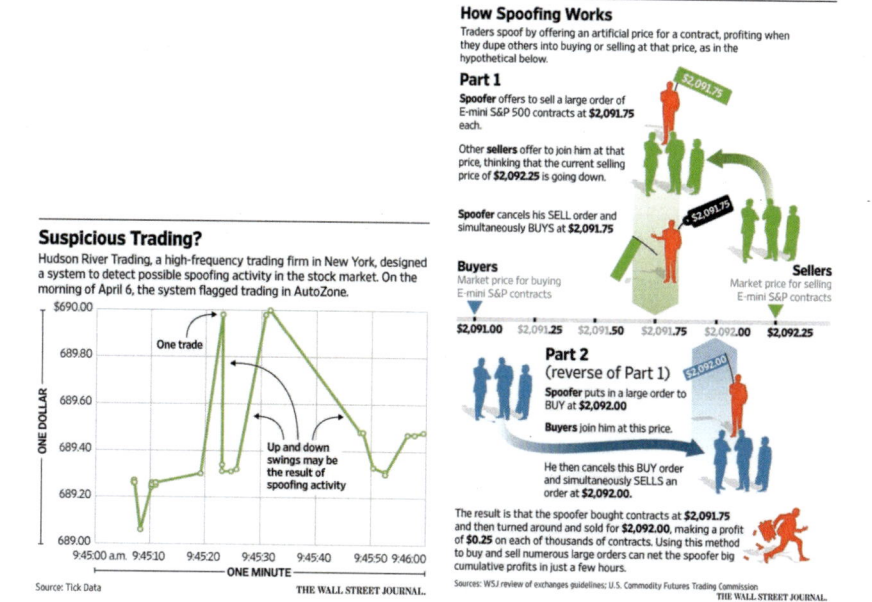

Chapter 26

The Greek Crisis and Why It is Important

Sandra and I have long had an interest in Greece. Sandra's Greek connection started with her 1964 year at the Centre of Economic Planning and Research. Her undergraduate and later PhD advisor, Roy Radner was involved with Andreas Papandreou, head of the centre, from an important family (at the time Sandra was there his father was prime minister, later he became prime minister as did his son). Through this connection, Sandra had a fellowship at the centre for academic year 1964/1965 following graduation from Berkeley with honors in Economics. In 1970, she toured me around Greece and I too became enamored with the country.[1]

The Greek crisis hit the US stock markets hard in early August 2011 with the Dow Jones average alternating up and down over 400 points for four consecutive days. The only previous time I recall four massive up down, up down days in sequence was the week before the 1987 crash. So I took note! While this was happening I was at Fidelity investments[2] in Boston giving a 5 hour series of talks on various investment topics including trying to explain to them why Professor Paul Samuelson, economics Nobel laureate and MIT professor, was critical of the Kelly betting approach. They and others in Boston and elsewhere were not using that strategy largely because of Paul's objections. It was the fact that he was negative even though they did not know the reasons for his skepticism. It turns out that Paul's theoretical points were correct but they are subject to interpretation and their impact on real applications is minor once you understand that short-term Kelly investing is risky and you can lower risk lowering the bet size and thus lowering the long-run growth rate of wealth. This approach dominates other strategies if used properly when its appropriate.

2004 Olympic sign *en route* to Athens, 2001

Full Kelly type strategies, which are used by many people including Buffett, Soros and many hedge funds, have the following characteristics:

1. Very large bets on a few of the very best assets,
2. Little diversification,
3. Much monthly variation in wealth including many losses,
4. Many months with very high returns, and
5. The most final wealth most, but not all of the time.

Once I explained this to the Fidelity group, they felt better about the approach. I decided to write a paper to explain this approach for others including a response to three letters Paul wrote to me in 2006 to 2008. The letters are on my website www.williamtziemba.com and the paper is Ziemba (2015). In Ziemba (2016) I try to explain why Kelly models are useful in practice, focusing on their good and bad points.[3]

The crisis in Greece resulted from bad investments by the banks and overspending by the government that essentially bankrupted the country. Huge spending on the 2004 Olympics was a factor. We saw that on the road from the airport. The worry in the US was that the Greek problem would spread to many other countries in southern Europe such as Portugal, Spain, Italy, Cyprus and Greece. Germany (mainly) plus France and some other northern European countries got put into the position of being the bailout solution to *save the euro* because if Greece left there would be huge losses to them and others, largely because of derivative securities based on Greek assets, plus the Greek people would be hurt more. Deep down the real problem with the euro defense was that it is a flawed union: yes, the currency is the same but there is no real economic or political union. These bailouts have been pumping billions into the failed banks in Greece and other countries while at the same time asking for extreme austerity measures. (They had been gaining a lot by exports to and investments in Greece without buying from Greece.) As a result, Greece, Spain, Portugal and Cyprus are depression economies with youth unemployment in the 50% area and much hardship for all. Italy and Portugal are not much better. Overall Greek unemployment remains about 26% more than the 25% in the US depression in the 1930s.

The crisis continued and Nicolai Battoo was trying to time the market's ups and downs in the futures markets and I had a rough period managing his hedge fund. Finally, I gave up on his timing which did not work because of the extreme volatility and went back to my own strategies which worked fine despite the turbulence.

The austerity in Greece: Sandra and I saw it first hand on a trip in 2011 from Athens to Mykonos, to Santorini to Rodos to Izmir where I was speaking to the Izmir stock exchange about derivative trading. They are set to be the derivative trading market place in Turkey. It was a lovely trip and there were strikes and other demonstrations in Athens with threats elsewhere. Talking to the people showed us first hand the austerity on the people of the country. The ferries these days are very luxurious. Syriza, a left wing party led by Alexis Tsipras won the election on January 26, 2015 on a platform to moderate austerity and lower the debt. It is in Germany's interest not to have Greece default so most likely a compromise on the debt repayment schedule with the austerity reduced and the debt pushed back. With continuing massive unemployment especially for the young, a whole generation has been negatively affected. This continues with peaceful demonstrations at least so far. On February 20, 2015 a tentative compromise was reached pushing back the problem for four more months. The Greek people overwhelming prefer to stay in the euro but want the austerity to be reduced.

The main Greek negotiator has been their colorful finance minister Yanis Varoufakis who has become a media star. Brash, yet sexy, with strong demands from a weak position he is championing Greece's case which is not an easy job. Greece has been running budget deficits since 1980. These have been in the 5–15% GDP range or $10–50 billion. Even in the boom times going into 2007, they had a deficit of 6.7% of GDP, some $21.455 billion. During the 2008–2009 financial crisis in the US and elsewhere, the deficits were higher: 2008 was −9.9% or $35.292 billion; and 2009 was −15.2% or $50.416 billion. 2010–2013 have been better as austerity kicked in at −11.1%, −10.1%, −8.6% and −12.2%. Just in this period the deficits totaled nearly $100 billion. Austerity did lower these deficits in 2014 and 2015 bringing the current government budget into surplus in 2014. Greece's 2015 budget projects a primary surplus (not counting debt repayments) of €3.3 billion or 3.3% of GDP. Overall, counting debt, the government will have a budget minor budget deficit of 0.2% of GDP. It has been more than 40 years since the government had a budget surplus. Greece with a population of 10,735,557 (July 2014) has a GDP of $2,843 billion. The troika (the ECB, IMF, and the Euro Commission) wants Greece to cut an additional €1.8 and €3.8 billion. Meanwhile, the hard line of Varoufakis has led to his demotion in the negotiating team with Christos Staikouras taking the lead.

This has been at a great cost. When austerity was first proposed as a solution for Greece, the expectation was that it would lower GDP 4–5%. In fact GDP has fallen by about 25%. Despite surpassing its budget targets for 3 years, Greece is in a stalemate with the troika over additional fiscal austerity measures as well as a number of promised overhauls. The basic problem is rising debt and a shrinking economy.

The Options and Comments[4]

- Throughout history debtor European nations have sold land to wealthy nations who own the debt. Greece has over 6,000 uninhabited islands and prime Mediterranean beach front land would possibly raise a large amount of money. There is talk of selling the Athens port of Pireus
- Running out of options to keep Greece from defaulting, Tsipras ordered local governments to move their funds to the Central Bank. With negotiations over more bailout aid deadlocked, cash is needed for salaries, pensions and IMF repayment. This raised about €2 billion.
- A third bailout of €30–50 billion is rumored but denied by the Euro Commission president Jean–Claude Juncker. Should there be this bailout, the play would give Greece more flexible payback terms and

is through to be a last resort. The second bailout of €172 billion still has monies tied to performance so all the monies may or may not be released.
- Credit default swaps were priced at an 81.8% chance of Greece being unable to repay its debt in 5 years (April 20), compared with 67% in the beginning of March. The 3 year bond yield jumped to 28.7%.
- Others such as Mohammed El Erian put the probability of an accident in the 55–60% area. So they might default as it is clear they are running out of money to repay their debts to the IMF in particular.
- The Greek debt is about €240 billion, owed mostly to the troika. Within the troika there are different views. Christine Lagarde, the head of the IMF, is hardline, expecting Greece to payup and meet agreed terms. But the other members are softer and more concerned for keeping the EU together. Later though she softened her position and, along with the French and Italian ministers, favors a haircut to bring the debt to a sustainable level. However, German prime minister Angela Merkel and especially German finance minister Wolfgang Schaeble have a much harder line that could actually result in a Grexit from the euro.
- The extent of the contagion if Greece were to default, while unknown, is likely substantial.
- Finally, there is the concept of forgiving some of the debt. Indeed some of the 2012 debt has been forgiven by other parties. After World War II bankers forgave half of Germany's debt after all the deaths and destruction it caused and the reconstruction needed but Greece caused no war. Hedge funds which bought discounted Greek bonds are holding out for full value.
- Greeks feel entitled but some like Germany who worked hard do not want to pay for Greece's life style though they like to vacation there. There is lots of resentment in Germany to a perceived view that Greeks want to live beyond their means.
- Agreements to continue austerity have in the past been broken with government workers rehired.

What Greece needs is a way to improve the economy and collect taxes and get productive Greeks back into the country. By the time this book goes to press we will likely know the outcome, but likely the whole situation will have its ups and downs.[5]

Why is Greece important?

Greece, China head the list of uncertainties, Janet Yellen, the FED chair[6]

Lets review why this is important and what has happened to the summer of 2015. First, Goldman Sachs, bless their souls, played a substantial role in messing up the situation by giving advise that backfired, shorting the resulting securities and taking a $150 million fee for their service.[7] The derivative securities legally circumvented the EU Maastricht deficit rules. When these cross currency swaps mature they add to the Greek Debt. The rules are that euro members must limit debt to a maximum of 3% of their GDP and 60% of total debt. But in 2009 the deficit was 12% way above the 3% limit if you use the Eurostat (the European Unions statistical office) numbers. Hospital and Military debt are routinely left off the Greek debt. These and other numbers are adjusted to meet the 3% limit. In 2005, Goldman sold these swaps to a Greek bank.

Goldman showed Greece's debt managers how to push their liabilities into the future. US and yen debt was swapped for euro debt to be re-exchanged back to the original currencies later. Greece was issuing bonds in yen, US dollars and Swiss francs. But Greece's debts and revenues are in euros. Goldman devised fictional exchange rates so Greece got more euros than the actual euro market value of 10 billion dollars or yen. So the debt for Greece increased by $1 billion in 10–15 year bonds which is not in the Greek figures. This manipulation was used in Italy before by a different bank. In 2002, the Greek debt was 1.2% of GDP. In 2004 it was 3.7% and in 2010 5.2%.

There is great fear of contagion to other weak countries and the trade and derivative contracts that Germany, France, Italy and others have is hard to evaluate but there is great fear that it is substantial.

The Troika wants to keep Greece in the euro but punish and discredit the left wing Syriza party and especially its "bull in a china cabinet" finance minister Varoufakis, who is an economics professor specializing in game theory and its leader, the very polished but forceful Tsipras. Some headlines show the importance

- Greece pledges to get rid of tax evasion as a way of life, *Yahoo*, June 14, 2015.
- Greek game of chicken is turning into pass-the-parcel, Ben Wright, *The Daily Telegraph*, June 25, 2015.
- In Greek referendum campaign, a barrage of doomsday ads, Suzanne Daley, *New York Times*, July 3, 2015.

- Ending Greece's bleeding, Paul Krugman, *New York Times*, July 5, 2015.
- Greece has 5 days to avoid Grexit, EU leaders signal, Andrea Rignier, *Investors Business Daily*, July 8, 2015.
- World markets brace for Greek outcome, *USA Today*, July 13, 2015.
- Greek crisis worsens after IMF quits talks.
- Greek talks deadlocked over reform to pensions.
- Markets rising on Greece bailout deal, Adam Shell, *US Today*, July 14, 2015.
- A debt haircut is "out of the question", Angela Merkel.
- Greece's creditors tighten the screw, Mehreen Khan, *The Daily Telegraph*.

The Greek stock market fell 23% after being closed 5 weeks. It was now down 85% since 2007.

Given all the uncertainty about whether the bailout talks would succeed, it was prudent of Greece to try to have a backup plan that could be quickly implemented should they be pushed out of the euro and need to resurrect the drachma. Their plan B was kept secret and only made public on July 27 causing an immediate outcry. Some opposition leaders called it treason but really it is simply a stage two stochastic programming strategy. Former finance minister Yanis Varoufakis worked on this after being asked by Prime Minister Alexis Tsipras prior to election. Varoufakis and a five man team (which included University of Texas professor James Galbraith) devised the plan which would have allowed a quick switch to the drachma since it set up a parallel system of receipts and payments. It required widespread hacking of individual and corporate tax registration numbers so they had information on all taxpayers. Also he proposed collecting information on foreign tourists as a way to avoid tax fraud. The legality of some of this is questionable on confidentially and other grounds. A staff of about 1,000 would be needed if it were actually implemented. The question of Grexit or not Grexit was handled. While Tsipras authorized the research, there was no intention of doing this unless the negotiations failed. It was simply a backup plan and still could be used.[8]

Some events following the referendum:

- Yanis Varoufarks finally threw in the towel and resigned right after the no-vote on July 5, 2015 and became a hostile critic of the deal.
- The new finance minister, Euclid Tsakalotos, was involved in the final stage of the negotiations with a more humble softer approach.
- Tsipras took a bold step. He did not like the tough additional austerity measures and the inflexibility of the Troika so he had them make a proposal. He did not like the terms and things like the inability to cut military spending to replace other cuts in social benefits and pensions. Of course, a factor here is who supplies the military — it is other euro members and the US. Also the party supported privatization as a public–private partnership with some continued public ownership and some infusion of capital by the investor. So he put it to a vote of the Greek people suggesting that a "Yes" meant his government would/might resign and urging a "No" vote. No might have kicked Greece out of the euro as well if the Troika demanded it.

  Paul Krugman, in a July 5, *New York Times* column, was in the No category and argued that Yes would have more of the same failed policies. He pointed out that Iceland's 2008-05 and Argentina's one peso-one dollar devaluation were successful.

  Yes to the bailout package meant that Greek banks would be solvent and in the Eurozone with more taxes and pension cutbacks. No meant the voters wanted to demand a better deal with risk of having to exit the Eurozone. The Troika did not guarantee the original conditions of the bailout, so in either case it would be back to the negotiating table.

- The vote was held and gave a solid 61% No. The unemployed and youth were heavy on the No side and the pensioners on the marginally on the yes side (52%). The Troika did not take well to this but stopped short of a Grexit. So there were negotiations and finally Tsipras agreed to harsher austerity terms than in the previous proposal. This time he accepted it conditional on approval by the Greek parliament and the Troika.

It was agreed on July 11 and on Friday July 12 and Monday July 13 the S&P500 rallied strongly. Previously there were days with enormous swings of optimism and fear. This was rather good for my trading as there were terrific mean reversion days to buy low set sell high limits then short at highs and have very low GTC buy orders. By July 25, the S&P500 had lost most of its recent gains, falling for a variety of reasons with the small cap Russell2000 falling more. With background positions and this tinkering, my AlphaZ fund, which won the Battle of the Quants futures contest in New York in 2015 and beat the equity winner (see page 184–186) based on results from February to April also had a strong May, June and July.

The agreement was only the first step and the proposal had to be approved by Greek parliament and the ECB and the individual countries in the Eurozone as well and the IMF. The next payment owed is 3.2 million euro on bonds held by the ECB on August 20, 2015. The creditors are in Athens trying to agree on the details of the agreed bailout plan. Tsipras has only been able to pass legislation with the aid of opposition parties as many of his party are opposed.

The IMF announced, finally pushed by the US, the they could not support a bailout with an unsupportable debt.

Despite an agreement with Tsipras and the troika signing off on the agreement, there are many dangers and risks ahead. Tsipras must sell the deal to the parliament. Hardliners in his party are not happy with the concessions agreed to. Energy Minister Panagiotis Lafazonis accused Germany of using the threat of expulsion form the Eurozone to get Tsipras to agree to their demands. With his party split he got parliamentary approval.

The next payment was on July 20 when $3.5 billion is owed to the ECB. Unlike when Greece skipped the June 30 IMF payment, Greece must pay as its the ECB that has kept the banks afloat and they did.

Economics Nobel Prize winner and Columbia University Professor Joseph Stiglitz (2015) sums up the thoughts after talking to people in Greece. His experience as chief economist at the World Bank reinforces my concerns that, in his words "heavy austerity moves downturns into recessions and then depressions." This happened in 1998 in Indonesia and later in Argentina and now in Greece. The Greek–Troika agreement is unsustainable because the debt is too high and the further austerity measures and difficult to meet goals are essentially impossible to meet. The IMF chief Christine Lagarde understands that the debt is too high and calls for a debt restructuring. France is sympathetic but the Germans have a hard line.

Provisions like high taxes even on the poor, a 3.5% budget surplus versus 1% this year, and structural reforms which favor some over others, the hundreds of petty conditions, weakening of the unions through changes in collective bargaining are not really feasible goals. Other changes — forcing Greece to give up labeling of milk as fresh to increase their exports, reflect selfishness on the part of the northern Europeans. So look for more trouble as this unfolds in the coming months and years.

The saga continues with further discussions trying to iron out specifics of the deal. For me, the major uncertainties on my trading are

1. The Greek situation along with
2. A crash in the Chinese stock market (the Shanghai composite lost 32%, the Shenzhen Tech Index lost 41% from June 12 to July 6, 2015 after a spectacular increase in 2014 and early 2015, There are 90 million trading accounts in China, more than the number of those who carry communist cards. The Chinese government manipulates their stock markets through monetary and other policies. The level of manipulation is greater than that of the Fed.
3. A possible bankruptcy in Puerto Rico which has some $73 billion in debt, a drop in the oil price, and
4. Fear over a FED rate hike and other worries.

A New Election

After some weeks of passing bills based on the even higher level of austerity than the people had voted down, Tsipras had to obtain opposition party votes as his party is split. To try to strengthen his position he resigned in late August and is called a new election for September 20.

Tsipras won the election so his party is still in power, but the discussions continue with no end in sight. There is dissension at the IMF where some staff point to an IMF debt-sustainability analysis on July 14 that concluded that the latest deal would result in Greek debt at 200% of GDP. They believe the IMF should not participate unless the Europeans offer debt relief — what they do not want to do. That was a €82–86 billion third bailout that Euro lenders agreed to on July 13. The Euro commission and Angela Merkel want the deal to go through and Lagarde seems to concur yet her staff will not support it. This was exactly the outcome former finance minister Yanis Varoufakis and others predicted.

The latest move from the government is to dramatically increase the admission prices to the major Greek sites. For example, the Parthenon moves from €12 to €52 plus the extra sties are no longer included in the ticket so one has to pay separately for them. Basic economics suggests that the demand to these sites will drop and total revenue may not increase. Also, more importantly, many tourists are likely not to come to Greece at all so hotels, restaurants and airlines likely will suffer. This policy seems very ill advised.

The Continuing Results, April 2016

The two sides were close to a deal concerning the third tranche of support. Issues are (see Guarascio, Strupczewski and Bacznska, 2016):

1. Will there be a haircut on the debt, and
2. What conditions, such as spending cuts, savings targets like 3.5% of GDP and reforms will be imposed on Greece

The IMF is pushing for debt relief but as Tagaris (2016) reports, they are still negotiating. The opposing views are giving debt relief as the IMF prefers and no debt relief as German Finance Minister Wolfgang Schaeuble demands (see Chrysoloras, Galanopoulos and Buergin, 2016) The biggest areas of contention are:

1. The management of bad loans that increase the debt and Schaeuble suggests moving to a competitive economy would make the debt manageable.
2. The overhaul of the Greek pension system; the Greek government insists that it will not cut current pensions.
3. Protection for people who cannot pay back bank loans.

Greece would like reduced interest rates and extended repayment schedules on previous rescue loans which started in 2010. This is even more important to them than possible write down of the debt (see Associated Press, 2016). Prime Minister Tsipras insists that the debt relief talks must start on completion of the tranche 3 negotiations. He said Greece will do everything it has committed to but argued that countries should be free to choose their own means of meeting agreed fiscal targets. He also accused the country's creditors of persisting in demanding austerity measures which have proven ineffective. Tsipras's government, which was elected on 2015 on promises to reverse painful austerity measures and lead the country out of budgetary supervision by its creditors, performed a U-turn in the summer of 2015 and, facing the alternative of leaving the Eurozone, signed a third €86 billion bailout. The IMF wants salary cuts in the public sector, lifting restrictions on layoffs, and cuts to the main pensions. These measures would kill the economy and the usefulness of a debt cut which they can't even guarantee.

In late May 2016, the Greek parliament approved a new batch of creditor mandated austerity cuts which unlocked a €10.3 billion bailout. These include cuts to come civil service salaries and repayment of non-performing loans. This followed tax hikes and other so-called reforms to reduce government spending. The sales tax went to 24% from 23%.

As big a problem as the Greek debt crisis is, the refugee exodus from Syria and other countries is going on at the same time and adds further pressures to the Greek financial situation. While other countries such as Turkey are receiving credit and concessions for helping refugees, little has been offered Greece. The situation in end of May 2017 was little changed the crisis and talks continue.

Notes

[1] Sandra and others like fellow PhD student Larry Nordell signed petitions for the colonels who led a coup to let Papandreou out of prison.

[2] I had just flown in from Seoul Korea having given one talk there to the business school and fifteen hours of ALM research to the financial engineering department in Taejon some two hours away and the center for Korean research facilities. So I was a bit asleep at the wheel when the crisis hit. Nowadays i react imediately to crises and that works better. and the results show it.

[3] The Samueson response paper and many other very useful papers published in the journal of portfolio management are in the 2016 book paper and hardback e- and m- books = smart cell phones like i-phone called Great Investment Ideas, World Scientific.

[4] The Greek debt is staggering as shown in this table as of the end of May 2017.

Date	Creditor	Type	Amount (mln €)	Cumul. (bn €)
05-Jun	IMF	repayment	307	1.274
12-Jun	IMF	repayment	345	1.619
16-Jun	IMF	repayment	575	2.195
19-Jun	IMF	repayment	345	2.54
19-Jun	ECB	GGB coupons	85	2.625
June	private	repay non tradable debt	190	2.996
03-Jul	private	Intl bond coupon	4	3
13-Jul	IMF	repayment	460	3.46
14-Jul	private	Intl bond coupon+ redemption	91	3.551
17-Jul	private	Intl bond coupon	16	3.567
17-Jul	private	new GGB coupons	71	3.638
19-Jul	ECB	GGB coupons	85	3.724
20-Jul	ECB	GGB coupons	608	4.331
20-Jul	ECB	GGB redemption	3491	7.822
25-Jul	private	Intl bond coupon	24	7.846

Bank of America Merrill Lynch, Business Insider

⁵ Greek debt and interest timeline

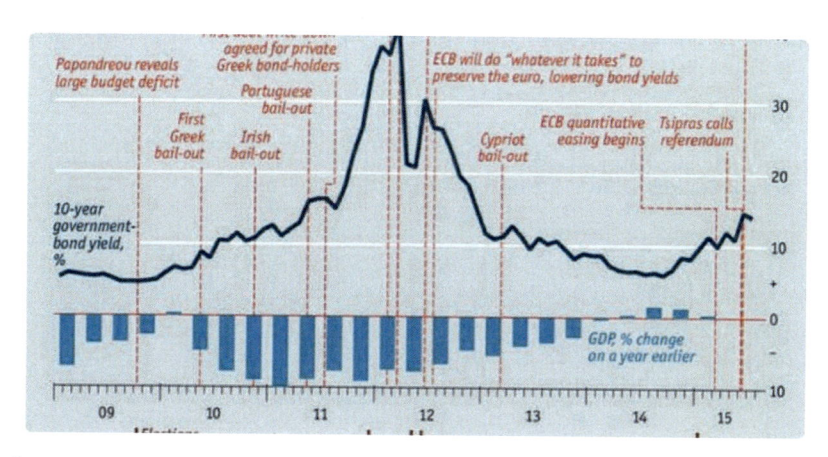

[Figure: Greek 10-year government-bond yield (%) and GDP % change on a year earlier, 2009–2015, with annotations: Papandreou reveals large budget deficit; First Greek bail-out; agreed for private Greek bond-holders; Irish bail-out; Portuguese bail-out; ECB will do "whatever it takes" to preserve the euro, lowering bond yields; Cypriot bail-out; ECB quantitative easing begins; Tsipras calls referendum.]

⁶ Mauldin (2015) discusses the problem of China and its impact on the west. The graph shows the stupendous rise in the Shanghai stock exchange and the collapse in 2017.

[Figure: Shanghai Composite Index, daily, Sep–Jul, with values ranging from 2,000 to 5,200; dated 7/31/2015.]

⁷ See B. Balzli (2010). How Goldman Sachs helped Greece to mask its true debt, Spiegelonline, February, 8.

⁸ A. Evans-Pritchard (2015). Secret plan for instant switch to drachma creates political storm, *Vancouver Sun*, July 27.

Chapter 27

Inefficiencies and Anomalies: Other Crashes and How They Fit the Models

Predictable Crashes versus Those that are Surprises

I focus on four large crash prediction measures: The first is my BSEYD (discussed in Chapter 14) which compares the long bond interest rate with the reciprocal of the trailing price earnings ratio which is an earnings yield. The second measure is my T-option, a measure of market confidence sentiment related to puts versus calls prices. The third is Warren Buffett's value of the economy to the value of the stock market. The fourth is the Sotheby's behavioral finance measure based on the enthusiasm for the Sotheby's stock. In this chapter, I discuss nine possibly anticipated declines that none of these measures predicted but we can deal with, namely:

1. September 11, 2001,
2. May to June 2006,
3. February 27 to April 6, 2007,
4. August 2011,
5. October 2014,
6. August 18 to September 18, 2015,
7. January 1 to February 12, 2016, and
8. Brexit vote, June 23 to June 28, 2016.
9. Trump election risk, Ocotber 24 to November 10, 2016[1]

The BSEYD is able to predict many, if not most, of the big crashes. Those are over 10% and average 25%. But there are a lot of mini declines in the

5–15% range that occur. Some are explainable or predictable and some are not. Examples include the 1991 attack on 9–11 on New York's World Trade Center. Then the market was limit down in futures, some −6%, then with trading suspended for a week, it fell −14% in total. Besides these bad scenarios, there can be declines that simple feed on themselves. In October 2014, there was constant talk in the business news "we have not had a −10% correction is a long time." So selling started with no other news. It never quite got to a −10% in closing prices, but was −9.86% on the close of the market at the bottom. The market turned when −10% was hit in the middle of a trading session and it was straight up from there for a huge retracement.

That was a **V** shaped decline that's relatively easy to deal with. In my trading, I shift from largely *C* trades, that is short puts deep out of the money with a large amount of capital behind each position to an **A** trade where you short futures to delta neutralize the long positions in the short puts. Then when it rallies, you eliminate the short futures which are not losing money. A full **A** trade buys long calls, so if that's the move, one does not get hurt on the rally by the short futures.

The August 2015 worldwide massive decline began on August 18 and had similar elements with many individual stocks including Apple Computer, indices such as the Russell2000 small cap index, and countries, actually in 20% plus decline bear markets. The spot VIX was 28.03 (up 46.45% on Friday August 21) with the future VIX lower, up 8.89 versus 19.14 on Thursday August 20. It was 13 on Tuesday August 18.

On Wednesday (August 19), options on the September 1700 S&P500 puts, which were 30 cents, closed at 1.15 on Thursday then $8.20 on Friday then 27.50 before they fell to $8.30 on Wednesday. They are 3.40 on Thursday. I bought some back at $3 and others at $1.80. Later on September 8, I closed the position at $0.95 so the trade made a profit. I also bought some 1650 September puts for $2 that I sold on Wednesday for $8. These closed at $2.40 on Thursday. The VIX peaked at 40 in the spot but the futures VIX was much lower, below 30. Historically, after a 40+ VIX, the next 12 months has very large gains, see Ziegler and Ziemba (2015). All the puts were trading at huge premiums. The DJIA was more than 10% below its May high. So again *sell in May and go away* was working.

On Thursday August 20, the DJIA fell 358 (2.06%). On Friday August 21, it fell 530.94 (−3.1%) to 16,459.75. Meanwhile, the S&P500 was down some 7% from its recent peak and it then fell 64.84 points on

Friday, August 21, an option expiry day. It seems clear that some type of flash crash — or computerized selling, was going on. The Nasdaq fell 3.5% (−171.45) to 4706.04 on Friday. The VIX rose more than 10% on each of Wednesday, Thursday, Friday and Monday. The VIX rose 118%, the largest weekly gain since 1990. On Monday August 24, the VIX actually rose an additional 90% with the DJIA down 1000 points at one stage, similar to the flash crash bottom. There were an enormous number of forced buying of short puts because of margin calls. For example, 1850 puts sold for $3–5 rose to $28 or $30 and were bought in for many customers including me in an Ameritrade account. In Investorline of the Bank of Montreal which uses very strict rules to limit positions, a small number of mine were bought in for $14.80 and $13 (13) in two accounts on August 30. I had bottom fished and bought some AAPL stock a few days earlier which increased the margin and was partially responsible for the buy in. These losses ate up some months of previous gains, but occur from time to time with put selling, if one is not hedged or fully capitalized and does not anticipate the decline, which was hard to do here.

The brokerage firms are ruthless in this. They eliminate their risk by being super conservative at the expense of the client — me in this case, buying in with no notice to the client. Bank of Montreal is even more conservative and will not allow many positions at all. Ameritrade is better allowing more positions but are ruthless in buying back short options in a crisis with no notice to correct the problem. I correct this problem with future gains. Fortunately there are only very few such buybacks so the gains outweigh this problem.

On Tuesday there was a big rally of about 35 S&P500 points only to lose it on the last hour to close −25 (3.9%) on the S&P500. But an encouraging sign was a drop of 5 points in the VIX to the 35 area. For example, the September 1700 puts fell from 27.50 to 20 despite the S&P500 falling. Then on Wednesday the market stabilized and was up about 35 then dropped to +12 and then there was a massive rally with the S&P500 up 72.9. Thursday was much the same with a big rally of 45+ S&P points then to fall to almost even and then it rallied to close up 50 points. It was quite a roller coaster.

What was the trigger or twig that got this multiple day decline with Thursday, Friday and Monday being the big down days?

It seems to be nothing really new but a final recognition of a bunch of current worries. There had been a long period of low volatility with cheap money fueling the market rise with an accommodating Fed. Then once the market started falling, it fell on itself and accelerated on Thursday through Tuesday and finally seemed to bottom out. Chinese markets fell into a 20% plus bear market and this suggested that global growth was slowing and then that drove the US market lower.

Is this a tempest in a teapot that will pass or an end to the 6 year bull market?

One observer said it has been 75 years since such a percent drop occurred. The drop in closing prices was about 11% from an August 17 high to a low on the 25th. Many such as young people with 3 times S&P long ETF's got blown out.[2]

This decline instead of being **V** shaped was a sequence of **W**s, WWWW, up, down, up, down with fast violent moves in both directions. That made the market very difficult to trade. In my case, I basically moved most positions to December at high volatility premiums way away from the money. So selling high volatility rather than the low volatility before the crisis hopefully will work out well.

So the drop in the week was 118 S&P points (−5.65%). The drop to the bottom on Monday was 334.83.

We will see how this plays out.

Then, finally in the options expiry week, September 14–18, the market began to stabilize and gently rise. Monday September 14 had a loss of −8 S&P500 points. Then on Tuesday, September 15, the day before the 2 day September Fed meeting, the S&P500 rose 25.70 points to 1979.75 in the September futures. These Fed induced rallies are as expected given the past data, see the discussion on that in Chapter 14. Finally, there was the Fed announcement. As usual in the Fed week, the market rallied in options expiry weeks. Also, in options expiry weeks the market usually rallies, so there were the two effect. The odds favored no rate rise because of the troubles in the US and especially abroad.

Following the announcement of no change for largely due to the overseas economic downtown, especially China, the market made various up and down moves in a violent reversing fashion. It then became weak in the period during Fed chair Janet Yellen's speech after the announcement. The market closed down −5 in the S&P500. Subsequently, during the night before the Friday morning settlement, it fell. Then on Friday, September 18, the stock market fell sharply, down 1.61% or −32.12 S&P500 points. Monday, September 21 has a 0.45% gain, then Tuesday had another 1.23% drop in the S&P500. The rest of that week was slightly down with Wednesday, Thursday and Friday falling from 1942.74 on Tuesday's close to 1931.34, some −11.4 S&P500 points. Then on Monday, September 28, it was rumored that Saudi Arabia and Norway were selling equities to make up for oil revenues not received due to the low oil prices and needed to cover expenses. That led to a −2.57% S&P500 decline. The market then stabilized during the turn of the month of October with rallies on September 29, 30 and October 1, 2, and 3. This took the S&P500 from 1881.77 to 1987.05, gain of over 100 points. In this period, the VIX decreased from 27.63 to 19.54. Mohamed el Erian and others predicted continuing high volatility.

We are soon coming to the best part of the year, namely the end of the sell in May and go away period. This is by my definition, the −5 day of November which is the 25th of October. There is a lot of conflicting opinions and analyses. Also there is record short positions in the market comparable to 2008. For example Blair Hull's new ETF product, 6 month model, is predicting −10% for the next 6 months. I was asked to comment on this model and gave some suggestions, some of which were used. The model then suggested −20% allocation and later −30%. Finally, after many days of gains, it is at zero. It is difficult for these models to be accurate all the time and this model has been successful in the past. My current positioning in my futures fund is cautiously optimistic using high VIX option sales of deep out of the money options, hedged with short futures so that the delta is close to zero. As of October 12 we have had nine consecutive days of falling VIX.[3]

The worries:

- Earnings have been dropping so the stock market is adjusting to the new pricing,
- Oil: oil has been dropping for months. It was now at the $40 level, it is so low that many companies and countries are in serious financial trouble.
- China: the stock market and currency are in decline and global growth may be declining, hence it impacts the US stock market. China's Caixin purchasing managers index fell again this week. The rmb was devalued in early August by the largest amount since 1994. Neighboring countries currencies are greatly affected. Kazakhstan floated its currency and it fell 25%. To maintain the rmb, China is selling dollars but its not enough.

China did nothing until a rate cut on Tuesday and some buying on Thursday. Also they forbade negative comments on stocks and halted many from trading.

- Commodities: China was stockpiling many commodities and is now dumping them to raise cash which affects stock markets and currencies.
- Fed: worries regarding the start of interest rate rises and their paths up. They continue to say "the data will tell us what to do." Interest rates have not increased in 9 years. There is much worry about when they will raise rates and the pace up.
- August: there seems to often be seasonal troubles in August. Historically September and October have been the weakest months. But August now seems to anticipate the September drops.
- Six year bull run fed by easy money putting $10 trillion into stock markets.
- Other markets (from 2015 intraday highs): Japan −7.2%, Germany −17%, Hong Kong −21%.

In my trading I use various corrective actions, here are two of them:

1. If net long: one can short futures but then you must adjust the positions to get out of these positions as the rally unfolds. This, in my terminology, is what I call an A trade. The A trade has three or four elements. Doing them all simultaneously is complicated but they can be approximated. One shorts a ridge of puts, call the sum of the premiums P. At the same time buy a ridge of calls of value C. Then short futures so the short puts are delta neutralized. If $T = P - C$ is over 100, there have been no quarterly losses since 1985 when you rule out BSEYD crash danger signals. Then it is a good play as T is a measure of how good the play is. But if T is less than zero then it is a short-term crash signal. There have been six cases with T less than zero from 1985 to 2015. The sum of the S&P500 changes in the next quarter was −41.7%. The last such signal was in 2003. If you think that the market is very very weak then you can delta neutralize the long calls as well. The fourth element is to short very deep out of the money calls. There is no risk here as you are long other calls closer to the money and they have expected return as low as 1.7 cents per dollar invested.
2. Alternatively, you can move positions to make your portfolio a safer one with similar premium to be made but later in time.

If net short: one can do similar things but in reverse for (1) or (2).

There have been additional small corrections including several 6–9% declines from July to September 2004 and March to June 2005. In an April 9, 2007 Barrons article, Michael Santoli notes that there has been one such pullback each year since 2004. In each case, a recovery quickly followed each decline and each retreat has been shallower than the preceding one and a faster recovery of the loss. Buying on the declines has been rewarded as bidders try to beat the crowd and speed up the recovery. Buying on these dips has worked so far, as has selling put options during the greatly expanded volatility which returned to low levels after the decline. The 2007 decline followed this pattern. As of April 6, 2007, the futures market returned to predecline levels with the VIX at 13.23.

Some Background on Crash Measures

Historically, the bond–stock crash measure has been successful in predicting 10%+ market corrections, including the declines in October 1987 (U.S. and Japan), the 1990 Japan, the 2000 US and the 2002 US. In Japan, from 1948 to 1988, there were 20 10%+ declines even though the market went up 221 times in yen (and 550 times in US dollars). The bond-stock measure had a 12/12 record in predicting crashes in that period, that is, whenever the measure was in the danger zone, there was a fall of 10%+ within 1 year from the time the measure went into the danger zone. This is a very good forecasting record, but eight declines in Japan during these 40 years were not predicted by this measure and were caused by other reason than high long term interest rates and high price earnings ratios.

Declines and Crashes not Predicted by the Measures

Although the measures have a good record, there are some key episodes which it did not predict. Studying these declines and their triggers helps us to assess shocks. The September 11, 2001 attacks and the stock market decline of 14% in the S&P500 that followed after a 1 week market closure was largely a random, that is unforeseen event. But the size of the decline was exacerbated due to the then weak stock market and US economy which had a recession starting in spring 2001. The stock market was weak because although prices had fallen, earnings had fallen more. The bond–stock model which had been in the danger zone in April 1999, predicting the April 2000 decline, then returned to the danger zone in the fall of 2001 predicting the 22% fall in the S&P500 in 2002. The T-measure for 3Q2002 at -142.8 predicted the 12% fall in the S&P500 that quarter.

The S&P500 fell 37% from 1460.25 at the end of December 1999 to 885.76 on 31 October 2002.

In May to June 2006 the S&P500 fell 7% and markets in some emerging economies fell 20% or more. Worries that valuations of some emerging market stocks were too high enlarged their losses. For example, the closed end emerging market fund Russian New Europe (RNE) was at a very high 37%+ premium on May 10 to net asset value — an amount way above historical values. The trigger for the decline was a rumor that the Bank of Japan would raise interest rates. These higher interest rates did not materialize but the fear that they would spark a rally in the yen led some yen carry trade players to unwind their short yen, long higher yielding non-Japanese asset positions, especially emerging market currencies. In turn this led to sales of various stocks and indices including the S&P500 and the decline was largest (elements of mean reversion) in those areas that had gained the most, namely the emerging markets. The VIX volatility index, rose from around 10% before the crisis to the 22% level before dropping back to 10% after the sell-off.

The third decline was February 27 to April 6, 2007 with the early April S&P500 is well above its February 27 and March 13 lows of 1399.04 and 1377.95, respectively. For months, there was talk of the current period being the longest time without a 2% decline in one day or a large monthly decline. The stock market had low volatility since the 2006 decline.

The paper of Lleo and Ziemba (2012), which discusses the bond–stock earnings yield predictions of three market crashes in the 2006–2009 period, namely China, Iceland and the US, had a clear sell signal on June 14, 2007 and a huge decline occurred this discussed in Chapter 14.

An example of these sentiments was made by Bob Stovall, a 50-year Wall Street veteran, in a talk on November 15, 2006 to investment students at Stetson University. Stovall argued that given the current real economic growth in 2006, it would be very difficult for stocks in the S&P500 to continue to increase in price (Moffatt, 2006). Without economic growth, companies would have trouble meeting earnings expectations. He said that the average bull market in US history lasts approximately 56 months. At that time, the US was approaching the 50th month of the bull market. He concluded that a shift toward steady cash flow stocks with dividends was preferable to large capital gains stocks.

It is known that bull markets start with low PE ratios and end with high PE ratios, see Chapter 14, footnote 5, page 319.

On Tuesday, February 27, 2007, the S&P500 fell 50.33 points or 3.47% to 1399.04. On that drop, the VIX volatility index rose from 11.15 to 18.31%, a jump of 64.22%. Several concurrent triggers have been mentioned for the fall, which were exacerbated by the confused reaction of market participants to these events. The first was a 9% fall in the Shanghai and Shenzhen stock markets, itself triggered by rumors that the Chinese government was going to raise the bank's reserve requirement and make regulatory changes to slow speculative activity in the soaring Chinese equity markets. The Chinese market drop triggered substantial sell-offs in Asia (where most equity markets were near peaks) and Europe as well as in the US While *I* believe that China is one of the most interesting financial market to study now, I also feel that this drop is **not** the underlying cause of the S&P persistent weakness. The Shanghai index was up more than 100% in 2006 and way up in early 2007 so the 9% fall is a minor blip in the long run growth trend, and likely motivated by profit-taking and a concern about over-valuation. Furthermore, it is not an indication of slowing of the Chinese economy which is expected to grow around 9–10% in 2007. Chinese markets tend to be quite volatile. Several weeks before the February 27 decline, the Shanghai exchange fell 11% in 1 week in early February, a decline which received little attention in international markets because it was spread over a week (Vincent, 2007). These two declines were the greatest since February 1997, when news of Deng Xiaoping's ill health triggered a sell-off. Thus, the Chinese decline may have determined the timing of the global equity decline, and return of increasing volatility and risk aversion but is not the underlying cause. Indeed in early April 2007 the Chinese market indices rose to new highs well above the February 25 interim high.

I expect that just like Japan, whose Nikkei stock average rose 221 times in yen and 550 times in US dollars from 1948 to 1988, but with 20 declines of 10%+, China will likely have higher gains in dollars than rmb, be overpriced like Japan, propelled up by fast growth and low interest rates and high liquidity and still experience many corrections.[4] The BSEYD crash signal was in December 2006. But the *market* did not understand this. Rather many market actors tend to react as a herd to such events, seeking to minimize their losses, but the more recent response appears to be buy on dips.

Other news also contributed to the fall in the S&P500 and worldwide markets on that Tuesday included a statement by former Fed Chair Alan Greenspan that a recession in the US was a possibility although it was not probable as well as some weak economic numbers.

Greenspan later said the probability of a recession was 25%. At the time, bond prices were actually estimating a higher probability. I assume, that even though it might be wise for a former Fed chair to let the current Fed chair do the talking, audiences like the one in Hong Kong, require that Greenspan say something interesting to earn his $150,000 speaking fee.

The decline was exacerbated by a large unwinding of yen carry trades who sold stock and created a short covering rally in the yen that moved the USD/JPY exchange rate from 127 to 116 on the yen dollar rate from March 30, 2006 to March 30, 2007. However, it appears that those who foresaw the end of the yen carry trade spoke too soon. Although the Bank of Japan recently doubled interest rates (in February 2007), the benchmark rate of 0.5% remains far below other interest rates — encouraging Japanese retail and institutional investors to continue to seek higher returns abroad, and foreign investors to use the weak yen as a financing currency — even if Morgan Stanley recently argued that yen-denominated loans to retail investors remain very small.

Accentuating the tension were political as well as economic risks. Many commentators such as Lawrence Summers (former Treasury Secretary and Harvard President and DE Shaw hedge fund consultant) have argued that the market was not pricing in the worldwide risks in most assets including the S&P500. However, both of my large crash 10%+ measures were not in the danger zone. The decline in February 27 to early April, and possibly beyond, had not reached a 10% fall and the VIX which reached 19% was bouncing around the 13–16% range most of the time.

The Mini Crash, January 1 to February 12, 2016

The Fed finally raised short-term interest rates by 1/4% at their December meeting. The 1/4% is arguably trivial but it sends a message that there is more to come. Indeed, the Fed chair, Janet Yellen, suggested that they might raise rates gradually but have up to four raises in 2016 and more later. This might eventually in 2–3 years yield a short interest in the 3.5% area. All this spooked the emerging markets especially. Starting on the first trading of 2016, the US stock market fell and in the first 5 days of January the S&P500 fell 113.47 S&P500 points or −5.57%. This was the largest fall in the first 5 days of January in the past 50+ years, from 2035.50 at the close of December 31, 2015 to 1922.03 on January 8, 2016. Meanwhile, the VIX rose from 18.21 to 27.01. These are very negative signals, see Ziemba (2012). In addition, the full January 2016 was down 4.68%, closing at 1940.24 with the VIX at 20.20, another negative signal. Another factor was China slowdown fears and a possibly lower growth rate.

The market bottomed on February 12, 2016 at 1864.78, down 170.72 or −8.39% in 2016 year to date, with the VIX at 30.90 intraday high, closing at 28.14. From there, the market began to rally with the VIX starting to fall, it signaled the end of the crisis. The market reached 2049.58 with the VIX falling to 14.02 on March 18.[5]

Brexit Vote, June 23 to June 28, 2016

British Prime Minister David Cameron made a huge mistake. To win the election in 2015 and appease a wing of his party, he promised a vote, he thought he could win, on remaining in the European Union. Former London mayor Boris Johnson and cabinet member Michael Gove among others campaigned for Brexit promising control over immigration and more money for the National Health Service among other issues. One of the cornerstones of the EU is free movement of people. This has made it more difficult for even highly educated people from non-EU countries, like me, to get visas. I found getting a UK visa to teach a course more work than actually teaching the course. The UK polls had the vote close but the London bookmakers had it about 70–30 for remain.

During the day of the Vote June 23, 2016, the preliminary polls had it looking like remain was winning and the S&P500 rose sharply from 2076.75 to 2105.75 with the VIX falling to 17.25 from 21.17. The market players assumed remain would win and the S&P was flying during the night. I was following this while in France. I covered most of my short puts which had fallen in value and hedged the portfolio with S&P futures short setting buy back limits on them assuming that there would be trouble at some stage. In the morning, I saw that as the vote came in, Brexit was winning and there was a huge reversal. My short futures got bought back at a small gain. Had I not had limits, I could have made more because the VIX went up almost 50% to 25.76 and the S&P500 fell to 2018.5, a drop of 87.25 points or nearly 5%. The short puts that I had went up in value with the higher VIX but I did not have too many of them. The next day, June 27, the S&P fell further to 1985 but the VIX dropped to 23.85. Thus, the crisis was over and a big rally ensued. The market assumed that the Fed would not raise rates and the low interest rates would favor stocks. My fund went back to its old high and is shown in the endnote.[6]

The Trump Election Risk, October 24 to November 10, 2016

Throughout the presidential election campaign Donald Trump used a strategy that tested the boundaries of acceptability: he insulted opponents and called them derogatory names. He argued that only he could save the country. He appealed to the uneducated and poor white while insulting many groups of color. But he developed a following that did not care about his actions and thought he could help them.

He made markets jittery by threatening to tear up alliances and trade deals. He kept a focus on Clintons's emails though nothing indictable was found and he has court cases pending threats to Clinton and a sexually explicit tape that infuriated women.

About a week before the election, the FBI director said there were more emails to be checked and Trump rallied in the polls. Then, near the election day, the FBI director said there was nothing indictable in them but Clinton didn't recover and many had already casted their votes in the interim. Whenever it looked like Trump was winning the market got nervous and fell.

As the vote came in the markets first rallied when it looked like Clinton would win and then fell, especially worldwide as it became clear Trump would win. The Dow Jones was down 800 points. Noted investor Carl Ichan bought $1 billion of S&P500 stock and futures near the bottom. Noted short seller George Soros was reported to lose $1 billion. I bought more as well. Then the market rallied when Trump gave a very conciliatory acceptance speech praising Clinton. The VIX then fell and the S&P rallied sharply. These movements are on the VIX-S&P500 graphs in the notes.[7] In the companion book on Stock market Crashes I view the President as two Trumps. Number one is the one that insults people, fires at will and appears very dangerous. End of May polls have more US people wanting to impeach him than favor him. But Trump numbr two who calmly reads a speech written by his aides is very bullish for the stock market. My futures fund made 5% that night.

Trump won the electoral college and thus the presidency while Clinton won the popular vote by over 2.5 million votes with 4 million who voted for Obama not voting. Thus making for a very divided country.

The market does not like uncertainty and they are uncertain about Trump's policies — some are potentially good like infrastructure and bringing jobs back to the US. The claim is that for the wealthy, the tax will be the same with fewer deductions but this is not realistic given his cabinet choices.

But he wants both to reduce taxes on corporations and the wealthy while pursuing a jobs and building program which would vastly increase the deficit.

He seems to want to run his empire with the help of his children from the Oval Office. Conflicts of interest and nepotism are wide spread. We will see the result.

Already daughter Ivanka is in trouble with her businesses and her husband Jarod Kushner is at the center of the current Trump-Comey et al. Russian interference bad scenario.

Small caps outperformed large cap stocks in the post election rally. For 15 consecutive days, the Russell2000 gained and beat the S&P500 which also rallied. This led me to two types of trades:

(1) long March Russell2000 short Russell2000 calls for a covered call position with the calls on the steep part of the decay curve in January. This is for a basically rising market partially hedged
(2) long Russell2000 short S&P500 spreads to capture the effect of small caps outperforming large caps. This is normally what I do for the January turn-of-the-year effect which occurs in December. This trade was successful 20 out of 20 times until the December 2015-January 2016 period which was in chaos because of the first quarter point increase by the FOMC. The real fear then was a large number of rate increases which never materialized. My presidential effect research with Chris Hensel is that during Democratic regimes, the small caps greatly outperform the large caps during the year not only at the turn of the year. So far, the Trump transition to the presidency seems to suggest policies that are more like the Democratic policies that favor the small caps over the large caps.[8]

My futures fund did well, making 5% on the night of the Trump victory. We can see from the vix-S&P500 graph,[5] once the vix turned, the S&P500 turned and I was able to keep my cool in the crisis and did not panic, so my futures fund went to another new high in early December 2016 and ended the month at a new high as shown in the footnote.[9]

Throughout December the market rallied through the options expiry and the Fed FOMC decision to raise short term interest rates by $\frac{1}{4}$%. The Fed chair Janet Yellen announced that they plan to increase interest rates three more times in 2017. This departure from an expected two raises caused a little selloff and then the market resumed its rise. The small cap stocks did not continue to outperform in December with the large cap S&P500 outpacing it. We will see if the traditional turn-of-the-year period has the Russell2000/S&P500 spread gaining. I decided not to play it. March options expiring with the FED meeting on the same days worked well. My fund gained 12% for the month with a private account up 22%. Anomalies are a very hard sell but they do seem to work. I am pleased to be the top futures trader in the US in my category.

The French election is discussed in our Crashes book. The main idea was that once it was clear after the first vote with five of the ten candidates advocating a Frexit that a moderate Macron would win the markets rallied. It was my best trading day ever with my four futures accounts, my fund and three private accounts gained over $550,000 US.

Notes

[1] While this book was being finished there were two more such crises namely the French election and the Trump-Comey-Kushner Russian interference bad scenario. These are covered in the companion World Scientific 2017 book on Stock Market Crashes Preictable and Unpredictable and What to do about them. A brief synopsis is at the end of this Chapter.

[2] The DJIA, the S&P500 and the VIX moved as follows during the crisis:

Date	DJIA	% change	S&P500	% change	VIX	% change
14-Aug	17,477.40		2091.54		12.83	
17-Aug	17,545.18	0.39	2102.44	0.52	13.02	1.48%
18-Aug	17,511.34	−0.19	2096.92	−0.26	13.79	5.91%
19-Aug	17,348.73	−0.93	2079.61	−0.83	15.25	10.59%
20-Aug	16,990.69	−2.06	2035.73	−2.11	19.14	25.51%
21-Aug	16,459.75	−3.12	1970.89	−3.19	28.03	46.45%
24-Aug	15,871.35	−3.57	1893.21	−3.94	40.74	45.34%
25-Aug	15,666.44	−1.29	1867.61	−1.35	36.02	−11.59%
26-Aug	16,285.51	3.95	1940.51	3.90	30.32	−15.82%
27-Aug	16,654.77	2.27	1987.66	2.43	26.10	−13.92%
28-Aug	16,643.01	−0.07	1988.87	0.06	26.05	−0.19%
31-Aug	16,528.03	−0.69	1972.18	−0.84	28.43	9.14%
1-Sep	16,058.35	−2.84	1913.85	−2.96	31.40	10.45%
2-Sep	16,351.38	1.82	1948.86	1.83	26.09	−16.91%
3-Sep	16,374.76	0.14	1951.13	0.12	25.61	−1.84%
4-Sep	16,102.38	−1.66	1921.22	−1.53	27.80	8.55%
8-Sep	16,492.68	2.42	1969.41	2.51	24.90	−10.43%
9-Sep	16,253.57	−1.45	1942.04	−1.39	26.23	5.34%
10-Sep	16,330.40	0.47	1952.29	0.53	24.37	−7.09%
11-Sep	16,433.09	0.63	1961.05	0.45	23.20	−4.80%
14-Sep	16,370.96	−0.38	1953.03	−0.41	24.25	4.53%
15-Sep	16,599.85	1.40	1978.09	1.28	22.54	−7.05%

(*Continued*)

Inefficiencies and Anomalies 311

(*Continued*)

Date	DJIA	% change	S&P500	% change	VIX	% change
16-Sep	16,739.95	0.84	1995.31	0.87	21.35	−5.28%
17-Sep	16,674.74	−0.39	1990.20	−0.26	21.14	−0.98%
18-Sep	16,384.58	−1.74	1958.08	−1.61	22.28	5.39%
21-Sep	16,510.19	0.77	1966.97	0.45	20.14	−9.61%
22-Sep	16,330.47	−1.09	1942.74	−1.23	22.44	11.42%
23-Sep	16,279.89	−0.31	1938.76	−0.20	22.13	−1.38%
24-Sep	16,201.32	−0.48	1932.24	−0.34	23.47	6.06%
25-Sep	16,314.67	0.70	1931.34	−0.05	23.62	0.64%
28-Sep	16,001.89	−1.92	1881.77	−2.57	27.63	16.98%
29-Sep	16,049.13	0.30	1884.09	0.12	26.83	−2.90%
30-Sep	16,284.70	1.47	1920.03	1.91	24.50	−8.68%
1-Oct	16,272.01	−0.08	1923.82	0.20	22.55	−7.96%
2-Oct	16,472.37	1.23	1951.36	1.43	20.94	−7.14%
5-Oct	16,776.43	1.85	1987.05	1.83	19.54	−6.69%

[3] This graph shows the VIX during the period August to October 12 and you can see that the multiple **W** type crisis ended at the turn of the month of October with the VIX declining in the last 9 days.

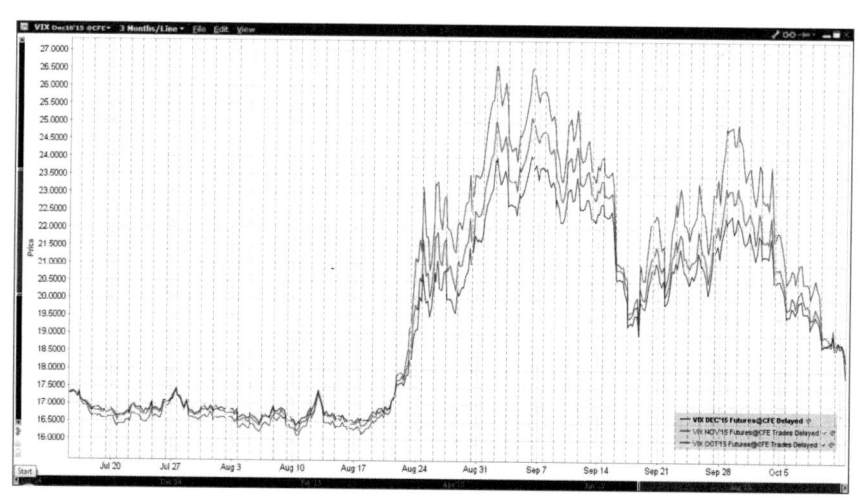

[4] See Ziemba and Schwartz (1991, 1992) and Stone and Ziemba (1993) regarding Japan and Lleo and Ziemba (2012) regarding the crash in 2008 of the Shanghai index.

[5] The S&P500 and the VIX in 2016 evolved as follows:

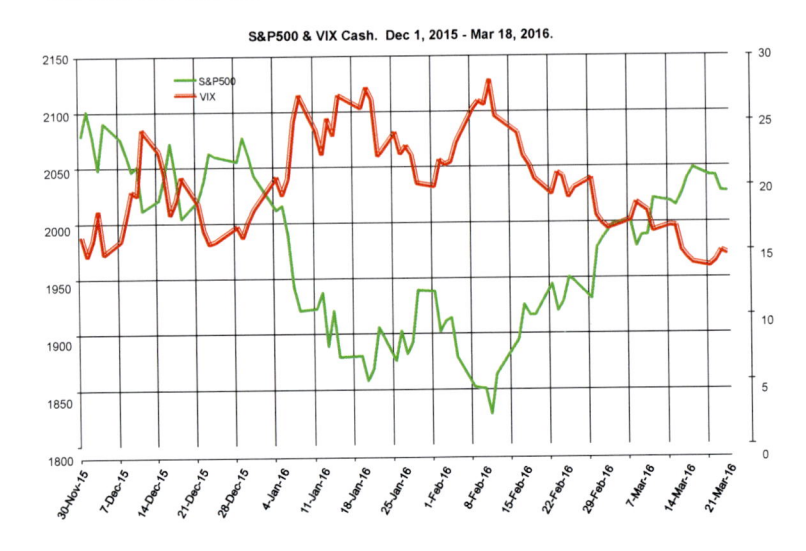

S&P500 & VIX Cash. Dec 1, 2015 - Mar 18, 2016.

[6] The S&P500 and VIX graphs were as follows:

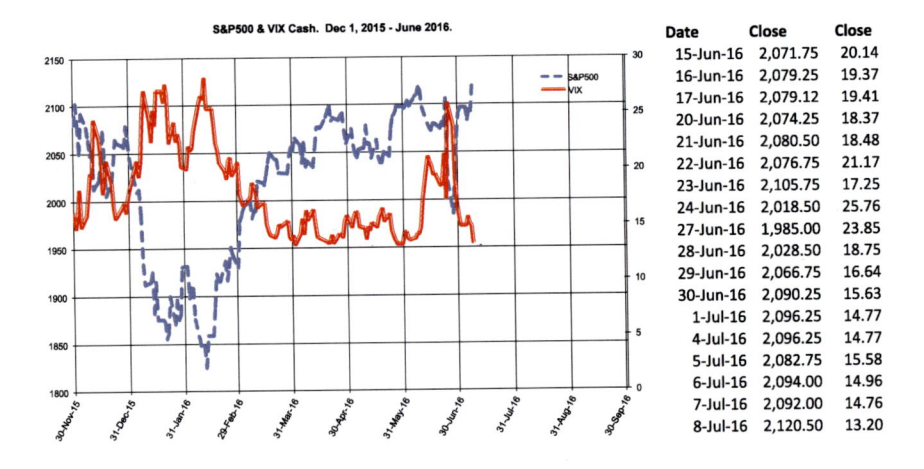

S&P500 & VIX Cash. Dec 1, 2015 - June 2016.

Date	Close	Close
15-Jun-16	2,071.75	20.14
16-Jun-16	2,079.25	19.37
17-Jun-16	2,079.12	19.41
20-Jun-16	2,074.25	18.37
21-Jun-16	2,080.50	18.48
22-Jun-16	2,076.75	21.17
23-Jun-16	2,105.75	17.25
24-Jun-16	2,018.50	25.76
27-Jun-16	1,985.00	23.85
28-Jun-16	2,028.50	18.75
29-Jun-16	2,066.75	16.64
30-Jun-16	2,090.25	15.63
1-Jul-16	2,096.25	14.77
4-Jul-16	2,096.25	14.77
5-Jul-16	2,082.75	15.58
6-Jul-16	2,094.00	14.96
7-Jul-16	2,092.00	14.76
8-Jul-16	2,120.50	13.20

Inefficiencies and Anomalies 313

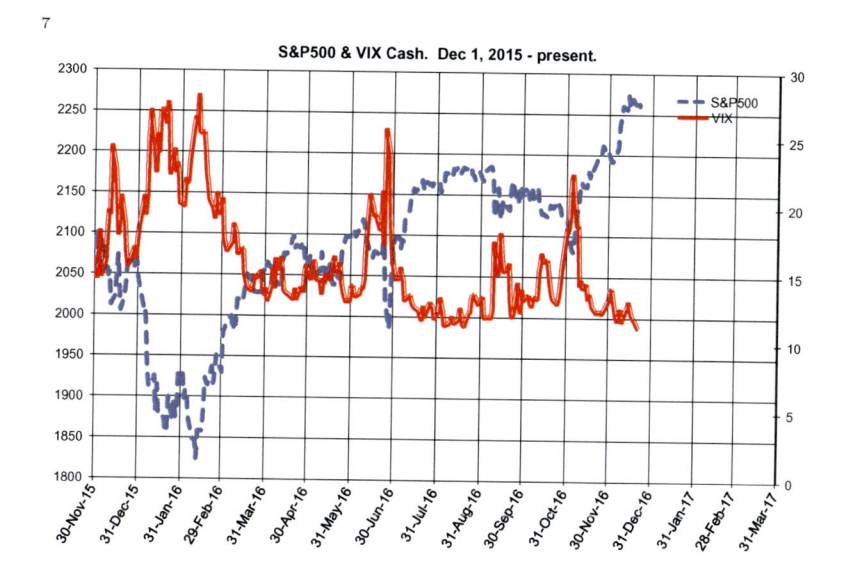

7

S&P500 & VIX Cash. Dec 1, 2015 - present.

8 7 Russell 2000 - 8 S&P500 Cash Spread x $100. Dec 1, 2015 - Dec 23, 2016

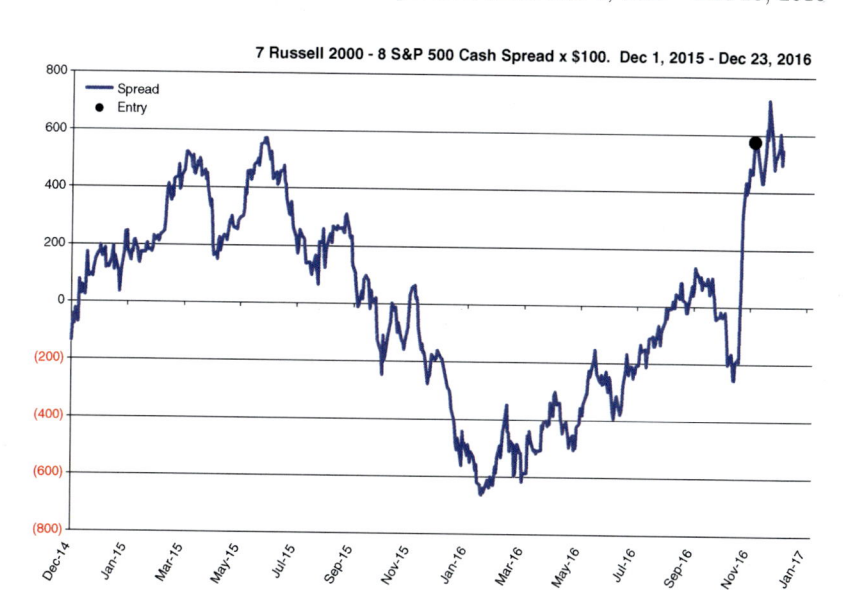

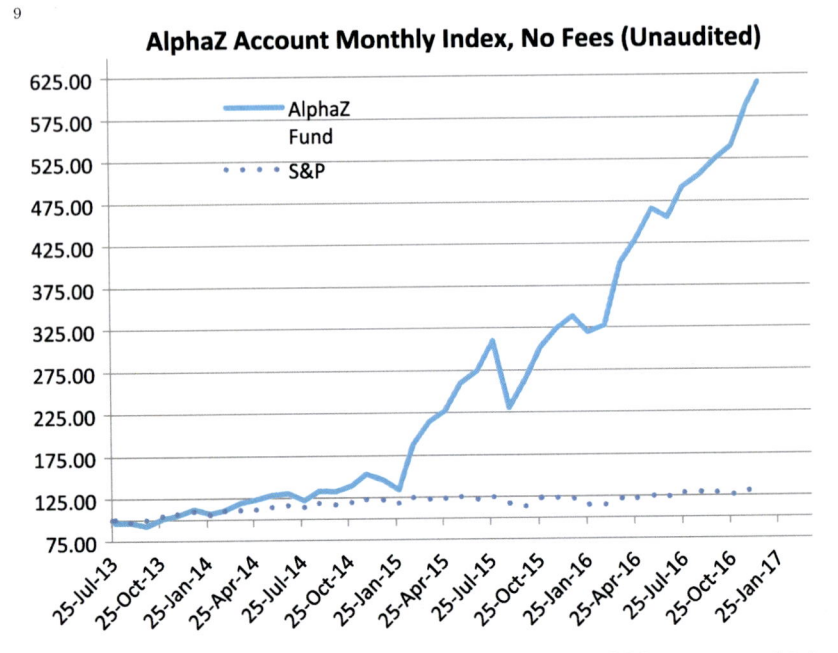

AlphaZ Account Monthly Index, No Fees (Unaudited)

The alpha z fund has continued gins in 2017 and closed May at a new high.

Chapter 28

Dealing with Madoff and Other Swindlers

Throughout history there have been countless ponzi and other swindles to cheat people out of their money. Sometimes the perpeturators get away with it for a long time or are never caught and exposed. Other times they are found out, disgraced and once in a while put into prison. Misinformation and false claims are at the heart of many of these swindles. The greed of the investors fuels the greed of the swindler. Low penalties for such activities make it easier for these swindlers to operate. These low penalties are all over the place in today's financial markets and are a major reason for the blowouts in hedge funds and bank trading departments. Since the 2007/2009 financial market crisis there has been some progress in revamping the rewards and penalties for losses in financial markets but much remains to be done.

Notable historical examples are John Law and the Mississippi land bubble which represented a quarter of the land in the US and much of the wealth of France.

Bernard Madoff has been in the news.[1] On Thursday, December 11, 2008, it was made public that his fund with over $50 billion was in fact a ponzi scheme and the superior results were simply made-up and the actual money his funds had was only a small part of the amount the clients supposedly had in their investment accounts. He supplied thick reports on the results of his supposed investments to each investor. The problem was that these investments and the trades involving them did not exist. A list of those who lost money and there were huge amounts and in many cases the entire investment portfolio of the victim appears in the *New York Times*.

Nikalai Battoo, for whom I was organizing and trading a BVI based offshore hedge fund told me on the phone that he lost $180 million, some 3% of his various funds and Harry McPike lost $48 million of his personal money. These and many of the others swindled are supposedly smart people who normally do proper due diligence on their investments. Madoff was well connected as the chairman of the Nasdaq Exchange and other high positions and claimed his clients came to him begging him to take their money based on the good results that their friends had received.

But not everyone was fooled or did not do their homework about the fund. In 1991, some 18 years before Madoff was exposed, my colleague Ed Thorp was asked to evaluate a group of hedge funds that included Madoff for a New York firm. In his report, Ed found that trades that Madoff claimed to have made simply did not exist. Since this was a private consulting report this information was not generally known to the investment industry. Later Ed wrote a column about this in *Wilmott* magazine where we both have regular columns. Ed explains the Madoff strategy called *split strike price* as follows. You buy a stock, sell a call option higher on it and use those proceeds to buy a protective put at a lower price. As Ed notes "according to financial theory, the long run impact on portfolio returns for many properly priced options with zero proceeds should be zero". The returns Madoff reported were way too large and too steady. In months with stock market losses, Madoff should have had losses but did not show them. They were made winners by supposedly shorting S&P500 futures and the winning months' returns were lowered to create the fictitious smooth returns. Ed also could not find the trades which led him to believe they were "made up".[2]

In 2014, JP Morgan Chase had to pay over $2.5 billion for failing to ignoring their information on the fraud.

It's hard to be in the investment business and not get cheated or swindled or misled at some point. Great investors like Warren Buffett, Ed Thorp and others have faced this and dealt with it and gone on to other successes.

Battoo turned out to be the worst one for me and his case has not still been settled. Some 30 lawyers are dealing with his failed empire in deliberations that started in 2012. It is painful but in this book I want to be realistic and tell the full stories good and bad.

It was early 2007, the phone rang. Nikolai Battoo called me saying there were a few elements that drew him to me. First, he was friendly with Harry McPike and I mentioned him in a *Wilmott* column on great investors. Second, Harry had financially backed the top racetrack betting syndicate in the world — Sydney's Jelko, and both Harry and Jelko were investors in Battoo's BVI-based hedge funds as were other racetrack syndicate people who at least partially used my race track ideas in my books with Donald Hausch. Third, he was looking for some entrepreneurial person with strategies to provide computer progress to trade markets based on good research. He boasted that he had 38 classes of funds with value US$7 billion of which $4.5 billion was his personal money. After a long first talk — I talk a lot but he went into all sorts of things he was doing to impress me. And he did! I went to Fort Lauderdale to meet him and we laid out plans for three projects that would hopefully lead to several hedge funds I could manage and collect some of the fees.

The projects were:

Trend following. He wanted me to essentially duplicate McPike's trend following system in futures. He told me that Harry was "worried I would steal his secret formulas somehow" so that was part of the reason for my departure from there. I had a colleague, Art Warburton, who I did a paper with many years ago and Art was in my PhD class at UBC. Art was always clever but not very motivated so did not do much research. But he was very good at computer work and was fascinated with trend following. So I brought him into the project — it was a big step up for him to the big time! The aim there was to build a computer model to go long and short various futures contracts and to weight them based on the Kelly capital growth investment criterion. I knew how to do the latter as I helped the young Cal Tech student Andrew Mart working for Harry McPike to devise a similar situation. That one took a year and a half of a smart person's time working part time. Art with my help came up with a model to predict the first part — which commodities to buy long and which to short. The Kelly optimization was difficult because the means estimates were not accurate. We could tell if the trend was positive or negative but not by how much. So instead of a Kelly optimization we used a crude weighting system that worked successfully. Using a trading program the model was able to in a few minutes determine daily the new positions to take and those to alter. Sandra actually ran the program for more than a year on paper trading while Warbuton concentrated on research with me helping a bit and supervising. As time went on Warburton and Battoo moved away from Sandra and I and then completely left. When I asked Battoo for some compensation for Sandra who checked this daily and me who checked it once in a while, he refused to pay anything. We did receive some consulting along the way but this was not a good development.

Equity model. The second project was an equity model trying to determine the best stocks in the S&P500 index. The model schema is discussed in

Chapter 13. We made a new model using such variables to predict monthly price changes of individual stocks. The model was operational but we were never able to implement it as Battoo's empire was collapsing. These models are useful in various ways for long, long–short and short trading in cash, equities and in various futures and options trading.

Racing project. The idea in the racing project was to make a factor model to predict the probability of each horse finishing first, second, third or fourth. Basically all you need are the probability of first because using the discounted Harviille formulas one can generate the probabilities for all possible finishes.[3] The prediction model for win is not easy to develop since close to 100 factors and data on each horse is needed.

The other aspect is to get optimization model to decide how much to bet in different wagers. That is actually the easier part of the work.

We had such factor models but never quite finished this project as the Battoo relationship cooled and the management of the project was very complicated with much to do. Once one has a reliable model it can be used in various wagers with the optimization models such as win, place and show, quinella (1–2 or 2–1), exacta (1–2), trifecta (1–2–3), superfecta (1–2–3–4) in a single race and pick 3, 4, 5, 6 across races. Behavioral biases are important here as bettors tend to over long shots and underrate favorites in high probability low payoff wagers such as win, place, show, quinella and exacta. But the bias reverses in low probability, high payoff such as the other bets listed above. In principle this is a license to print money. All you need to do is break even on the bets and win the rebate. For example, one group in St Kitts in the Caribbean, who are close to one of the rebate shops, bets $800,000 per day, breaks even on the bets but makes $20–40 million per year on the rebate. This is a project I would like to return to especially after getting most of the codes ready to use for various wagers and finishing the 2017 book *Exotic Betting at the Racetrack* for World Scientific and writing a chapter on professional racetrack betting (Ziemba, 2012b). In these publications, I discuss bets I actually made on various types of wagers in the US and elsewhere.

Currently, I have a consulting contact to supply factor and bias models and optimization codes for Hong Kong racing. That project and research on U.S. racing continues with a new group of people helping me with research which is in progress. To slow the rate of increase of real estate prices in Vancouver, the provincial and federal governments have created some new rules designed to slow the purchases by foreigners especially from China.

They include an additional 15% tax for foreigners in addition to the current 2% for property purchases plus elimination of the free capital gains tax on property sales by foreigners. In addition mortgage rules have been tightened and under consideration is a tax on vacant properties held by foreigners. The net effect so far is dramatically less sales by foreigners with a small decline in price, although I expect them to fall more later.

Notes

[1] See Bloomberg (2009) and US Attorney for the Southern District of New York (2009).

[2] See E O Thorp (2009), My encounters with Madoff's scheme and other swindles, *Wilmott*.

[3] The Harville (1973) formulas are the simple idea that the probability of an ij finish is the probability that i is first times the probability that j wins the race that does not contain i. It is similar for ijk and $ijkl$. These formulas are useful but they have a bias in reality, namely, if a favored horse does not win, his chance of coming second is less than the Harville formulas predict. So these the probabilities of these favored horses need to be reduced slightly. Meanwhile, the probabilities of a longshot coming in second, third or fourth are increased slightly. For the technique, see papers by Benter, Bacon-Shone and Lo, Henery, and Stern in Hausch, Lo and Ziemba (1994, 2008).

Chapter 29

An Adventure in the Bed and Breakfast Business, British Columbia Real Estate over the Years

When I arrived in Vancouver in 1968, my salary at UBC, which was all my income, was C$12,000 per year less the taxes.[1] Rochester offered more as did Northwestern in the US$13K range. In the first year I rented a house with a French psychiatrist, Pierre Flor Henry. The rent was $250/month or $125 each for a house that was way up Prospect Road in North Vancouver. The house we shared was a nice one and you could only see one house nearby with all the trees and shrubbery. At that time the lot next door was selling for $13,000, about the same as my salary. Lots at Whistler, the ski resort which was just opening up were $2,500 with $250 down and 3% interest. In those early days salaries were low but prices were too. A few of my colleagues bought houses in nice view areas near the university in the $30,000 area. Those houses in 2017 are worth about $3 million or more, a rise of more than 100 times in 48 years.

After Sandra and I married in 1970, we rented houses in Vancouver and we finally bought a house for $60,000 in 1973 after our trip to Afghanistan. That was on the other side of Vancouver and worked well for us. House prices were always moving and usually plateaued for a while then resumed their rise. Basically to have a house you needed two good salaries, one job was not enough. It was hard to stay ahead of the market prices.

In those days, there were few restaurants, and except for the Chinese, most were closed on Sundays because of the liquor laws which required no liquor after midnight on Sunday until Monday. The UBC faculty club and a few other restaurants were good ones, but the pickings were slim. Finally, a top Italian restaurant Il Duca du Mantova was opened and Bruce Fauman told us about it. At $25 for a full meal, it was at the high end in cost and was top quality. Bruce actually spent $600 there one month. Now in 2017, with three people in a top Vancouver restaurant, a five course meal with wine pairings is almost as much. Expo 86 changed all that and since then Vancouver has built a strong restaurant profile as good as the top cities in the world. Shops closed Wednesday afternoon and there was no Sunday shopping nor late night shopping, when pregnant Sandra liked to spend Sunday at Banyen Books, one of the few places open and a great book store and institution in Vancouver.

In 1981/1982, we were both visiting professors at UCLA and I was consulting for the Canadian Sports Pool designing lottery games based on sports outcomes. Ian Howard, my boss, took me to the Mexico City Fronton and that led to the risk arbitrage paper I did with Dan Lane.[2]

Ian had me come to Vancouver in the winter and we continued our work. A friend Ulrike Hilborn asked me to appraise a rug at a friend's house. It was a large Russian sumak in the living room of a great house near the Locarno Beach on Belmont Street. It was a block away from the beach but very close — an ideal location with a terrific view. I said to the owner "don't ever sell this house unless you sell it to me." They said they were thinking of selling with a price in the 700's. Wow! That was three or four times the value of our house that was then worth maybe $200,000. Next door was Nelson Skalbania's $3 million house. He was a top Vancouver entrepreneur. So the area was tops.

I went back to UCLA and we returned after our teaching finished. We decided to look possibly to move closer to the beach area. Our real estate agent then pointed out that there was a nice big house a lot higher than we were considering in the $450,000 area near the beach. Of course it was the Belmont house. That was the time of very high interest rates imposed by Paul Volker's policy as the head of the FED. These rates approached 20% and indeed one could buy long dated T-bills for 15% plus. That was one of the greatest investments in history. Sandra did not want to bid more than 400K as our Alma house was then worth about 150K. Anyway after discussing with the UBC top applied real estate Professor Stan Hamilton who had wisely advised us on Alma, we bid 425K to close the deal. To cover the cost we privately sold Alma for 160K but gave up some months at a high interest. We got it but Sandra, still untenured, remained worried.

In 1984, I interviewed at the Stanford Engineering Economics Systems Department. Stanford rules are that you must be one of the top three in your field and if you are not number 1 they want to know why numbers 1 and 2 don't want to come to Stanford. Anyway I designed a field where

I was in this group but in the end once again they went with a person they later did not give tenure to. I was in the full professor hire with tenure category so that's a harder position to get hired into.

At the same time, Mike Brennan proposed me as a joint appointment with finance at UBC. I was the *Management Science* Departmental Editor for Finance plus active in portfolio theory and other areas. But the others did not agree. In their words, "we cannot have a guy like you." Anyway, pretty mean. So UBC looked worse and I arranged a visit at Stanford and sold the Belmont house which Sandra never liked for $488,000. I knew then that I would never be able to replace it. But UBC was at a low point and it was nice to be again at Stanford on sabbatical. After that visit we bought a a house on Laburnum and sold it and rented a place near UBC but got poor advise from Stan this time before going to Japan for a year.[3] When we returned in 1989, Vancouver had been discovered after the 1986 World Expo, a wonderful world fair. Along with the impending turn over of Hong Kong to China, brought an influx of Chinese buyers including especially Hong Kong women buying houses like candy for their children. One bought 13. Another bought 4 but found out later that the local school was not acceptable so she bought 4 more. This pushed up prices. In 2017, the Vancouver housing market and its suburbs are on fire price wise. Our old Belmont house is worth well over $10 million and there are 10 houses on that street over $20 million. Ordinary houses are worth their land which has gone from $25–30,000 when I arrived in 1968 to the $3–4 million area, a rise of fully 100 times in 48 years. Whistler, which has lagged has gone from $2,500 a lot to over $1 million. For Vancouver, the forecast is for more of the same — the suburbs re up 40%+ in the past year. The game here is for people to move further and further away and to improve the transit system so they can get to the downtown fairly quickly. Now that the horse has been stolen — that is the prices are out of whack for what people in Vancouver can afford, the governments of British Columbia and Canada are moving to slow or stop the price rises. These include an extra 15% tax on the value of a property purchased plus the usual 2% for foreigner buyers, elimination of the no capital gains taxes for foreign sales gains, plus more stringent mortage qualification rules for all buyers. The effect of the latter is that some marginal buyers do not qualify for mortgages. The effect of the other two measures which are being legally challenged are unclear. What is clear is that there has since been a slowdown in sales, and prices may fall later.

In Japan we had two jobs so lots of savings. We bid on one very good house but missed it because of timing. The real plus was that the Japanese experience turned me into a valuable finance consultant then led to the work with Buchanan, Russell and other places. We bought a house after Japan which we have kept since.

In 1982, I corrected the Whistler mistake of not buying at Lake Tahoe for US$6,000 or C$2,500 at Whistler in 1968 by buying a four bedroom condo which meant we could have Sandra's two brothers and their families visit around Christmas time. In 2002, when Vancouver awarded the 2010 Olympics, Whistler prices doubled. Whistler is a convenient two hour easy drive or bus ride from Vancouver and has developed into one of the world's top ski resorts and summer destinations. In 1996, Sandra's brother Gene had a heart attack at 48 and died. Her father had died at 43 this way so that was a risk for her other brother and her as well. Fortunately they are in good health. But that and the fact that the children were growing older ended the Xmas trips. So we accumulated points at Intrawest (now called EMBARC by the new owners) and now rent out the Whistler condo. The last 4 years have seen huge price rises in Vancouver but declining prices of secondary recreational properties such as the Whistler condo.

In 2015, there was a massive drop in the price of oil down from a $147 high[4] to under $30 per barrel. This and other factors such as a Chinese slow down in the economy which led to lower commodity prices and subsequently a sharp decline in the Canadian dollar versus the US dollar. In February 2017, it was around 1.31 having bottomed at 1.47. Whistler prices in Canadian dollars have increased about 20%. The buyers are not foreigners

The Plumbush Inn

**Fine Lodging by the Sea
on Salt Spring Island, B.C.**

Bed and Breakfast
Private Baths in all Rooms,
Gourmet Breakfasts
Working Farm with Exotic Sheep
Pond, Trails, 1000 feet of Waterfront

The Plumbush Inn is a peaceful retreat by the sea on picturesque Salt Spring. The Inn's beautiful estate setting encompasses 22 acres of forest and meadows. Walk along the one thousand feet of private ocean front. Walk through pastures amongst sheep and goats. Secluded gardens provide a tranquil environment for your relaxation. Our spacious living room provides a warm meeting ground. As your hosts we strive to provide a private quiet hideaway.

The Inn decor is French Provincial with fine antique furniture. Each room has a special charm and decoration. All rooms have a queen bed and private bath.

The Plumbush Inn is an easy drive from the three ferry terminals on Salt Spring Island.

Explore the shops and galleries in nearby Ganges. The many crafts-people on the island open their studios to visitors and there is a summer arts fair. There are tennis and golf courses and parks, boating and cycling on the island. Pubs and a variety of fine dining restaurants are easy driving from the Inn. Salt Spring is a convenient base from which to visit the other Gulf Islands and Vancouver Island.

Gourmet farm breakfast, which is included in the price, is served in the dining room. Special diets can be accommodated.

Reservations are held with one day's deposit. Master Card, Visa, US, Cdn checks accepted.

We at **The Plumbush Inn** look forward to welcoming you

For reservations contact
Sonia and Darren Schneider
The Plumbush Inn
600 Walker Hook Rd.
Salt Spring Island, B.C. V8K 1N6
or call or fax 250-537-4332

---

with US dollars, pounds or euros but rather Vancouver area people who made large gains on their Vancouver properties. In 2017 I was finally able to sell Whistler for more or less the 2002 price.

To replace Belmont, in 1992 we bought a Bed and Breakfast Inn and Farm on Salt Spring Island. It had 984 feet waterfront, a large Inn and a cottage. In the beginning we ran the B&B ourselves going over when we had guests. We bought two llamas, mohair goats, Jacob and Merino–Leicester sheep, plus chickens so it was a functioning farm. We needed to have someone there all the time. We had a number of B&B farm managers but unfortunately the economics are poor and this cost us money. So we moved to just renting the property. We rent it now unfurnished to a family, storing our belongings in the basement and also rent the cottage. There is a road cutting the property so I separated out the waterfront lot from the 22 acre farm — this took an astounding 8 years to do.

Vancouver real estate has continued higher and higher and waves of people from China and other places have raised prices to extremely high levels comparable with New York, San Francisco, London and other top locations. Meanwhile Vancouver has grown into a very sophisticated city with top restaurants, opera, theater, etc., and a ranking, along with Melbourne and Geneva, as the world's most liveable city. But it is ranked third in the world as most expensive real estate relative to incomes behind Hong Kong and Sydney.

Notes

[1] We did get a tax break for two years.

[2] The idea is to bet on A then later on B, the opponent so that you make a profit regardless of who wins. That's not always possible but often is. This paper discusses exact arbitrage and approximate risk arbitrage. See Ziemba and Ziemba (2013) for many applications of this, especially in NFL playoff and Superbowl football betting on Betfair. I do the same in S&P500 futures market in the alpha Z Futures Fund.

[3] We rented from a famous math professor, Maurice Sion. His wife Emily and Sandra wrote a woman's book together. Sion was retiring and offered us the house for 500k and he would carry most of the paper. I had bid up to 450k and asked Stan if I should go to 500 assuming he knew the market. He said no. Then I asked again, are you sure? Still no. With two against me I gave up. Two months later it sold for 670k. It is probably worth 4 million now in 2017.

[4] Rachel called the top in a major financial newspaper.

Chapter 30

Two Tries in the Horse Ownership Business

My first foray into racing was somewhat accidental, and at the low end. Not a good combination for any investment! Things started off beautifully, however. In September 2005, I was invited to speak to the management at one of America's great classic racetracks, Keeneland. It is a beautiful site and I have used their library for research on several occasions. I spent 3 hours covering key issues facing the industry in the US, including rebating, betting exchanges and demand elasticity. I felt that the talk gave senior management plenty of food for thought, and a lively discussion ensued.

Keeneland is America's richest race track, particularly in terms of average purse, as it hosts several major horse sales each year, including its worldclass September sale of select yearlings. Spending totals hundreds of million per sale. The track gets 4.5% — a rather profitable sideline. The select sales are the thoroughbred equivalent of a major Sothebys art auction, and attract a similarly monied clientele. They are well worth watching, even as a spectator.

Several days prior to my talk, I met a trainer from Bay Meadows, CA, named Greg Vartanian, who was talking up a recent $2,700 yearling purchase he had just made. The horse seemed a potential bargain: his sire's yearlings generally went for $20,000 or so, but his dam's foals had never won a race (despite her having good earnings and wins on the track). I figured the risk was worth my Keeneland speaking fee and air fare as well as a nicely symmetrical arrangement — so I took a 50–50 share in ownership.

The young horse's first big race came in early 2006, and went better than I could have ever hoped: he broke the track record for $4^1/_2$ furlongs at Golden Gate! Greg seemed to run his tiny stable on a shoestring, and was keen to follow up on a few feelers he had from potential buyers in the 200K range, but I felt like we had plenty of upside with the horse and was in no hurry to hedge. In retrospect, a Mistake!

After a second good race, there was talk of a $500K offer for our horse from the Zayat stables, based in Del Mar, but nothing firm materialized. Still, feeling good at this point about my initial foray into ownership, I returned to Keeneland in September 2006 for the select sales and partnered up with Greg to buy five more horses for a total of $57,000. The agreement was for 50–50 ownership, but it quickly became apparent that my trainer was long on talk and short on assets so I had to pay for all the horses.

My wake-up call came a month too late, when the California Horse Racing Board opened a case against Vartanian for illegal doping: he was using methamphetamine to make his horses run faster! As it turns out, exiting a horse-ownership arrangement as with other illiquid securities can be a lot harder than entering it. By the time the whole fiasco was over, I was out $100K and more than a bit disillusioned. [Final note: Greg V was barred from training in California in 2008, and has dropped from sight.]

If winning at the betting windows is hard, winning from the ownership box seemed an even more daunting challenge.

A Second Try at a High Level

After a half-dozen years on the ownership sidelines, I opted to get back involved in the spring of 2013 this time with a top-flight group of trainers and fellow owners, and some top-notch young horses. No more bargain-hunting with scoundrels! What got me interested was the huge drop in stud fees of top quality stallions from the 2007 high. Stud fees are usually correlated with the US stock market so when it fell in 2007–2009 (see Lleo and Ziemba, 2012, for a correct prediction of that crash on June 14, 2007), the stud fees fell as well. In 2013, there was a depression-like atmosphere in the Blue Grass with many farms in financial trouble and stud fees at the top farms a third or so of the 2007 level. The correlations had decoupled so with a rising stock market, it seemed a good time to get into this market.

We have top trainers like Shug McGaughey, trainer of many top horses including Kentucky Derby winner, Orb and the personal trainer for the famous Phipps stable and John Sheriffs, the trainer of Zenyatta, who won 19 of 20 losing her final race by a nose to Blame in her second Breeders' Cup classic in 2010. She won the year before and remains the only female winner of this $5 million race.

Keeneland was again the source for the yearlings. But this time I went in as part of an ownership pool. My investment got me a share in group of nine yearlings from the 2012 crop: two fillies and seven colts. Each year a number of horses are bought at the Keeneland select sale in the $100,000 plus range totaling about $800,000 for the whole group which might include some horses jointly owned with the farm or others. So about $1.5 million is raised trying to sell about 30 $50,000 shares with about $700,000 for training and other expenses. But in my group I have a 1/22$^+$ share for my $52,000 less $4000 that was paid back but there should be stud fees that over time will hopefully turn the investment into a gain. My account has over 20,000 as well so this comes later too.

Five of the horses in the 2012 group are only one eighth owned by our group because of their high cost. It was these horses, by super star stallions, that got me interested in being part of the group. These include colts by Smart Strike, the sire of $10+ million champion Curlin and many other top runners who had an $85,000 stud fee, which was increased to $100,000 in 2015,[1] Medaglia D'Oro ($100,000 fee, $125,000 in 2015+), a personal favorite of mine who sired horse of the year Rachel Alexandra, as well as undefeated Songbird, Street Cry ($100,000) who sired Zenyatta[2] and a filly and a colt from the last crop of newly retired champion sire AP Indy. AP Indy at $300,000 (later $150,000) stud fee was the sire of many top runners including Mineshaft, Benardini, Dreaming of Julia, Pulpit, Rags to Riches, Malibu Moon (the sire of Orb, the 2013 Kentucky Derby winner) and Majestic Warrior.

Candy Ride, May 2015   Tapit, May 2015

The top sire in the US and likely the world, along with Galileo and the undefeated Frankel, both in the UK, is Tapit who has produced over 30 grade I winners plus many other top horses. He is at Gainsway standing for

$300,000 and possibly more to actually get a season in 2016 and a reputed $350,000 in 2016.

Later, I bought a share in five horses in a 2013 crop of yearlings. These are all running in 2016 as 4 year olds. They include:

1. Arbitrator by Quality Road ($35,000 fee), Out of Code Book by Giant's Causeway ($40,000 cost), in ten races he earned $86,985 with two wins in his last two races, three seconds and one third. His trainer, Christophe Clement had him at Belmont and he was sold for $40,000.
2. Candour by the undefeated Argentinean Candy Ride out of Valid Warning by Valid Appeal (125,000 for a half). Candy Ride is standing at Lane's End for $60,000 in 2017 and was the sire of Shared Belief, the top 4 year old in the US before his injury and later death. His first start was in a one mile 75K maiden special weight race at Belmont for 3 year olds and up on September 18, 2015. He finished fifth at 9–1, collecting $2,250. He was never in contention. His next race was a $1^1/_{16}$ mile at Belmont in which he finished seventh. His earnings were $2,625 so he was not covering expenses. He was given away for nothing.
3. Marine One by Malibu Moon a son of AP Indy and sire of 2013 Kentucky Derby winner Orb out of Datts Our Girl by Kentucky Derby winner, the dual qualifier Thunder Gulch. To show how tough the business is Marine One cost $185,000 plus expenses, he won one race and was out of the money in 3 other races, he was then put in a $40,000 claiming race which he won and collected a $33,000 purse but we then lost the horse having collected $47,660 plus the claim money when he was claimed. This was done as he was very slow and the assumption was that he could only run in low level claiming races. So we have collected some money and cut our losses.

   The next two purchases were both fillies.
4. Mio Me by Kentucky Derby future book favorite Eskenereya out of Missle Bay by Yes Its True ($130,000), ran at Santa Anita. She began her career with a win and won $89,462 in her first eleven races. She had one win, one second and two thirds. Unfortunately, she died of an unknown cause on April 29, 2016. There was a $130,000 insurance policy and after an autopsy, we were paid $7678.68.
5. Season Ticket by the dual qualifier, Belmont Stakes winner Lemon Drop Kid ($40,000 fee in 2017) out of the French mare Game by European superstar Prix de l'Arc Triomphe winner Montjeu (120K) was the star of this group. She ran in Canada in top races, including a third in a $500,000 Woodbine Oaks stakes which earned her C$50,000 (US$40,000). In her

next race, the $150,000 one mile Ontario Damsel on July 18, she finished second and collected $30,000 more. Season Ticket next won the 51st running of the $250,000 Canadian Wonder Where Stakes at Woodbine on August 9, 2015 ridden by Patrick Husbands. She was the 2–1 favorite and collected C$150,000 (US$114,195). After her 14th race, her earnings were US$280,171. She was then shipped to Belmont but finished out of the money in two starts. So with thirteen starts she has earned $279,861 with two wins, three seconds and one third. She seems more suited for top level Canadian grass races so was returning there. She won one race in Canada and finished eleventh in the grade II $200,000 Dance Smartly Stakes on July 3. She does not want to train so she was sold at the November 2016 Kneeland auction for $155,600.

This group cost me $55,000 for a 1 in 16.93 share (total cost for the five horses was $600,000). So far, as of December 20, 2016, they have collected purses of $506,903 plus $40,000 for the claim plus the 40,000 and $155,000 sales less expenses. Mio Me, Season Ticket Arbitrator and Marine One won races, and Candor has earnings of $2625. As the late economics Nobel laureate James Tobin has argued: economics is about incentives, these groups have many pluses and two drawbacks. First the trainers get paid a daily fee so their incentive to race frequently and raise money for the owners is limited. They do however seem to have a plan. The organizers of the groups may or may not own shares, but they get a fee just like hedge fund managers and if there are profits, they get a percent of the profits. But there is nothing forcing them to invest their own money in the group. They do have their reputations on the line, so I hope that that is enough to have a situation where we do not lose money. In early 2017 we were cashed out and received $14,635.31. So I have a loss of about $32K on the group 9 since I only received this plus the insurance money.

Many of these horses trace back to AP Indy as sire or damsire and therefore back to Secretariat. Secretariat ran the fastest times since 1950 at least and likely back to Man O'War in the 1920s.[3]

The only recent competitor was Ghostzapper in 2004, who ran four zeros on Ragozin's scale, four 84s on Equiform (the highest I ever saw) and his 2004 Breeders' Cup Classic $1\frac{1}{4}$ mile victory was under 2 minutes. He was faster than Secretariat's Kentucky Derby. Secretariat still holds the records in the Kentucky Derby, Preakness and Belmont Stakes from his 1973 triumphs. In breeding, he produced over 600 offspring. The males were average or poor and many never ran a race except that three of them had one super race each: (1) General Assembly won the $1\frac{1}{4}$ mile 1979

Season Ticket at the Wonder Where Stakes

Ghostzapper provider of the superfecta for WTZ

Travers in a record 2.00 until Arrogate won the 2016 Travers in 1:59:2; (2) Risen Star was second only to Secretariat in the Belmont Stakes at 2.26.4 versus Secretariat's record 2.24 in 1973 and (3) Kingston Rule who won the Melbourne Cup in record time in 1990.

Secretariat's female offspring were more successful and include Lady's Secret, Summer Secretary and Super Staff. But his real forte was the sons of his daughters. Super sires AP Indy and Storm Cat were his best and others include Tinner's way, Giants Causeway and Gone West. Storm Cat's stud fee of $500,000 in his prime was then the highest in the world at that time and at 116 breeds, he collected about $58 million per year for his owners — see the photo of my visit to him. The noted trainer D Wayne Lukas said

Two Tries in the Horse Ownership Business 333

Storm Cat at Overbrook Farm, Lexington, Kentucky

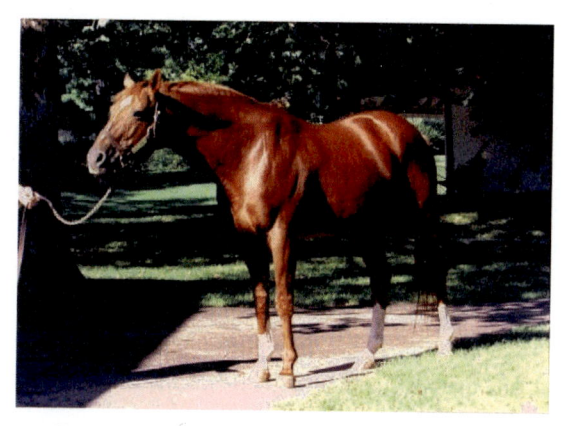

Secretariat at Claiborne Farm, Paris, Kentucky

that Terlingua, the dam of Storm Cat, was the fastest horse he ever trained. Secretariat was the top broodmare sire in the world following Alleged who won the Prix de l'Arc race at Longchamps in Paris twice. Alleged was so unruly that, when I visited him at Walmac Farm near Lexington, he had to be led out of his stall with two chains attached to his bridal and held by two grooms, one on each side.

Secretariat's Heart

They say that the great horses have a lot of heart. Scientifically, a big heart is carried only by the X-chromosome which is only transmitted through

Class Leader at the Preakness undercard

daughters. A normal horse heart is about 8 pounds. Sham who broke the record in the Kentucky Derby and Preakness, finishing second to Secretariat, had an 18 pound heart. The famed jockey Laffit Pincay, Jr. said that in 40+ years, Sham was the best horse he ever rode and Pincay rode the triple crown winner Affirmed as a 4 year old after jockey Steve Cauthen moved to England to ride. Secretariat's heart was estimated at 22 pounds, the largest on record. Eclipse and Pharlap had 14 pound hearts. So maybe size matters in the greatest thoroughbreds.

Peace Mission: A Case of Good Breeding

Peace Mission, trained by famed Zenyatta trainer John Sherriffs was a $50,000 purchase sired by Harlan's Holiday out of Royal Parade by St Ballado. His first start of Belmont Park was in Race 3 on October 27, 2013 in a maiden $90,000 race. He was not one of the top picks and his odds on Betfair (where I was betting) and at the track varied from 5–1 to 17–1 with the high odds at the end of the betting period.[4] Junior Alvarado rode him well on the outside and he looked very strong and won the race paying $27 at the track; an even money shot was second. The $54,000 first place money and excellent showing, with a time faster than Honor Code's first race (see below), provided great promise that we would not lose money with this horse. Unfortunately, he suffered a minor injury in training before his next start. The prospects for recovery were good. However, in July 2014 it was determined that he was too fragile to run again so he was donated as a gelding to a central Kentucky farm to be a show horse.

Class Leader Looks Promising

Class Leader, by Smart Strike out of Class Kris with damsire Kris S, was sixth in his first race at Churchill Downs on October 27, 2013. That was a maiden race and he got a very low 42 Beyer speed rating and $192 in earnings for the effort. He is trained by Neil Howard. His second race was on February 17, 2014 at the Fair Grounds, in New Orleans in a maiden special weight race of one mile and 70 yards for the purse of $45,000. This time was more successful when he won the race at 6.1–1 by two lengths running an 82 Beyer. He collected 60% of the purse or $24,000.

His third race was also at the Fairgrounds on March 13, 2014. Again it was at the same distance of 1 mile 70 yards. After I studied the past performances and the PSR and HTR ratings, Class Leader was my pick so I bet win, place and show along with some small exactas and this time the second choice in the betting behind #2 Candy Dandy.

The finish was 1–3–5–2 so it was another nice win for Class Leader. I won my across the board bet but lost the small exactas and trifecta bets because I had the 3–5 shot #2 in them along with #1 first or second and #3 second or third. I did not put #5 in despite being third in the PSR because he never ran a Beyer rating competitive with horses 1, 2 or 3. Then #2, the favorite, ran fourth. I won my bets plus the rebate and collected the rebate on the lost exacta and tri bets for a small profit in total.

Neil reported that Class Leader came out of the race in great shape and he thought that he was very professional and "workmanlike." Class Leader relaxed and simply waited for James to give him his cue. James Graham was equally enthusiastic about Class Leader's performance. Neil said James walked into the paddock before the race and simply said, "This is going to be a lot of fun Neil."

Class Leader's next race was the $500,000 grade III Illinois Derby on April 19, 2014. This was a big step up in class and money and brought many top 3 year old males to the race even though they could not accrue any Kentucky Derby points. So horses trying to get enough points for the Kentucky Derby field would not be in this race so the competition might be less tough.

The favorite in the Illinois Derby was Midnight Hawk, trained by legendary superstar trainer Bob Baffert who always seems to know where to ship his horses. While Midnight Hawk has enough points to qualify for the Kentucky Derby, California Chrome and others appear stronger so he did not to run there. Also this race is very close in time to run a horse in two tough races. So the Illinois Derby was preferred.

On paper Midnight Hawk with four consecutive 90 plus Beyers (95, 93, 95, 98) and none of the other horses in the 90s, was the clear standout at 3-5 in the morning line. He was first or second in all the races starting in December 2013. He had basically no 2 year old form, another reason not to run in the Kentucky Derby.[5] Another was despite his low dosage, very acceptable for the Kentucky Derby but in his last three races he faded near the finish. Class Leader with Beyers of 42, 82 and 86 with wins in the last two races was the second choice. The only other horse with a Beyer above 80 was Dynamic Impact who had an 88 in a mile race at Keeneland. Dynamic Impact ran a 102 Beyer and went to the Preakness. Midnight Hawk's next race in uncertain.

The obvious bets were on #3 at 2-5, #8 at 9-2, #1 at 9-1, #5 at 9-1, and #4 at 22-1. Specifically Win on #1, Place on #3, Exactas on 8-3, 1-3, 5-3, and Tris and Superfectas with 1-3-4-5-8 with #3 in first, second and third position and the others all over the place with some of #1 and #4 as well as #8 in first position. The finish was 1-3-4-8, the four highest PSR ratings and the top three HTR ratings. The payoffs were $2 win $21.20, $2 exacta 1-3 $38, $2 tri 1-3-4 $423.40, $1 super 1-3-4-8 $897.40.

Class Leader won $30,000 for his 4th place finish to boost his career earnings to $70,482.50 so far. His fifth race was on the Preakness undercard in a $100,000 race, the Sir Barton Stakes, race 10 at Pimlico on May 17, 2014. Class Leader was again ridden by James Graham. This race was for 3 year olds who have never won a stakes race. The top horses were #2 Six Spot, #3 Life in Shambles, #10 Class Leader and #11 Change Now (who was scratched).

Class Leader won, despite his poor post position, at 9-5 odds, followed by #3 Life in Shambles at 7-2 and #2 Six Spot at 5-1 and #1 Sea Vie Chico at 14-1. The win, place, show payoffs on Class Leader were 5.60, 3.40 and 2.80. The $2 exacta paid $27.80 and the $2 trifecta $37.10.

It was a great outcome for Class Leader and the partnership with his $60,000 share of the purse. His earnings in his five races with 3 wins and 2 out of the monies, now totaled $136,332. He was scheduled in the Matt Winn Stakes at Churchill but unfortunately got a lung infection. He should be fine but will be away from training from 30-45 days. He is nominated to all the summer stakes for 3 year olds. He then ran in race 8, a $43,000 allowance/optional claiming race for 3 year olds and up going one mile on the dirt at Churchill Downs on September 19, 2014, with regular jockey James Graham. This was his first time facing older horses after his time off. Unfortunately, it was an out of the money finish, a dead heat for fifth place at odds of 11.5–1, beaten by $4^1/_2$ lengths. He won $752 for his efforts. James Graham commented after the race that Class Leader was not able to get in a good running rhythm with balance in the beginning. He started to get his stride going at the top of the stretch but could not quicken and got a little tired in the end. Neil Howard was disappointed but thinks that Class Leader will be better when he can go around two turns which will allow him to settle, get in a running rhythm and make his sustained run. This field was very solid.

This race set up Class Leader well for a start at Keeneland. But that was a flop when he finished ninth on October 18, 2014 at 10.4–1. He was third in an allowance optimal claiming race at Santa Anita on January 8 earning $7,800. His next race was better when he ran second, beaten by a neck at the finish after taking the lead in a $42,000 allowance race at the Fairgrounds on February 1, 2015. He collected $8,400 for his efforts. His next race was the $125,000 Mineshaft Handicap for 4 year olds going $1^1/_{16}$ mile on the dirt at the Fairgrounds on Saturday February 21, 2015. Unfortunately that was another flop with Class Leader finishing eleventh. On April 3, Class Leader was second at Santa Anita in the $100,000 Tokyo City Cup earning $20,000. On April 18, 2015, Class Leader ran a 98 Beyer finishing third in a $80,000 allowance race at Keeneland. He also ran in similar allowances on May 28 and June 20 finishing fifth and third, respectively. His thirteenth race was the $100,000 Michael G Schaeffer Memorial at Indiana Downs on July 18 at one mile and 70 yards, where he finished third and earned $11,006 and a current total of $173,389.

He was shipped to Del Mar to run in the $1 million grade I Pacific Classic on August 22, 2015, hoping that the field would be weak. But the talented mare, Beholder, who just easily won the Clement L Hirsh, was the favorite, along with Bayern, Red Vine, Catch a Flight, Imperative, Hard Aces, Hopportunity and Midnight Storm, all who have run 100+ Beyers, easily won the race. Class Leader did get a 98. Although outclassed, one positive was a jockey switch to the legendary Mike Smith.

Beholder was the favorite of the betting public but not the handicappers who favored Red Vine. But she won easily by $8^1/_4$ lengths. She ran the $1^1/_4$ miles in 1:59.77, just below the track record. This under 2 minutes joining the elite at this classic distance: Secretariat, Ghostzapper, Monarchos and very few others. Red Vine was third behind Catch a Flight. Bayern led from the start but faded to ninth. Class Leader was seventh and collected $250 of the $1 million purse. He was sixth in the $1 million grade I Big Cap at Santa Anita earning $10,000. In his next race he was second in a $100,000 race, earning 20%, or $20,000. He was still in training for the summer 2016 campaign and later sold for $40,000.

Honor Code: We Might have a Kentucky Derby Horse

The star of our group so far and potential Kentucky Derby horse is Honor Code who we own one eighth of. I was especially high on Honor Code watching him train in Saratoga with trainer Claude McGaughey III known as Shug. He trained Lure, Personal Ensign, Easy Goer, Seeking the Gold, Coronado's Quest, Inside Information, and then Vanlandingham (his first colt), Point of Entry and Orb. With a 22% win rate he is a well respected trainer and is the personal trainer for the legendary Phipps family.

Honor Code runs with his head bobbing like his sire, AP Indy. In the 1992 Breeder' Cup Classic, AP Indy rallied strongly from far back to win the race and become horse of the year. He had also won the Belmont Stakes that year. Later, he became one of the world's top stallions with a $300,000 stud fee, which was lowered to $150,000 prior to his retirement in 2011. Honor Code's pedigree is spectacular. His dam was the Storm Cat mare, Serena's Song. He is big and strong with a terrific presence. His first race was in a $80,000 maiden race on August 31, 2013 at Saratoga. I remember Tom Durkin's call "and Honor Code is no where to be seen." The track was muddy and JR Velesquez, the jockey, made a brilliant run along the rail from 22 lengths behind to win by $4^1/_2$ lengths. Honor Code made this run in the last 3 furlongs. He made a huge impact as he was the only horse that day who made a big closing move. The final time was fast but the final 3 furlongs were blazing fast.

So it looked promising with this horse. His next race was October 5, 2013 in the $500,000 Champagne, a grade I race. This was now the big time. Again he put on a spectacular run in the last 3 furlongs but had to go eight wide so did not quite make it. The winner, Havana, had a good trip and won by part of a head. But Honor Code finished ahead one jump later! So with a better trip or longer race he looked superior. The next race was the $2 million Breeders Cup Juvenile. The trainer and major owner decided not to ship Honor Code for the November 2, 2013 race but go for

AP Indy at Lane's End, 2009

the grade II Remsen Stakes at Aqueduct on November 30, 2013. The idea being not to have him stress the trip with yet another race so soon at Santa Anita in which he would run two turns for the first time facing other horses that had already done this. It would also prepare him better for the 2014 races.

My first reaction was disappointment as winning, and he likely would have been the favorite, would have brought in $1.2 million plus a lot of prestigue had he won or placed second. So we will see how this decision works out. Shug did have Orb in 2013, the Kentucky Derby winner, who was the favorite in all the triple crown races, finishing in the money in the other two. Training horses and determining when to run them is a very complex business. For some reason, winners of the Juvenile do not seem to be able to do well as 3 year olds. For example, of the 29 Juvenile winners since 1984, only one, Street Sense in 2006, won the Kentucky Derby. Also of these 29 winners, only one, Timber Country in 1995, won the Preakness, and no Juvenile winner has won the Belmont. So out of 87 triple crown races, winners of the Juvenile have only won two races!

Why is this? The answer seems to be this is too much to expect from a 2 year old and many of the horses are either injured, worn out or out of form. So the evidence supports the decision made to skip the Juvenile. New Year's Day, trained by Bob Baffert, won the Juvenile, beating Havana and the D Wayne Lucas trained, Strong Mandate. None of these three were in the 2014 Kentucky Derby.

Then Honor Code won the $400,000 grade II Remsen Stakes of Aqueduct, narrowly defeating Cairo Prince who headed Honor Code before Honor Code was able to come back for the win which showed his tenacity. This added $240,000 to his earnings and his reputation which made him the future book favorite for the Kentucky Derby. His next races were scheduled to be at Gulfstream in early 2014 beginning with the $400,000 grade II Fountain of Youth on February 22. Honor Code has a lot of competition. The fastest 2 year old horse of 2013 was Shared Belief who won the $750,000 Cash Call Futurity on December 14 at Hollywood Park by 5 and $3/4$ lengths. The gelding, Shared Belief, by the undefeated Candy Ride out of a Storm Cat mare was trained by Jerry Hollendorfer. He had an abscess on his right foot so he missed a workout. He is scheduled to run February 8 at Santa Anita in the Robert B Lewis Stakes. Honor Code has a minor injury which looks not serious but he will miss 10 days training so he will miss the Fountain of Youth on February 22. He was to follow Orb's 2013 plan: Fountain of Youth then Florida Derby on March 30 then the Kentucky

Orb now in stud at Claiborne farms for a $25,000 fee

Derby. Instead, he may possibly run in the Grade II $600,000 Rebel Stakes race at Oaklawn on March 15. He still could make the Kentucky Derby. with a different set of races. Fortunately, there are many possibilities. He is still the second choice at 6–1 after the 5–1 Cairo Prince in the second Derby future book. Cairo Prince shined in the Holy Bull Stakes at Gulfstream, winning by more than five lengths.

Special Agent

I was excited about our fourth horse, Special Agent, by Medaglia D'Oro with the dam Secret Status by A P Indy. Medaglia D'Oro sired 2009 horse of the year Rachel Alexandra. Special Agent, also trained by Shug, ran his first time at Aqueduct on November 9, 2013. He finished fourth, a bit of a disappointment. Then in his next race he was sixth and in a third try he finished fifth, again out of the money. So far he shows little promise in relation to his excellent pedigree, but we will see. I thought the current plan was to try him on the grass. Orb, the 2013 Kentucky Derby winner was way back in his first three 2-year old races then blossomed as a 3 year old. Special Agent ran again on the dirt on April 16, 2014 in a $58,000 maiden race and finished sixth at 8.3–1. So that's four straight poor races. His earnings from these four races total $4,309 so with expenses there is a

Medaglia D'Oro, sire of Special Agent, at Darley

big loss on him so far. We will see what the future brings. The plan is to try him long on the grass.

The move to the grass in a long race worked. Special Agent's win odds were 11.2–1 as #6 in the $1\frac{1}{4}$ mile Maiden Special Weight $75,000 race 5 at Belmont on May 18, 2014. He won the race, finally showing his terrific breeding and handling by trainer Shug McGaughey and the move to leading jockey JJ Castellano. Special Agent added $45,000 to his lifetime winnings to total $49,309. Special Agent's sixth race was the eighth race at Belmont on June 18, 2014 in a $1\frac{1}{4}$ mile turf $77,000 allowance with JJ Castellano riding him again. This race was for 3 year olds and up who never won $10,000 other than in maiden or a claiming race. It is a mixture of 3, 4 and 5 year old horses, several with higher Beyers than Special Agent. Three of them have run $1\frac{1}{4}$ miles before but for Special Agent and the others, this is a new, longer distance. The result was good with Special Agent finishing second and picking up 20% of the $77,000 purse. Special Agent's seventh race was the fifth race at Saratoga on July 18, 2014. That was an $85,000 allowance at $1\frac{3}{8}$ on the turf with JJ Castellano. The result was a fourth place finish and a payoff of $4,250. He was close then weakened. Special Agent's eighth race was on August 30, 2014 in an $85,000 allowance run over $1\frac{3}{16}$ miles at Saratoga. Special Agent with JJ Castellano was close most of the race but faded to dead heat for fifth place with Golden Soul who was second in the 2013 Kentucky Derby. His next race was to be at Belmont, hopefully at a shorter distance, but he has an enlarged suspensary ligament on one of his hind legs. Once the shockwave treatment was completed, he resumed training at Win Star. He next race was on Saturday, February 21, 2015 in an $38,000 allowance for 4 year olds on the dirt at the Fairgrounds. That was a flop with a last place finish. The decision was to sell him for $10,000. He had won $70,234 mostly in 2014 so was not covering his cost.

Stockholder

Our fifth horse Stockholder, who cost $280,000, is trained by famed Zenyatta trainer John Sheriffs. His sire was Exchange Rate out of the dam Looking After and damsire Broad Brush. His first start was in race 4 on May 17, 2014 at Belmont in a $75,000 maiden special weight race. He was the fourth choice of five runners at 7.10–1. Stockholder got some good experience finishing third and collected $7,500.

His second race was on July 14, 2014 in a $85,000 maiden special weight race for 3 year olds and up for one mile on dirt at Belmont Park. He was

Stockholder wins at the Fairgrounds

ridden by Javier Castellano. His morning line odds were 4–1 as the third choice in the betting and in the PSR and HTR. But he finished seventh and last and collected $750. The plan is now to gled Stockholder and try that as he seems not interested enough in running and was hard to load in the gate. He was then moved to trainer Neil Howard. He ran on January 18, 2014 at the Fairgrounds finishing fifth in a 7.5 furlong turf race. He ran in a maiden special weight dirt taken off the turf race at the Fairgrounds on February 5, 2014 finishing sixth at 6.1–1 odds. His next race was in a $1\frac{1}{16}$ $20,000 maiden claiming race at the Fairgrounds on February 20, 2015 with a purse of $16,500. The idea was to get him claimed and exit the losses from his career, but he was the favorite at 3–1 in this race and won convincingly by 5 lengths. I did not bet nor did anyone claim him in that race. His next race was in the $15,000 claiming are for 4 year olds and up going 1 mile on the turf. He won again but was disqualified to second place because of a bumping incident. He won 20% of the $12,000 purse or $2,400 and was claimed so now is gone.

Ready Reply

Our sixth horse, Ready Reply, a filly by More than Ready out of Leos Pegasus by Kentucky Derby winner Fusaichi Pegasus,[6] was ready for her debut on Thursday June 19, 2014 at Belmont. But she had soreness from a small chip in her left front ankle so needed 60 days away from training. Then trainer Christophe Clement decided to stop training. She was sold at the November Keeneland sale of brood mares and fillies for $40,000.

Mingle

Our seventh horse, Mingle, a bay filly by City Zip out of the Dixie Union filly Rumari, who cost $90,000 has weak knees and was sold at the November Keeneland sale of brood mares and fillies was sold for $1,500.

Native Talent

Our eighth horse, the AP Indy filly Native Talent by Unbridled's Song out of Rare Gift was being prepped by trainer John Shirreffs to debut at Belmont in their fall meet. She has been slowed in her training by a small popped splint. She has now had two races, both were out of the money. Her first race was at the Fairgrounds and she finished fifth. In her second race at Keeneland, she finished seventh and last. Her third was a maiden special weight race at Keeneland on April 18, 2015, going two turns. In four starts she has only one third place finish and the other three races she was out of the money. In total she has earned $7,357 so so far is not covering her cost. Once again, great pedigree is not a sufficient condition for a good racing career, so it is not surprising that she will be sold at the November Keeneland Broadmare sale. She brought a surprisingly high $140,000 at the sale, this was below the about $200,000 initial cost, but does lower the loss on her racing career.

Communicate

Our ninth horse, Communicate, had the same sire, Street Cry, as Zenyatta with dam West Talker and the damsire was Stormin Fever, has not been trainable. Sadly the decision was made to donate him as a 3 year old to a steeplechase trainer for a career there. Since Zenyatta did her best running at 4, 5 and 6. I was surprised about this decision to give away an expensive horse.

Honor Code and the Derby and Beyond

Shug McGaughey had been bringing Honor Code along carefully. Comparing Honor Code to Orb, he said that the reason Orb was so successful in 2013 was that everything went smoothly. "We never missed a work, never missed a race, never had a single setback with Orb all winter."

Things went smoothly for Honor Code in 2013 and his early training in 2014. Then he suffered a minor injury and was out of training for 10 days in January for some bruising of an ankle. That put the schedule behind and the Orb route Fountain of Youth grade II and Florida Derby grade I would not work. It was announced that Honor Code would go to the grade II Rebel stakes at Oaklawn on March 15. Then Shug made a U-turn and entered Honor Code in an allowance at Gulfstream on March 12. That meant no Kentucky Derby points, less money, a $75,000 race rather than the $600,000 Rebel, but no travel. Meanwhile, Shug's other top 3 year old, Top Billing, did well winning the Fountain of Youth and became one of the Derby favorites. It seemed Shug was not into running the two head to head as trainer Todd Pletcher would do with his 250+ horses. So they would take separate routes with the April 5 Wood Memorial grade I being a potential target for Honor Code. Then Top Billing suffered a cannon bone injury so was out of the Florida Derby and the Kentucky Derby. So then maybe after the allowance race Honor Code will go back to the Florida Derby plan.

The race arrived and Honor Code was a 3–5 favorite with a top Beyer of 93 as a 2 year old. The main competition was from Social Inclusion who won his only start by $7^1/_2$ lengths also with a 93 Beyer. That was in a short 6 furlong race on February 22 at Gulfstream. Both were rated 104 on the PSR scale and HTR picked Social Inclusion over Honor Code.

The handicappers Mike Beer and Dan Ullman of the *Daily Racing Form* had an analysis close to my thinking. Honor Code was the class of the field, had run long races and had a top trainer and the top jockey JJ Castellano who won all four of his races on March 12. The allowance was $8^1/_2$ furlongs. Honor Code gave a weight advantage of 5 pounds to Social Inclusion and Were all Set and 10 to a Special Night and 15 to Ta Bueno. There was a possibility of a wire to wire by the 3–1 Social Inclusion. The bet on 3–5 shots is usually to place and the Dr Z bets on the exacta are usually the favorite in second place but with a super horse at low odds you also bet the favorite in first position.

The suggested bets were placed on #4 and on 1–4 and 4–1 exactas. I made those bets at the rebate shop and a win bet at better odds at Betfair plus the place bet there which, with only five horses in the race, only two horses placed in the UK system.

An interesting event occurred. In 1990, Donald Hausch and I wrote two racing arbitrage papers (reprinted in my 2012 book *Calendar Anomalies and Arbitrage*, World Scientific). One dealt with creating an arbitrage by betting the horses at different racetracks at different prices. Nowadays all the money for a race is only in the pool at that horse's racetrack. All the money gets shipped there. So that will not work any more. The other paper called *locks at the racetrack* is the situation where one super horse has so much bet on it to place or show that there exists a weighting such that no matter what is the finish you cannot lose.[7]

So if the super horse is in the money the place or show bets on those that collect are the minimum $2.10. And if the super horse is out of the money, the small bets on the so-called weaker horses have huge payoffs. In either case there is a profit and in fact it is equal by construction of the model. Such a lock or arbitrage occurs maybe 10 times a year in US racing. Well Honor Code just about made the list in this race. Honor Code opened up at 1–9. The opening pools had Honor Code with 53,170 out of 56,140 for 94.7% in the show pool, well above the level for a lock, namely 91.5%. That's for a 5 horse field with a 11% track take (the actual track take of 15% with a 4% rebate). By the end of betting, there was was virtually still a lock but not quite.

The succeeding pools kept the lock as Honor Code moved to 1–5 then 1–2 and Social Inclusion to 3–1 then 2–1 then 7–5. Social Inclusion got the late money, usually a good sign as that money is usually more informed. At the end there still was close to a lock with Honor Code at 347,778 out of the total 390,377 show pool or 89.1%. This was 3 times the win pool and more than 11 times the place pool. At 1–2 my place bet was all right with Honor Code having 21,046 of the 37,247 or 56.5% of the place pool versus 66,989 out of 123,752 or 54.1% in the win pool. Meanwhile, the Betfair win and place odds were as shown in the figure. I lost the Betfair win bets and won the smaller place bet.

Social Inclusion ran wire to wire and broke the Gulfstream track record running a Beyer 110. This was quite impressive given that many great horses have run at Gulfstream. It was also the highest Beyer by all 3 year olds in 2014 including Kentucky Derby and Preakness winner California Chrome who was named horse of the year. Honor Code ran a 93, the same as his Champagne grade I second and above his 88 in the grade II Remsen. Honor Code had a decent but not spectacular race but could not keep up and finished second. He added $13,200 to his earnings which then totaled $401,200, This is the majority of the $535,990 of the four horses of the nine in this group that have run races.

It will take a few years to get into profitability given lots of costs off these earnings and 1/8 for Honor Code, Special Agent and Class Leader.

Chances are good that with his super pedigree and terrific 2 year old form and a decent 3 year old year so far, that eventually Honor Code can be a moderately priced stallion. His only not excellent race saw Social Inclusion breaking the track record at Gulfstream, scoring the third fastest 3 year old time on chef-de-race scale at 65 and vaulting Social Inclusion into being very valuable.

Despite my place bet being a pretty good one, the place and show payoffs were the minimum $2.10 with the show being a minus pool where the track does not get its full track take. Then they pay the three first finishers the $2.10 payoffs. Social Inclusion paid 4.80 to win, 2.20 to place and 2.10 to show. The 1–4 exacta paid $7 per $2 bet. The superfecta 1–4–2–3 paid $8.20 per $1 bet showing how favored these horses were in a 5 horse race.

Trainer Shug McGaughey was impressed with the winner but also satisfied with Honor Code's effort. He remarked to the Daily Racing Form after the race "I'm disappointed we didn't win but not that disappointed in his race. We got a race into him and Javier obviously didn't beat him up."

The big winners were the trainer Manny Azpura and owner Ron Sanchez of Ronjos Racing Stable of Social Inclusion. By breaking the track record and beating the star Honor Code, there was a lot of interest by others to buy part or all of the horse. He was a $60,000 Keeneland September yearling purchase and now was worth close to $10 million. The top offer

Honor Code at Winstar Farm, May 2014

was $5 million for 75%. Before the race, the 85 year old trainer said:

> I really like this horse and I like everything he's done since I've got him. I'm so pleased with him and I believe he's going to keep improving, I told my wife before the race, 'You're going to see him break out of the gate and they're never going to catch him. They'll be 10 lengths behind.'

And he was right. There was a possibility that Honor Code and Social Inclusion would meet in the Kentucky Derby. It is hard to wire the field in the Derby but its been done a few times such as by Spend A Buck in 1985 and the filly Winning Colors in 1988.

Unfortunately, Honor Code suffered another minor injury and must rest with no training for 2 months and then restart training and hopefully compete in the fall races. Meanwhile, Social Inclusion ran in the April 5, 2014 Wood Memorial finishing third earning 20 Derby points so he did not have enough points to qualify for the Kentucky Derby. But he was in the Preakness and Belmont Stakes.

As of mid August 2014, Honor Code was essentially ready to be back in training with Shug McGaughey. What we need to complete his dossier to prepare for a top level breeding career is a grade I win. There are not many grade I's in the late fall so the plan was to run him as a 4 year old.

Honor Code was doing well and breezed a $1/2$ mile in 29 seconds on the dirt, second best of 14 at the Fair Hill Training Center in Elkton, Maryland. The plan is to ship him to Belmont so Shug can train him over a deeper surface and watch him train daily.

Honor Code is back

Honor Code finally made it back to racing on Saturday November 22, 2014. That was a 6$^1/_2$ furlong allowance optional claiming race on the dirt with a purse of $69,000 at Aqueduct. Just like in his first race of 7 furlongs, he started slow, was way behind and then had a tremendous finishing kick to win by a length plus. He earned $41,400 but the real gain was getting his reputation back. The NYRA commentators were impressed so the old Honor Code seems to be back. His 106 Beyer was one of the top races by 3 year olds in 2014. This was an improvement over his previous Beyers which were 89, 93, 88 and 92.

In his 2 year old races he beat top 3 year olds Wicked Strong, Ride on Curlin and Cairo Prince. His 2014 second place finish behind Social Inclusion's 110 Beyer is higher but that was higher than any horse achieved in any of the triple crown races. Wicked Strong was fourth in the Kentucky Derby, third behind Honor Code in the Remsen, won the grade I Wood Memorial beating Social Inclusion and was second in the Travers. Cairo Prince, who is now retired, won the grade II Holy Ball and Nashua Stakes and was fourth in the G1 Florida Derby. Ride on Curlin, who was third behind Honor Code's second in the G1 Champagne, was second in the G1 Arkansas Derby and Preakness, seventh in the Kentucky Derby and eleventh in the Belmont Stakes. So Honor Code seems competitive with these and other top 3 year olds. We will see what the next move is and his 4 year old year. The current plan was to run him in the G2 $300,000 Gulfstream Handicap on March 7 and hopefully later in the year in some G1 races such as the grade I Met Mile or the grade II Suburban at Belmont Park and later the grade I Whitney at Saratoga in August culminating with the 1$^1/_4$ grade I Breeders' Cup Classic at Keeneland on October 31, 2015.

Honor Code charging in the Gulfstream Handicap; Honor Code winning the Gulfstream Handicap

The Gulfstream Handicap had six horses running with #5 Private Zone the favorite. He was rated the best on HTR and at 126 on PSR rating systems. Valid was second in both and at 125. There are very high rankings to put them at the top of the 3 year olds. In PSR, Honor Code was ranked third and Wicked Strong fourth and in HTR they were reversed. The other two horses, East Hall, a closer like Honor Code and Loverbill. Private zone had won three grade I races and been second in two others. He had a jockey change to a less familiar and top jockey (Carlos Marquez) when his regular riser (Martin Pedrosa) could not get a Florida license. Honor Code had beaten Wicked Strong as a 2 year old in the G2 Remsen.

So this was tough competition after Honor Code's 6 month layoff. I was hoping that Honor Code could win and bet him accordingly in all the pools but I had to hedge in case Private Zone beat him and a little bet should Valid win. I assumed that Wicked would not win or be second so downgraded him. The race was vintage Honor Code. He was way at the back. Meanwhile, Private Zone and Valid were leading and having a speed dual. One plus for Honor Code was he was ridden by JJ Castellano, America's top jockey and the pilot of Honor Code's last four races.

According to the *Daily Racing Form*'s Mike Welsh, trainer Shug McGaughey, while watching the Gulfstream Park Handicap on the tv monitors and not seeing Honor Code anywhere near the leading horses said "I was about ready to go home ... I was watching it on tv, and down the back side there wasn't a (1) on there for a long time. Then I saw him swing to the outside. It was the same thing when he broke his maiden at Saratoga. I was watching on tv there and he wasn't ever in the picture and I was thinking up excuses already."

Fortunately he stuck around to watch the rest of the race, otherwise he would have missed an incredible performance by Honor Code who rallied down the center of the track from more than a dozen lengths behind to run down the favorite Private Zone and Valid. Honor Code stumbled at the start then dropped far off the early pace set by Private Zone and pressed from the outset by Valid. The leaders posted early splits of 23.51 and 45.96 seconds for the opening quarter and half mile with Honor Code about 15 lengths behind. Jockey Javier Castellano eased Honor Code outside to start his rally from the back stretch as the two leaders continued to battle upfront. But behind them, the rest of the field was hitting them best strides. At the 3/4 mile in 1:10.09, Honor Code had just one horse beat. But a furlong later he had moved into fourth and had the front runners firmly in his sites. Honor Code responded to steady urging while gaining steadily. In the stretch Private Zone and Valid still were ahead but Wicked Strong and Honor Code were gaining. With less than a furlong to run, Wicked Strong's rally stalled and Honor Code swept past him and took aim at the lead. With one final surge he passed the two leaders to win the race. The photos show him gaining ground and then winning. He beat Private Zone by half a length with Valid third, ahead of Wicked Strong for the 1–5–6–2 finish.

Jockey Javier Castellano admitted that their trip was worrying despite his mounts typical running style. "I didn't mind it (being far back), because he is a come from behind horse and the pace set up perfect for him." Private Zone and Valid hooked up together all the way but Castellano was worrying on the back side because Honor Code wasn't picking it up. At the 3/8 pole Honor Code turned around and took off at the top of the stretch. According to Castellano, it was amazing the way he did it.

Honor Code got 60% of the $300,000 purse or $180,000 so he was then 4 wins and two seconds winning $626,740. I did well in my betting at the rebate shop. Betting Wicked in third and fourth spot and focusing on Honor Code with some Private Zone and less Valid hedging paid off well in all the betting pools. His value is increased and chances to be a good stallion at Land's End now a very good possibility that would turn my investment into a profit.

His seventh race was the G2 $400,000 Alysheba Stakes at Churchill Downs on May 1, 2015 on the Kentucky Oaks undercard. The main competition was the Todd Fletcher trained Protonico. JJ Castellano chose Honor Code to ride. Somehow it was not Honor Code's day. He apparently did not like the track and finished fifth, although the slow pace was a factor. He had a bit of kick but was not his in his usual form of blazing at the end. A slow pace hurt Honor Code, but still he ran the last 1/4 mile in 23 seconds. This was a big disappointment. He collected $11,520 for his effort so now has won $638,260. I was there in an owners section of the vast track facility that Churchill has become. Fortunately, Honor Code came out of the race in fine shape.

Triple Crown 2015

I did not have any horses in the running for the 2015 Triple Crown but I watched and traded it and toured the horse farms. Elyse Mach, a music professor from Chicago and a racing enthusiast toured with me. We visited a number of the major farms, including Lane's End. The story of the 2015 Triple Crown follows.[8]

With Elyse Mach at Lanes End

Kentucky Derby, 2015

The organizers of the Kentucky Derby have altered the criterion to enter the race.[9] It has always been for a long time a maximum of 20 horses with a main and auxiliary gate to fit them all in. The 2014 and beyond rules give very little weight to 2 year old performance and focus on the major races just prior to the first Saturday in May with the last two races having the most weight. Hence, horses with top 2 year old form but weak 3 year old performance will not qualify. Horses such as dual qualifiers Lemon Drop Kid, Birdstone and Union Rags, all of whom won the Belmont stakes after poor Kentucky Derby performances, and skipping the Preakness, would be excluded from the Derby field. Of course, they could run in the Preakness and/or Belmont stakes.

I followed the handicapping services PSR, HTR, SuperScreener, Wizard, Beyer Speed Figures, Chef-de-Race and my own handicapping. Each service has a different take on it The Wizard had American Pharoah as the best bet, Dortmund second, the Dubai invader Mubtaahij next and Firing Line fifth.[10]

The favorites were the Bob Baffert trained Dortmund and American Pharoah who he rated equal going into the Derby. HRT favored American Pharoah (highest PSR at 117), Dortmund was second (116 PSR), Firing Line was the third (116 PSR), fourth was the lightly raced Materiality

(116 PSR) who won his three races but had no 2 year old races, fifth was Carpe Diem (111 PSR) who won the Blue Grass and sixth was Frosted (111 PSR) who won the Wood Memorial. The lack of a 2 year old race was a big strike against Materiality as the last horse horse who won the Derby with no 2 year old races was Apollo in 1888.

The top horses were, according to Super Screener's Super 7 for the Kentucky Derby:

Frosted **Dortmund** **Carpe Diem** **American Pharoah**

Upstart **Materiality** **Mubtaahij**

Super Screener provides suggested bets which combine the top horses in various ways in the exacta and trifecta.[11]

It was expected that one of the two Baffert horses would win. What actually happened was AP did win easily, followed by Firing Line (ridden by Hall of Fame and triple crown money jockey Gary Stevens), with Dortmund third and Frosted fourth. I collected on some of the exacta and tri bets plus the rebate but this was not enough to break even as four short priced horses were the top four. There were no big payoffs like in the past 6 years where both the tri and the superfecta were huge payoffs in the tens and hundreds of thousands.

The Preakness, 2015

The Preakness 2 weeks later had eight starters including the second and third place Derby finishers Dortmund and Firing Line. Again I used the same handicappers adding also Timeform.[12] Again the handicappers favored American Pharoah followed by Dortmund and Firing Line with the others rated much lower.

The track conditions were perfect — 82F and sunny. Then just before the start of the Preakness thunderstorm blew in so the track was sloppy for the race. That favored American Pharoah, who was already at 4 to 5 odds, even more as he had won the Rebel Stakes in the mud previously. None of the other seven horses had run in such conditions. He won wire to wire easily. Dortmund, who I focused on in the betting, got mud in his face for the first time, didn't much like the track and finished fourth. Firing Line, who was second in the Derby and the third of the big three, stumbled at the start, was never in contention and jockey Gary Stevens eased him as he finished seventh.

Trainer Wayne Lukas wanted to run Mr Z but his owner Ahmed Zayat, who also owns American Pharoah, did not. Since both are fast starters, he did not want a speed duel so Lukas arranged for another client, Calumet Farms to buy the horse. In the race, Mr Z did go with American Pharoah and later Pharoah moved ahead to win the race.

My analysis, following Super Screener, that Dortmund would recover from his minor injury that he had in the Derby and American Pharoah be tired because of the three races in 6 weeks did not work. In the mud, two long shots, #5 Tail of Verve and 28.5 to 1 and #7 Diving Rod at 12.6 to 1 finished second and third. I had the first, second and fourth horses on the ticket but not the third in that position. The slam dunk betting of the three top horses in the the first three positions never materialized.

Besides being a dominant horse, never really tested, American Pharoah had an advantage in the mud, springing out of hole one never to be headed and winning by seven lengths as a legitimate final odds 9 to 10 shot.

American Pharoah

The big question now is can Bob Baffertt and American Pharoah win the triple crown? He was in this same position with Silver Charm (1997), Real Quiet (1998) and War Emblem (2002) and they all lost the Belmont. Real Quiet lost by four inches! My colleague George Hofmeister bought the breeding rights (paying $1.1 million) for Real Quiet after he had won a grade I and finished last in his next race. After one more year of racing as a 4 year old, he sold 2/3rds for $16.5 million and kept 1/3rd, bravo for George.

Last year, I shorted California Chrome for the Belmont Stakes because his dosage was in the high 3s and that worked as he lost. Now we have a dominant horse, never tested with three races in 6 weeks and four races in 9 weeks with an even higher dosage of 4.33. While I was concerned that the last 12 Belmont Stakes winners have had dosage indices 3 or lower, Steve Roman points out that actually American Pharoah is on his trend line since 1940.[13] 2012 was no exception as the lone dual qualifier, Union Rags, with a dosage index of 2.14 won the race and the favorite, Dullahan, with a 4.20 dosage, finished seventh. In 2013, Palace Malice won with a DI of 2.64. In 2014, Tonalist won with a 2.78 dosage.

There have been horses with DI above 3.5 who won the Belmont such as Commendable (5.00 in 2000) and Sarava (4.50 in 2002). But, the winners from 2014 back to 2003 had dosage indices of 2.56, 1.75, 2.56, 2.43, 3.00, 3.00, 2.11, 1.77, 1.88, 2.14, 2.64 and 2.78. Even the great Sunday Silence with a 3.80 dosage got crushed in the Belmont by Easy Goer. It is believed that the breed has changed toward speed and that shows up more in the Kentucky Derby and less in the Belmont. Gramm and Ziemba (2008) study this as well.

AP's dosage profile is 2–3–3–0–0 so he has no solid or professional points with a dosage index of 4.33, which is high even for the Kentucky Derby and super high for the Belmont. His sire, Pioneer of the Nile, was second in the 1999 Kentucky Derby and is from the Raise a Native sire line. and the Northern Dancer dame sire line. He had 5 wins in 10 races, 1 second, 1 third and 3 out of the money, winning $1.634 million. Empire Maker and Yankee Gentleman are the second generation sires and Unbridled, Lord at War, Storm Cat and Ecliptial are the third generation sires.

It is not obvious that there is a missing Chef-de-Race to lower the dosage so I must assume that the 4.33 is correct. So the script favors a loss in the Belmont, but the ease with which he has won all his races except the first loss and with little rest argues for a strong performance. So right now I am neutral and would not short him.

The 2015 Belmont Stakes

The Betfair odds for the Belmont Stakes 2 weeks before the race had American Pharoah as a 4–5 favorite to win the triple crown.[14] This indicates what a favorite American Pharoah had become.

From 1948 when Citation won the Triple Crown to 1973 when Secretariat won it, there was a 25 year hiatus, then Seattle Slew and Affirmed won in the 1970s. Since then, there has been a 37 year drought with 12 gone into the Belmont having won the previous two legs. There is controversy concerning new shooters and we have American Pharoah the only horse running in all three races. It is said that the three most difficult things in sports to overcome are Wilt Chamberlain's 100 point game in 1962, Joe Dimaggio's 56 game hitting streak 1941 when he beat Ted Williams' 4.06 batting average for the MVP and the Triple Crown. Williams' average was 399.5 going into the last day of the season. So he could have closed the season rounded to 400 and not risk missing 400. But the great hitter felt he wanted to earn the 400 legitimately. He was 6 at 8 in that double header to end up at 406. No one has bettered that since.

For me, a trader, I am always thinking about how not to lose money. So, in this case, given the track record of the 12 near misses and the 37 years, there were a number of reasons to short American Pharoah, they include: a 4.33 dosage, the only horse that had competed in all three races, the freshness of the new shooters and the long 2015 campaign.

In the Belmont, there have been three horses, Birdstone, Lemon Drop Kid and Union Rags, that had the following pattern: a very good 2 year campaign, a weak 3 year old year, poor in the Kentucky Derby (way out of the money), skipping the Preakness and winning the Belmont Stakes as the lone dual qualifier (Birdstone and Lemon Drop Kid went off at long odds of about 30 to 1). So a logical pick of an upset was the lone dual qualifier Carpe Diem. So I bet Carpe at 21 to 1 on Betfair and a bit more at 14 to 1. Unfortunately, his connections thought he was only 90% so they scratched him and I lost these bets which were locked in at these odds. Too bad they are not dosage advocates. Indeed very few know about dosage despite years of research by Roman and myself.

The handicappers favored American Pharoah (PSR 119), with Frosted (102) and Madefromlucky the only ones over 100 at 101 with Materiality at 97.[15] Wizard and Timeform had similar ratings.

In my betting I favored Frosted and Materiality with a little bit in the tris and supers on the 3 to 5 favorite American Pharoah. The 4.33 dosage scared me. The race turned out to be vintage American Pharoah. Victor

Espinosa got him out in front with a small lead which was maintained throughout, then near the finish AP pulled away and the 37 year drought was over. AP was a Triple Crown winner. He ran a dream trip as planned by Bob Baffert and Espinosa: go to the front, slow the pace to a crawl and have plenty of energy left for the stretch run. The 1:13.41 for 6 furlongs was much slower than the two Honor Code races. As Sandra from the beginning and John Swetye later pointed out: could the dosage be wrong. Both his sire Pioneer of the Nile and grandsire Empire Maker are not rated chefs or is he simply an outlier? The −58 Roman rating versus −72 for Honor Code and a time of 2.26+ was not exceptionally fast or slow and about the same as his previous races including the Derby and Preakness. He just beat the other horses and what else need he do?

Steve Roman informed me that by his PFs ranking system these three combined classics have the third poorest speed figures since at least 1997. American Pharoah's Derby ranks 13th, his Preakness seventeenth and his Belmont tenth. Andy Beyer rated his Derby the eighteenth fastest since at least 1991, his Preakness the twenty second fastest and his Belmont the thirteenth fastest. It was the fastest fast track Belmont since 2001 in terms of raw time, not in terms of speed figures like Beyer's or Roman's where the raw time is adjusted for track speed on the day. His Beyers were 105, 102 and 105. Honor Code's 112 is much higher on the same track but he had a super fast pace. Honor Code has a chance to win if they meet but would not be favored. One thing is for sure, AP won the Triple Crown but he is not Secretariat breaking the track record in each of the three races. AP easily won the $1.75 million Haskell at Monmouth on August 2, 2015. Again, it was against weak 3 year old competition but again he was never even threatened.

I won a few tris and supers that did not pay too much with the favorite first, the second pick second and two longshots third and fourth. Fortunately the Honor Code gains swamped the small loss in the Belmont.

Back to Honor Code: The Met Mile on the Belmont Stakes undercard, June 6, 2015

His next race was a tough challenge for Honor Code, especially coming off the disappointing Churchill Downs race, but the $1.25 million 1-mile, 1-turn race was more suitable for him and it was fast: 1:08.74 for 6 furlongs (good enough to win most 6 furlong races) which compares with the 1:12.4 in the Churchill race. He has done well at Belmont, almost winning the G1 Champagne.

He was the last pick in Betfair as the public viewed him mostly by his last race. So I got 13 to 1 there, plus more later at 9 to 1. At the track he was 7-1 US odds. Almost nobody but me picked him first (and I'll admit to some wishful thinking!). Timeform supplied by Alydar did pick him first as well. In PSR, HTR, Wizard and the odds he was an also ran, so they thought. How could he beat the Breeders' Cup Classic winner Bayern, or Private Zone favored here despite Honor Code beating him in Florida, or last year's Belmont Stakes winner Tonalist? And there were *weaker* horses ridden by hall of fame jockeys Gary Stevens and Mike Smith.

Super Screener and the Wizard had a more positive view. Super Screener in his analysis of the Met Mile rated Honor Code third behind Tonalist and Bayern and that Honor Code "will be closing fastest of all and a certain board hitter, plus, deadly at one turn miles."

Wizard wrote,

> Like Tonalist, this stalker/closer is expected to benefit from a fast pace. He was a G2 winner last year in his third start, and missed in the G1 Champagne over this track and distance by just a neck in his second start. Plagued by layoffs after those first three races, he came back with an impressive win over Private Zone March 7 in a G2 race at today's 1-mile distance. However, when he next raced in the G2 Alysheba on May 1, he was stuck trailing a very slow pace, with no chance to make up appreciable ground in the stretch. Nonetheless, he did past four rivals with an extremely fast final 5/16 of a mile. With a more advantageous pace set up expected today, he could be sitting on a peak performance in this third start off the layoff.

I figured that the fast pace, no matter how good the opposition would set it up for JJ to let him loose and finish strong to beat them all. The race started and Sandra said "where is he"? It looked like he had no chance being 15 lengths behind. Then as the fast pace softened he made his run, a brilliant one, getting a −72 on Steve Roman's score, which was higher than Shared Belief, California Chrome and all the others in his cohort. It was a gem to watch, very similar to his Saratoga fall comeback race and his Florida race. This was the sixth fastest Met Mile in 120 years. This score compared to mid 60s for the best other top races and a −58 for American Pharoah's Belmont that won him the triple crown. Honor Code's Beyer was 112, the highest of any horse in 2015.

I did fine in my bets making enough on Betfair and two betting shops to cover some nice embroidery and tile bought in Istanbul the previous week.

Honor Code is tied for the nineteenth best 3 year old and up in the world in Longine's ratings in June 2015. This was his first time on the list.

Honor Code winning the Met Mile

Shared Belief, who is still injured was tied for second behind American Pharoah, the leader. Firing Line, who was second in the Kentucky Derby and out of the money in the Preakness, is ninth. California Chrome, who is out for a number of months with a cannon bone injury, is tied for eleventh. Dortmund and Main Sequence are tied with Honor Code for nineteenth.

That puts Honor Code back on top, competitive with the best 4 year olds and hopefully he runs in the $1.25 million Whitney at Saratoga and the $5 million Breeders' Cup Classic in Keeneland. His status now as a brilliant G1 winner with five wins, two seconds and one fifth with about $1,308,260 in earnings ($680,000 from the Met Mile), makes him a good stallion prospect for Lane's End. Hopefully, Honor Code can meet American Pharoah in the Breeders' Cup Classic on October 31, 2015 at Kneeland. It will be interesting to see who wins and who the competition is. American Pharoah is scheduled for the Grade I Haskell at Monmouth Park in New Jersey and possibly the Travers in Saratoga or the Pennsylvania Derby and then the Classic. From a money point of view all this is a big risk for American Pharoah — he's already reported to be a $200,000 stallion[16] and these fees swamp all but the $5 million purse in the Classic with $3 million going to the winner. So retiring him now at the peak of his fame as the number one horse in the world and triple crown winner, might be optimal. Zayat is in a bit of a bind: "I can't win no matter what I do. I am either a greedy owner for running him or I just retired the horse, people would say

I deprived the racing public of the horse". It seems that Zayat wants to run him in more races.

That is however a non-event because the breeding rights were sold to Coolmore-America for $6 or $9 million plus some bonuses when he was the champion 2 year old. So Zayat gets these purses such as the $1.1 million he got from winning the August 2, 2015 Haskell. AP is still worldwide #1 with even higher 131 pound rating as of late July 2015. So he should run the horse to collect the purse in the Travers or one or two other races before the October 31, 2015 Breeders' Cup, the natural retirement date. Meanwhile, at 150 or so breeds in Kentucky at his effective $100,00 stud fee for about $15 million plus Australian fees, based on a reduced $60,000 Australian dollar stud fee, Coolmore-America looks like they made a very good deal with a current value over $100 million. He was shipped to Australia in his first and now second breeding year.

Honor Code at the Whitney, August 8, 2015

The talk of all the *Daily Racing Form* analysts was "is Honor Code a one turn horse or can he do two turns?" His two losses were on two turns and all the one turn races were spectacular runs where he looked impressive. Also on the Sunday before the race he did not want to run on the Oklahoma training track and had to be brought to the main track. So there were lots of queries about his ability.

Honor Code was the favorite at 3–1 with Tonalist at 4–1, Noble Bird at 5–1, Liam's Map at 6–1, V.E. Day at 8–1 and Lea at 9–2 with long shots Wicked Strong and Normandy Invasion at 30–1.[17]

We had seats at the 3/8th pole far away from the finish line but with a great view of the two turns (and the large screens) so we could see when Honor Code got moving. It was, as expected, in the middle of the second turn and he moved up fast from his usual last place position. He was blazing fast gaining with each stride on Liam's Map who was five lengths ahead of Honor Code as they passed by us.

One of my colleagues for the syndicate I participate in which owns 1/8th of Honor Code wrote as follows:

> Honor Code broke alertly and had a little early foot as he did in the Met Mile but quickly went to the back of the pack around the first turn while racing with Tonalist and V.E. Day. Down the backside Honor Code did what he does and dropped further back even though there was plenty of early pace set by Liam's Map. The first 1/4 mile in $22^{3}/_{5}$ and the 1/2 mile

in 46 seconds flat. Honor Code trailed by 19 lengths. As the field reached the 1/2 mile pole Honor Code was starting to improve his position but still had plenty to do. Half way around the turn for home he started to gather his momentum but the margin was still 12 lengths. Honor Code approached the top of the stretch while running along the inside but still had much more work to do. With an 1/8th mile to run the deficit was still 4 1/2 lengths as Javier moved Honor Code to the outside of the early pacesetter Liam's Map. With a 1/16th to run, Honor Code was all out and gaining. He just managed to get past Liam's Map two jumps from the wire to when by a remarkable neck!!!!

Honor Code winning the Whitney

So he won with rather good win, place and show payoffs of 9.50, 5.90 and 3.50. Tonalist at 7-2 was the actual favorite with slightly more bet. A $200 win, place and show bet on Honor Code at one rebate shop returned $1,890 plus rebate and at the other rebate shop I had two $50 wps bets plus some small losing exacta bets with Honor Code first or second. He collected $670,000 earnings so now has hit the $2 million mark. The jockey JJ Castellano did not whip him at all and rode a perfect race. He was sure pleased as the photo shows. The pace was fast at 1:09.72 for 6 furlongs with Liam's Map 5 lengths ahead of Honor Code. So it set it up for the late running Honor Code.

Only seven horses have won the Met Mile–Whitney double and that includes such greats as Tom Fool (1953), Kelso (1961), Criminal Type (1990), In Excess (1991) and Tizway (2011).

Honor Code's chef-de-race rating for the race was −67. He was now more or less at or near the top of the older male horses in training. California Chrome and Shared Belief were still on the injured list but likely will run in 2016. They were ahead of Firing Line, Dortmund and Main Sequence.

Materiality had been retired. Honor Code moved to the top 10 worldwide. The next moves for Honor Code were the $400,000 grade II Kelso Mile at Belmont on October 3 and then the $1\frac{1}{4}$ mile Breeders' Cup Classic on October 31. The Whitney was a *you win and you're in* for the Classic. American Pharoah ran in the Travers where he had a speed duel with Frosted and then was narrowly beat by Keen Ice and later scheduled to run in the Breeders' Cup Classic.

Regarding syndications and possible stud fees on retirement, Steve Roman pointed out that Honor Code shapes up well against American Pharoah both in terms of pedigree and performance. The ratings for Honor Code and American Pharoah respectively: BRIS 110 versus 109; Equibase 126 versus 112; Beyer 113 versus 109 and chef-de-race -72 versus -70.

Rebecca Ruby Cameron's (2010) Emory University honors economics thesis studies factors affecting stud fees. The major factor that yields high stud fees is having many successful offspring including stars. Tapit has Untappable, Tonalist, and four eligible for the 2016 Kentucky Derby. Uncle Mo had in his first crop of runners, three in the 2016 Kentucky Derby including the winner Nyquist and four in the Preakness. I saw him at Ashford in April. His fee of $75,000 was raised to $150,000 for 2016 and 2017. Breeders prefer stallions that produce winners of stakes and graded stakes races, have high stallion ratings, high comparable stallion ratings and have a pedigree dominated by speed. Location in Kentucky provides an average 55% premium. Fully 90% of the top race horses in North America are from the Northern Dancer line with the remaining 10% from Mr Prospector or Seattle Slew. Important variables are the sire index, comparable sire index, number of foals sold at auction and the running behavior of the foals than the running behavior of the sire. Variables that Cameron found insignificant in her regression equations are the number of crops the stallions have had, the average number of foals per crop, the average earnings per runner and the average auction price of the stallions offspring. The attributes of some of these seemingly important variables which are not important are captured in other significant variables. The stallion's height and best Ragozin number capture the importance of the stallions own importance at the track on his fee. Height is meant to capture physical characteristics that raise fees. Stallions producing a higher percentage of offspring that are stakes winners have higher fees.

Tapit in 2015, with 30 or more grade I winners, is at the top with a $300,000 stud fee and probably more to actually get a season. At the August 2015 Saratoga Select Sale, one Tapit sold for $2 million, another for $950,000 was bought back. In total, seven Tapit's sold for $6.35 million. Fasig Tipton made a big deal that American Pharoah was sold at Saratoga. In reality he was consigned by Zayat and did not make the $300,00 reserve price so was bought back. He had several horses in the 2016 Kentucky Derby field.

At the September Keeneland select sale, a gray/roan Tapit colt out of Silver Colors by Mr Greeley sold for $2.1 million. The colt's second dam was 1988 Kentucky Derby winner Winning Colors. Mandy Pope bought the colt with Bob Baffert (with Kaleem Shah and John Sikura) being the underbidder. Pope bought the colt's full sister for $700,000 at the 2014 Keeneland September sale. The second highest price was for a chestnut colt by Tapit out of the grade I winner Pure Clan by Pure Prize that sold for $1.65 million to Roy and Gretchen Jackson in partnership with Three Chimneys Farm. Tapit is at the top. Close by are War Front who had a $1.15 million colt out of Grate by AP Indy and Benardini, a son of AP Indy whose colt out of Pilfer by Deputy Minster sold for $1.5 million. My colleagues in group VIII bought two Tapit offspring, one for $850,000 and another for $1.8 million for another partnership.

Cameron compares why A.P. Indy's fee was $150,000 while Birdstone's was $30,000 back in 2009. Each of the variables contributes to the higher fee. AP has a higher percentage of foals that are stakes and graded stakes winners of 8% and 4%, respectively. Also the sire and comparable sire indices are higher and there is more speed in his dosage profile. His is also more popular with more foals sold at auction.

Carpe Diem won the grade I Blue Grass and was the lone dual qualifier for the Belmont until he was scratched with a minor knee chip injury and retired by the Winstar and Stonestreet owners. They bought him as a 2 year old in training for $1.6 million. He was a $550,000 yearling and earned $1,519,800. Investment in horses in training is risky and in most cases is a losing proposition. With a star like Honor Code, one might make a profit. More promising is owning shares in horses that breed. I am doing that with Carpe Diem who won grade I races at 2 and 3 years old and was one of the top 3 year olds. He had 4 wins, one second and was 10th in the Kentucky Derby in six races. His last race was the Preakness. As a two year old. Carpe Diem won the grade I Breeders Futurity at Kneeland. He earned $1,519,800. Carpe Diem, like American Pharoah, and Dortmund won grade I races as a 2 and 3 year old. Those and Honor Code are likely to be competitors in the new sire superior mare mating game. Dortmund did not run in the Breeders' Cup Classic in 2015 but is still training. He was rated close to American Pharoah going into the Kentucky Derby.

I bought a half share in Carpe Diem. There are 50 shares, the Winstar 25 and the Stonestreet 25, plus 8 to the farm Winstar plus one to the trainer Todd Pletcher and one to another supporter of the stallion, Stonestreet advisor John Moynihan. He was syndicated for $10 million with major owners Winstar and Barbara Banke, the owner of Stonestreet, Curlin and Rachel Alexandra. So it's $200,000 per share. Observe how much the farm gains but they and Stonestreet took considerable risk. Our share gives us two breeds for each of the next 4 years plus one in succeeding years, plus about 2% (1/50) of the net other live foal breeds. That is the excess over about 110 breeds owed to the shareholders and the farm, trainer etc. in years one to four which is about 30-40 live foals. After year four, it is about 2% of about 70-100 extra breeds for the live foals, which is our share of the other stud fees beyond the ones from the other 50 shares who get one breed each. We also receive possible South America (Brazil, Argentina) breeds in the off season if he is shipped there. Carpe Diem was sired by Giants Causeway who was by Storm Cat with dam Rebridled Dreams and damsire Unbridled Song. Extra costs are insurance, some interest as we bought with some debt, maintenance fees, etc. Winstar and Stonestreet, like Lanes End are terrific operations so the risk seems worth it. Hopefully, most or all of the investment will be paid back from the proceeds of the breeding before the first horses are running in 4 years. Then if they do well, there would be gains on the investment about 2% (1/50) of the net other stud fees.

We will see in the next few years how this plays out.

There is a futures book for the Breeders' Cup on Betfair. Honor Code was about 10-1, with the favorites American Pharoah at 2-1 and Beholder at 3-1. My betting strategy was to go long Honor Code, long the brilliant Irish shipper Gleneagles at 18-1, later 12-1, who won a number of group I races and was sired by Galileo,[18] the sire of Frankel and many other top racers. All four of these horses are rated in the top 10 worldwide. The other contenders were Frosted (who easily won the Pennsylvania Derby), Keen Ice (who beat American Pharoah in the Travers), Firing Line, Tonalist (whose Betfair odds dropped to 8.8-1 from 16-1 after he easily won the Jockey Club Gold Cup), Dortmund, Bayern (who has had a spotty record lately but won the Breeders' Cup Classic in 2014), Texas Red (who is now injured and out the rest of 2015) and Palace Malice (who was retired to 3 Chimneys). My strategy was to bet enough on the other possibly winners so if Honor Code and Gleneagles both lose, I at least break even.

California Chrome at Dubai

California Chrome: A Case of Good Breeding at a Cheap Price

We saw with Secretariat, his greatest offspring were the sons of his daughters as well as his daughters. A great example of this third, fourth and fifth generation success is California Chrome who become the world's highest earning horse by winning the 2016 Dubai $10 million World Cup on March 26, 2016. The $6 million winners share plus subsequent wins puts California Chrome above $14 million, more than Curlin's $10+ million and all other horses in the US and Europe. Steve Coburn and Perry Martin bred the $8,000 claimer Love the Chase to the $2,500 stud fee Lucky Pulpit and got the 2014 Kentucky Derby and Preakness winner. When California Chrome lost the Belmont, Coburn complained bitterly that other horses were fresh in the race and California Chrome had to run all three triple crown races. Once that low point passed, they were smart and kept the horse in training. A try at Ascot failed but he was second earning $2 million in the 2015 Dubai World Cup.

Coburn sold his share of California Chrome to Taylor Made for his breeding career.[19] The next step was to run in the 2016 Breeders' Cup Classic in the fall. What is interesting is that the low cost breed worked out well likely because of the pedigree of California Chrome which three generations back includes AP Indy, Cozzene and Mr Prospector. Four generations back includes Dantzig, Seattle Slew, Northern Dancer and Raise a

Native. Secretariat and other greats are in the fifth generation.[20] Actually they were lucky because, except for California Chrome, Lucky Pulpit has been a very poor sire with most everybody who is breeding to him losing money. He had only two stakes winners from 168 starts. His stud fee, which was raised to $20,000 after California Chrome's success, was now $7,500, three times the fee when California Chrome was bred. This is on the list of poor stud values since he has not produced anything else besides California Chrome.[21] Chrome keeps winning and at 6, has earned $14,752,650 with 16 wins, 4 places and 1 show in 27 races when he retired to Taylor Made to stand for $40,000. He was second in the 2016 Breeders' Cup Classic to Arrogate. Chrome was voted horse of the year with Arrogate second. They were rated first and second worldwide by Longines with Arrogate on top. In Chrome's final race, the $12 million Pegasus, he was ninth in a race won by Arrogate who has now earned $17,084,600 in only eight races. After a first loss in a short race, the other seven were wins at long classic distances.

This breeding cheap to cheap to get a champion was pioneered in the 1930s to 1950s by Federico Tesio in Italy who bred three of the four undefeated horses namely Braque, Nearco who was the grand sire of Northern Dancer, and Ribot, and the recent Frankel. Recently I saw the grave of Ribot who was 16/16 winning the arc twice at Darby Dan farm where he was leased late in his breeding career. And on June 2, 2017 was able to visit and have a marvelous tour of Tesio's Dormello farm on Lake Majjoiri where he lived. That was one of seven farms Tesio and his partner had. Tesio had other great horses too and many of them are ancestors of the many horses and foals on the property. For the full story wait for my Wilmott column and a co-authored breeding book in progress. There have been only two US undefeated horses: Colin in 1907 and Personal Ensign in 1988.

Honor Code at the Kelso Grade II Mile Race, October 3, 2015

Honor Code's next race was the $400,000 Kelso mile to Belmont on October 3 where he was the 3–5 morning line favorite. Trainer Shug had Easy Goer in 1989. He ran in the $1^1/_4$ mile JCGC which he won but he lost the Breeders Cup to Sunday Silence. The choice of race is important for success. Sunday Silence's trainer, Charley Whitingham said before the JCGC that, if Easy Goer ran there, then Sunday Silence would beat him in the Classic which was exactly what happened. So Shug sent Honor Code to go the

1 mile Kelso rather than the 1 1/4 mile classic which was on the same day at Belmont.

It had been raining since Friday at Belmont and the track was muddy. This should not be a major factor for Honor Code as he easily won his first race at Saratoga on a muddy track. The competition seemed to be Red Vine, who was third behind Beholder in the Pacific Classic, and Appealing Tale, who won his last race in Santa Anita's grade II Pat O'Brien at 7 furlongs. PSR, HTR favored Honor Code but the Wizard picked Red Vine and wrote:

PGM #	Horse Name	M/L	Jockey	Trainer
5	RED VINE	5-1	ROSARIO J	CLEMENT C

Has a solid chance at an upset today dropping a bit in class and cutting back in distance from a good 3rd in the G1 Pacific Classic behind Beholder, a mare who may be the best horse in the country. Prior to that, Red Vine finished 2nd in his first graded stakes race, beaten by next-out repeater Bradester. Stalker/closer has put in three more works over this track since then and has won 3 of 5 over all on dirt, including 1 for 1 on wet tracks.

2	HONOR CODE	3-5	CASTELLANO J	MCGAUGHEY III C

Honor Code has won back to back G1 races, including the Met Mile over this track and distance, and has proven himself to be one of the best 3 or 4 horses in the country. However, he's coming off a 2-month layoff in what appears to be a 'prep' for the Breeders' Cup, and at expected very short odds today, he may be vulnerable. He comes from far back, and the pace in this race projects to be average, which may compromise his chances a bit. His lone wet track start was a spectacular debut win, so the expected wet weather won't hurt, but he must give from 6 to 11 lbs. to all rivals as well.

1	APPEALING TALE	6-1	TALAMO J	MILLER P

Figures to control the pace, although he may get some pressure from Scarly Charly. 5yo gelding enters in career-best form, having finished first or 2nd in four straight, including his first graded stakes win last time out in the G2 Pat O'Brien at 7F on dirt. He's 1 for 1 on wet tracks and could spring a front-running upset if able to slow down the pace enough at a distance where he's won 4 of 8.

HTR had it Honor Code, Red Vine and Appealing Tale. PSR had Honor Code 121, Appealing Tale 102, Scarley Charley 108, Mylute 102, Matterhorn 104 and Tamarkuz 104. So Honor Code was the pick. At 3–5 Morning Line and 1–5, then 2–5 then 1–2 then 3–5 with Appealing Tale getting the late money. My bet was Honor Code to place.

Well, the Wizard script was right and Appealing Tale won wire to wire with a slow pace with Red Vine second. Honor Code was not too far back and made a run but finished third, beaten by 3 3/4 lengths, Tamarkuz was fourth, Mylute fifth, Scarlay Charly sixth and Matterhorn seventh and last.

The Breeders Cup Classic, October 31, 2015

Honor Code came into the race with terrific workouts at Belmont and was shipped to Keeneland a few days before the race. The picture shows him working out there in the rain which does not bother him. The Longines world's best racehorse ratings still have American Pharoah first at 131

Honor Code working out at Keeneland

American Pharoah winning the Classic

with Arc winner Golden Horn the 4–5 favorite in the turf at 130, two time Arc winner Treve is third at 126, Able Friend is 125, Shared Belief, who will race in 2016 is also at 125, Solow who beat Gleneagles (20–1 in the Classic) in the grade I Queen Elizabeth II stakes at Ascot on October 17 is sixth at 129, then there were eight horses at 123 tied for seventh. The seven include Honor Code,plus the Great Gatsby, Order of St George, Lankan Rupee, Jack Hobbs, Free Eagle, Flintshire (who is not in the Breeders' Cup Turf and I had to hedge out, as best as possible, my Betfair long bet on him) and Designs on Rome. Not there are California Chrome, Beholder the second choice in the Classic above Honor Code, Tonalist, who won the Jockey Club Gold Cup (also 6–1 in the Classic as is Honor Code), Keen

Ice (12–1, who beat AP in the Travers) and Frosted (15–1, who won the Pennsylvania Derby). Besides those mentioned Effinex (107) and Smooth Roller (111) have run races with high Beyers.

My feeling in the betting was that at 10–1 on Betfair, Honor Code was my first pick. He had never run 1 1/4 but his sire AP Indy won this race and the 1 1/2 mile Belmont, so his breeding should be ok. My other pick was Gleneagles at prices around 18–1. All his races were on the grass but he won several group I's.

Then I tried to hedge out the possible winners. I assumed that AP and Beholder would be over bet so I was slightly long Beholder and slightly short AP.

Noted TV handicapper Randy Moss who has created his own pace figures saw it on a webcast: "AP leading followed by Beholder with the late chargers Tonalist, Honor Code, Keen Ice and Smooth Roller making a late run and any of these could win."

The various handicappers favored American Pharaoh for a variety of reasons that he has easily won every race except the Travers second place and his first race fifth. He just ran as fast as he needed to win! His high 4.33 dosage confused me in the Derby and Belmont, but he had plenty of stamina to win those races. He became even more favored when the 5 year old mare Beholder was scratched. She was thought to be the main competition to AP and was a speed horse who would push him on the lead. I was hoping that Honor Code might win to finish his career. He had great workouts, his regular jockey JJ Castellano, and looked wonderful. His trainer took the route to run him in the mile race that was a prep instead of tiring him out with a mile and a quarter race. He along with Tonalist were the second or third choice of the handicappers. A worry was his not having run at this distance before, but a bigger worry was that AP was the only speed horse and could easily go wire to wire slowing it down. The handicapping information is in the notes.[22]

In the end, the race was as expected. AP won easily in a fast time of 2:00.07. Secretariat, Monorchos, Beholder and a few other have run in the 159s. Steve Roman reminded me that Spectacular Bid holds the world's dirt record for 1 1/4 miles at 1:57.4, about 10–15 lengths better than AP. He retired with the public thinking he is a super star comparable to the greats of the past including Affirmed, Seattle Slew and Secretariat, but some of us feel that he just had a sequence of good pace trips and won some good races. Except for losing Travers and the Classic, he did not face much competition.[23]

Roman's ranking for the Classic was −73, the best of AP's career but that is way below Ghostzapper's −98 and a −124 best. Ghostzapper had four zeros on Ragasin's scale. On Fotias's Equiform he had four 84s. In comparison, Medaglio D'Or's best was an 82. Zenyatta's was an 81. Mineshaft, Candy Ride, and Invaser all Lane's Ends stallions all had 83s. So the evidence points to a very good horse but comparisons with Secretariat, who broke the track record in all three classic races seems not supported by the facts.[24] Only Ghostzapper is competitive with Secretariat and possibly the underrated, unchallenged, super on the grass, Frankel, who never ran in the US and the current superstar Arrogate.

AP's stud fee is $200,000+. But he is two for one so the fee is really $100,000. His sire, Pioneer of the Nile, had his stud fee raised from $60,000 to $125,000 and that was before this final brilliant grand slam. At a reputed 175 breeds per year, we are talking here of gross income of $17.5 million for the owners of AP. Coolmore America's reputed $6 or $9 million purchase (plus possibly some performance adjustments) of the breeding rights for AP as a 2 year old sure looks like a jackpot! And as mentioned above there are Australian Fees too of $60,000 Australian. That's a lot of breeds but it shows the high demand for AP offspring.

Mike Smith with 22 Breeders' Cup wins, many more than any other jockey, guided Effenix, who was 33–1 at the track and a whopping 119–1 on Betfair, to a second place finish. Honor Code made his run but there was just too much ground to make up given the perfect setup for AP but he did get third. The payoffs at the track on AP were 3.40 to win, 3.00 to place (the wise bet) and 2.40. Effinex paid 14.20 and 6.20 to place and show. Honor Code paid 3.40 to show. That was worth $500,000 in earnings so he now retires having won $2,518,260. The chart for the race is in the notes.[25]

In the betting, I was able to get AP at 2–1 up to 2.8 US odds on Betfair in the futures and 9–1 on Honor Code. He was much more favored at the track. I was long mostly Honor Code, some Tonalist, some Gleneagles and Keen Ice and slight net short on AP on all the bets which were some 6 pages on my Betfair account. My goal was to have it such that a group of four or five horses I was long on or neutral so that I was hedged like the stock market but the result of some 20 small win bets on AP even at decent odds made me slightly net short.

Just prior to the race, I made a large bet to show at US odds of 1.6 to 1 on Honor Code or $5.20 equivalent. That made up for my slightly short win bet on AP despite those win bets on AP at odds a lot higher than at the track. A mistake was not betting a lot on AP to place, the usual less than even money bet.

So Honor Code goes to a stud career at Lane's End and hopefully I make a gain on my $52,000 investment with some of the net earnings of the nine horses in the group with most of it from Honor Code, plus a share of Honor Code's future stud fees. During the week before the Breeders' Cup, Liam's Map was sold. As part of the deal our group 8 traded one half share of our four and a half shares of Honor Code for one share of Liam's Map. Honor Code had narrowly beaten Liam's Map in the Whitney with both horses running 113 Beyers. Later Liam's Map ran a 114 in the $1\frac{1}{4}$ mile grade 1 Woodward which he won by 4 lengths. This along with Beholder's 114 in the Pacific Classic, were the fastest races of 2015.

Liam's Map was a 1-2 favorite for the Breeders' Cup Las Vegas Dirt Mile run on Friday, October 30. His trainer, Todd Pletcher, and owners wanted a Breeders' Cup win so they put him in an easier race than the Classic. The script was wire to wire like AP but he stumbled at the start, was third behind Bradester and Mr Z who set fractions of 23.10 seconds for the quarter and 46.23 for the half mile. Liam's Map was fighting with jockey JJ Castellano and had a lot of traffic problems but still won easily by $2\frac{1}{2}$ lengths, again showing why JJ is America's top jockey in money earnings.

Lea finished second $3\frac{1}{4}$ lengths ahead of Red Vine who finished $3\frac{1}{4}$ lengths ahead of Wicked Strong. So the top four finished in order of their odds. Valid, Mr Z, Street Strategy, War Story, Bradester, and Tapiture completed the order of finish. He won $550,000 of the $1 million purse and set the track record in 1:34.54 a lot below the previous track of 1:36.23 set by Street Strategy on October 9.

Liam's Map was an $800,000 yearling purchase by Unbridled Song out of Miss Macy Sue by Trippi. He retired to stud with six wins and two seconds in 8 starts with $1,358,940 earnings. Both he and Honor Code are now at Lane's end. Their stud fees are $25,000 and $40,000, respectively. Their books with about 150 matings planned, are full and over subscribed. Tonalist is the latest to be retired for stud duty at Lane's End. He won the Belmont beating California Chrome and three other grade I races. In their two meetings, Honor Code prevailed. His stud fee at $25,000 is the same as Liam's Map and Carpe Diem. Like the others, Carpe Diem is also is great demand and over subscribed. With his better pedigree, more explosive style and, likely, more left to prove in his brief injury plagued career, Honor Code has a certain edge over Liam's Map and Carpe Diem and his mares in foal

372   *The Adventures of a Modern Renaissance Academic*

Liam's Map winning the Breeders' Cup Dirt Mile

Honor Code and Liam's Map arriving at Lane's End

Seize the Hay at one and four days with his dam Summer Chant at Overbrook Farm sold for the second highest behind only American Pharoah at the November 2016 Kneeland sale.

After the Classic

Honor Code, Liam's Map and American Pharoah were retired for stud duty. Honor Code is scheduled to breed to about 145 mares with the best first year book of mares ever at Lane's End. Our group has 4 of the 40 shares so we receive four breeds which we are selling as seasons in the $40,000 stud fee area plus we will receive a portion of the funds from the rest of the breeds. But there are considerable costs associated with the breeding including injury or death and fertility insurance. Hopefully the net revenue stream plus the net racing winnings mostly from Honor Code's more than $2.5 million earnings and Liam's Map's earnings in the Breeders' Cup plus proceeds from our one share of the 50 shares. Our group sold one Liam's Map season for $30,000, above the standard stud fee with no guarantee plus 2% of the net pooled revenue for mares breed outside the syndicate.

Both Liam's Map and Honor Code are champions. Honor Code was AP Indy's fifth champion following Mineshaft (older male and Horse of the Year), Benardini (3 year old male), Rags to Riches (3 year old filly) and Tempura (2 year old filly). Tonalist, at $25,000 fee, was also retired to stud at Lane's End. He, Liam's Map and Honor Code were the three horses nominated for Eclipse (older male and horse of the year), with Honor Code the winner as he had beaten both Liam's Map and Tonalist.

We sold one Carpe Diem season and bought a mare called Summer Chant who was sired by Belmont-Stakes winner Summer Bird for $37,000 to breed to Carpe Diem. Our plan was to sell the mare in foal at the November 2016 Keeneland sale. But on the day of the auction in November 2016, prices were poor so she did not make her reserve price. So we waited for the foal called Seize the Hay to be born. See his picture at one day and four days with his dam summer chant. Summer Bird was sired by Birdstone who also won the Belmont with sires Grindstone and Unbridled who won Kentucky Derby. On the dam side, are such greats as Summer Squall, Storm Bird, Northern Dancer, Secretariat, Alydar and Nijinsky. Since Unbridled's Song sired our Liam's Map and Arrogate, our foal Seize the Hay looks promising with Unbridled's Song the second dam with the sire being the great Giants Causeway sired by $500,000 stud fee Storm Cat. We also bought for $55,000 in a private sale at the Ocala auction a 2 year old daughter of Zenyatta's sire, Street Cry, with dam sire Dynaformer which we named Via Frattina

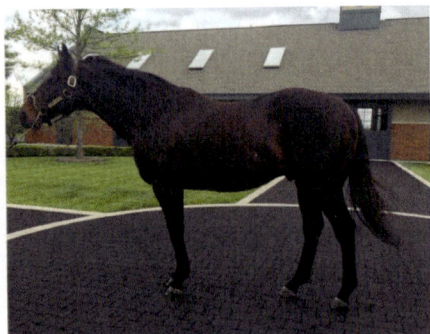

Blame at Clairborne and Benardini at Darley

which is a major street in Rome for haut couture. We planned to run her at Saratoga and possibly breed to Carpe Diem in a couple years.

In a workout at the Oklahoma training track she worked 3/8th in 37.3 seconds, second best of 27, which was encouraging. See her photo. She was 7th in her first race but only three lengths behind the Winner against tough competition. In her second race, again against tough competition, she was last. These were at top tracks. Then moving to the lesser track, Laurel in Maryland, she was second. The winner then won a grade III at Del Mar so interest in Via Fratina picked up. So we cashed out for 110K less 10K expenses to the trainer and selling agent thus clearing 100K so we made a slight profit after all costs.

Running these tens of millions farms can be very profitable if they are adequately capitalized and have a good product. Just like risk control in the options market, if one over bet, one can get into serious financial trouble. The top farm, 3 Chimneys, took too large a stake in several stallions including Preakness and Belmont stakes winner Point Given who looked like a super star but was so big that his offspring were not successful. This over betting caused them financial trouble. So they had to restructure with a new partner.

In the Spring of 2016, I went to Kentucky to visit the horses I co-own mostly in breeding duties. Honor Code and Liam's Map are at Lanes End. The filly Summer Chant is in foal to Carpe Diem at Overbrook — the farm of WT Young the richest person in Lexington. This massive gorgeous property is on the east side of Lexington in the area of top notch homes, each better than the rest. Young, who owned Storm Cat, actually made his fortune in peanut butter. Besides controlling the market, he invented part of the processing. He died 11 years ago and his son having no interest

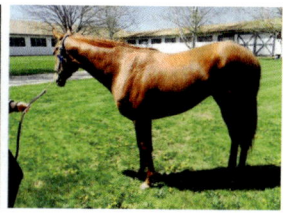

Summer Chant at Overbrook Farm, Carpe Diem at Winstar, Via Frattina at Saratoga

in horses, sold them. The farm, impeccably kept, is leased out. Summer Chant looks great and we were pleased to have her in foal to Carpe Diem who is at Winstar, another gorgeous facility. Carpe Diem is a $25,000 stud fee. Our one share of which I have half entitles us to two seasons, we sold one and used the other for our daughter of Belmont Stakes winner Summer Bird. I also went to three other farms. Claiborne is always nice and gave a terrific tour mostly about their glorious past but they do have War Front who has became a $200,000 stallion (and $250,000 in 2017) and was bred twice to Zenyatta but both of these foals died. They also have Blame and a few other minor stallions. The glory days are over and the farm is run in its traditional conservative manner. At Darley, they lost Street Cry who died at 16 but have top sires Benardini at $100,000 and Medaglia D'Oro at $150,000 per season. Darley is owned by Sheik Mohammed and is another top organization.

We bought a three year old filly named Beginners Luck who was sired by Breeders' Cup Classic winner, Awsome Again with dam sire Holy Bull for $20,000 plus the other expenses. She was being bred to Carpe Diem and our plan is to have the foal born in New York to qualify for their state benefits. Our other Carpe Diem season this year is being used to foal share breeding to Vitellia who was also sired by Awsome Again. The plan is to sell the resulting foal in a 50-50 foal sharing arrangement. Summer Chant had a tough time producing Seize the Hay who was very big as the pictures show. So if she is healthy enough we will breed her to Commissioner who was second in the Belmont stakes and whose sire and dam sire also won the Belmont.[26] But that did not work so she will rest till next year. We also bought a Mucho Uno two year old filly whose dam sire was the great grass horse Theatrical named Marida, in honor of my friend, Marida Bertocchi who died this year. Marida was a Professor at the University of Bergamo where I visited many times. Marida the filly is scheduled to run at Saratoga trained by Tom Morley.

Notes

[1] In April 2015, Smart Strike had laminitis and had to be put down. Also Street Cry died while in Australia in the Kentucky off season breeding period.

[2] Zenyatta, a national treasure, won 19 of 20 races, including the 2009 Breeders' Cup Classic against the males. Her only loss was in her last race, the 2010 Breeders' Cup Classic. There Blame beat her by a nose after she got a slow start. More on Zenyatta is in my racing book Ziemba (2017). She is stabled at Lane's End Farm, Kentucky. She has produced four offspring, one of which died from a paddock accident. She has been bred to Benardini, War Front, Tapit and now to War Front again. Unfortunately, this foal has also died.

[3] If you actually compare times in the same races, Secretariat was much faster than Man O'War. But it is a 1920s versus 1970s comparison. At the Kentucky horse farm near Lexington, one sees the long stride of John Henry (24 ft). Secretariat's (25.5 ft) was a bit longer and Man O'War's (28 ft) was a lot longer still. Man O'War won one race by 100 lengths at odds of 1 to 100. Secretariat won the 1973 Belmont by 31 lengths at odds of 1 to 10. Both were greats but in different eras. Which would have won a match race is unclear?

[4] My bets on various horses along with more detail on this business is in Ziemba (2017).

[5] The last horse to win the Kentucky Derby without a 2 year old race was Apollo in 1888.

[6] Fusaichi Pegasus was one of the 5 Kentucky Derby winners who grew up on the *Magic Field*, a section of the property owned by my friend George Hofmeister in Paris, Kentucky. He is the only Kentucky Derby winner sired by the top speed horse Mr Prospector. He was sold as a yearling for whopping $4 million. After the Derby win, Coolmore, very wise business people from Ireland, bought him for a reputed $70 million. To show how they would get their money back, he was standing for $200,000 stud fee at the start and bred to more than 100 mares in Kentucky and more in Australia. They would then have gotten all their money back before they even knew if the offspring were good runners (that's 4 years). Fusaichi Pegasus turned out to be a very good sire but his stud price has dropped all the way to $5,000 in 2015 and $7500 in 2017. But he is a worthwhile sire and is the damsire of a horse I co-own.

[7] The Hausch and Ziemba 1990 condition for a lock is

$$k > 1 - \frac{Q(n-1)}{21(n-3)} = 1 - \frac{0.98(5-1)}{21(5-3)} = 0.915.$$

Also the bet on $x =$ the favorite must equal

$$\frac{x}{y} = 2 + \frac{Q(n-1)}{1.05(1-k)} = -2 + \frac{0.89(4)}{1.05(0.085)} = 37.89.$$

This formula guarantees a profit of $0.05(x + 2y) - (n-3)y$ which is positive if a lock exists. So with a bankroll of say $W_0 = \$2,500$, $x = \$2,260$ and the four y's $= \$60$ each, and the profit $= -\$1$ as the lock did not quite exist.

In *Dr Z's Beat the Racetrack* (1987), I presented a way to use the Dr Z place and show systems in England. There they only have place which has a different number who collect based on the number of horses in the race. For $4 \leq n \leq 7$, two collect, for $8 \leq n \leq 15$, three collect as in the US show, and for larger n, four collect. I saw a flaw in the way they computed these payoffs. Instead of giving back the stake and then sharing the profits, they simply share the proceeds. Hence, with a big favorite, one can get payoffs less than the stake. But the track must pay the minimum. My Dublin colleagues Patrick Waldron and David Jackson saw this independently and used the Hausch–Ziemba locks idea to create an arbitrage. I discussed this with them and said "you will be able to do this once then they will change the rules." Indeed they made GBP 50,000 in one big play and then they changed the rules. See Jackson and Waldron (2003) and on the general concept of arbitrage, see Edelmann and O'Brian (2004).

[8] For those who would like more detail on various Triple Crown campaigns, please see my *Exotic Betting at the Racetrack*, World Scientific, 2017.

[9] The rules for obtaining a spot in the race with at most 20 starters are in my May 2015 column in *Wilmott*. Basically, most of the points needed to qualify are in the last two races prior to the Derby. Hence, horses with top 2 year old form but weak 3 year old performance will not qualify. Horses such as Lemon Drop Kid, Birdstone and Union Rags, all of whom won the Belmont stakes after poor Kentucky Derby performances and, skipping the Preakness, would be excluded from the Derby field. Of course, they could run in the Preakness and/or Belmont stakes.

[10] The following table has PSR, HTR, Super Screener and Wizard ratings:

PP	Horse	PSR	HTR	Super Rank	Screener Score	Wizard
1	Ocho Ocho Ocho	99	13	T	33	
2	Carpe Diem	111	5	TWC	90	
3	Materiality	116	4	TBH	70	
4	Tencendur	100	9	MP	78	
5	Danzig Moon	93	10	TLS	79	
6	Mubtaahij (IRE)	0	8	TBH	NA	fourth
7	El Kabeir	100	15	MP	64	
8	Dortmund	116	2	TWC	100	second
9	Bolo	101	12	T	60	
10	Firing Line	116	3	TBH	70	fifth
11	Stanford	97	18	T	36	
12	International Star	99	11	TBH	62	
13	Itsaknockout	87	10	T	20	
14	Keen Ice	86	14	TLS	62	
15	Frosted	111	6	TWC	100	third
16	War Story	93	16	T	50	

(*Continued*)

(*Continued*)

PP	Horse	PSR	HTR	Super Rank	Screener Score	Wizard
17	Mr Z	95	17	T	14	
18	American Pharoah	117	1	TBH	81	a best bet
19	Upstart	108	7	TBH	78	
20	Far Right	97	21	MP	44	
21	Frammento	96		TLS	62	
22	Bold Conquest			T	38	

TWC = top win contender
TBH = top board hitter
TLS = top long shot
MP = midpack
T = tosses
/ = scratched

[11] Super Screener, Budget (medium) for the Kentucky Derby.

Amount	Wager	1st	2nd	3rd	4th	Cost	$0.50
$10	Exacta box	Win Contenders 2,8,15				$60	
$10	Exacta part wheel	Win Contenders 2,8,15	Best Pace/Pressers 3,8,18			$80	
$1	Tri part wheel	Win Contenders 8,15	Super 7 2,3,6,8,15,18,19	All Closers 5,12,14,15,20,21		$65	$32.5
$1	Tri part wheel	Super 7 2,3,6,8,15,18,19	Win Contenders 8,15	All Closers 5,12,14,15,20,21		$65	$32.5
$1	Tri part wheel	Best Pace/Pressers 3,8,18	Win Contenders 2,8,15	Top 13 + Bolo 2-10,12,15,18,19,21		$96	$48
$1	Tri part wheel	Top Closers 5,12,15	Top 13 2-8,10,12,15,18,19,21	Best Pace/Pressers 3,8,18		$99	$49.5
$0.50	Tri part wheel	Super 7 2,3,6,8,15,18,19	Top 10 2,3,5,6,8,10,12,15,18,19	Top Closers 5,12,15,21		$112	$56
$1	Tri part wheel	Win Contenders 8,15	Top 13 2-8,10,12,15,18,19,21	Super 7 2,3,6,8,15,18,19		$132	$66

[12] The PSR, HTR, Super Screener, Wizard and Timeform ratings were as follows:

PP	Horse	PSR	HTR	Super Screener Rank	Score	Wizard	Timeform
1	American Pharoah	122	1	TBH	63	1	1
2	Dortmund	117	2	TWC	88	3	3
3	Mr Z	93	7	T	na	4	4
4	Danzig Moon	100	5	TBH	56		
5	Tale of Verve	86	8	TLS	56		
6	Bodhisattva	100	6	TLS	44		
7	Divining Rod	105	4	T	33		
8	Firing Line	115	3	TBH	75	2	1

TWC = top win contender
TBH = top board hitter
TLS = top long shot
T = tosses

[13] It is not clear how useful Steve's regression line is here as there is a lot of noise in the system, but here it is.

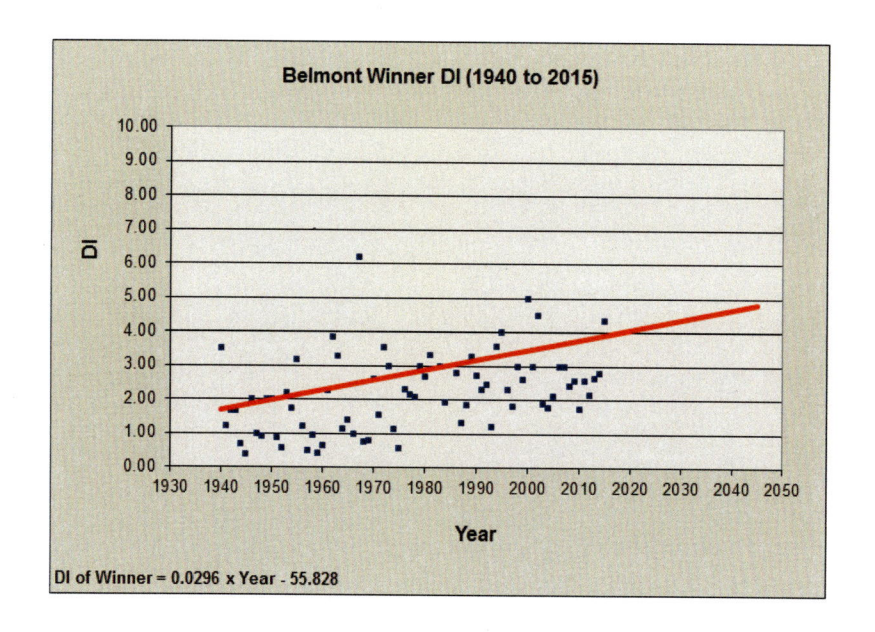

Belmont Winner DI (1940 to 2015)

DI of Winner = 0.0296 x Year − 55.828

[14] SuperScreener for the Belmont

		Back all	Lay all
9 selections		2.14 £33	2.16 £715
	American Pharoah		
	Frosted	5.1 £38	
	Materiality	6.8 £16	7.2 £10
	Divining Rod	28 £4	48 £4
	Mubtaahij	14.5 £4	55 £4
	Madefromlucky	21 £8	
	Tale Of Verve	27 £4	95 £3
	Carpe Diem	14.5 £8	21 £5
	Keen Ice	25 £4	55 £3

[15] The PSR, HTR, Super Screener, Wizard and Timeform ratings were as follows:

PP	Horse	PSR	HTR	Super Rank	Screener Score	Wizard	Timeform
1	Mubtaahij (IRE)	88	5	TBH	88		
2	Tale of Verve	97	6	T	71		
3	Madefromlucky	101	4	TBH	88		
4	Frammento	84	8	TLS	71		
5	American Pharoah	115	1	TBH	87	1	3
6	Frosted	102	3	TWC	94	3	1
7	Keen Ice	88	7	MP	66		
8	Materiality	97	2	TWC	89	2	2

TWC = top win contender
TBH = top board hitter
TLS = top long shot
MP = midpack
T = tosses

[16] He is 200,000 but you get 2 for 1 so its really 100,000 and he is 60,000 aussie down there.

[17] Other stats for the Whitney contenders: The chef-de-race ratings from Steve Roman of the main contenders including seven grade I winners were:

HORSE	PF	FIN	DATE	RACE	GR	AGE/SEX	TRK	DIST	SURF	TRK COND
COACH INGE	-55	1ST	06/06/15	BROOKLYN INVITATIONAL S	G2	4YO&UP	BEL	12.00	DIRT	FST
COACH INGE	-64	3RD	07/04/15	SUBURBAN H	G2	4YO&UP	BEL	10.00	DIRT	FST
HONOR CODE	-53	1ST	03/07/15	GULFSTREAM PARK H	G2	4YO&UP	GP	8.00	DIRT	FST
HONOR CODE	-72	1ST	06/06/15	METROPOLITAN H	G1	3YO&UP	BEL	8.00	DIRT	FST
LEA	-44	1ST	01/10/15	HAL'S HOPE S	G3	4YO&UP	GP	8.00	DIRT	FST
LEA	-76	2ND	02/07/15	DONN H	G1	4YO&UP	GP	9.00	DIRT	FST
LEA	-66	2ND	06/13/15	STEPHEN FOSTER H	G1	3YO&UP	CD	9.00	DIRT	FST
MORENO	-66	2ND	03/07/15	SANTA ANITA H	G1	4YO&UP	SA	10.00	DIRT	FST
MORENO	-54	3RD	03/28/15	NEW ORLEANS H	G2	4YO&UP	FG	9.00	DIRT	FST
MORENO	-65	1ST	04/18/15	CHARLES TOWN CLASSIC S	G2	4YO&UP	CT	9.00	DIRT	FST
MORENO	-46	2ND	05/30/15	CALIFORNIAN S	G2	3YO&UP	SA	9.00	DIRT	FST
NOBLE BIRD	-56	2ND	05/01/15	ALYSHEBA S	G2	4YO&UP	CD	8.50	DIRT	FST
NOBLE BIRD	-67	1ST	06/13/15	STEPHEN FOSTER H	G1	3YO&UP	CD	9.00	DIRT	FST
TONALIST	-73	1ST	05/02/15	WESTCHESTER S	G3	4YO&UP	BEL	8.00	DIRT	FST
TONALIST	-53	2ND	06/06/15	METROPOLITAN H	G1	3YO&UP	BEL	8.00	DIRT	FST
TONALIST	-70	2ND	07/04/15	SUBURBAN H	G2	4YO&UP	BEL	10.00	DIRT	FST
V. E. DAY	-54	2ND	06/06/15	BROOKLYN INVITATIONAL S	G2	4YO&UP	BEL	12.00	DIRT	FST
WICKED STRONG	-39	3RD	04/25/15	EXCELSIOR S	G3	4YO&UP	AQU	10.00	DIRT	FST

Honor Code was actually the morning line favorite at 3–1 with the others odds, PSR, HTR, Wizard as follows:

PP	Horse	ML	PSR	HTR	Wizard
1	Honor Code	3–1	122	3	2
2	Tonalist	4–1	124	1	1
3	Noble Bird	5–1	118	4	
4	Liam's Map	6–1	124	5	
5	Moreno	12–1	107	6	
6	V.E. Day	8–1	102	7	3
7	Lea	9–2	123	2	4
9	Wicked Strong	20–1	107	8	
10	Normandy Invasion	30–1	112	9	

[18] 500,000 euros stud fee and fully booked.

19 Elyse Mach and I visited Taylor Made to see Chrome and he looked terrific having been overbooked at $40,000. Joe Taylor and his cousin told me that a share was for sale for $288,000, the original share price. I bid that but the seller Martin wanted more, arguing that Chromes $12,000,000 valuation was too low given a $4 million deal to breed in Chile so nothing happened. But I was able to buy a nice property for 1/7th of Vancouver prices using the funds obtained from equity futures trading using largely racing bias ideas.

20 The pedigree of California Chrome.

CALIFORNIA CHROME (USA) ch. H, 2011 {A4} DP = 7-9-14-0-0 (30) DI = 3.29 CD = 0.77 - 27 Starts, 16 Wins, 4 Places, 1 Shows **Career Earnings:**$14,752,650

LUCKY PULPIT (USA) ch. 2001	PULPIT (USA) dkb/br. 1994 [IC]	A.P. INDY (USA) dkb/br. 1989 [IC]	SEATTLE SLEW (USA) dkb/br. 1974 [BC]	BOLD REASONING (USA) — dkb/br. 1968
				MY CHARMER (USA) — b. 1969 *
			WEEKEND SURPRISE (USA)* b. 1980	SECRETARIAT (USA) — ch. 1970 [IC]
				LASSIE DEAR (USA) — b. 1974 *
		PREACH (USA) b. 1989	MR. PROSPECTOR (USA) b. 1970 [BC]	RAISE A NATIVE (USA) — ch. 1961 [B]
				GOLD DIGGER (USA) — b. 1962 *
			NARRATE (USA)* dkb/br. 1980	HONEST PLEASURE (USA) — dkb/br. 1973
				STATE (USA) — b. 1974
	LUCKY SOPH (USA) b. 1992	COZZENE (USA) gr. 1980	CARO (IRE) gr. 1967 [IC]	FORTINO (FR) — gr. 1959
				CHAMBORD (GB) — ch. 1955
			RIDE THE TRAILS (USA) b. 1971	PRINCE JOHN (USA) — b. 1953 [C]
				WILDWOOK (USA) — b. 1965
		LUCKY SPELL (USA) b. 1971	LUCKY MEL (USA) ch. 1954	OLYMPIA (USA) — b. 1946 [B]
				ROYAL MINX (GB) — ch. 1948
			INCANTATION (USA) br. 1965	PRINCE BLESSED (USA) — br. 1957
				MAGIC SPELL (USA) — b. 1954
LOVE THE CHASE (USA) ch. 2006	NOT FOR LOVE (USA) b. 1990	MR. PROSPECTOR (USA) b. 1970 [BC]	RAISE A NATIVE (USA) ch. 1961 [B]	NATIVE DANCER (USA) — gr. 1950 [IC]
				RAISE YOU (USA) — ch. 1946 *
			GOLD DIGGER (USA)* b. 1962	NASHUA (USA) — b. 1952 [IC]
				SEQUENCE (USA) — b. 1946
		DANCE NUMBER (USA) b. 1979	NORTHERN DANCER (CAN) b. 1961 [BC]	NEARCTIC (CAN) — br. 1954
				NATALMA (USA) — b. 1957 *
			NUMBERED ACCOUNT (USA)* b. 1969	BUCKPASSER (USA) — b. 1963 [C]
				INTRIGUING (USA) — ch. 1964 *
	CHASE IT DOWN (USA) ch. 1997	POLISH NUMBERS (USA) b. 1987	DANZIG (USA) b. 1977 [IC]	NORTHERN DANCER (CAN) — b. 1961 [BC]
				PAS DE NOM (USA) — br. 1968
			NUMBERED ACCOUNT (USA)* b. 1969	BUCKPASSER (USA) — b. 1963 [C]
				INTRIGUING (USA) — ch. 1964 *
		CHASE THE DREAM (USA) b. 1984	SIR IVOR (USA) b. 1965 [IC]	SIR GAYLORD (USA) — br. 1959 [IC]
				ATTICA (USA) — ch. 1953 *
			LA BELLE FLEUR (USA) b. 1977	VAGUELY NOBLE (IRE) — b. 1965 [CP]
				PRINCESS RIBOT (USA) — b. 1964

21 See Thoroughbred: Sire Watch.

22 The Handicapping Information for the Classic

		Odds			Highest'Last		Ranking			
Horse	ML	Betfair	US Track	PA•	Beyer	Roman	SS∓	Alydar	HTR	PSR
1 Tonalist	6–1	9–1	6–1 6–1		111/105	73/72	5–1 B	2	3	120
2 Keen Ice	12–1	14.5–1	8–1 7–1		106/106	62/62	8–1 B	3	5	105
3 Frosted	15–1	23–1	12–1 9–1		106/106	63/63	15–1 C		4	108
4 American Pharaoh	6–5	0.72–1	3–5 5–1		109/105	70/59	3–1 B	1	1	120
5 Gleneagles	20–1	8.4–1	8–1		124/114 RP*	124/114	20–1 X		6	na★
6 Effinex	30–1	119–1	33–1		107/92	70/31	20–1 C		7	100
7 Smooth Roller	15–1	**			111/111	73/73	30–1 X			113
8 Hard Aces	50–1	61–1	61–1		103/92	59/27	50–1 X		8	95
9 Honor Code	6–1	9–2	9–2 5–1		113/101	72/50	15–1 C	LP±	2	120
10 Beholder	3–1	**			114/99	66/60	2–1 A			119

•PA = Pace Advantage, ∓SS = SuperScreener, A = Must, B = Logical, C = Toss, X = Toss
*RP = Racing Post, ** = Scratched
±LP = Late Pace, ★na = not rated

23 I was consulting for a powerful family in Little Rock, Arkansas who used Bob Baffert, and D. Wayne Lukas to train some of their many horses. They said Baffert told them he was furious at an excercise rider who ran AP too fast right before the Travers so that may have contributed to his loss.

24 Steve Roman argues that had AP been in a very fast pace with suicidal fractions, he likely would have collapsed and got beat — maybe by Honor Code. Steve points out, as two examples of wire to wire greatness, Spend a Buck's

1985 Jersey Derby run 3 weeks after his wire to wire Kentucky Derby win (which I recall as I was there and the dosage theory had a perfect 1–2 finish with the exacta paying paying \$118 for \$2). After fractions of 45.2 and 1.09 for 6 furlongs keeping up with speed ball Huddle Up, Spend a Buck beat future Belmont winner Creme Fraiche, who was a top quality classic runner, by a neck. The second was Affirmed's 1979 Hollywood Gold Cup. He went wire to wire despite fractions of 45.3, 1.09.3 and the mile in 1:34.1. Affirmed was never more that a head in front of Sirlad, a three time champion in Italy. Sirlad set records at Hollywood Park on the prior and succeeding races at 9 and 12 furlongs. Affirmed was also able to beat Alydar by close margins in all three triple crown races with the two of them close together all the race.

25

ELEVENTH RACE
Keeneland
OCTOBER 31, 2015

$1\frac{1}{4}$ MILES. (2.00^{00}) 32ND RUNNING OF THE BREEDERS' CUP CLASSIC. Grade I. Purse \$5,000,000 FOR THREE-YEAR-OLDS AND UPWARD. Northern Hemisphere Three-Year-Olds, 122 lbs.; Older, 126 lbs.; Southern Hemisphere Three-Year-Olds, 117 lbs.; Older, 126 lbs. All Fillies and Mares allowed 3 lbs. \$50,000 to pre-enter, \$50,000 to enter, with guaranteed \$5 million purse including travel awards of which 55% to the owner of the winner, 18% to second, 10% to third, 6% to fourth and 3% to fifth; plus travel awards to starters not based in Kentucky.

Value of Race: \$4,550,000 Winner \$2,750,000; second \$900,000; third \$500,000; fourth \$300,000; fifth \$100,000. Mutuel Pool \$8,269,736.00 Exacta Pool \$4,553,714.00 Superfecta Pool \$2,411,198.00 Super High Five Pool \$290,125.00 Trifecta Pool \$4,070,105.00

Last Raced	Horse	M/Eqt.	A.	Wt	PP	¼	½	¾	1	Str	Fin	Jockey	Odds \$1
29Aug15 ^{11}Sar^{2}	American Pharoah	L	3	122	4	1^{1}	1^{1}	1^{2}	$1^{3\frac{1}{2}}$	1^{5}	$1^{6\frac{1}{2}}$	Espinoza V	0.70
3Oct15 ^{10}Bel^{3}	Effinex	L b	4	126	6	$2^{\frac{1}{2}}$	2^{3}	2^{1}	2^{2}	$2^{3\frac{1}{2}}$	$2^{4\frac{1}{2}}$	Smith M E	33.00
3Oct15 ^{5}Bel^{3}	Honor Code	L	4	126	8	8	8	8	$5^{\frac{1}{2}}$	$5^{1\frac{1}{2}}$	$3^{1\frac{1}{2}}$	Castellano J J	4.70
29Aug15 ^{11}Sar^{1}	Keen Ice	L	3	122	2	$5^{1\frac{1}{2}}$	$5^{1\frac{1}{2}}$	$5^{\frac{1}{2}}$	7^{2}	6^{hd}	4no	Ortiz I Jr	9.70
3Oct15 ^{10}Bel^{1}	Tonalist	L f	4	126	1	$3^{1\frac{1}{2}}$	3^{hd}	$4^{6\frac{1}{2}}$	4^{4}	4^{2}	5no	Velazquez J R	6.00
26Sep15 ^{10}SA^{6}	Hard Aces	L b	5	126	7	7^{3}	7^{5}	$6^{\frac{1}{2}}$	6^{1}	7^{4}	6^{hd}	Talamo J	72.80
19Sep15 ^{10}Prx^{1}	Frosted	L b	3	122	3	$4^{1\frac{1}{2}}$	$4^{4\frac{1}{2}}$	3^{hd}	3^{1}	$3^{\frac{1}{2}}$	$7^{12\frac{1}{2}}$	Rosario J	11.30
17Oct15 ^{4}ASC^{6}	Gleneagles-Ire	L	3	122	5	6^{hd}	$6^{\frac{1}{2}}$	$7^{2\frac{1}{2}}$	8	8	8	Moore R L	11.10

OFF AT 5:52 Start Good For All But GLENEAGLES (IRE). Won driving. Track fast.

TIME :23^{4}, :47^{2}, 1:11^{1}, 1:35^{2}, 2:00 (:23.99, :47.50, 1:11.21, 1:35.47, 2:00.07)

(New Track Record)

\$2 Mutuel Prices:				
	4-AMERICAN PHAROAH	3.40	3.00	2.40
	6-EFFINEX		14.20	6.60
	9-HONOR CODE			3.40

\$2 EXACTA 4-6 PAID \$76.40 \$2 SUPERFECTA 4-6-9-2 PAID \$1,224.00 \$1 SUPER HIGH FIVE 4-6-9-2-1 PAID \$1,715.10 \$2 TRIFECTA 4-6-9 PAID \$322.60

B. c, (Feb), by Pioneerof the Nile - Littleprincessemma, by Yankee Gentleman. Trainer Baffert Bob. Bred by Zayat Stables (Ky).

26 That breeding did not happen so the current plan is to breed Summer Chant to Awsome Again in 2018.

Chapter 31

Travels to Universities and Academic and Professional Conferences over the Years

I end this book with pleasant memories of the opportunities I had, through the academic lifestyle helped by sabbaticals and summer breaks, NSERC and my own initiative to visit and make friends with people all over the world. This continues to the present day.

My first conference talk was the International TIMS in Mexico City in 1967. I was an instructor in my last PhD year at Berkeley which was a prestigious part time appointment. I flew from San Francisco. The conference and my talk went well and it was good to participate. At that time the pyramids were far out in the countryside, that and the National Archeological Museum were highlights. That trip was on my own money and I was short coming back so I cashed in my ticket and took buses back. There were chickens and other animals on the buses and a lot of nice stops such as Acapulco which was a lovely place full of greenery at that time. Later, in 1994, while I was consulting at Frank Russell, Doug Stone and I gave a 4 day course on various financial theories and models to the Mexican Bolsa in Mexico City. By then the city had grown so much that it was all city out to the pyramids.

Since I was productive from the start, I got many invitations and NSERC provided travel funds. My Berkeley PhD thesis on stochastic programming and the theory of economic policy extended the work of Dutch greats, Jan Tinbergen (economics Nobel Prize winner) and Henri Thiel. That led to five chapters I was able to present and publish in good journals.

In my first year at UBC I received the first National science and engineering research council (NSERC), Canada's NFS, grant in the Commerce Faculty (as it was then called) for research in stochastic programming.

That was for $4,000 for 1 year, a big sum since my salary was $12,000 and lots at Whistler that are now several million were $2,500 with 10% down at 3% interest.[1] (I had offers at Northwestern and Rochester, both good schools, for slightly more money but chose UBC instead.) Subsequently, I got renewals each year and eventually the grants were for 3 and 5 years and my last grant was for $52,000 per year for 5 years or $260,000 in total. NSERC encouraged theoretical methodological research and, if published in top journals, that's exactly what they wanted. The money was earmarked for research assistance, namely graduate students, secretarial assistance, supplies such as computers and travel to major conferences was encouraged. You could not pay yourself a stipend or use the money to buy off courses to teach less, but it was very valuable in these other ways such as extra secretarial assistance and extra travel funds for computer equipment and travel to conferences. Later, I received several Social Science and Humanities Research Council (SSHRC) grants for projects. These were less valuable as they were more restricted. I served on the committees for a few years giving out these grants. Unfortunately, at UBC Commerce, traveling too much, even if all other aspects of your job were done well according to the faculty handbook, was not appreciated. Administration was highly rewarded at the expense of research.

When I left UBC losing the NSERC was probably more important than the low and heavily taxed salary. Now on occasion I referee for NSERC and it is usually a proposal for a lot of money at an eastern Canadian university to do some research I did better 30 years ago.

Starting in the summer of 1968, I went to many conferences for the next 36 years on the UBC faculty with the NSERC money lasting two more years. Not all travel expenses were covered but most were. Some invitations provided support and there were some other grants for special conferences and limited support form the university. My first such conference was in San Remo, Italy. Since I am half Italian with my mother's side from Trento above Venice and there are only 400 great places in Italy, I connected with the people. Italy has 43% of the world's art treasures and there are gems like Florence, Rome and Venice plus many others, though overshadowed by these big three, also have many treasures. My portfolio theory and stochastic programming research was in high demand. In the early years, the Italian universities had funds for visiting professors that would cover most costs and afforded the opportunity to travel to interesting places and meet interesting people. They would set up lectures in various cities. They would basically cover expenses and allow travel to interesting places and to meet and become friendly with the research elite.

My other half on my father's side is Polish. The Ziemba name means bird. I had never been to Poland but when I was 55 I got two invitations. One was to be the first speaker to the business school at Notre Dame, a new university founded by physicist who simply wanted his own university. So he bought and painted buildings then hired professors part time and was in business. It is now the top private school in the country. The second one on the same trip was to be keynote speaker at Jaap Spronk's Conference on the European Working Group on Financial Modeling. Actually there were two keynotes and I was both of them! That was kind of them. They are now on their 56th semi-annual conference which I attended in Dubai in November and was the lead speaker in a panel discussing the August–October 2015 stock market mini crash.

There were interesting trips to Eastern Europe in the 70s and 80s, a time when it was easy to travel there. There were great trips to Hungary with a marvelous host, Professor András Prékopa, on the left in blue, the late distinguished probability theory and stochastic programming expert running a powerful mathematical programming group in Budapest. In the picture is Prékopa who organized the conference which was the second of the stochastic programming international conference[2] following the Oxford 1974 organized by Michael Dempster, now of the University of Cambridge,

Participants at Stochastic Programming Summer School, Koseg, Hungary, 1981

officially, like me, retired but very active in stochastic programming and financial modeling. Behind Prékopa is Janos Pintner author of a top code for non-convex optimization working out of Halifax, Nova Scotia. Several visits to the statistics department were arranged by the late Jitka Dupačová. One in May 1998 was a seminar sponsored by local banks in Prague organized by Jitka on the progress in developing and implementing asset-liability models.[3]

In August 1981, we went for a month to the International Institute for Applied Systems Analysis (IIASA). The institute was a cold war idea of Harvard professor and decision theory expert, the late Howard Raiffa. He arranged international funding and it was an east–west cooperative venture designed to try to solve or make progress on important global problems such as pollution, water availability, environment, etc. Top stars from the US, Russia and other countries went there. In December 1980, Sandra and I attended an energy conference at IIASA organized by our Stanford friend Alan Manne. We remember this as our energy work on self sufficiency for Canada indicated we would not have lots to export so I was ignored! (we were a bit wrong on that as tar sands were developed without all of the costs we had included so came on stream at a lower cost.) Following that we went to Israel and our luggage was lost en route to Athens! Later, we visited IIASA for the month of August 1981 when I worked on the Kusy–Ziemba asset-liability paper that later was published in *Operations Research* in 1986. I also attended some technical conferences. The setup had theory people along with applications people with a mixture of east and west. It was a plum job for eastern Europeans and Russians. Most visitors were short term but some were able to make a career of it. One of my colleagues from Kiev, Yuri Ermoliev, has been there more than 30 years and also arranged for his daughter Tatania to be there for a long time. Both are good researchers and are involved in theory and applications. A few local professors, notably Georg Pflug, a University of Vienna statistics decision theorist, consult 1 day a week. As the cold war ended, IIASA's role became less important and funding became more difficult. Now in 2017 it is a shadow of the salad days occupying only about a third of the office spaces in the wonderful Schloss Laxenburg buildings, but in those days, IIASA was a top research place.

My visits to Italy began in 1984 with a countrywide tour organized by Jacopo Patrizi. It started in Rome and included Siena and Bologna. We knew so little about Italian food at the time that we asked why Bologna and were told it had the finest food and top class hospitality. Indeed it was a great visit. Later Piera Mazzoleni in Venice set up lectures there and in other universities in northern Italy.

Over the years I gave many talks in Bergamo, thanks to my host, the late Professor Marida Bertocchi, and Venice, thanks to Professor Elio Canestrelli as well as other universities in Florence, Turin, at a Supercomputer Center at the University of Calabria, Catania, Bolzano in the mountains where a 5,000 year old body was found and other universities across the country.

The Bergamo visits started in November 1993 and continue to the present. In May 2015, I lectured on portfolio theory and asset-liability management to the students in their new PhD program and on May 29,2017 we had a memorial day in her honor organized by Giorgio Consigli and Rita D'Eclessia with many speakers including me. we then had a nice conference on computational stochastic optimization in Bergamo. After we had a walk into greatness visiting the Dormello horse farm of Federico Tesio the worlds greatest trainer on Lake Majjoiri in northern Italy. Though Tesio died in 1954 his horse of the century two time arc winner Ribot ran after that to finish undefeated 16/16. Tesio had any other great horses including

Me with students at Bergamo, May 2015

undefeated Nearco the sire of Neartic who sired $1 million stud fee stallion Canadian Northern Dancer who sired many top stallions. Descendants of many great Tesio horses are on the property now and his house and stables are still there in his charistic stone buildings. The horses are fenced with chestnut railings designed so as not to hurt the horses. It was a rare treat and the current farn manager was very gracious showing us around once I said I was a co-owner of Honor Code.

The initial visit to Bergamo was for a conference on real time trading and financial modeling. To get a flavor of the scope of my visits here are some of the highlights and titles of the talks[4]: In 1993, I spoke on the turn of the month effect on the S&P500 and its use in the design of a seasonal index fund. In October 1997, there was a conference and I spoke on large scale financial planning models. In October 2006, I spoke to a symposium on financial instability in international equity markets and the predictability of the bond stock yield difference model and risk management of insurance companies using asset-liability models. On that same trip I spoke in Verona on risk measures and risk control of investment and hedge fund portfolios. Also at the University of Venice, I gave talks on the symmetric downside Sharpe ratio and incentives and risk taking in hedge funds. In April 2007, I spoke on intertemporal surplus management and in June 2009, I spoke on advances in portfolio theory and asset management in the tradition of HM Markowitz. Sandra and I collaborated with Marida Bertocchi on a book on pensions and retirement for Wiley in 2010 which was reissued in 2015. In 2013, I attended the international stochastic programming conference in Bergamo.

In Bergamo, I met Anatassios (Tassos) Malliaris who was teaching a doctoral seminar on stochastic calculus for Marida's students in the early 1990s. He then invited me to Loyola for a seminar on calendar anomalies. I invited him to present a paper at the 1998 stochastic progamming conference in Vancouver. We remained connected over the years and I value our friendship. We recently completed together a *Handbook of Futures Markets*, which covers this field very well. I co-wrote two chapters, one on how to lose money in derivatives and examples of many who did and the returns from buying puts and calls in bear, bull and normal markets, hedged and unhedged from 1985 to 2012. The latter idea I use in trading and the former gives ideas of how not to lose money.

My strength and weakness has always been that I am interested in everything. So I applied to graduate schools in 5 fields and took Berkeley which was the best university. That was a smart move.

Tassos Malliaris

Colleagues at an energy conference in Vancouver

Just like financial modeling and hedge fund type management is popular with operations research/management science trained professors in 2017, back around 1980 it was energy modeling. So as our part of this, Ernest Koenigsberg, at the time an instructor at Berkeley who I knew from my days there and we taught courses at the same time (he is seated in the front, the third from the left)[5] and I organized a conference on energy modeling which we held in a North Vancouver hotel. Notable speakers included John Mulvey of Princeton with whom I would later edit an asset-liability book for Cambridge University Press from the 1995 Issac Newton program on financial modeling, Berkeley PhD student colleague Richard Grinold, then a UC Berkley finance professor and later a major player at BARRA and Barclays, my stochastic programming PhD student Chanaka Edirsinghe, now a chaired financial modeling professor at RPI. Also in the picture far left next to John is Loring (Jack) Mitten, who was then chair of the UBC management science division and a dynamic programmming expert and on the far right next to Sandra is Klaus Spreemann from the University of Ulm, Germany who had arranged several wonderful visits there and to St Gallen, Switzerland where he taught next.

In 1991, I was fortunate to be a keynote speaker in a major international conference in Rio de Janeiro and also give lectures in Santiago, Chile and visited Buenos Aries, the Paris of South America, to see the horse racing hippodrome and eat their wonderful beef. That was the era of rampant inflation in Argentina and I saw it in action ordering the same exact meal on 3 of my 4 days there and paying always more the next day in Argentine pesos using an updated menu with new prices. The tango was invented on a well-known street there and great shows are at the Casa Blanca (the white house). Rio is dangerous but I had no trouble and an added plus was very good gems and jewelry to bring back for my wife. I was scheduled to go again in late June/early July 2016 to the international conference on stochastic programming where I organized two financial modeling sessions at Bezos, a beach resort about 2 hours north of Rio. I would also give 2 weeks of lectures in Chile hosted by Professor Alexandro Joffre. In the end due to a number of factors I canceled Brazil — there was the Zita fear plus very long expensive flights plus other considerations including the crime, deep recession and the government scandals. So in the end, I canceled going to Brazil and Chile replacing it with a trip to France. There I worked with Sebastien Lleo on some of our delayed papers and, as I am part of the economics of wine handbook team, attended the economics of wine conference in Bordeaux instead.

Once I was phasing out of UBC I did a lot of teaching over 3 to 6 weeks in excellent places. Excellent has two dimensions: quality of the school and how great the place is to be. Some schools excel in both but at least one makes it worthwhile.

Gems were Luiss Guido Carli in Rome where we visited on four occasions. I taught anomalies, applied investments, applied stochastic programming and asset-liability management. The students were good and they were fun to teach as they were very interested in the subject. Rome and

Travels to Universities and Academic and Professional Conferences 393

In Cyprus 2003 with stochastic programming colleagues, George Pflug of the University of Vienna and Marida Bertocchi from Bergamo, Italy and Jitka Dupacova form Prague who have now died.

Rita D'Ecclesia of Rome with Marida Bertocchi and Jitka Dupačová

Me relaxing in Rome

all the major universities in Italy have always had top academics in the finance mathematical programming area. For example, Bruno de Finetti who made many discoveries very early, some were credited to him and others rediscovered later. de Finetti was a legend among his many contributions where discovering quasi concave functions and formulating mean-variance tradeoffs in 1940 a decade before the famous paper of Roy in Econometrica and Harry Markowitz in the Journal of Finance (see Harry's 2010 Collected Works from World Scientific). Currently there are many top academics. One colleague is professor Rita D'Ecclesia who is an expert in bond portfolio analysis who we saw at the Borghese Gallery in June 2015. She organizes top conferences in Rome and I been fortunate enough to have gone to some of them.

Rome as a site seeing place is the top of the top in Italy with the Vatican, Borghese Gallery, Doria-Pamphilj Gallery, the Capitoline Museum and of course all the ancient Roman sites and a myriad of other interesting events. You walk near the Spanish Steps and several of the small churches there have paintings by Raphael. The Borghese is in a beautiful large building in a huge park in the north of the city. It was founded by Cardinal Scipione Borghese in the early 17th century. Besides being wealthy and a tremendous patron of the arts, he was relentless in going after the best pieces of art. One method he used for those who would not sell to him was to show up at their home in the middle of the night and tell them to sell for a low price for he would put them in jail for some trumped up charge. This

Sebastien Lleo in Nantes

Rita in Dubai

tactic was very effective in building a great collection. The tables were turned later, at the beginning of the 19th century, Napoleon, whose sister Paolina was married to a descendant of the Borghese family, legally stole much of the collection by buying it cheap. These many pieces are now in the Louvre. Still the Borghese collection has marvelous Bernini carvings and there are nice Caravaggio paintings and many other great treasures, among them a beautiful Canova white nude carving of Paolina resting on a bench. The Doria-Pamphilj which is little known in the guide books has a marvelous collection of paintings and sculptures formed 400 years ago and never altered due to an Italian law that required collections to be kept complete. It is a great example of superior risk management to have been able to afford to keep all of these great art pieces for more than four centuries. The Vatican with the Raphael rooms and Michelangelo's Sistine Chapel and the neighboring St Peter's Basilica are the top sites with a fantastic collection of which everything is of top quality. It is comparable to the Louvre in Paris, the Hermitage in St Petersburg, and the British and Victoria and Albert Museums in London. The lesser known but wonderful speciality museums are a way to avoid the horrendous crowds and still see fine collections.

Another great museum is the archeological museum in Naples. We were fortunate to go there again in June 2015 and enjoyed the museum with its huge statuary, fine mosaics and frescoes from Pompeii. In a previous visit we had also spent a long day walking around the ruins at Pompeii. This time we stayed in a lovely hotel in the old city and were pleasantly surprised at the good food at low cost compared to other places such as Rome (about a 50% discount). The local pizza place is actually famous for its owner who has won numerous prizes which are displayed on the walls.

I always published many papers and starting in the early 1970s I began to write books. The first, *Stochastic Optimization Models in Finance* (1975) did me a lot of good. It was way ahead of its time and many top scholars studied it in their PhD work. It helped me to be promoted to full professor, which I made in 8 years. Only UCLA finance star Michael Brennan made it in seven. Later, *Turkish Flatweaves* (1979) was one we co-produced with Scorpion. I bought some copies and they produced a British version for their sales.

I was associate editor with departmental editor Marty Gruber of NYU of finance department of the journal *Management Science* and then in 1982 I became departmental editor which I did for 10 years. That department had ten top associate editors including Darrell Duffie, Mark Rubinstein, Suresh

Pizza in Naples

Sundaresan, Donald Hausch, Gordon Sick, Vojislav (Max) Maksimovic, and Hiam Levy and produced strong papers. We accepted papers that made good contributions to the theory and practice of finance using management science operations research techniques. In 1995, I was asked to organize a finance handbook for North Holland which I edited with Max Maksimovic of the University of Maryland and Bob Jarrow of Cornell University. North Holland, a top publisher gave us high prestige but they basically grabbed most the royalties. We did get a $1,000 fee each for editing this handbook. The finance handbook was a terrific success and became a major research reference book.

In 1999, as a result of its success, I was asked to become the series editor for North Holland's Handbooks in Finance. They did give series editors and volume editors fair royalties. This was a prestigious offer because the economics series was edited by Kenneth Arrow and Michael Intrilligator, statistics was edited by C S Rao of the Indian Statistical Institute and operations research series, which included the Handbook of Finance, was edited by George Nemhauser of Georgia Tech and Alexander Rinnooy Kan. So I was flattered to be asked. Arrow who died in the spring of 2017 was the smartest person I ever saw in action. Rao it was said was not only a member of the Indian Statistical Institute he WAS the Institute. George

Mike Intrilligator, his wife with John Swetye & me at Santa Anita Racetrack

With Constantinides at the multinational finance conference in Istanbul, 2004

was the best student of UBC colleague Jack Mitten and Alexander was a top discrete optimization expert and departmental editor with me of a part of the journal Management Science and became a huge executive in Holland.

I was at Stanford organizing a conference with Alan Manne on planning under uncertainty for George Dantzig which was held at the Electric Power Research Institute, Kenneth Arrow attended and I asked him to be an advisor. Besides being brilliant, he is modest, replying "I am not sure I am qualified in finance." I simply replied "I think you are." The *Journal of Finance* gave him a well-deserved award as one of the pioneers in modern finance. Later at the January American Economics Association meetings I asked MIT professor Paul Samuelson if he would be an advisor as well. Then I asked Stanford's Bill Sharpe, Harry Markowitz of UC San Diego, Bob Merton also from MIT and Merton Miller of the University of Chicago to advisors and I had a full house of six economics Nobel Prize winners as advisors. When Miller died I replaced him with George Constantinides also from the University of Chicago and Stewart Myers of the MIT Sloan School of Management, and later ex-UBC empirical corporate finance expert Espen Eckbo, who is at Dartmouth College. From the start Mike Intrilligator was very helpful in discussing ideas to make the handbooks in finance series better. I miss him now. Unfortunately, he had a lingering illness and recently died.[6]

In 1995, George Constantinides arranged a visit to the University of Chicago finance department where I taught Japanese finance at the Gleacher Center in the downtown. I was friendly with Merton Miller as we viewed finance similarly. Common subjects were Japanese markets and futures markets. While Miller did not do anomalies himself, he appreciated what I was doing. In his words "you are coming at it from a different angle but I have respect." While I was there, I attended the finance seminars and Richard Thaler's behavioral finance workshops. I actually commuted from Vancouver most weeks with one trip to Europe staying at the Faculty Quadrangle Club while there. George was very helpful with the North Holland Handbooks in Finance series and during my visit to Chicago and with other advise over the years. He also has continued supporting the Cypriot universities where he came from.

Rachel was looking for a college that year and visited many schools in the US and Canada and she came to Chicago for a visit. She was impressed

Rachel & her colleagues at RGE

with Nobels and in the top floor of the Gleacher Center are pictures of all those who taught, visited or were somehow affiliated with the University of Chicago. This wall includes a whos who of economics, physics, chemistry, medicine and other fields. When Rachel met Miller she asked "what did you do to win the Nobel Prize?" He replied let me explain it this way, a pizza delivery man arrives with the pizza and asks how many pieces you would like, the reply is I'm very hungry, cut it into eight pieces. Rachel immediately grasped the main idea of the Modigliani–Miller theory that it doesn't matter how you finance the corporation, you get the same result. Miller added, "but we proved it rigorously." That was one of the first applications of arbitrage in finance. Rachel did attend the University of Chicago studying medieval history with a minor in French. There she got excellent training in analytical skills which helped her in her masters study at Oxford in international relations and world political economy. Her undergraduate thesis was on the Bayeaux tapestry and her masters thesis was on currency unions.

In 1998, the year I organized the 7th International Conference in Stochastic Programming in Vancouver, we went earlier in the year to the University of Cambridge where I had an Arthur Anderson fellowship for 4 months at the Judge Institute, their business school. There we stayed at Wolfson College, one of the newer (about 50 years old) but great colleges there. While UBC had one then no faculty lunch places, they had 50 or more. You never knew who would sit next to you at dinner but they were always interesting. Later in 2003, I had a similar 4 month Christiansen fellowship to Oxford University and St Catherine's College. Although I was attached to the mathematical institute, my use of math for real world problems was a great interest and I gave five talks all over the campus. They invited me to teach pension fund management models and Kelly optimization in their mathematical finance masters program. There were terrific students, possibly the best I ever had and I continued to go 1 week a year to teach this until they changed the program in 2011.

In 2012 one of the Chinese PhD students, Changling Xu, wrote me saying I was the best teacher in the Oxford mathematical finance masters program having taken my half day Kelly lecture and half day pensions and retirement lecture that I gave from 2003 to 2010 to the mathematical finance masters students. Even if not true, it is a nice complement. I do try to give good lectures with excellent slides that my wife prepares. Judging how students like lectures is difficult at best as their utility functions may be very different what one might expect. I did find the Oxford masters students in the mathematical finance program to be super ones to teach.

In any event he invited me to speak to a multi-day event for Chinese company owners, and following my suggestion they invited my daughter Rachel to participate as well. I was able to stay at St Catherine's and my daughter also spoke and stayed at the big Randolph hotel in the center of Oxford which cost for one night what my 4 day stay cost at St Catz. It was great to get back to Oxford again as I missed it since my last 2010 teaching visit. Apparently they changed the program so my lectures were dropped. It was homecoming for her as well as she got her masters in political economy at the spy training ground for MI6, St Antony's. Rachel has met a lot of famous people in her life including having invited Sean Connery to their Spy Ball and giving a lecture with Bill and Hilary Clinton in the audience who were visiting their daughter Chelsea, also a masters student in Rachel's class. After high school, she went to Paris, as did Ivanka Trump who was there as well in the same event. My lectures went well and I enjoyed listening to Rachel who spoke about the current economic situation in the world. It used to be I was ahead of her on common topics but now her work with Nouriel Roubini and his firm has moved her to new heights. We did two books together, both based on our *Wilmott* columns. I started in 2002 when Paul Wilmott began his magazine and have written a bimonthly column since then. Rachel was in Egypt after her Oxford masters degree and wanted to attend an interesting conference with a 1400 euro attendance fee. She wrote Paul on her own asking if she could be the magazine's correspondent. That led to an article in *Wilmott* and since then we have had some joint columns, she has some of her own as do I and the two books, Ziemba and Ziemba (2007, 2013) which have reworked, updated versions of the columns which cover a lot of valuable topics.

Rachel spent two years in Egypt following Oxford. And we went too, taking a cruise on Lake Nasser and visiting Cairo and Abu Simbel, the temple that was taken apart and moved when the area was flooded. We visited the hotel where Agatha Christie spent a lot of time and write some of her books in Jordan. The pyramids are nice and their construction is still a mystery. The Photo shows Sandra and I near one of them.

The next pages show some memorable remembrances of our visits to Egypt and Jordan.

In Jordan we visited the main city Amman and the ancient city of Petra which was lost for a thousand years. There is a lot of driving there, much like Arizona. To get to Petra, you walk down a narrow winding path with high walls for several hundred meters then you see the temple where Indiana Jones (Harrison Ford) saved his father, Henry Jones, played by Sean Connery. It is a façade and has some entry rooms. Along the area are other structures and a path to some upper level buildings. It's quite a sight. In the movie Lawrence of Arabia Anthony Quinn's character invites Lawrence and his entourage to have lunch in the vast field Wadi Rum (the Valley of the moon). Close by are some natural covered bridges and the small house where the real Lawrence stayed to hide from his enemies. Camping out there in tents was memorable but really cold in the desert.

Ruins in Jordan   Our car in Wadi Rum

Travels to Universities and Academic and Professional Conferences 403

Near where Lawrence hide out from his enemies

Reputed to be the remains of Lawrence of Arabia's hideout house

Tents where we camped in Wadi Rum (the Valley of the moon)

Sandra and Rachel have lunch at the entrance to the path to Petra

On the pathway to Petra

Rachel near the end of the long path to Petra

Petra carved out of the rocks

Sandra at the path to the upper part of Petra

In Petra

Donkey and rider in upper part at Petra

Designs on walls at Petra

It was nice to visit Egypt and see the pyramids and reminded me of my Mexico City visit in 1967. I recall Sandra and I having dinner in the hotel at the second cataract of the Nile river. It was there that Agatha Christie wrote some of her books. It is also a scene from the wonderful Death on the Nile movie which had an all star cast led by Peter Ustinov, David Niven, Angela Lansbury and others. The site of Tutankhamun's grave which you can go inside brings memories depicted in the Robert Taylor, Eleanor Parker movie on the Valley of the Kings. Recall the lovely Eleanor was the other woman in the Sound of Music. We took a tour on Lake Nasser, the huge lake made to provide for the dam. It was less crowded there than Nile boat tours and had very large fish and ten meter crocodiles because of the availability of food in the lake.

In Cairo, the main Egyptian museum is a gem with great artifacts even better than the wonderful British museum's fabulous collection; see also the great Egyptian collection in Turin. There are some good Egyptian carpets so we were able to get a couple. The famous Mamluk carpets from circa the 16th century are from there. For these carpets, an excellent place to see them is in a Vienna museum.

Throughout the country are the great statues we associate with Egypt.

406 *The Adventures of a Modern Renaissance Academic*

Interesting designs

Tutankhamun (King Tut) in Egyptian museum, Cairo

At entrance to the tomb of the Tutankhamun (King Tut)

Designs depicting religious beliefs

Travels to Universities and Academic and Professional Conferences 407

Five people working on a large carpet

Egypt makes nice oriental rugs too

Coptic 6th century weaving in Cairo's Egyptian museum

A rather large carving

Sandra and I near pyramid

Sandra on Lake Nasser small boat

408 *The Adventures of a Modern Renaissance Academic*

Hotel at second cataract where we stayed in the footsteps of Asath Christie

Lake Nasser (also called Lake Nubia) on the Nile river in upper Egypt and Northern Sudan. It was named for Egyptian President Gamal Abdel Nasser

Sandra and I in Egypt

Travels to Universities and Academic and Professional Conferences 409

The hotel at the second cataract of the Nile river where we had dinner, a place where Agatha Christie wrote some of her books

The Spinx of Giza near a pyramid

An Egyptian temple

Me going into an Egyptian tomb

Rachel in an Egyptian Temple

Rams guarding a temple

The Abu Simbel temple complex at the second cataract of the Nile river

Egyptian symbol

Remains of a giant carving

Small temple

The two temples at Abu Simbel were created during the reign of Ramesses II (c1279–c1213 BC). It took 20 years to create the complex dedicated to the gods Ra-Horakhty, Ptah and the deified Ramesses II (The Great Temple) and the goddess Hathor and Queen Neferate, Ramesses' favorite wife (small temple). The name, Abul Simbel was the name of the boy who led Swiss explorer, Burckhardt to the site in 1813 CE. But he did not see it as it was buried in sand. He then mentioned this to fellow explorer Giovami Belzani who found it in 1817 CE. Between 1964–1968 CE both temples were dismantled and moved 65 meters higher onto the plateau of the cliffs above and rebuilt 210 meters to the north-west of its original location at a cost of US $ 40 million.

The Chinese group was a lot of fun. During our dinners they frequently cheered themselves with wine and a special liquor they brought from China. The events, such as lunch and dinners were in various colleges, some of which I had not visited before, like Queens College.[7] The highlight was the lunch at Balliol College which was founded by a knight in 1263. He and his wife in their 13th century outfits (his being armor) were depicted on oil paintings on the walls. There was a trip to Waddesdon Manor, the Rothschild's English estate a gem 40 minutes from Oxford in the countryside, now part of the National Trust. The five Rothschild brothers in five major capitals of Europe were astute traders, often distorting information for their trading benefit. The highlight was a wine demonstration by their rather talented sommelier, one of the top 300 wine experts in the world. Besides the top French wines, the Rothschilds produce similar, mostly bordeaux-style red wines in Australia, Argentina and other countries. We got to taste nine of them ending with the US$2,000 per bottle Mouton Rothschild 1990. I was sitting next to an impeccably dressed

Beijing woman. She passed on the first 8 wines in their small glasses and told me she only drinks the 1990 Mouton Rothschild and buys it in Beijing for 5,000 pounds a bottle. Somehow, more of these expensive red wines are sold in China than produced in France. There is some serious cheating there!

At the same time I was teaching at Oxford I also taught a short course on applied investment at the ICMA Centre of the University of Reading. I was at Reading until 2013 when my 20% part time appointment at high pay ran out. That was my highest academic salary at full market price. Getting a visa in the UK is very complicated and I did it three times. It was more work to get the visa than to teach the course! The Reading students were not the best but they were pleasant and I was very friendly with the staff there. Over the years, in the UK, I had short course teaching at the University of Warwick, London School of Economics, Imperial College and University of Manchester. I also gave lectures at conferences in the UK including the University of Sussex, University of Salford, Brunel University, the University of Southhampton and Edinburgh University. I also had two visits to Trinity College, Dublin. In Dublin, the library has fantastic items related to the Book of Kells. Patrick Waldron, a racing colleague and member of Trinity, took us around to various racetracks and farms including the famed

Vancouver post conference social, 1996

Travels to Universities and Academic and Professional Conferences

At an ORS conference, Alba

In Barbaresco, Italy with one of my Alba colleagues near one of the great vineyards

Coolmore. Ireland is like Australia, most people are into racing as it is a national sport. In consulting for the Ford family of Little Rock, Arkansas who were gracious to me having bought most of my books and I gave them many others. They said their ancestors were from Ireland and around 1850

Koray Simsek, his wife & daughter with us at dinner at Matbah, June 2015

the three brothers split up with one founding racing in Australia, one to Arkansas and the other going elsewhere.

While at Oxford in 2003, I wrote a monograph on *The Stochastic Programming Approach to Asset Liability and Wealth Management* for AIMR. At that time, AIMR gave a hefty fee of $31,250 for writing the monograph which, along with a 72-page appendix, was free to AIMR members. The fee was one quarter of the $125,000 budget for four books — rather generous at the time. Later it was available as a free download for everyone. Mark Kritzman was my editor and helped move the monograph along. He runs Windham Capital Management, a small financial consulting firm in Cambridge, and teaches financial engineering part time at the MIT Sloan School of Management. We have kept in contact over the years.

There were many who contacted me regarding the ALM software but the hard sell made them all fizzle. The most fun one was in Alba, Italy, with Operational Research Systems. They did various consulting jobs. We had a number of nice visits usually staying at a local agritourism bed and breakfast. Alba is a truffle center and is close by two wine mountains: Barola and Barbaresco. Sunday dinner in Barbaresco, starting at 1 pm ending at 5:15 with top food and wine, looking down at the grapes was especially memorable.

One of my hosts had an apartment in Menton, on the French Rivera. One year we stayed there to enjoy the beautiful gardens the city is famous for plus all the other great activities including a nice Picasso museum.

I taught a similar course on applied investments for 4 years during June at Sabanci University outside Istanbul on the Asian side. Our host was Koray Simsek, who we knew from our EDHEC visit in Nice. Koray was a student of Mulvey's at the Princeton Financial Engineering Department. Three of biggest billionaire industrialists each formed their own university which have very good facilities and top quality museums. Koç is the most famous, located on the Bosphorus close to the Black Sea. Istanbul, some 40 minutes away by bus, is always a delight to look at oriental carpets, good copies of 15th and 16th century Iznik tiles, weavings and pottery and other nice items to buy including gems to make beautiful necklaces. A plus are several restaurants serving meals from 16th century Ottoman Sultan recipes. The teaching sadly ended with changed economic circumstances and now there are no foreign visitors at the university as far as I know. Also political unrest has accelerated and there is a massive influx of refugees from Syria and other countries, so we now go as tourists as we did in 2015 and 2016 and Koray has moved to a private university in Florida.

Recep Bildik, another dear friend in Istanbul, had contacted me years ago to discuss anomalies. He works for the Istanbul stock exchange and teaches part time at Koç. He spoke several times in my Sabanci classes and we have contact on many issues.

There were many visits to Germany to universities including Ulm and Augsburg in the south and recently to the mathematics powerhouse at the University of Bonn where many of my math finance colleagues were also speaking. One of the best, and where I spoke again in 2016, is the Campus for Finance Program at the WHU, Otto Beisheim School of Management, a private school. They have a unique program for students who cannot afford the tuition, they get to go to the university and later pay a fraction of their salaries to the school. Professor Markus Rudolf, who had visited me as a post doc at UBC, is a chaired professor who became the Dean there and helped organize this unique program. The annual program in January is organized by the students and they have companies coming to look for candidates to hire and have various invited speakers.

In my 2010 visit, the other speakers were the head of the London stock exchange, who thought her 1.5 million pound salary low, and the economic Nobel Prize winners for game theory: John Nash, who was popularized in the movie *A beautiful mind* and Israeli Professor Robert Aumann. Nash gave a talk on a gold standard proposal for a monetary union. Aumann had research on the threats of war, namely, if you threaten and are powerful war might be avoided. I had heard his talk at the ETH on one of my visits

Professors John Nash and Robert Aumann, their wives & me

Conference in Germany, 1981

to Zurich. WHU assigns students to take care of the visitors. Mine was Maureen Benk, a German PhD student of Markus who was extending a paper he and I wrote on intertemporal asset allocation, extending to asset prices with jumps.[8] Sadly, in May 2015, as I was working on this book, it was announced that John Nash and his wife were killed in an auto crash while in a taxi returning home from receiving an award.

Many visits to France were also memorable. The highlight from an academic viewpoint was lecturing at the famous College de France in Paris. Their seminar is organized by five top universities. There I spoke on Kelly investing to determine appropriate bet size to yield high final wealth most of the time. In 2000, there was the first of the Bachelier Finance conferences held in Paris. Paul Samuelson, Bob Merton and Steve Ross were among the major speakers, organized by Helyette Geman. There I met Raphael Douady and his father who they say was a member of the famous secret Borbaki. Pure mathematics books by N Borbaki are written by a secret group of famous mathematicians. Raphael was invited to be a member but preferred another career path, that of quantitative finance. Currently he is taking up a chair at Stony Brook and continuing activities with many other ventures including his Paris based data company and involvement with the finance group at the Courant Institute in New York. I am an advisor to a new data company he is starting. He had a nice conference at the University and in New York focusing on financial regulation and quantitative methods. I spoke on stock market crashes, big and small and what to do about them.

We went numerous times to the burgundy wine area above and below Beaune. The best whites are from the Montrachet area in the south. We stayed many times at the wonderful inn Le Montrachet which had terrific food and atmosphere. The great red wines are in the north. A favourite lunch place was the rotisserie at Chamberton near where the photo was taken. Gevrey Chamberton wine bottles with no labels covered

In Chambertin, the heart of the famous burgundy red wines

with dust are served which are terrific as is the food which focuses on very good beef.

At Christmas 1993, I along with John Board of Reading University taught short courses at the Pont et Chausses, Paris. We stayed New Year's Eve at the Trianon Palace, Versailles. I received a US$5,000 fee (in french francs) for teaching: 1,000 went for two 200 dinners, a 400 hotel and a 200 lunch. It was well worth it and I had $4,000 left. Later John and I along with Charles Sutcliffe did joint research on portfolio theory and published four joint papers. Later, John invited me to teach at Reading for a number of years.

For a while I was visiting professor of finance at the University of Monaco which is housed in their soccer stadium. They are an upstart new university founded by a Geneva hedge fund trader. In June 2015, at a conference in Nantes, France, I saw Gregory Moscato, a former colleague who is still teaching there.

Two other visits for about a month each were especially pleasant. Lionel Martellini invited me to teach an MBA course for EDHEC in Nice and also to stay in their home close by in Giot. Lionel is currently scientific director of EDHEC-Risk Institute and Senior Scientific Advisor ERI Scientific Beta. Another memorable visit was to the powerful economics department at the University of Toulouse. That was a research visit and my host was Christian Gollier, who is an expert in resource economics including the determination of discount factors for long dated assets.

In recent years I had several visits to the University of Reims working with Professors Oliver Gergaud and Sebastien Lleo. Oliver has subsequently moved to the Hedge Business School in Bordeaux and we had a pleasant visit there. Besides the university work we had various tours in Reims and Bordeaux to the champagne and wine areas. After giving lectures at the university we toured the famed Bordeaux wineries such as Lynch Bages.

Four of us, including Oliver, Princeton wine guru Orley Ashenfelter, NYU Professor Karl Storchmann and I are working on a Handbook of the Economics of Wine for World Scientific. In 2014, we drove to Walla Walla, Washington for the International Wine Economics Conference. The talks were interesting and use economic and statistical tools applied to wind questions. The annual conferences are an off shoot of the Economics of Wine Journal edited mainly by Karl. We did not attend the 2015 conference in Mendoza, Argentina but did attend in 2016 when it was held in Bordeaux. Bordeaux is a nice historic clean city with a network of easy to use trams to get around. The wine area is an hour away and we had several excellent tours of top producers. One interesting thing is that some of the very best not only command a high price but sell a huge amount. The conference was fine. The 2017 conference is to be in Padua. Their representatives had a fabulous presentation. After the Bordeaux conference, we trained to the chateaux area in the Loire valley near Tours and visited three of the great castles nearby.

Paris was less hectic on our return but on our arrival to Paris on a good direct flight it was a zoo at the airport taking two hours to get through passport control. We went up to Reims to visit with Sebastien and discuss our joint papers and his other research and gave a lecture together on crashes at their Paris campus. Paris is always fun. We went to l'Organgerie to see the Monet water lilly paintings as well as others and the new Picasso museum. The Picasso exhibit in Vancouver was equally impressive. We also made our usual exhibit to the wonderful impressionist painting at the Orsay and had lunch at their nice restaurant.

Teaching in Asia was also rewarding. I am still affiliated with KAIST the Korean MIT where I go periodically to Taijan, the city with all the major R&D centers of the famous Korean companies. It is similar to Tsukuba, Japan where we spent academic 1988/1989. Professor Woo Chang Kim, who I co-author with, is my host there. He has a PhD from Princeton's financial engineering department as does Koray Simsek, my host at Sabanci. Woo Chang is also a partner in a hedge fund founded by his PhD supervisor and my colleague John Mulvey which has now been sold.

KAIST, the Princeton University financial engineering department, China's Tsing Hua University and EDHEC—Risk Institute have organized a two day conference on robotic investing which I look forward to. Samsung and Alibaba are major sponsors reminding again of the Asian financial power. The conference was interesting. I did not like the EDHEC continuous time straight finance theory for portfolio management but with their aggressive marketing they have much business. Would you like a portfolio changing from 100% equities to 30% in 5 minutes and back? Not me. The MIT etc computer science whizzes working for Google, Facebook, Amazon and Alibaba on financial services reporting were sure impressive. Want to deal with 300 million credit cards — well these people can do it. I was my usual self in the question period. My highlight was getting efficient market guru Burton Malkiel interested enough to invite me to lunch and I got in a debate with ex treasury secretary about the crash of 1987. A brilliant professor and the co youngest Harvard full professor and ex-president of

Harvard. He is fully confident but in this case he would benefit by reading my chapter in the Handbook of Futures on how to lose money and not lose it in derivatives. Rachel got his email and I have sent him some things which he might read. He is involved in her Roubini Global Economics company.

I have had three visits to Singapore, two at the National University and one at the National Technological University that is connected to Carnegie Mellon University. The third, the Singapore Management University, the last built, is in the downtown and emphasizes business and economics. One of my colleagues, Kian Guan Lim, who was in the 1994 *Efficiency of Racetrack Betting Markets* with a paper on Singapore racing was a dean there. The three universities are very competitive and that strengthens all of them. Singapore has very good students and is nice to visit with very good food. The major drawback is hot muggy weather all year long.

I also had five trips to China. One was a trip to Shanghai where I gave a course on investment research. Like Japan, I talk for 3 minutes and the translator talks for 6–8 minutes. That was all enjoyable and Rachel and Sandra were on that trip with our star tour guide Rachel arranging our post lecture tour by train all the way the Xian. After the visit to the underground army I got a lesson in bargaining. I used to be a good bargainer from my days in Turkey, Iran and Afghanistan, but clearly was out of practice. I saw some small models of the soldiers, a package of about six of them. The asking price was rmb400, I got to 200 and then to 50 where I bought them.

Visiting the underground soldiers in Xian, China

Then we went outside and there was a booth asking 10 — the real price turned out to be 5!

Later, I was invited to a conference in Beijing. My most fun was palling around with my friend the late Arnold Zellner, just a prince of a person and probably the world's top Bayesian statistician. Later, when I was giving a talk on Kelly investing at the University of Chicago, he guided me across the campus. He is one I sorely miss. He was the supervisor of a number of finance PhDs who studied anomalies or other violations of the strongly held belief, strongly held in the Chicago business school, in efficient markets. Chicago Booth is right at the top in quality covering efficient markets led by Gene Fama, behavioral finance led by Richard Thaler and many other subjects.

In Beijing, I met Professor Ren Rouen who was a very good econometrician working with my Berkeley (now Harvard) Professor Dale Jorgensen and others. I had some good times at his Behang University and was invited also to Chengdu which is billed a small city with hot spicy food. Small is a relative term, so 7 million in China qualifies. Subsequently, I returned to Chengdu and visited the panda breeding center where the mothers are 1,000 times as heavy as the babies and they cannot recognize the babies as they are being born so the staff pulls the babies away as they are being born so the mothers don't trample on them (for subsequent birth, the mothers understand what's going on and the babies don't need protection). I also went to see the giant Buddhas a bit north of Chengdu which was a good experience, but even 2 hours away from this major city the air was quite polluted.

For students of black swans, as you walk on the breeding center grounds, you pass a lake filled with these lovely birds. They are not rare in China or Australia where it is reported they come from.

In December 2015, I went to the 4th International Conference on Intelligent Finance in Chongquin for the Chinese Academy of Sciences. Professor Heping Pan is the main organizer and I am helping in the organization and will give a keynote talk and read an endorsement of the conference from Harry Markowitz.

Other Trips and Other Places

In August 2011, I was fortunate to visit two of the world's top racetracks that were running at that time. I missed Deauville in France as my visits there were out of racing season, but went to Del Mar in California, then to Korea (to give a week long series of lectures on portfolio theory and asset-liability management) then to Saratoga. Del Mar, is a very good place with a Hollywood flavor, founded by movie stars Bing Crosby and Pat O'Brien. It is 100 miles south of Los Angeles. The last part of the drive is very beautiful through beach towns, making up for the miserable car congestion leaving Los Angeles. This was the first of two visits to Del Mar. A frequent visitor to Del Mar was the 1940s movie star and pinup girl with her legs insured for $1 million, Betty Grable. At her funeral, more track people attended than the Hollywood crowd as she was such a favorite at Del Mar. In late July 2012, I flew directly from London which avoided the tough drive to visit Del Mar again.

The Boston trip which was a side trip from my annual visit to the Saratoga racetrack in late August through Labor Day. Before that I went to Korea for a week of lectures to the financial engineering department of the Korean Advanced Institute of Science and Technology (KAIST) which is located in Taejon, the center of the research departments of the major companies in Korea. In that way, Taejon is similar to Tsukuba in Japan with large research center all over the city. This was followed by visit and talk to the KAIST Business School finance department in Seoul. The Korean students are top notch. Indeed, KAIST is modeled after MIT and has some former MIT faculty in charge. The Korean companies are very innovative with good electronics, cars and other products. A danger there is always the threat from the North, which likes to saber rattle making wild claims of retaliation. Hence, the stock market in Korea trades at price–earnings rates that reflect current tension.[9] This was my first visit to Korea. I taught again in August 2012 and that time the emphasis was on stock market anomalies and applied investments and I spoke again to the business school finance department in Seoul.

In 2011, the focus was on portfolio theory and practice and other investment methodology emphasizing the theory. A lot of this material is in a survey paper Ziemba (2015) in a Wiley book edited by Constantine Zopoundus, a Hania, Crete professor, and the great papers including a number of mine are in the two volume handbook of the *Fundamentals of Financial Decision Making* which I edited with Leonard MacLean in 2013. Len and I have finished a book of problems, taking some from the Ziemba and Vickson (1975, 2006) *Stochastic Optimization Models in Finance* and adding new ones based on the papers, introductions and commentary in the 2013 volumes.

Given strong interest in Kelly investing, it was nice to give the 2013 Hallsworth Lectures at the University of Manchester Social

Studies/Economics Department. My host Igor Evstigneev organized a mathematical conference emphasizing game theory and had me speak as well. I heard a talk by one of his PhD students Mikhail Zhitlukhin, whose thesis on stopping rule problems was joint University of Manchester with Igor and the Russian Stecklov Institute with Alexander Shirayaev. I immediately observed that this had great applications to exits from bubble type markets. Later we wrote three papers. One was on when to sell Apple Computer stock in 2012 when it was flying upward, gaining points day by day. The model exited at 680 with the ultimate high not much over 700. Later Apple traded down to the 380 area and has rebounded to well over 900 equivalent after a 7 to 1 split, an increased dividend and a stock buy-back program. The famed investor Carl Ichan has championed Apple stock since the 2013 bottom. As I have argued, they have always had a very low price earnings ratio, with a sequence of innovative products with high demand, high profit margins and very loyal customers including my family. Ichan views APPL in June 2015 as the next Netflix a stock he made $2 billion on. By jawboning the Apple board, he had some influence in boosting the dividend and stock buy back program and the increased price of the stock which he and I argue is still cheap given the huge cash hoard of close to $200 billion. The PE once cash is taken out is currently about 10 versus 18 for the S&P500 and much higher for many stocks.

I am very interested in predictions of how to exit these bubble-like markets. It is not easy to get these correct. In 2000, the internet index fell 17% in one day and then preceded to reach new highs later. My BSEYD model predicted that the S&P500 would fall in that period. The related index for the Nasdaq 100 that Soros shorted too early and lost a reputed $5 billion, was exited by the model Mikhail and his thesis advisor Albert Shiryaev built that we were applying. The second paper dealt with circa 1990 Japan and we studied the golf course membership market which had a market cap larger than the Australian stock market of A$250 billion. That was a much bigger bubble than the Nikkei and Topix stock exchanges and the model was very good at providing exit strategies. Professor Shiryaev, who was the top student of the legendary probability theorist A N Kolmogorov, invited me to speak at a conference in Moscow in the summer of 2013. So I got to see first hand all sorts of papers on optimal stopping rules. Moscow is expensive and has top sights and very good restaurants. We returned to St Petersburg to revisit the Hermitage and other museums and sights. As in our 1992 visit, we searched out the famed Parzyryk carpet. It was still hard to find but well worth the effort, see page 31 for a discussion.

Our third paper is in a special issue on bubbles and crashes in the journal *Quantitative Finance Letters* with editors Leonard MacLean, Sebastien Lleo and me. In this issue, I had five short papers. One with racing colleague John Swetye on using the late Marty Sweig's forecasting methods based on Fed movements and momentum. Another paper, discussed in Chapter 27, was on stock market crashes you cannot really predict but can deal with. Sebastien and I wrote two papers on the BSEYD model. Finally, the paper with Mikhail applies the model to the 1929 and 1997 as well as other crashes. We are summarizing all this in a book on stock market crashes which is in press now with World Scientific for a low $35 paperback price for terrific material. Mikhail and Sebastien Lleo worked with me on that and we added some Yale research about how many crashes are there and how many do investors expect — in short a lot more. We concentrate on predictions and what to do and I discuss big events like Brexit, the Trump election, the French election and the recent Trump-Comey-Kushner bad scenario which is on going regarding possible Russian interference in US politics. I was pleased that alpha z gained on all of them — Trump nearly USD400k and french election USD554K that night in my four futures accounts.

Visiting China Again

In December 2015, I helped Professor Heping Pan organize the IV International Conference on Intelligent Finance held in Chongqing.

Chongqing is one of about 10 major centers in China that are growing rapidly. To get there I flew from Vancouver to Hong Kong on Cathay Pacific a rather good airline which takes 13 hours going and about 11 returning followed by a 2 hour flight on China Airlines to the city which is up toward Tibet. Chongqing is vast with the area measuring one and a half hours drive in a fast car in a mountainous area filled with sky scrappers and 33 million people. Large portions of it are open spaces and then there is a big cluster of buildings. The main downtown and the old city is extremely congested. The colorful shopping district of the old town is so filled with so many people that you can hardly move. There are thousands and thousands people moving around, many with interesting characteristics. Some are trying to sell things. Chongqing is called fog city as it is usually overcast. With thousands of cars moving all the time there is smog. It was never really clear but I was able to breathe ok.

The day before the conference Peter Liao, Trade Commissioner (education, S & T, innovation and life sciences), Consulate General of Canada,

At the Teahouse with Jianu Lin

With Trade Commissioner Peter Liao

arranged to take me around Chongqing. We toured the downtown and had a very nice lunch and then visited the Three Gorges Museum. The area of the Three Gorges and the damming of the hydro power is so vast it would take 3 days to see it all. More than one million people were moved by the damming. Peter is a great host and representative for joint Canada–China business relations.

The conference was held in the Chinese Academy of Sciences Headquarters and we stayed in a nearby five star hotel which was about an hour away from the city center. The hotel was fine and had nice rooms and the internet and my phone worked reasonably well and I was able to keep up with my trading. Somehow with my schedule, being able to watch the markets through the night works out. There are three night traders in Chicago who split the night shift and I am very chatty with them. It continues to be a strong year for my accounts especially the ones I trade on the phone.

The food was very limited as not many people were staying at the hotel so they did not stock much food in the restaurants. The main restaurant was a Korean barbecue and there was also a Chinese restaurant but other than noddles and rice it was hard to get any food. The food at the conference was not much better as it was cafeteria style. I was so hoping for Peking duck or similar but I got along ok. In China there are always a whole host of people to help serve you. They mean well and it is helpful even though it is not part of my US–Canadian culture.

Professor Pan organized the previous three conferences in Melbourne (2004), Chengdu (2007) and Beijing (2009). I was involved in the Chengdu conference and went to another conference in Beijing in this period. For the

Professor Pan

2015 conference, I helped organize some talks and gave my own presentation on predictable and non-predictable stock market crashes. Also, to introduce the conference, Professor Pan had me present the welcoming remarks of Nobel laureate Harry Markowitz.

Harry Markowitz's Opening Remarks

Harry Markowitz Company
August 28, 2015

Dear Professor Pan,

I regret that I cannot attend your important conference on Intelligent Investing. Permit me to summarize the gist of the remarks I would make if I were with you. I understand that the principal concern of you and your speakers is new results. But there may be one or more among you who can write in Chinese or to be translated into Chinese important lessons for the typical Chinese investor. Please teach that it is foolish to view the stock market as a get-rich-quick opportunity. In the first instance (in an IPO) the function of the stock market is to facilitate Adam Smiths "Invisible Hand" that moves resources toward where they are most productive. In the present instance it serves to move capital from those who wish to save to those with investment opportunities. The after-market adds liquidity to the market, so investors with different needs or views can exchange claims against firms.

The investor should invest wisely. This entails diversification, of course. It also means selecting a risk-return opportunity for the investors portfolio-as-a-whole that the investor will stick with through the inevitable declines in the market that will occur. The chief mistake of the small investor is that he or she buys when the market goes up, assuming the market will go up further, and sells when the market goes down, assuming that the market will go down further. Thus the naive investor buys high and sells low. In contrast, the professionally managed portfolio rebalances at these times, profiting from the naive investors errors.

If the typical Chinese investor can be educated on these matters, it would benefit the investor, the Chinese economy and the world.

Best wishes,

Harry

The Chengdu Conference I prefaced my remarks by relating the great ideas that changed fields often face resistance. For example, the paper describing the famous Black–Scholes option pricing model was published in 1973 in the *Journal of Political Economy* only after Professors Merton Miller and Gene Fama pushed to have it published after it had been rejected by four other journals. In the end it transformed the industry of options which is now in the trillions of dollars. The formulas provide fair pricing of contracts. While the assumptions are strict and not really valid in most cases, the pricing is accurate enough to be useful most of the time. Similarly, Harry Markowitz, also at the University of Chicago, went on a dark path as well, developing his diversification, risk and return ideas. At that time, Economics Nobel laureate Milton Friedman did not consider his work to be economics. Even after Markowitz won the Nobel Prize in 1990, Friedman did not change his views. Yet, Markowitz's ideas caught on and changed, for the better, the way people invest. Despite the fact that more sophisticated investment technology exists, the majority of quantitative portfolio selection uses mean-variance techniques. In the handouts for the conference there was a Markowitz paper with Van Dijk discussing his methods reprinted from the 2006 *Handbook of Asset Liability Management* which I edited with Stavros Zenios of the University of Cyprus and the University of Pennsylvania Wharton School, who is in the photo with frequent co-author, Leonard MacLean, of Dalhousie University. Also included was a paper of mine with extensions of models with Markowitz type ideas such viewing risk as losing money rather than variance. These models are discussed in other chapters in this book. The photo shows Markowitz's collected works volume published by World Scientific. Among other things, Harry's collected works has much discussion on the historical development of portfolio theory and its applications from 1600 to 2010, its publication date. See also MacLean, Thorp and Ziemba (2010, 2011) and MacLean and Ziemba (2013). We plan a portfolio theory and practice handbook and intend to extend this to more recent contributions. Originally that was supposed to be a collection of my papers but many are in MacLean and Ziemba (2013) so we are expanding the coverage into other new and reprinted papers.

In my talk at the conference, I discussed stock market crash models of the type where you can predict the declines and other models where it is hard to predict the decline *ex ante* but *ex post* it is well understood. This talk was similar to those I gave in Dubai at the financial modeling conference and London to 7 City Fitch.

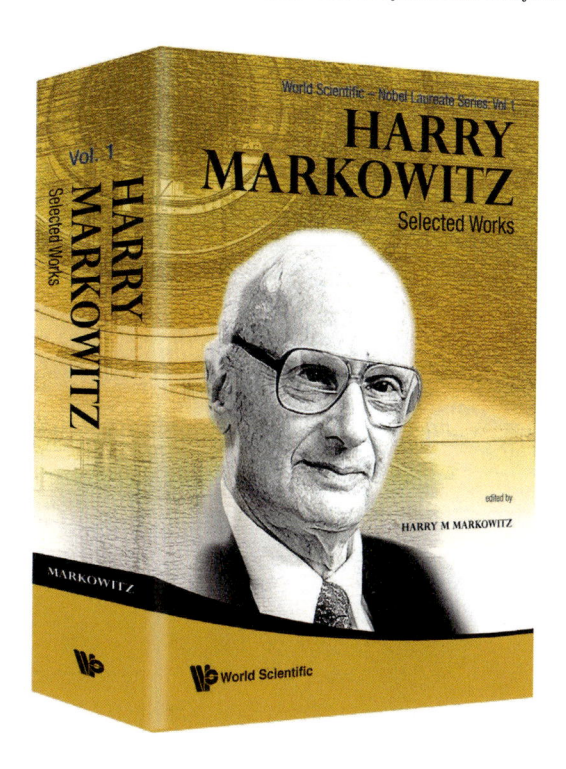

Two of my colleagues were able to come and speak: Leonard MacLean of Dalhousie University spoke about our joint paper concerned with developing a model so that the investor's wealth will stay above a specified path while, at the same time, maximizing the growth rate. The paper, published in *Quantitative Finance*, makes the Kelly criterion more acceptable by toning down the risk behavior and developing a method to create a smooth wealth path. Mikhail Zhitlukhin spoke on a method to modify the Sharpe ratio to make it consistent with stochastic dominance as the current standard Sharpe ratio has the property that one return can dominate another return yet have a lower Sharpe ratio. In my own modification,[10] I focus on not losing money and that procedure allows me to evaluate the greatest investors. My talk went over well and I had a long time to speak so I could cover everything I wanted to.

There were a number of very strong Chinese speakers, many with US connections. Some of the talks were in English and other was a mixture of English subtitles and Chinese words. In general the talks were very good quality.

After the conference, Professor Pan arranged for me and Professor Rodney Wolff of the University of Queensland specializing in mining economics to stay at the Sheraton and be hosted by a Chinese billionaire. Our generous host was one of three brothers who are mostly in the commercial paper business. We gave discussions of our trading strategies. There was a Chinese stock broker there who suggested a strategy based on volatility that has, according to the simulations and a small number of real trading results, produced smooth returns with only small drawdowns. The idea is to create synthetic puts and calls for each stock using cash, interest rates and stock data. They must be synthetic as actual options are not traded. Then for each of the 2000+ stocks, create a strangle by adding the put to the call. Then one wins if the stock rises or falls sufficiently. This is where the volatility comes in. With so many stocks, it is diversified. It all works because the typical Chinese investor is talking very risky positions hoping for a big gain and this creates considerable volatility. I presented my AlphaZ strategy and results to the billionaire and his colleagues. The meetings were successful and it looks like we might do something starting with Chinese equities and then later in the US.

The Australian professor discussed how one might took at an overall plan to build a large mining operation in southern Australia. The costs are extremely high, including $1 million to drill 100 meters and you must drill much deeper than that and have many holes to determine what is actually

Our generous host at his company

under the ground. There are many considerations including which types of minerals to look for including precious minerals like gold and silver or less valuable minerals. There also are many constraints including environmental consideration, scheduling people, how to handle discounting of asset returns in the future and building infrastructure as the area is remote and one must fly there. It seemed to me this is an asset-liability problem like the models I discussed earlier in the book.

We then, after a long drive through the city, had a fabulous lunch with beautiful food and a top Bordeaux wine at a very attractive sunken garden restaurant. A real treat, especially since our food on the previous few days was not so great. Later, we had a similar dinner. The move to the hotel was pleasant and the Australian professor and I had a nice Peking duck dinner there. My Chinese hosts were very kind taking care of us visitors. The trip back to Vancouver was long but smooth. Our next trip was the San Francisco AFA/AEA conference after a few days in the Napa Valley wine district.

Spring 2016 Trips

In April, Sandra and Rachel went on a tour organized for Oxford–Cambridge Alumni to Central Asia. It was Sandra's way of doing what I had been able to do in 1982 while we were visiting professors at UCLA. They had a marvelous time with a well organized trip to Uzbekistan and Turkmenistan visiting Tashkent, Samakand, Bukhara, Shakhrisabz and other places like my earlier trip. Much has changed but the old sites are as glorious as ever.

I went to Kentucky to visit the horses then flew to Chicago and London where I had a few days before our Hali organized tour of Georgia and Armenia. Georgia was a big success with wonderful people, good sites and good food emphasizing vegetables. While they have had a rough past from the Soviet occupation, the people are forward looking and treat their guest well. Armenia was an interesting visit as well but much rougher. It started with much rougher, bumpy roads through the mountains. The 1915 massacre is paramount in their national story and colors their behavior. Earlier, much of eastern Turkey was Armenia which as part of the Ottoman Empire stretched Kayseri east including Van, Erzurum and Erzinican. So the pile rugs and kilims from these areas, like the Kars kilim I bought, are thought to have been woven by Armenians. The guides have their stories down pat with everything Armenia. The Armenian museums have excellent older pile rugs as well as some nice embroideries I had thought were from the Greek Islands. Well, maybe they were but perhaps they were made by Armenians. Our tour guide, Vladimir Grigoryan, and the Hali staff, editor Ben Evans and assistant Rachel Meek were very helpful as was our Georgian guide Tatiana. As expected, the group had a lot of interesting people, some with a vast knowledge of carpets and kilims and embroideries and some novices. The border with Turkey is closed as is the border with Azerbijan, but you can, as we did, fly to Istanbul from Yerevan. The flight on AtlasGlobal Airlines was smooth and we had a nice 5 day visit to Istanbul, where the food, especially the 15th century Ottoman Sultan recipes, was marvelous. We bought our usual selection of hand woven towels, tiles and Armenian embroideries.

Notes

[1] It was a big mistake not to buy one. Throughout my career at UBC the big payoff has been housing — most people who did it well made more on their homes than their salaries. But it was difficult to be ahead of the game for us. That's a story my wife prefers me not to tell!

[2] Prékopa helped organize a strong group with much Eastern European talent like Peter Hammer and Andrzej Ruszczynski at Rutgers. He divided his time between Rutgers and Budapest and taught and continued research till he was 85 and was planning a Budapest retirement before he died in 2016.

[3] In june 2017 I organized memorial handbook volumes in my world scientific series of Handbooks in Financial Economics for Marida Bertocchi (edited by Rita D'Eclessia, Stavros Zenios, and me) and Jitka Dupacova (edited by Milos Kopa, Roger Wets and me) with pictures and most important research papers, In addition Dave Morton who postdoced in Prague is doing some special journal issues to honor our two late colleagues.

[4] A list of my presentations appears on the web at www.williamtziemba.com.

[5] Koenigsberg was promoted to professor in 1982 and taught there until his retirement in 1991. He died in 2009.

[6] Perhaps the issue became that universities were changing. In my 1972 class in statistics at Stanford the issue was calculators and the limited number of electrical outlets for running them during the exam. At the midterm, there were only four students with calculators, but by the final the whole class had them.

[7] In 1974, at the time of the first International Conference on Stochastic Programming, I visited Michael Dempster who was a young Professor with a position at Balliol College. He had three large rooms which was quite an office. Cambridge has similar huge quarters. In 1998, on a Dempster arranged visit to the Judge Institute, I visited Steve Satchell who had the multiple room

quarters at Trinity College once occupied by the philosopher Bertrand Russell and earlier by Isaac Newton. Steve was from Australia and wanted to do his PhD with the best econometrician in the world. That was J D Sargan, who had 23 papers in *Econometrica*. I had studied some of them, such as "Three Stage Least Squares", in my PhD class at Berkeley taught by Dale Jorgenson. Steve wrote to Sargan who wrote back come on over to the London School of Economics. Steve was Sargan's last PhD student and is now a major player in financial modeling and econometric studies of financial markets.

In 1974, Dempster had a 10th century door at his house and when you walked in there was a giant six foot on a side head of the statue of Liberty. These were castoffs from the Oxford archeology department. Again, showing what a great university it has been and continues to be.

[8] Benk's paper is in Gassmann and Ziemba (2012).

[9] See Chapter 35 of *Investing in the Modern Age* where I discuss the economies and financial markets of India, Russia, China and Cyprus. There I show the price–earnings graph of Korea versus similar countries during various threats of war with North Korea.

[10] Ziemba (2008) and Gergaud and Ziemba (2012) discussed earlier in this book.

Epilog

Great professors are those who want to remain students all their lives which I have tried to do.

My Berkeley PhD thesis advisor Willard I Zangwill kindly sent three provocative queries for me to consider which I respond to below. Bill was in the Navy then joined the PhD program in operations research at Stanford graduating in 1965. His class at Stanford, like Berkeley at that time, was loaded with top talent which you do not see now. At Berkeley, the PhD students included Ellis Johnson, Dick van Slyke, Richard Cottle, Roger Wets, Katta Murty, Romesh Saigal, Richard Grinold (of Barra and Barclays fame), Steve Jacobson, Steve Bradley, Saul Gass, Steve Stigler, Daniel Heyman and others. At Stanford, there were Arthur Geoffrion, Curtis Eaves, Steven Lippmann, Bruce Miller, Donald Morrison, Robert Hayes, Gene Durbin, William Pierskalla and others.

Bill Zangwill did his PhD supervised by Arthur F (Pete) Veinott, Jr, arguably the most talented of the best operations research group with Berkeley a close second once George Dantzig moved from Berkeley to Stanford. Bill's PhD was on inventory control model and nonlinear and network programming. He was the first of Pete's 28 PhD students. Wow that's a lot! Well, my dear friend Tom Cover, Stanford statistics and information theorist, had 64! Veinott used to say he was my grandfather as Zangwill supervised me as his only PhD student. Zangwill came to the Berkeley business school as an acting associate professor. That meant that instead of waiting 5–7 years to build a strong research record, he had to achieve tenure in 2 years. My colleague, Howard Kunreuther from our days at the Institute for Defense Analysis where we met in 1965 while I was working on the US supersonic aircraft project there and other times and now distinguished researcher in low probability earthquakes and other rare natural events at the University of Pennsylvania Wharton School put it this way to me: who is this guy Zangwill with six papers, all on different topics in six consecutive issues of the journal *Management Science*? So he easily got tenure.

I recall fondly the pleasant competition between Bill and Olvi Mangasarian who were both writing nonlinear programming books that are still valuable now. I was taking Oliv's three-term course in the OR department where he was a visitor on leave from a Bay area oil company research department. His approach was thorough building the theory carefully step by step. Zangwill was totally different and got to the bottom line fast after a brief motivation. I have used both books in lectures and research throughout the years. In Arkansas consulting for a very nice family who were super friendly they are doing well I suppose in their futures trading but did not know basic things like dosage, the favorite longshot bias or the Kuhn-Tucker Theorem. Well they know the first two now and for the third I suggested the Mangasarian, Zangwill and Luenberger-Ye books on nonlinear programming.

Later, Zangwill decided to move to a non-academic position. Then after a few years he wanted to return to academia and went to an operations research meeting and asked what's the most difficult field then I will go into that and be the best. Well he did that in fixed points which are the numerical solution of equations like $g(x) = x$. He got a tenured position at the University of Chicago business school. Later, his interests moved to Japanese production and productivity and he visited while Sandra, Rachel and I were in Japan. Later he and his wife Julia were helpful to Rachel when she went to the University of Chicago for her BA in Medieval History.

Bill has continued active in many areas of decision making and hopefully will tell his own complete story. Now to his provocative queries.

1. *What are the lessons of your life? Are there any insights you want to pass on to future generations? Is there a philosophy you think important that your life revealed? Does life have meaning? what does life mean to you?*

One is that you don't have to be the most technically talented to succeed. What's important is an inner confidence and a driven, healthy attitude, always striving to do good work and to work well with others. I have some parallels with Tom Brady, the five time superbowl winning quarterback of the New England Patriots. When the draft occurred he expected to be a top pick but he was the sixth quarterback chosen, number 199. His NFL competitor Peyton Manning was first, as was John Elway. When he arrived in New England he was the fourth string starting quarterback. Somehow he got to be the backup to starting quarterback Drew Bledsoe. Then luck helped him — he got his break when Drew got an injury. The rest is history — a quick set of three superbowls in 4 years and there is no way he would fail, be replaced or lose his confidence. At 39, having had yet another banner year in 2017 when he won his 5th Super Bowl more than any other quarterback to play until he is 45, he says he wants to play another 10 years. The point here is that talent sometimes is latent and needs to be discovered or can be wasted. Once discovered, it needs to be given a chance to prove itself and, therefore, academics and others need to be patient about achieving the success that is within them.

In my case luck was Keizo Nagatani asking me if I wanted to go to Japan as the first Yamaichi Visiting Professor of Finance, 1988–1989. The UBC straight finance, strict efficient market theorists would not let me teach their courses. Why give our good courses to an outsider, especially one who is top notch and a threat to show us up, and comes at it from another background, seemed to be their thinking. While I was departmental editor for finance for the top journal *Management Science*, with 10 outstanding finance associate editors, and publishing a lot in major finance and management science journals, there was a difference in approach. So there was a cultural difference against someone with a management science background.

To carve out my own territory, I manufactured courses in the management science division and this worked for many years. In the end, when I took early retirement, Major factors were health, the management science division going totally to production, then called supply chain management, the low salary, the finance hostility — and no matter what great things I did nobody cared. I had no group there where I was a good fit, despite being very active in the academic and professional world in many areas.

The Japan experience was tremendous and I was accepted in finance. It was a different and more open culture and they wanted to benefit from US research and experiences. There it was practical with theory to be used if actually useful. Stan Hamilton, a UBC dean, explained the finance group as "they live in their own world."

Learning which I always treasure was great and I enjoyed the teaching where I could do option pricing, futures and anomalies with a nice group of students from the university and from Yamaichi who came up to Tsukuba and were in my two study groups. Even better were my long talks with Mr Okada, one of the YRI managers. We chatted for hours about anomalies and the US and Japanese financial markets, etc. He in Japanese me in English with a translator. This experience led to three books, many research papers and led into the consulting job with Frank Russell.

In the famous 1960 *Magnificent Seven* movie which was based on the earlier 1954 Japanese movie *The Seven Samurai* directed by the great Akira Kurosawa, James Coburn's character was puzzling to some. If he is the best with a knife and a gun who does he compute with? Answer: himself. I think in my case it is my inner drive to understand things that drives my research. I like to write thing up and writing comes easy for me, in research articles, books, etc. I do like credit and enjoy statements like Zangwill's:

Your autobiography is very impressive. You have accomplished an enormous number of things. You get more done in a year than most people I know do in a decade. Part of this is your team since your wife and daughter have been highly involved and contributed immensely, and the love is apparent.

I have been greatly pleased how our daughter Rachel has flourished from her BA at Chicago, Masters in Political Economy at Oxford (her experience in Japan when she was 9 years old, including going to a local Japanese school which allowed join the class as she learned Japanese doing music and science first and work independently on the BC correspondence curriculum when she was lost in the Japanese. This taught her independent work habits and openness to new experience and this continued with a solid high school education at Crofton) to become a star working with Nouriel Roubini. She is much more in the media than I. When my paper with Sebastien Lleo on the Buffett stock market crash measure was written up in Bloomberg, it was my first citation there, Rachel had 14. A couple of times I have been at the same conference with her where I was the keynote speaker. People come up to me and look at my badge and say you must be Rachel's father. I was pleased to write the two books we did together based on our Wilmott columns. My wife, Sandra has helped in huge ways — always supportive, producing papers, presentations and books and standing up to me when she knows a better way to do it. Her brilliance I see all the time. One signal is her telling me something only to see it in Paul Krugman's column a couple days later. She actually learned real economics and applies it and there are very few who do that. One thing that's helped a lot is very good co-authors. I am usually the idea person and suggest papers and together we get them done. I have always had such co-authors as listed in this book. Now in my mid-70s I work closely with Len MacLean, Mikhail Zhitlukhin, Sebastien Lleo, Woo Chang Kim, Ed Thorp and am planning two books on horse breeding with a 6 foot one swiss miss, Lee Imboden who is super sharp. Her BA thesis is PhD level on nice surveys of yearling pinhooking etc prices. We plan a 1700s to now breeding book plus a monograph on why are some stallions 300k others 30k.

2. *Relative to the writing, many stories are a series of challenges. The protagonist has to overcome some challenges. The excitement is in the question, can he overcome this difficulty? Most novels are a series of challenges, perhaps one or two major challenges and then smaller ones along the way.*

A big challenge has been the UBC academic finance discrimination. Partly is was a different culture and a grab of very scarce resources and partly a difference of personality styles. Throughout, I have stuck to my research on anomalies, portfolio management, asset-liability management and became famous in these fields to lead to superior investment performance in these fields. I have always had good relationships with top people outside UBC and outside the UBC business school. The greats have always respected my work. These include six Nobels I had as advisors to the North Holland and World Scientific finance handbook series.

There is a serious catch 22. Academic finance is reluctant to accept new directions always with some sort of excuse. Then there is their club with editors accepting papers of their friends and students. Then these journals define the jobs, high pay and certain recognition. Still there is a real world out there and I have focused on doing good work in the papers and books. Publishing in the top journals has always been difficult, but I have had a strong record with many diverse and creative contributions. My books have made it to academic finance elite and many papers are widely cited. But other useful papers with results helpful to many investors are considered too useful so must appear in applied journals. Some of them have ideas worth millions or billions.

Perhaps I am too sensitive and expect too much. I know that some outlets have a 6% acceptance rate so the competition for space is very intense and a small proportion available for outsiders. In my case, I even referee for these journals and some of my papers have been published there. And essentially all the papers get published eventually. Anyway I did have a hand in a number of important research areas helping to define the fields. Creating new fields is the most fun and rewarding

3. *Is there any organization to your life? Can you specific various periods in it? For instance, for one period X was dominant. Then the next period was shaped by Y.*

Like Zangwill I always had many interests. That was a strength and a weakness. The academic world likes narrow people. I had several phases. Initially I was a theorist in stochastic and nonlinear programming. That led to lots of publications in top journals and quick promotions to associate and full professor. During this 8 year period, I started applying my technical training to finance via portfolio theory and later asset-liability management. It was much easier then. For example, in the 1970s, I submitted five papers to the Journal of Financial and Quantitative Analysis (JFQA) — all five were published. But now it is much tougher as the fields are more developed and the rewards are much greater for publication.

Going to Japan in 1988 was a major turning point and helped a lot and pushed me to more major applied as opposed to theoretical activities in financial applications and money management. I was already trading futures and writing portfolio theory papers but the Japan experience moved me to a higher level. That led into my 9 years as the main consultant to the Frank Russell Research Department and with many spinoff benefits. At UBC, there was no credit or recognition, even though I could have helped them a lot. I replaced an old friend and Economics Nobel laureate Bill Sharpe of Stanford University. Bill was doing mean-variance and CAPM research and I worked on stochastic programming asset-liability models, calendar and fundamental anomalies and Asian financial markets. Bill went on to found Financial Engines, a very successful financial advisory firm.

Editing and writing a series of books for publishers such as North Holland and World Scientific as well as the Cambridge University Press, SIAM-Mathematical Programming Society and Wiley, along with many papers in many journals has been very rewarding with much more to do. My books are available from the publishers or from amazon.com. Here is a collection of their covers. My website www.williamtziemba.com lists these and has links to those available from amazon.com.

Epilog

Love of writing books

Bibliography

Ariel, R. A. (1987). A monthly effect in stock returns. *Journal of Financial Economics 18*, 161–174.

Associated Press (2016). Greece, creditors in new bid to strike deal in reform talks, April 8.

Aumann, R. J. (2005). War and peace, Nobel Lecture, December 8, 2005 and {ETH}, Zurich Lecture, November 20, 2006.

Balas, E. (2000). *Will to Freedom: Journey through Fascism and Communism*. Syracuse University Press.

Balzli, B. (2010). How Goldman Sachs helped Greece to mask its true debt. Spiegel online.

Benter, W. (2008). Computer based horse race handicapping and wagering systems: a report. In D. B. Hausch, V. S. Y. Lo and W. T. Ziemba (Eds.), Efficiency of Racetrack Betting Markets, pp. 183–198. Singapore: World Scientific.

Bertocchi, M., S. L. Schwartz and W. T. Ziemba (Eds.) (2010). Optimizing the aging, retirement and pensions dilemma. New York: Wiley, February, 411 pages; 2nd edition 2015.

Bicksler, J. and E. Thorp (1973). The capital growth model: An empirical investigation. *Journal of Financial and Quantitative Analysis 8*(2), 273–287.

Bloomberg.com (2009). Bernard Madoff gets 150 years in jail for epic fraud. online, June 29.

Bodie, Z., A. Kane, and A. Marcus (2005, 2010). *Investments* (9th edn.).

Bolton, R. and R. Chapman (1986). Searching for positive returns at the track: a multinormal logit model for handicapping horse races. *Management Science 32*, 1040–1059.

Busche, K. (1994). Efficient market results in an Asian setting. In D. B. Hausch and W. T. Ziemba (Eds.), *Effciency of Racetrack Betting Markets*, pp. 615–616. New York: Academic Press.

Cameron, R. R. (2010). The determinants of thoroughbred stud fees, Economics Honors Thesis, Emory University.

Cariño, D. R., D. H. Myers, and W. T. Ziemba (1998). Concepts, technical issues, and uses of the Russell–Yasuda Kasai financial planning model. *Operations Research 46*(4), 450–462.

Cariño, D. R., and W. T. Ziemba (1998). Formulation of the Russell–Yasuda Kasai financial planning model. *Operations Research* 46(4), 433–449.

Chopra, V. and W. Ziemba (1993). The effect of errors in mean and co-variance estimates on optimal portfolio choice. *Journal of Portfolio Management*, 6–11.

Chrysoloras, N., A. Galanopoulos, and R. Buergin (2016). Greece points finger at IMF as Schaeuble sees deal in weeks. *Bloomberg* online, April 11.

Citigroup (2008). Form 8-k, Current Report. Filing Date November 26, http://pdf.oecdatabase.com/367/0000950123-08-016585.pdf.

Clark, R. and W. T. Ziemba, W.T. (1988). Playing the turn-of-the-year effect with index futures, *Operations Research XXXV*, 799–813.

Clark, R. and W. T. Ziemba (1987). Playing the turn-of-the-year effect with index futures playing the turn-of-the-year effect with index futures. *Operations Research XXXV*, 799–813.

Culp, C. and M. H. Miller (1995a). Hedging in the theory of corporate finance: A reply to our critics. *Journal of Applied Corporate Finance* 8(1), 121–128.

Culp, C. and M. H. Miller (1995b). Metallgesellschaft and the economics of synthetic storage. *Journal of Applied Corporate Finance* 7(4), 62–76.

Davis, A. (2006). How grant bets on natural gas sank brash hedge-fund trader. *Wall Street Journal*, 9/19/06.

Davis, A., H. Sender, and G. Zuckerman (2006). What went wrong at Amaranth. *Wall Street Journal*, September 20.

Davis, A., G. Zuckerman, and H. Sender (2007). Hedge fund hardball: amid Amaranth's crisis, other players profited. *Wall Street Journal*, January 20.

Dimson, E. (1988). *Stock Market Anomalies*. Cambridge, UK: Cambridge University Press.

Douglass, J., O. Yu and W. T. Ziemba (2004). Stock ownership decisions in defined contribution pension plans. *The Journal of Portfolio Management*, 30(4), 92–100.

Dunbar, N. (2000). *Inventing Money: The Story of Long-Term Capital Management and the Legends Behind It*. New York: John Wiley and Sons.

Durden, T. (2010), 21st Sequential Weekly Outflow Confirms Investors Refuse To Be Suckered Into Stock Market, Yahoo Finance, September 29.

Edelman, D. C. and N. R. O'Brian (2004). Tote arbitrage and lock opportunities in racetrack betting. *European Journal of Finance*, 10, 370–378.

Edwards F. R. and M. S. Canter (1995 spring). The collapse of metallgesellschaft: unhedgeable risk, poor hedging strategy or just bad luck? *Journal of Applied Corporate Finance* 8(1), 86–105.

Edwards, F. R. (1999). Hedge funds and the collapse of long-term capital management. *Journal of Economic Perspectives* 13(2), 189–210.

Englund, P. (2008). *Nobel Lectures: Economic Sciences, 2001–2005*. Singapore: World Scientific.

Epstein, L. G. and S. E. Zin (1989). Substitution, risk aversion and the temporal behavior of consumption and asset returns: A theoretical framework. *Econometrica* 57(4), 937–969.

Epstein, R. A. (1977). *Theory of gambling and statistical logic* (2nd edition, 2012). New York: Academic Press.

Evans-Pritchard, A. (2015) Secret plan for instant switch to drachma creates political storm, Vancouver Sun, July 27.

Fama, E. F. and F. French (1992). The cross-section of expected stock returns. *The Journal of Finance 47*(2), 427–466.

Figlewiski, S. (1994). How to lose money in derivatives. *The Journal of Derivatives 2*(2), 75–82.

Flood, R. and R. Hodrick (1990). On testing for speculative bubbles. *Journal of Economics Perspectives 4*(2), 85–101.

French, K. R. and J. M. Poterba (1991). Were Japanese stock prices too high? *Journal of Financial Economics 29*(2), 337–363.

Friedman, M. and L. J. Savage (1948). The utility analysis of choices involving risk. *Journal of Political Economy 56*(4), 279–304.

Fung, W., D. A. Hsieh, N. Y. Naink, and T. Ramadorai (2006). Hedge funds: Performance, risk and capital formation. Technical report, London Business School.

Gassmann, H. I. and W. T. Ziemba (Eds.) (2012). *Stochastic Programming Applications in Finance, Energy and Production*. Singapore: World Scientific.

Gergaud, O. and W. T. Ziemba (2012). Great investors: their methods, results and evaluation. *Journal of Portfolio Management 28*(4), 128–147.

Geyer, A. and W. T. Ziemba (2008). The Innovest Austrian pension fund planning model InnoALM. *Operations Research 56*(4), 797–810.

Glaeser, E., J. Gottlieb, and K. Tobio (2012). Housing booms and city centers. *American Economic Review, Papers and Proceedings 102*(3), 1–10.

Glaeser, E. L., J. Gyourko, and A. Saiz (2008). Housing supply and housing bubbles. Harvard University, Technical Report, July 16.

Gramm, M. and W. T. Ziemba (2008). The dosage breeding theory for horseracing predictions. In D. B. Hausch and W.T. Ziemba (Eds.) *Handbook of Sports and Lottery Markets*, in *Handbooks in Finance*, pp. 307–332, Amsterdam: Holland.

Greenberg, M. R. and L. A. Cunningham (2013). *The AIG Story*. New York: John Wiley and Sons.

Guarascio, F., J. Strupczewski, and G. Bacznska (2016). EU Commssioner says progress with Greece but reform talks ongoing. *Reuters* online, April 10.

Harville, D. A. (1973). Assigning probabilities to the outcomes of multi-entry competitions. *Journal of the American Statistical Association 68*, 312–316.

Haigh, J. (2008). The statistics of lotteries. In D. B. Hausch and W. T. Ziemba (Eds.), *Handbook of Sports and Lottery Markets*, in Chapter 23, In *Handbooks in Finance*, pp. 481–502. San Diego: Elsevier.

Hausch, D. B. and W. T. Ziemba (1984). *Beat the Racetrack*, Harcourt, Brace and Jovanovich; *Dr Z's Beat the Racetrack*, revised and expanded 2nd edition, William Morrow, 1987.

Hausch, D. B. and W. T. Ziemba (1985). Transactions costs, extent of inefficiencies, entries and multiple wagers in a racetrack betting model. *Management Science 31*(4), 381–394.

Hausch, D. B. and W. T. Ziemba (1990a). Arbitrage strategies for cross-track betting on major horse races. *Journal of Business 63*, 61–78.

Hausch, D. B. and W. T. Ziemba (1990b). Locks at the racetrack. *Interfaces 20*(3), 41–48.

Hausch, D. B. and W. T. Ziemba (Eds.) (2008). *Handbook of Sports and Lottery Markets*, North Holland Handbooks in Finance Series. Amsterdam: North Holland.

Hausch, D. B., V. Lo, and W. T. Ziemba (Eds.) (1994). *Efficiency of Racetrack Betting Markets*. New York: Academic Press.

Hausch, D. B., V. Lo, and W. T. Ziemba (Eds.) (2008). *Efficiency of Racetrack Betting Markets* (2nd edn.). Singapore: World Scientific.

Hausch, D. G., W. T. Ziemba and M. E. Rubinstein (1981). Efficiency of the Market for Racetrack Betting. *Management Science XXVII*, 1435–1452.

Henery, R. J. (2008). Permutation probabilities as models for horse races. In D. B. Hausch, V. S. Y. Lo and W. T. Ziemba (Eds.), *Efficiency of Racetrack Betting Markets*, pp. 219–224. Singapore: World Scientific.

Hensel, C. R. and W. T. Ziemba (1995). U.S. small and large capitalized stocks, bonds and cash returns during democratic and republican administrations, 1928–1993. *Financial Analysts Journal 51*(2), March/April, 61–69.

Hensel, C. R. and W. T. Ziemba (1995). The January Barometer: Swiss, European and Global Results, *Finanzmarket and Portfolio Management 9*(2), 187–196.

Hensel, C. R. and W. T. Ziemba (2000). Anticipation in the January effect in the U.S. futures markets. In D. B. Keim and W. T. Ziemba (Eds.), *Security Market Imperfections in World Wide Equity Markets*, pp. 179–202. Cambridge, UK: Cambridge University Press.

Hirsch, J. A. and Y. Hirsch (2016). *Stock Trader's Almanac.* Hoboken, New Jersey: Wiley.

Hope, Albanese and Viswanatha (2015). *The Wall Street Journal.*

Housel, M. (2012). The fed has a huge influence on the stock market, web.

Jackson, D. and P. Waldron (2003). 4 Parimutuel place betting in Great Britain and Ireland. In L. V. Williams (Ed.), *The Economics of Gambling*, pp. 18–29. Psychology Press.

Jagannathan, R., A. Malakhor and D. Navikor (2006). Do hot hands persist among hedge funds managers? An empirical evaluation. Technical report, Northwestern University.

Janacek, K. (1998). Optimal Growth in Gambling and Investing. M.Sc. Thesis, Charles University, Prague.

Jorion, P. (1997). *Value-at-Risk: The New Benchmark for Controlling Market Risk.* Burr Ridge, IL: Irwin Professional.

Jorion, P. (2000). Risk management lessons from Long-Term Capital Management. *European Financial Management 6*, 277–300.

Jorion, P. (2007). *Value-at-Risk: The New Benchmark for Controlling Market Risk*, 3rd Ed. Burr Ridge, IL: Irwin Professional.

Keim, D. B. and W. T. Ziemba (Eds.), (2000). *Security Market Imperfections in World Wide Equity Markets*. Cambridge, UK: Cambridge University Press.

Kindleberger, C. P. and R. Aliber (2011). *Manias, Panics and Crises, A History of Financial Crise*, New York: MacMillian.

Koivu, M., T. Pennanen, and W. T. Ziemba (2005). Cointegration analysis of the Fed model. *Finance Research Letters 2*, 248–259.

Kouwenberg, R. and W. T. Ziemba (2007). Incentives and risk taking in hedge funds. *Journal of Banking and Finance 31*(11), 3291–3310.

Kusy, M. I., and W. T. Ziemba (1986). A bank asset and liability management model. *Operations Research 34*(3), 356–376.

Kutler, J. (2015). A year after *flash boys*, high frequency trading lives on. *Institutional Investor*.

Lewis, M. (2014). *Flash Boys*. New York: Norton.

Lintner, J. (1965). The valuation of risk assets and the selection of risky investment in stock portfolios and capital budgets. *The Review of Economics and Statistics 47*(1), 13–37.

Litzenberger, R. and D. Modest (2009). Crisis and Non-Crisis Risk in Financial Markets: A Unified Approach to Risk Management, http://papers.ssrn.com/sol3/papers.cfm?abstract_id=1160273. Last accessed on 14 December 2016.

Lleo, S. (2010). Risk Management: A Review. In *Risk Management: Foundations for a Changing Financial World*, Research Foundation of CFA Institute John Wiley & Sons, pp. 73–112.

Lleo, S. and W. T. Ziemba (2012). Stock market crashes in 2007–2009: Were we able to predict them? *Quantitative Finance 12*(8), 1161–1187.

Lleo, S. and W. T. Ziemba (2014). How to lose money in financial markets: Examples from the recent financial crisis, *Alternative Investment Analyst Review*, *3*(3), 22–35.

Lleo, S. and W. T. Ziemba (2015a). Can Warren Buffet also Predict Market Downturns, Mimea.

Lleo, S. and W. T. Ziemba (2015b). Some historical perspectives on the Bond-stock yield model for crash prediction around the world, *International Journal of Forecasting*, 31, 399–425.

Lleo, S. and W. T. Ziemba (2015c). Utility functions for Rogue Investors, Mimeo, University of Reims.

Lleo, S. and W. T. Ziemba (2016a). The BSEYD crash prediction model: the basic idea and early applications. *Quantitative Finance Letters 4*(1), 19–25.

Lleo, S. and W. T. Ziemba (2016b). The BSEYD crash prediction model: additional applications and other models for stock market crash prediction. *Quantitative Finance Letters 4*(1), 26–34.

Lleo, S. and W. T. Ziemba (2016c). The Swiss black swan bad scenario: Is Switzerland another casualty of the Eurozone crisis? In J. Guerard (Ed.), *Portfolio Construction, Measurement and Efficiency: Essays in Honor of Jack Treynor*, pp. 389–420. New York: Springer.

Lleo, S. and W. T. Ziemba (2017). Does the bond stock earnings yield difference model predict equity market corrections better than high PE models? *Journal of Financial Markets, Instruments and Institutions*, in press.

Lo, V. and J. Bacon-Shone (2008). Approximating the ordering probabilities of multi-entry competitions by a simple method. In D. B. Hausch and W. T. Ziemba (Eds.), *Handbook of Sports and Lottery Markets*. Amsterdam: North Holland.

Lopes, L. L. (1987). Between hope and fear: The psychology of risk. volume 20 of *Advances in Experimental Social Psychology*, pp. 255–295. Academic Press.

Lucca, D. and E. Moench (2011). The pre-fomc announcement drift. Federal Reserve Bank of New York, Number 512.

Lucca, D. and E. Moench (2015). The pre-fomc announcement drift. *Journal of Finance* 70(1), 329–71.

Luenberger, D. (1998). *Investment Science*. New York: Oxford University Press.

Mack, B. (2015). The fast track to the futures: Technological innovation, market microstructure, market participants and the regulation of high frequency trading. In A. Mallarias and W. T. Ziemba (Eds.), *Handbook of Futures*, pp. 247–285. Singapore: World Scientific.

MacLean, L. C. and W. T. Ziemba (1999). Growth Versus Security Tradeoffs in Dynamic Investment Analysis, In R. J.-B. Wets and W. T. Ziemba (Eds.), *Stochastic Programming: State of the Art 1998, Annals of Operations Research 85*, 193–226, ResearchBalzer Science Publishers.

MacLean, L. C. and W. T. Ziemba (2006). Capital growth theory and practice. In S. A. Zenios and W. T. Ziemba (Eds.), *Handbook of Asset and Liability Modeling, Volume 1: Theory and Methodology*, in Handbooks in Finance, pp. 429–473. Amsterdam: North Holland.

MacLean, L. C. and W. T. Ziemba (Eds.) (2013). *Handbook of the Fundamentals of Financial Decision Making*. Singapore: World Scientific.

MacLean, L. C., E. O. Thorp and W. T. Ziemba (Eds.) (2010). *The Kelly Capital Growth Criterion: Theory and Practice* (paperback, 2011). Singapore: World Scientific.

MacLean, L. C., E. O. Thorp and W. T. Ziemba (2010). Good and bad Kelly properties. In L. C. MacLean, E. O. Thorp and W. T. Ziemba (Eds.), *The Kelly Capital Growth Criterion: Theory and Practice*, pp. 563–572. Singapore: World Scientific.

MacLean, L., W. T. Ziemba, and G. Blazenko (1992). Growth versus security in dynamic investment analysis. *Management Science, Special Issue on Financial Modelling* 38, 1562–1585.

MacLean, L., W. T. Ziemba and Y. Li (2005). Time to Wealth Goals in Capital Accumulation and the Optimal Trade-off of Growth versus Security. *Quantitative Finance* 5(4), 343–357.

MacLean, L.C., E. O. Thorp, Y. Zhao and W. T. Ziemba (2011). How does the Fortune's Formula-Kelly capital growth model perform? *Journal of Portfolio Management* 37(4), 96–111.

Malliaris, A. and W. T. Ziemba (2015). *Handbook of Futures Markets*. Singapore: World Scientific.

Manchester Trading, LLC (2006). MARHedge, San Francisco.

Mauldin, J. (2015). When China stopped acting Chinese. Thoughts from the front line, July 31.

Mello, A. S. and J. E. Parsons (1995, Spring). Maturity structure of a hedge matters: Lessons from the metallgesellschaft debacle. *Journal of Applied Corporate Finance 8*(1), 106–121.

Miller, B. and C. K. Ho (2008). Merrill Lynch cut to "sell" at Goldman on write-downs. Bloomberg.com, September 14.

Miller, M. H. and D. J. Ross (1997, Summer). The orange county bankruptcy and its aftermath: Some new evidence. *Journal of Derivatives 4*(4), 51–60.

Moffatt, C. (2006). Wallstreet week "hall of fame" inductee introduced to the George investment program class. Available at: thegeorgeinvestmentsview

Moffitt, S. D. and W. T. Ziemba (2016a). Can the Rich Get Richer? (Spoiler Alert: Yes!). *Social Science Research Network Working Paper Series*, Sept. 2016. URL http://ssrn.com/abstract=2848010.

Moffitt, S. D. and W. T. Ziemba (2016b). Does it pay to buy the pot in the Canadian 6/49 and other lotteries, Mimeo.

Mossin, J. (1966). Equilibrium in a capital asset market. *Econometrica 34*(4), 768–783.

Perold, A. F. (1998). Long-Term Capital Management. Harvard Business School Case N9-200.

Rachev, Z. (Ed.) (2003). *Handbook of Heavy Tailed Distributions in Finance.* Handbooks in Finance Series, Singapore: North Holland.

Reinhart, C. M. and K. S. Rogoff (2011). *This Time is Different: Eight Centuries of Financial Folly*, Princeton, New Jersey: Princeton University Press.

Rendon, J. and W. T. Ziemba (2007). Is the January effect still alive in the futures markets? *Financial Markets and Portfolio Management 21*(3), 381–396.

Ritter, J. (1988). The buying and selling behavior of individual investors at the turn of the year. *The Journal of Finance 43*(3), 701–717.

Ritter, J. R. (1996). How I helped make Fischer Black wealthier. *Financial Management 25*(4), 104–107.

Roberts, H. V. (1959). Stock market patterns and financial analysis: Methodological suggestions. *Journal of Finance 14*(1), 1–10.

Roberts, H. V. (1967). Statistical versus clinical prediction of the stock market. Technical Report, University of Chicago.

Rosenberg, B., K. Reid, and R. Lanstein (1985). Persuasive evidence of market inefficiency. *The Journal of Portfolio Management 11*(3), 9–16.

Roubini, N. (2011). *Crisis economics: A crash course in the future of finance.* New York: Penguin Books.

Rozoff, M. and Kinney (1976). Capital market seasonality: The case of stock returns. *Journal of Financial Economics 3*, 379–402.

Schwartz, E. S. and M. Moon (2000). Pricing of internet companies. *Financial Analysts Journal* (May–June): 62–73.

Sears, S. M. (2010). Flash crash is a game changer. The Striking Price, May 8.

Sharpe, W. F. (1964). Capital asset prices — a theory of market equilibrium under conditions of risks. *The Journal of Finance 19*(3), 425–442.

Shaw, J., E. O. Thorp and W. T. Ziemba (1995). Convergence to Efficiency of the Nikkei Put warrant Market of 1989–90. *Applied Mathematical Finance* 2, 243–271.

Shefrin, H. (2009). Ending the management illusion: preventing another financial crisis. *Ivey Business Journal*, 73(1), 7.

Shefrin, H. M. and M. Statman (1984). Explaining investor preference for cash dividends. *Journal of Financial Economics* 13(2), 253–282.

Shiryaev, A. N., M. V. Zhitlukhin and W. T. Ziemba (2014). When to sell Apple and the NASDAQ? Trading bubbles with a stochastic disorder model. *Journal of Portfolio Management* 40(2), 54–63.

Shiryaev, A. N., M. V. Zhitlukhin, and W. T. Ziemba (2015). Land and Stock Bubbles, Crashes, Entry and Exit Strategies in Japan Circa 1990 and in 2013. *Quantitative Finance* 15(9), 1449–1469.

Sjostrom, Jr, W. K. (2009). The AIG bailout. *Washington and Lee Law Review* 66(3), http://ssrn.com/abstract=1346552.

Stern, H. (1994). Estimating the probabilities of the outcomes of a horse race: alternative to the Harville formula. In D. B. Hausch, V. S. Y. Lo and W. T. Ziemba (Eds.) (1994, 2008), *Efficiency of Race Track Betting Markets*, pp. 225–235. Singapore: World Scientific.

Stiglitz, J. E. (Ed.) (1990). Symposium on Bubbles. The *Journal of Economic Perspectives* 4(2), 13–18.

Stiglitz, J. E. (2015). Greece, the sacrificial lamb. *International New York Times*. Available at: http://nyti.ms/1Mr3jcv, July 25.

Stone, D. and W. T. Ziemba (1993). Land and Stock Prices in Japan. *The Journal of Economic Perspectives* 7(3), 149–165.

Stutzer, M. (1998). Unpublished mimeo on the Kelly criterion properties, University of Iowa.

Stutzer, M. (2000). A portfolio performance index. *Financial Analysts Journal* 56(3), 52–61.

Stutzer, M. (2003). Portfolio choice with endogenous utility: a large deviations approach. *Journal of Econometrics*, 116, 365–386.

Stutzer, M. (2004). Asset allocation without unobservable parameters. *Financial Analysts Journal* 60(5), 38–51.

Stutzer, M. (2009). On growth optimality versus security against underperformance. In MacLean, Thorp and Ziemba (Eds.), The Kelly Capital Growth Investment Criterion: Theory and Practice. Singapore: World Scientific.

Tagaris, K. (2016). Greek PM says IMF insists on wrong polities in Greece. *Reuters*, April 10.

Thaler, R. H. and W. T. Ziemba (1988). Anomalies: Parimutuel Betting Markets: Racetracks and Lotteries. *The Journal of Economic Perspectives* 2(2), 161–174.

Thorp, E. O. (1997). The Kelly criterion in blackjack, sports betting and the stock market. mimeo, paper presented at the 10th international conference on gambling and risk taking, Montreal, June 1997, http://www.bjmath.com/bjmath/thorp/paper.ht

Thorp, E. O. (2006). The Kelly criterion in blackjack, sports betting and the stock market. In S. A. Zenios and W. T. Ziemba (Eds.), *Handbook of asset and liability management*, in Handbooks in Finance, pp. 385–428. Amsterdam: North Holland.

Thorp, E. O. (2009). My encounters with Madoff's scheme and other swindles. *Wilmott*.

Till, H. (2006). Comments on the Amaranth case: early lessons from the debacle. Technical report, EDHEC.

Tompkins, R. G., W. T. Ziemba and S. H. Hodges (2008). The favorite-longshot bias in S&P500 futures options: the return to bets and the cost of insurance. In D.B. Hausch and W.T. Ziemba (Eds.), *Handbook of Sports and Lottery Markets*, in Handbooks in Finance, pp. 161–180. Amsterdam: North Holland.

US Attorney for the Southern District of New York (2009, March 10). Bernard L. Madoff charged in eleven-count criminal information.

Vincent, A. (2007). China's stocks tumble. *BNP Paribas*, March 2.

Wallace, S. W. and W. T. Ziemba (Eds.) (2005). *Applications of Stochastic Programming*, SIAM — Mathematical Programming Society Series on Optimization, Philadelphia.

Walker, I. (2008). How to design a lottery. In D. B. Hausch and W. T. Ziemba (Eds.), *Handbook of Sports and Lottery Markets*, Chapter 22, in *Handbooks in Finance*, pp. 459–479. San Diego: Elsevier.

Wigmore, B. A. (1985). Greenwood Publishing Group.

Wilson, D. (2015). Buffett gauge's caution signal for u.s. stocks disputed in study. *Bloomberg Business* online, July 16.

Zadeh, F. (1998). My Life and Travels with the Father of Fuzzy Logic. New Mexico: TSI Press.

Zenios, S. A. and W. T. Ziemba (Eds.) (2006). *Handbook of Asset and Liability Modeling: Volume 1: Theory and Methodology*. Amsterdam: North Holland.

Zenios, S. A. and W. T. Ziemba (Eds.) (2007). *Handbook of Asset and Liability Modeling: Volume 2: Applicatons and Case Studies*. Amsterdam: North Holland.

Ziegler, A. and W. T. Ziemba (2015). Returns from investing in S&P500 futures options, 1985–2010. In A. G. Mallarias and W. T. Ziemba (Eds.), *Handbook of Futures Markets*, pp. 643–688. Singapore: World Scientific.

Ziemba, R. E. S. and W. T. Ziemba (2007). Scenarios for Risk Management and Global Investment Strategies. Wiley, November, in UK and January 2008 in US.

Ziemba, R. E. S. and W. T. Ziemba (2013). *Investing in the Modern Age*. Singapore: World Scientific.

Ziemba, W. T., A. Akatay and S. L. Schwartz (1979). *Turkish Flat Weaves*. London: Scorpion and Vancouver, Canada: Yoruk Carpets and Kilims.

Ziemba, W. T., S. L. Brumelle, A. Gautier, and S. L. Schwartz (1986). *Dr. Z's 6/49 Lotto Guidebook*. Dr. Z Investments, San Luis Obispo and Vancouver.

Ziemba, W. T. and D. B. Hausch (1986). *Betting at the Racetrack*. Dr Z Investments, Los Angeles.

Ziemba, W. T. and D. B. Hausch (1987). *Dr Z's Beat the Racetrack*. New York: William Morrow.

Ziemba, W. T., S. Lleo and M. Zhitlukhin (2017). *Stock Market Crashes: Predictable and Unpredictable and What to Do About Them*. Singapore: World Scientific.

Ziemba, W. T. and J. M. Mulvey (Eds.) (1998). *Worldwide Asset and Liability Modeling*. Cambridge, UK: Cambridge University Press.

Ziemba, W. T. and S. L. Schwartz (1991). *Invest Japan*. Chicago: Probus Publishing.

Ziemba, W. T. and S. L. Schwartz (1992). *Power Japan: How and why the Japanese economy works*. Chicago: Probus Publishing.

Ziemba, W. T. and R. G. Vickson (Eds.) (1975). *Stochastic Optimization Models in Finance*. San Diego: Academic Press.

Ziemba, W.T. and R. G. Vickson (Eds.) (2006). *Stochastic Optimization Models in Finance, Academic Press, 2nd edition*. Singapore: World Scientific.

Ziemba, W. T. (1988). Discussion of 'The Buying and Selling Behavior of Individual Investors at the Turn of the Year' by Jay R. Ritter. *Journal of Finance XLIII*, 717–719.

Ziemba, W. T. (1988). Synopsis of 'Playing the Turn of the Year Effect with Index Futures'. OR/MS Today XV: 37–38.

Ziemba, W. T. (1991a). Japanese security market regularities: Monthly, turn of the month and year, holiday and golden week effects. *Japan and the World Economy 3*, 119–146.

Ziemba, W. T. (1991b). The chicken or the egg: Land and stock prices in Japan. In W. T. Ziemba, W. Bailey and Y. Hameo (Eds.), *Japanese Financial Market Research*, pp. 45–68. New York: North Holland.

Ziemba, W. T. (1994a). Worldwide security market regularities. *European Journal of Operational Research 74*, 198–229.

Ziemba, W. T. (1994b). Investing in the turn-of-the-year effect in US futures markets. *Interfaces 24*(3), 46–61.

Ziemba, W. T. (1995). *Collection of Dr. Z Columns on Racing, Lotteries, Sports and Casino Gambling*. Dr. Z Investments, San Luis Obispo and Vancouver.

Ziemba, W. T. (2003). The Stochastic Programming Approach to Asset Liability and Wealth Management, AIMR Charlottesville, Virginia, December, 192 pages plus 72-page appendix.

Ziemba, W. T. (2007). The Russell Yasuda, InnoALM and related models for pensions, insurance companies and high net worth individuals. In S.A. Zenios and W.T. Ziemba (Eds.), *Handbook of Asset and Liability Modeling, Volume 2: Applications and Case Studies*, in Handbooks in Finance, pp. 861–962. Amsterdam: North Holland.

Ziemba, W. T. (2008). Efficiency of racetrack betting markets. In D.B. Hausch and W.T. Ziemba (Eds.), *Handbook of Sports and Lottery Markets*, in Handbooks in Finance, pp. 183–221. Amsterdam: North Holland.

Ziemba, W. T. (2012). Stochastic programming and optimization in horserace betting. In H. I. Gassman and W. T. Ziemba (Eds.), *Stochastic Programming*

Applications in Finance, Energy and Production, pp. 221–256. Singapore: World Scientific.

Ziemba, W. T. (2012a). *Calendar Anomalies and Arbitrage*. Singapore: World Scientific.

Ziemba, W. T. (2012b). Stochastic programming and optimization in horserace betting. In H. I. Gassman and W. T. Ziemba (Eds.), *Stochastic Programming Applications in Finance, Energy and Production*, pp. 221–256. Singapore: World Scientific.

Ziemba, W.T. (2013). The case for convex risk measures. *Quantitative Finance Letters 1*, 47–54.

Ziemba, W.T. (2013b) Portfolio optimization in A. Bell. In C. Brooks and M. Protopczuk (Eds.), *Handbook of Research Methods and Applications in Empirical Finance*, pp. 45–72. London: Edward Elgar.

Ziemba, W. T. (2015). Response to Paul A Samuelson letters and papers on the Kelly capital growth investment model. *Journal of Portfolio Management 42*(1), 153–167.

Ziemba, W. T. (2016). Understanding the Kelly Capital Growth Investment Strategies. *Alternative Investment Analyst Review, 5*(2), 49–54.

Ziemba, W. T. (Ed.) (2016b). *Great Investment Ideas*. Singapore: World Scientific.

Ziemba, W. T. (2017). *Exotic Betting at the Racetrack*. Singapore: World Scientific.

Index

15th–16th century Iznik tiles, 46
1981 Brazil-Germany-USA conference, 19
1984 Breeders Cup, 84
1984 Breeders Cup Classic $3 million, 78
2010 movie Secretariat, 86
4 standard deviation player, 62

A P Indy, 125, 339
Abdul Kadir Akatay, 42
Abu Dhabi, 52
Afghan carpets, 42
Afghan currency, 41
Afghanistan, 39
Ahmed Zayat, 53
AIG, 256
Ajanta and Ellora, 41
Alan Greenspan, 186
Alan King of IBM Research, 15
Alan Manne, ix
Alexandre Ziegler, 182
Alhambra, 58
Allied Irish Bank, 251
Alois Geyer, 197
Alpha Z Futures Fund LLC, 188
Alternative Investment Analyst Review, 13
Amaranth Advisors, 211, 228
amazon.com, 66
American Pharoah, 53
Amos Tversky, 209
An inability of speculators, 163
Andreas Papandreau, 29

Andy Lo, 201
Andy Rudd, 191
Angel Cordero, Jr., 117
Ankara, 38
Annals of Operations Research, 17
Annals of Statistics, 20
Anomalies and Arbitrage, 180
Anomalies Research at Frank Russell, 179
Antti Kanto of the University of Vassa, Finland, 89
Apple Computer, 138
Applications of Stochastic Programming, 196
applied stochastic programming and asset-liability management, 61
Arky Robbins, 42
Armenia, 49
Arrogate, 124
Art Frass, 3
Arthur (Pete) F. Veinott, ix
Arthur Geoffrion, 61
Arthur Goldberger, 29
Asian Financial crises, 220
assassination of John F Kennedy, 16
Aumann, 237
Average Mutual Funds, 204
aversion, 80
Axcom Trading Advisors, 205
Aya Sofya, 47
A N Kolmogorov, 149
a New Name, Dr Z, 61

BA in Medieval History, 138
Babe Ruth, 62
Bakti restaurant, 42
Baluchistan, 39
Bandi Amir, 42
Bank of New York, 247
bankroll, 121
Barings, 249
barometer, 180
Barr Rosenberg, 224
Bartlett McGuire, 2
basketball ±3 points is a tie, 62
Battle of the Quants in New York, 99
Bayakoa, 88
BC Lottery Commission, 61, 63
BC Lotto Director Guy Simonis, 63
Bear Stearns, 251, 260
Beat the Dealer, i, 108
Beat the Market, i
Beat the Racetrack, 83, 105, 189
beatable, 76
Beholder, 53
Bell Labs, 70
Belmont Stakes, 53
Beppie Weiss, 88
Bergamo, 38
Berkeley, 2, 41
Berkeley and Stanford were #1 and #2 ahead of #3 and #4 MIT and Cornell, 2
Berkshire Hathaway, 236
Bernie Sanders, 160
Bessarabian, 122
Bet, 120
Beth Nobel, 47
bets with a huge advantage, 67
Betting at the Racetrack, 45, 66, 83, 86, 103
Betting exchanges, 102
Betting System, 83
between the wall paper and the wall, 136
bias, 83
Bicksler and Thorp, 192

Bill Benter, ix
Bill Benter Letter, 165, 167
Bill Gross, 165
Bill Jewell, 17
Bill Niskanen, 3
Bill Sharpe, 33, 172
Bill Zangwill, ix
billionaires are very focused, 5
Bingo Games, 65
Black and Scholes, 34
Black Monday, 247
Blair Hull, ix, 165
Blind emotions versus reality, 163
Blue Mosque, 42
Bodie, Kane and Marcus, 202
Bokhara, 47
Bolton and Chapman, 126
bonds, 147
bonds and stocks compete for the money, 147
Booth School of Business, i
born, 134
Breeders' Cup, 4, 102, 105
Breeders' Cup Classic, 53, 120
Breeders' Cup day at Hollywood Park, 101
Brian Hunter, 210, 233
British Museum, 39, 72
broke her leg, 88
Bruce Fauman, 4, 101, 104
BS in Chemical Engineering, 12
Bubble investor Soros, 149
bubble trader George Soros, 148
Buffett's Berkshire Hathaway, 67
Bulbughoff carpets, 46
burials, 60
Burj Khalifa, 52
Burnham and Lambert, 247
Busche, 165
buy high, sell low, 135
buy Italy, sell Florence, 219
buy low, sell high, 135

Calendar Anomalies and Arbitrage, 98, 180, 189
California resident, 16

Cambridge University Press, 196
Canada, 73
Canadian, 41
Canadian criminal code, 63
Canadian speculators, 163
Canadian sports pool, 61, 65
Candy Ride, 84
Capital Growth Theory, 70
CAPM assumption is not needed, 82
Cappadocia, 32
carpets and kilims, 48
Cathryn Cootner, 49
Cato Institute, 3
cave in Deriyinku, 34
Center for Planning and Economic Research, 29
centimillionaires, 185
Chanaka Edirisinghe, 177
Chania, 30, 31
Charles Ying, 134
Chenery, 86
Chest Fund, 70
Chicago Quantitative Alliance, 99
Chiefs Crown, 105
Chinese slowdown, 98
Chopra and Ziemba, 80
Chris Hensel, 175, 180
circumstantial and statistical tests, 166
Citadel, 235
Citigroup, 257
Citron, 248
Claiming Stakes, 119
Clark Art Museum, 9
Class Leader, 335
Claude Shannon, 69, 70
co-authored lotto 6/49 book, 64
Commodity Corporation, 192
Condolezza Rice, 27
Connecticut, ix
consulting for the Canadian sports pool, 62
contango, 232
continuing Greek saga, 150
contract, 96
convex, 218

convex payoff structure, 66
convex risk measures, 17
convex shortfall penalties, 198
Cordoba, 57
Cornell and Stanford universities, 124
corporate policy to dump consultants, 176
correlations, 218
Cowles Commission, 19
crash model prediction project, 147
crashes, 133, 147
Crete, 31
cross track, 102
Culp and Miller, 242
C West Churchman, 36

Daily Racing Form, 114, 117
Daiwa Trading Scandal, 250
Dale Jorgensen, ix
Dan Rosen of Algorithmics, 25
Daniel Bernoulli, 69
Daniel Kahneman, 209
Daniel Mc Fadden, 3
Daniel Siegelman, 123
Danube in flood, 30
David Blackwell, ix
David Booth, 197
David Brown, 47
David Lucca and Emanuel Moench, 186
David Luenberger, 26, 172
David Myers, 174
David Pyle, 85
David Tranah, 196
De Young Museum in San Francisco, 49
Delhi airport, 42
Democratic presidential terms, 95
Democratic presidents, 98
Dennis Dodds, 42
Dennis Kira, 25
dependent, 218
designing games based on hockey, baseball, basketball, 62
Dick Cottle of Stanford, 15
Different credit risk, 162

Different currency risk, 163
Do not over bet, it is too dangerous, 218, 222
Does it Pay to Buy the Pot, 64
Doha, 52
Dollar, 120
Donald B Hausch, x, 26, 101
Donald Keim, 99, 140
Donald Trump, 160
dosage index, 125
Douglass Wilde, ix
downside symmetric Sharpe ratio, 203
Downtown Tokyo land values, 161
Dr Jon Thompson, 46
Dr Z, 4
Dr Z system, 84, 103, 106
Drexel, Burnham and Lambert, 247
Dr Z keys data, 109
Dr Z's Beat the Racetrack, 86
DSSR, 203
DSSR is 26.4, 206
dual qualifier, 125
Dubai airport, 52

Early Days in Berkeley, 15
Eastern Turkey, 39
Easy Goer, 128
economics of wine conferences, 208
Edward O Thorp, ix, 101, 104
Edelman Practice of Management Science Competition, xv
Edmonton Oilers, 62
efficiency, 83
Efficiency of Racetrack Betting Markets, 83, 189
Efficient markets, 182
Egon Balas of Carnegie Mellon, 25
Egypt, 47
Egypt makes nice oriental rugs too, 407
Elena Tsvara, 45
Ellio, 109
Ellis Johnson, 17
Elston Howard, 112
Elywn Berlekamp, 205
end effects, 174

engineering dean, 10
Enron, 245
Ephesus, Turkey, 24
Epstein, 61
Erik Fleten, 25
Erwin Diewert, 4
Erzurum, 48
Eugene Fama, 34
European Working Group on Commodities and Financial Modeling, 52
Evaluating the Greatest Investors, 201
Exchanging currencies in St Petersburg, 219
Exotic Betting at the Racetrack, 83, 125
Expected Value Per Dollar Bet, 120
expected value to show was 2.62, 89

favorite-longshot bias, 83
FED Chairman Janet Yellen, 193
Federal government sued them, 63
Figlewski, 211
Finance Theory, 61
Financial Analysts Journal, 140, 180
Financial Disasters Since The 1980s, 244
Financial Planning Model, 171
Fisher Black, 96
Fleet Nashrullah Stakes, 118
flood, 30
Foofraw, 114
Ford Foundation, 77
Forgetting that high returns involve high risk, 214
fork in the road, 129
Form, 114
Fortnum and Mason, 57
Fortune magazine, 123
Fortune's Formula, 69, 70, 262
fractional Kelly wagering schemes, 76
Frank Fabozzi, 207
Franz Edelman, 174
French and Poterba, 164
fugu, 137

fund, 211, 218
futures anticipation, 97
Futures Fund LLC, 188

Gallant Man, 128
Gambling Times, 106
Gate Dancer, 117
Gene Fama, 183
Gene Woolsey, 26
General Assembly, 124
Genius, 182
geometric mean, 70
Georg Pflug of the University of Vienna, 25
George Brett, 62
George Dantzig, 17, 173
George Elford, 38
George Soros, 5, 70, 138
George Soros' Quantum Fund, 77
George W Bush, 41
Georgia and Armenia, 47
Georgia Tech, 10
Gerald Debreu, 3, 139
German mathematician, 64
Ghostzapper provider of the superfecta for WTZ, 332
Ghulame Rubbaniy, 52
Giants Causeway, 125
Gibraltar website lottery expert for Mansion, 66
GJ Investment Fund, 207
Glenn Anderson, 62
Global Economics, 136
Go for Wand, 88
Go for Wand broke her leg, 88
Gold Coast of Australia, 127
Goldman Sachs, 96, 202, 236
Gone West, 125
Good and Bad Properties of the Kelly Criterion, 76
Gordon Sick, 24
Gorgeous, 88
grade II Remsen Stakes, 340
Granada, 58
Great Investment Ideas, 59, 210
Great professors, 435

Gretzky that year had 196 points, 62
Gretzky was simply the great one, 62
Gulf visit, 57

half Kelly, 77
Hali, 46
Hali editor, Ben Evans, 51
Handbooks on Asset Liability Management, 196
handicappers, 114
Hans Foellmer, 17
Harness Races in Finland, 89
harness tracks in North America, 91
Harold McPike, 165, 261
Harry Markowitz, 81
Harry Zhang, 25
Harvard, 2
Harvard's Fogg museum, 46
Harville formulas, 165
Hatay, 50
Hausch, 126
Hausch and Ziemba, 102, 164
Hausch, Lo and Ziemba, 102
hedge fund, 211
Hensel and Ziemba, 97, 187
Herat, 33
Herman Chernoff, 73
Hillary Clinton, 160
Hirsch and Hirsch, 99
historic come back, 63
Hog wash, 183
Hollywood Park, 106, 108, 115
Hong Kong betting, 165
Honor Code, 53, 338
Honus Wagner, 62
Horand Gassmann, 26
Horse, 327
Horse Ownership Business, 327
How the Pros Wager, 69
How to Lose Money in Derivatives, 211
How to lose money in financial markets, 13
Hunt Brothers, 245
Hunter, 233

I am not a gambler, 106
I stopped trading this, 98
Iguazu Falls, 37
In baseball, a one run game was considered a tie, 62
In Ho Kim, 2
inadequate, 218
increase in book value, 202
Index arbitrage, 135
Index funds have grown and grown, 204
India and Afghanistan, 41
indicating, 117
InnoALM, 195
Insider Monkey, 210
Institute for Defense Analysis, 2
Interfaces, 174
Invention, 83
Invention of the Place and Show Betting System, 83
Invest Japan, 203
Investing in the Modern Age, 99
Investment Science, 176
Investors, 201
Iran and Afghanistan, 39
Ishi, 234
Is Learning Possible, 234
Isaac Newton Institute, 195
Isfahan, 39
Istanbul, 47
Istanbul, Georgia and Armenia, 59

Jaap Spronk, 52
Jack Mitten, 27
Jacob Marschak, 15
Jacobs and Levy, 140
James Simons, 205
Janecek, 81
January barometer, 180
January effect, 95
January returns have been high, 95
January turn of the year effect, 78
Japanese Financial Market Research, 145
Japanese manufacturing, 137

Japanese stock and land prices, 179
Jari Kurri, 62
Jeff Yass, 129
Jeopardy, 119
Jerry Kallberg, 26, 61
Joe Biden, 160
John Birge of the University of Chicago, 15
John Campbell, 181
John Cox, 202
John Gaines, 120
John Harsanyi, 3
John Kenneth Galbraith, 244
John Maynard Keynes, 70
John Merriwether, 210
John Neff's Windsor, 77
John Swetye, 87
Joseph Mayo, 12
Joseph Schumpeter, 244
Joseph Stiglitz, 179
Josephine Powell, 48
Journal of Economic Perspectives, 145, 179
Journal of Investing, 180
Journal of Portfolio Management, ii, 59, 180
JP Morgan, 255
Julian Robertson's Tiger, 77
Julian Shaw, 160

Kabul, 42
Kandahar was full of bandits, 41
Karl Shell, 34
Karl Storchmann, 208
Kats Sawaki, 26, 137
Kayseri, 31
Kazak, our second samoyed, 85
Keeneland select sale, 329
Keim and Ziemba, 99, 145
Keizo Nagatani, 133
Kelly betting, 77, 186
Kelly betting has essentially zero risk aversion, 80
Kelly betting system, 102
Kelly bettor has an optimal myopic policy, 78

Kelly criterion, 260
Kelly investing, 80
Kemal Mustafa Attaturk, 38
Kenneth Arrow, ix, 34
Kentucky Derby, 101
Kentucky Derby favorite Nyquist, 87
Keynes did not believe in market timing, 71
Keynes emphasized three principles of successful investments, 70
kilim as a door, 32
Kindleberger and Aliber, 244, 259
Kingdom of Denmark, 162
Kings College Cambridge's Chest Fund, 70
Kingston, 124
Kings College Cambridge, 70
Kneeland Racetrack, 53
Kontriner, 198
Konya, 38
Kouwenberg and Ziemba, 210
Kuşadasi, 32

LA Kings–Edmonton Oilers game, 63
Lady's Secret, 124
Laffit Pincay Jr, 87
Las Vegas, 64
Las Vegas Dirt Mile, 53
Las Vegas odds maker Michael (Roxy) Roxborough, 63
Lawrence Siegel, 202
Learning Possible, 234
led to a panic in the S&P500 futures, 221
legendary owner Penny Chenery, 86
Lehman Brothers, 254
Leland–Rubinstein, 134
Leonard C MacLean, x
Leonard MacLean, 25
Leonardo di Vinci, 1
Lev Pontryagin, 36
Liam's Map, 53
linear programming, 2
Liquid Assets, 208
Litzenberger and Modest, 260
Lleo and Ziemba, 187

Lloyds of London, 67
Lo and Ziemba, 126
log is the most risky utility function, 69
London, 67
London school of economics, 130
long a small cap futures, 96
long term capital management, 211
LOR was born, 134
Los Angeles, 115
lottery design, 72
lottery design errors, 72
Lotto, 66
lotto design, 65
Lotto games are in principle, 76
Lotto Guidebook, Ziemba, 67
Lotto players are different than horse players, 66
LSE Systemic Risk Research Centre, 59
LTCM disaster, 198
Lucien Polak, 36
Lutfu Bayhan, 43

MacLean, Thorp and Ziemba, 80
MacLean, Ziemba and, 81
Madoff fraud, 257
Malibu Moon a son of AP Indy, 330
Management Science, 23, 83, 126, 172
Manchester Trading, 225
Manhattan Fund, 234
many visits to Finland, 90
Marcus, 12
Mark Kritzman, 196
Mark Messier, 62
Mark Rubinstein, 85, 122
market for win was fairly priced, 83
Markets are beatable, 183
Markus Rudolf, 25
Martin Kusy, 26, 61
Marty Zweig, 134
Mashad, 39
Massachusetts, 1
Matador fund, 227
matrices, 218

Matti Koivu, 90
MBA program at Berkeley, 2
mean reversion, 160
Mello and Parsons, 242
Memhet Çetinkaya, 48
Mercin, 39
Merrill Lynch, 252
Merton Miller, 148
Met Mile, 53
Mettallgeselschaft, 241
Mettallgeselschaft Refining and Marketing Inc (1993), 241
Mevlana Rumi, 38
Mexican Default, 246
Mexican Tequilla Crisis, 249
MF Global, 258
Michael Spence, 36
Michelangelo, 58
Middle East Technical University, 38
Midnight Sun Empirical Finance conference, 90
Mikhail Zhitlukhin, 138
Miller and Ross, 248
mispriced place and show opportunities, 101
MIT mainframe, 109
MIT's Chemical Engineering Department, 2
Mitt Romney, 160
model prediction project, 147
Moffitt and Ziemba, 64, 131
Mohammed El Erian, 150
monasteries, 30
Montclair State University, 131
Monti Pashi, 258
most unpopular numbers in Canada, 73
Motley Fool, 187
Mugatea, 120
multiple correlation matrices, 198
My father, 8
My mother, Mary Moser, 8
Mykono, 38

Nashrullah, 118
Nationwide Life Insurance, 181
NATO conference, 33
natural gas market, 231
Nemrut Dag, 52
never pays to bet more than the Kelly strategy, 77
Nick Leeson, 249
Niederhoffer's Hedge Fund Disaster, 220
Nikkei Put Warrant Market, 160
Nikkei stock average, 161
Nobel prize winner George Stigler, 19
nonlinear programming algorithm, 102
Northeast Anatolian prayer kilim, 32
Northern Dancer, 104
Northwestern, 21
Norwegian Computing Centre, 3
Nouriel Roubini, ix
nouveau riche, 75
NSA Puts and Calls, 162
NSERC, 22
NY Yankees, mid-1950s, 130

odds on favorite offers, 113
Office rents in Tokyo, 161
Oil and Natural Gas Market, 230
Omalos, 30
Operations Research, 23, 172, 175, 199
Optimal Kelly, 120
optimal Kelly bet, 79, 120
optimally, 86
Orange County, 247
Orestes in Vancouver, 58
Oriental Carpet Conferences, 48
Orley Ashenfelter, 208
Other fast Belmont's, 128
Ottoman empire, 48
Over betting, 223
over betting Yields Frequent Trading Disasters, 223
Ownership Business, 327
Oxford Cambridge Club, 59

Paine Webber, 163
painted monasteries, 30
Pan Am, 2
panned for gold, 30
panic in the S&P500 futures, 221
Paris Pike, 120
Parzyryk carpet, 149
Pat Day, 79
Paul A Samuelson's critique, 80
Paul Coffey, 62
Paul Cootner, 49
Paul Samuelson, 34, 138, 184
Pazyryk, 60
Pazyryk burials, 60
Pazyryk carpet, 46
Pebble Beach golf courses, 139
Pec Pass, 31
penalties, 218
Penn State University, 1
Persepolis the city of Cyrus the Great, 39
Perspectives, 179
Peter Hammer's, 17
Peter Kall, 36
Peter Muller, 98
Petroleo Brasileiro, 70
PhD sequence on nonlinear programming and portfolio theory, 61
Philip Wolfe, 17, 33
phone calls with Benter, 166
Pierre Trudeau, 63
Place, 83
Plitvici Lakes, 37
Point Given, 128
pool, 65
Portfolio insurance, 134
Postscript by Ziemba, 120
Potash Corporation of Saskatchewan, 70
Poterba and Summers, 160
Power Japan, 145
prayer carpet, 31
presidential election effect, 181
Princess Rooney, 113
Professor Sidney Schoeffler, ix

Qatar, 55
Quants on Wall Street, 135
Quantum Funds, 218
Quebec, 63
Quebec game was skill not luck, 63
quinella, 91

race, 78
Rachel in Samarkand, 47
Rachel Ziemba, ix
Racing Form, 117
Rand Corporation, 2
Raphael Sangre, 126
Raymond Vickson, 34
Real correlations are scenario dependent, 218
rebate, 102
rebate shops, 102
rebates from betting shops, 86
Refining and Marketing Inc (1993), 241
Reinhart and Rogoff, 259
Renaissance Medallion, 193, 205, 207, 237
Rendon and Ziemba, 99
restaurant, 42
Richard Bellman, 36
Richard Dennis, 262
Richard Feynmann, 36
Richard Grinold, 19, 174
Richard Roll, 95
Richard Zeckhauser, 224
Risen Star, 124
Risk premium, 182
risky, 67
Rita D'Eclessia, 52
Ritter, 96
Robert Hall, 29
Robert Oliver, 17
Roberts, 92
robot jockey, 55
Rochester, 21
Roger Wets, ix, 173
Rogoff, 259
Rogue Trader, 229, 233
Romania, 30

Romesh Saigel, 15
Ron Dettero, 93
Ron Howard, 26
Ron Wolff, 17
Rose Kurpiel, 13
Ross Clark, 96
Roubini, 136, 259
Roubini Global Economics, 136, 188
Roy Radner, 3, 29
Rozoff and Kinney, 99
RPI presidents outrageous salary, 177
Ruffian, 89
Russell Yasuda Kasai, 23
Rustem Pasha, 45
Ruth was also high in batting, 62

Salomon I puts, 162
Samaria Gorge, 29
Samuelson letters, 59
Sandra Schwartz, ix, 4
Saratoga Spa, 84
Scandal, 250
scenario, 218
scenario dependent correlation matrices, 218
Scorpion, 42
Scott Peterson, 135
Scythian culture, 60
Seabiscuit, 119
Seabiscuit Claiming Stakes, 119
Seattle Slew, 116
Secretariat, 53, 87, 104, 333
Secretariat's heart, 334
See Grinold's paper, 177
Seljuk, 46
Seljuk carpets, 47
Sell in May and Go Away, 181
sell the tails, 67
Seville, 57
Shah Abbas hotel in Isfahan, 40
Shah's jewels, 39
Shakhrisabz, 47
Sham broke the record in the 1973 Kentucky Derby and Preakness Stakes but was beaten, 87
Shanti, a pure white Samayoed., 41

Shared Belief, 84
Sharpe ratio, 77
Sharpe ratio of 1.68, 206
Sheik Mohammed, 53
Sheikh Faisal Private Museum, 55
sherries, 57
Shelby Brumelle, 66
Shelby Brumelle, another professor in my UBC department, helped me make the model I used, 63
sherry center Jerez, 57
sherry winery, 58
Shiraz, 39
Shiryaev, Zhitlukhin and Ziemba, 138
shops, 102
short the large cap S&P500 index futures, 96
Show, 83
SIAM-MPS, xvi
Siberian Ice Maiden, 60
Siemens Austria InnoALM, 23
Silver Charm the best, Captain Bodget second and Free House third. So that was my picks announced, 125
Singapore, 18
Singapore pools, 63, 65
sire, 124
Sistine Chapel, 72
Slew O'Gold, 78, 116
small cap effect, 95
small cap stocks, 95
so long has he has an advantage, 117
Société Generalé, 211, 242
Sports Illustrated, 106
sports lotto games, 63
SSHRC, 22
Stakes, 118
Stanford, 21, 41
Stanley Druckenmiller lost $5 billion shorting the Nasdaq, 148
Stavros Zenios and Leonard MacLean, 197
Steve Bradley, 19
Steve Roman, 124, 125
Steve Stigler, 19

stochastic optimization, 188
stochastic programming, 18
Stochastic Programming and the Theory of Economic Policy, 15
Stochastic Programming Approach to Asset-Liability and Wealth Management, 196
stocks and bonds compete for the money, 147
stock market, 133
stock market anomalies, 133
stock market crashes, 133
Stock Trader's Almanac, 99
stocks, 95
Stone and Ziemba, 145, 164
Storm, 125
Stutzer, 81
Subprime Loan, 243
Sumitomo, 250
Sun Empirical Finance conference, 90
Susquehanna, 129
Suvrajeet Sen, 15
Suzani from Uzbekistan, 50
swindles and Ponzi schemes, 208
Swiss franc over time, 59
Syndicates exist, 102
syndicates in the US, 102
system, 120

Tabriz, 39
Taj Mahal, 41
take large risky bets with a huge advantage, 67
Tau Beta Pi, 12
Tblisi, 48
teaching at UBC, 61
teaching Simons, 205
teaching visit to UCLA, 95
Ted Williams, 7, 62
Teheran, 47
Testing the Dr Z System with Ed Thorp, 101
the 19 most unpopular numbers, 76
the 1997 blowout, 226
The 2 Minute Sprint, 123
The 6/49, 67

The Breeders' Cup Distaff, 1990, 88
The Classic, 116
The Distaff, 112
the Dr Z name came out of this, 63
The Juvenile, 103
The Juvenile Fillies, 104
the preface to Beat the Racetrack, 122
the Racetrack, 86
the racetrack is a financial market, 105
the recipe for disaster, 244
The Russell–Yasuda Kasai Financial Planning Model, 171
The Sprint, 107
The Turf, 114
the typical mutual fund does not beat the market, 204
They say it cannot happen again, 226
Thomas Jefferson, 72
Thomas Sargent, 29
Thomas Schneeweis, 207
Thorp, 81, 122
Thorsten Hens, 37
three divided cities, 29
Three to Beat the Breeders' Cup, 103
Till, 233
Tokyo stock exchange, 131
top broodmare, 124
top broodmare sire, 124
Top camels are worth US$1–10 million, 55
Topkapi Palace Museum in Istanbul, 47, 58
Toronto, 25
Totals, 120
tower above all other players in his era, 62
tracks in North America, 91
Trading, 225
Trainer Ron McAnally, 89
Trend Following in the Bahamas, 261
Trento, 13
Troy, 38
Turkey, 31
Turkish and Islamic Arts Museum, 47

Turkish Flat Weaves, 42
Turkish kilims, 32
Turkmenistan, 47
two reasons, 98
Ty Cobb, 62

UBS, 257
UCLA Anderson School, i
UMass Hedge Fund Database, 207
UMASS *Alternative Investment Analyst Review*, 80
undefeated champion, 119
Understanding the Kelly Capital Growth Investment Strategy, 13
University of British Columbia, 21
University of Chicago, i
University of Connecticut, 1
University of Massachusetts, ix
University of Texas, 1
University of Tsukuba, 189
University of Zurich, 36
Unpopular Lotto Numbers, 71
unpopular number six-tuples, 74
Unpopular numbers, 65
US Savings and Loan Crisis, 246
using, 69
Utility Functions of Hedge Fund Traders, 237
Uzbekistan, 47, 49

valley of Bamiyan, 42
Vancouver bingo parlors, 66
VaR type systems are inadequate, 218
Varig in Miami, 42
Various Efficient/Inefficient Market Camps, 182
Vas ist dat, 95
Venice, 24
Victor Niederhoffer, 210
Vinci, 1
visiting professors at UCLA, 61, 63
volatility exploded, 221

Wall Street Week with Louis Rukeyser, 134

Walter Denny, 47
Walter Oi, 2
Warren Buffett, ix, 70, 184
We stated the the following trading rule, 97
weak form violation of the efficient market hypothesis, 101
weak market efficiency, 83
Weiss, 88
Werner Roemish, 17
What is Japan Doing Right, 133
white pigeons of Mazari, 43
Whitney Stakes, 53
Wild Again, 79
Wild Week, October 20–25, 1997, 220
William T Ziemba, xv
Wilmott columns, ix
Wilt Chamberlain in the 4th grade, 173
Winners and Losers, 238
Winning the Battle of the Quants Trading Competition, 188
Wolfgang Herold and Konrad Kontriner, 198
World's Greatest Hedge Fund, 205

Yale University, 19
Yamaichi Research Institute, 189
Yamaichi went bankrupt, 222
Yamichi Research Institute's, 136
yellow Uzbek suzani, 50
yoghurt in Bulgaria, 30
Yogi Berra, 131
Yoruk carpets and kilims, 43
yurt-type tents, 39

Zari Rachev, 45, 138
Ziegler and Ziemba, 191
Ziemba and Hausch, 102
Ziemba and Mulvey, 145
Ziemba and Ziemba, 164, 181
Ziemba, Lleo and Zhitlukhin, 145, 190
Ziemba–Schwartz, 222

Made in the USA
Lexington, KY
04 December 2018